Lecture Notes in Artificial Intelligence   12057

Subseries of Lecture Notes in Computer Science

Series Editors

Randy Goebel
University of Alberta, Edmonton, Canada
Yuzuru Tanaka
Hokkaido University, Sapporo, Japan
Wolfgang Wahlster
DFKI and Saarland University, Saarbrücken, Germany

Founding Editor

Jörg Siekmann
DFKI and Saarland University, Saarbrücken, Germany

More information about this series at http://www.springer.com/series/1244

Petra Hofstedt · Salvador Abreu ·
Ulrich John · Herbert Kuchen ·
Dietmar Seipel (Eds.)

Declarative Programming and Knowledge Management

Conference on Declarative Programming, DECLARE 2019
Unifying INAP, WLP, and WFLP
Cottbus, Germany, September 9–12, 2019
Revised Selected Papers

 Springer

Editors
Petra Hofstedt
Brandenburgische Technische Universität
Cottbus-Senftenberg
Cottbus, Germany

Ulrich John (iD)
hwtk Berlin
Berlin, Germany

Dietmar Seipel
Universität Würzburg
Würzburg, Germany

Salvador Abreu (iD)
Universidade de Évora
Évora, Portugal

Herbert Kuchen (iD)
Westfälische Wilhelms-Universität Münster
Münster, Germany

ISSN 0302-9743   ISSN 1611-3349 (electronic)
Lecture Notes in Artificial Intelligence
ISBN 978-3-030-46713-5   ISBN 978-3-030-46714-2 (eBook)
https://doi.org/10.1007/978-3-030-46714-2

LNCS Sublibrary: SL7 – Artificial Intelligence

This Springer imprint is published by the registered company Springer Nature Switzerland AG
The registered company address is: Gewerbestrasse 11, 6330 Cham, Switzerland

Preface

These proceedings contain a selection of reworked papers of the DECLARE 2019 conference that took place during September 9–12, 2019, at the Brandenburg University of Technology (BTU) Cottbus-Senftenberg in Cottbus, Germany.

A central topic were methods, technologies, and applications of declarative programming and modeling, a fundamental subdomain in the area of artificial intelligence. The conference consisted of three events, each with a long-standing tradition: INAP – 22nd International Conference on Applications of Declarative Programming and Knowledge Management, WLP – 33rd Workshop on (Constraint) Logic Programming, and WFLP – 27th International Workshop on Functional and Logic Programming.

INAP covers all aspects of applications of important methods and technologies around declarative programming, constraint problem solving, and related computing paradigms. It comprehensively contemplates the impact of data and knowledge engineering, programmable logic solvers on the internet society, its underlying technologies, and leading edge applications in industry, commerce, government, and societal services. Previous INAP conferences have been held in Japan, Germany, Portugal, and Austria.

WLP serves as a scientific forum of the annual meeting of the Society of Logic Programming (GLP, Gesellschaft für Logische Programmierung e.V.). They bring together researchers (not only from Germany) interested in logic programming, constraint programming, and related areas such as databases, non-monotonic reasoning, knowledge representation, and operations research. WLP focuses on research in theoretical foundations, implementation, and applications of logic-based programming systems. Previous workshops have been held in Germany, Austria, Switzerland, Egypt, Japan, Denmark, Spain, Brazil, Italy, and France.

WFLP aims at bringing together researchers, students, and practitioners interested in functional programming, logic programming, and their integration. WFLP has a reputation for being a lively and friendly forum, and it is open for presenting and discussing work in progress, technical contributions, experience reports, experiments, reviews, and system descriptions. Previous WFLP editions took place in Germany, Japan, Denmark, Spain, Brazil, Italy, France, and Estonia.

Declarative programming as the main topic of the conference is an advanced paradigm for modeling and solving complex problems. With their contributions, participants presented current research activities in the areas of declarative languages and compilation techniques, in particular for constraint-based, logical and functional languages and their extensions, as well as discussed new approaches and key findings in constraint-solving, knowledge representation, and reasoning techniques. Furthermore, academic and industrial applications were subjects of the scientific exchange.

DECLARE 2019 was jointly organized by the BTU Cottbus-Senftenberg and the Society for Logic Programming (GLP e.V.). We would like to thank the authors of the submitted papers, the presenters of the invited talks, and all conference participants for their fruitful and interesting contributions and discussions. Furthermore, we thank the members of the Program Committee and the reviewers for their time, effort, and contributed expertise. We also would like to thank the BTU Cottbus-Senftenberg for hosting the conference. Ultimately, we specifically thank the local organization team at BTU Cottbus-Senftenberg: Sven Löffler, Katrin Ebert, Denny Schneeweiß, Gudrun Pehle, Daniela Schramm, and Ilja Becker. The event would not have been possible without them.

February 2020

Petra Hofstedt
Salvador Abreu
Ulrich John
Herbert Kuchen
Dietmar Seipel

Organization

Program Chair

Petra Hofstedt   BTU Cottbus-Senftenberg, Germany

Program Committee of INAP

Salvador Abreu (Co-chair)	Universidade de Évora, Portugal
Christoph Beierle	FernUniversität in Hagen, Germany
François Bry	Ludwig-Maximilian-University of Munich, Germany
Vitor Santos Costa	University of Porto, Portugal
Agostino Dovier	University of Udine, Italy
Thom Frühwirth	University of Ulm, Germany
Ulrich Geske	University of Potsdam, Germany
Gopal Gupta	UT Dallas, USA
Michael Hanus	University of Kiel, Germany
Petra Hofstedt (Co-chair)	BTU Cottbus-Senftenberg, Germany
Tomi Janhunen	Tampere University, Finland
Gabriele Kern-Isberner	TU Dortmund University, Germany
Herbert Kuchen	University of Münster, Germany
Sven Löffler	BTU Cottbus-Senftenberg, Germany
Vitor Beires Nogueira	Universidade de Évora, Portugal
Ricardo Rocha	University of Porto, Portugal
Dietmar Seipel (Co-chair)	University of Würzburg, Germany
Helmut Simonis	University College Cork, Ireland
Theresa Swift	Universidade Nova de Lisboa, Portugal
Hans Tompits	Vienna University of Technology, Austria
Masanobu Umeda	Kyushu Institute of Technology, Japan
Armin Wolf	Fraunhofer FOKUS Berlin, Germany

Program Committee of WLP

Slim Abdennadher	German University in Cairo, Egypt
Christoph Beierle	FernUniversität in Hagen, Germany
Thomas Eiter	Vienna University of Technology, Austria
Daniel Gall	University of Ulm, Germany
Ulrich Geske	University of Potsdam, Germany
Michael Hanus	University of Kiel, Germany
Petra Hofstedt (Co-chair)	BTU Cottbus-Senftenberg, Germany
Steffen Hölldobler	TU Dresden, Germany
Tomi Janhunen	Tampere University, Finland
Ulrich John (Co-chair)	hwtk Berlin, Germany

x   Contents

**27th International Workshop on Functional and Logic
Programming - WFLP 2019**

Invited Talks

GPU-Based Parallelism for ASP-Solving

Agostino Dovier[1], Andrea Formisano[1,2(✉)], and Flavio Vella[3]

[1] Dipartimento di Scienze Matematiche, Informatiche e Fisiche, Università di Udine, Udine, Italy
{agostino.dovier,andrea.formisano}@uniud.it
[2] Dipartimento di Matematica e Informatica, Università di Perugia, Perugia, Italy
[3] Facoltà di Scienze e Tecnologie Informatiche, Libera Università di Bolzano, Bolzano, Italy
flavio.vella@unibz.it

Abstract. Answer Set Programming (ASP) has become the paradigm of choice in the field of logic programming and non-monotonic reasoning. With the design of new and efficient solvers, ASP has been successfully adopted in a wide range of application domains. Recently, with the advent of GPU Computing, which allowed the use of modern parallel Graphical Processing Units (GPUs) for general-purpose computing, new opportunities for accelerating ASP computation has arisen. In this paper, we describe a new approach for solving ASP that exploits the parallelism provided by GPUs. The design of a GPU-based solver poses various challenges due to the peculiarities of GPU in terms of both programmability and architecture capabilities with respect to the intrinsic nature of the satisfiability problems, which exposes poor parallelism.

Keywords: ASP solvers · ASP computation · SIMT parallelism · GPU computing

Introduction

Answer Set Programming (ASP) is an expressive and purely declarative framework developed in the last decades in the Logic Programming and Knowledge Representation communities. Thanks to its extensively studied mathematical foundations and the continuous improvement of efficient and competitive solvers, ASP has become one of the most popular paradigms in many fields of AI. It has been fruitfully employed in many areas, such as knowledge representation and reasoning, planning, bioinformatics, multi-agent systems, data integration, language processing, declarative problem solving, semantic web, robotics among the others [5,9,10].

The clear and highly declarative nature of ASP enables excellent opportunities for the introduction of parallelism and concurrency in implementations of

This research is partially supported by INdAM-GNCS-20 project and by Univ. of Udine PRID ENCASE. The authors are member of the INdAM Research group GNCS.

P. Hofstedt et al. (Eds.): DECLARE 2019, LNAI 12057, pp. 3–23, 2020.
https://doi.org/10.1007/978-3-030-46714-2_1

ASP-solvers. Steps have been made in the last decades toward the paralleliza-
tion of the basic components of Logic Programming systems [15]. Such implementations aimed at exploiting multicore architectures, distributed systems, or
portfolio in order to provide efficient ASP solvers [6]. In this direction, a recent
new stream of research concerns the design and development of parallel ASP
systems that can take advantage of the massive degree of parallelism offered by
modern Graphical Processing Units (GPUs) [7,8].

GPUs are many-multicore devices designed to execute a very large number of concurrent threads on multiple data. They also exhibit a hierarchical
memory organization which strongly impact on memory-intensive problems like
ASP-solving. Therefore, to take full advantage of GPU architecture, one has
to adhere to specific programming directives, in order to proficiently distribute
the workload among the computing units and achieve the highest throughput in
memory accesses. This makes the model of parallelization used on GPUs deeply
different from those employed in more "conventional" parallel architectures. For
these reasons, existing parallel solutions are not directly applicable in the context
of GPUs.

This paper illustrates the design and implementation of a conflict-driven
ASP-solver that is capable of exploiting the *Single-Instruction Multiple-Thread*
parallelism offered by GPUs. The overall structure of the GPU-based solver
is reminiscent of the conventional structure of sequential conflict-driven ASP
solvers (such as, for example, the state-of-the-art solver CLASP [13]). However, substantial differences lay in both the implemented algorithms and in the
adopted programming model. Moreover, we avoid two hardly parallelizable and
intrinsically sequential algorithms usually present in existing solvers. On the one
hand, we exploit *ASP computations* to avoid the introduction of loop formulas
and the need of performing *unfounded set checks* [13]. On the other hand, we
adopt a parallel conflict analysis procedure as an alternative to the sequential
resolution-based technique used in CLASP.

The paper is organized as follows. Section 1 recalls basic notions on ASP,
GPU-computing, and the CUDA framework. The approach to ASP solving based
on *conflict-driven nogood learning* is described in Sect. 2. Section 3 illustrates
the difficulties inherent in parallelizing irregular applications, such as ASP, on
GPUs. The software architecture of the CUDA-based ASP-solver YASMIN is outlined in Sect. 4. In particular, the new parallel learning procedure is presented in
Sect. 4.2. Section 4.3 outlines an extension of the basic ASP-solver to exploit the
asynchronous concurrency enabled by CUDA streams. An experimental section
(Sect. 5) compares the new learning procedure against the standard resolution-
like procedure. Finally, conclusions are drawn in the closing section.

1   Preliminaries

We briefly recall the basic notions on ASP needed in the rest of the paper (for
a detailed treatment see [13,14] and the references therein). Similarly, we also
recall few needed notions on CUDA parallelism [21,22].

Answer Set Programming. An ASP program Π is a set of ASP rules of the form:

$$p_0 \leftarrow p_1, \ldots, p_m, not\ p_{m+1}, \ldots, not\ p_n$$

where $n \geq 0$ and each p_i is an atom (i.e., a propositional basic unit). If $n = 0$, the rule is a *fact*. If p_0 is missing, the rule is a *constraint*. Notice that, under the answer set semantics (described below), such a constraint can be rewritten as a headed rule of the form $q \leftarrow p_1, \ldots, p_m, not\ p_{m+1}, \ldots, not\ p_n, not\ q$, where q is a fresh atom. Hence, constraints do not increase the expressive power of ASP.

A rule including first-order atoms (i.e., involving variables) is simply seen as a shorthand for the set of its ground instances. Without loss of generality, in what follows we consider the case of ground programs only. (Hence, each p_i is a propositional atom.)

Given a rule r, p_0 is referred to as the *head* of the rule ($head(r)$), while the set $\{p_1, \ldots, p_m, not\ p_{m+1}, \ldots, not\ p_n\}$ is referred to as the *body* of r ($body(r)$). Moreover, we put $body^+(r) = \{p_1, \ldots, p_m\}$, $body^-(r) = \{p_{m+1}, \ldots, p_n\}$, $\varphi^+(r) = p_1 \wedge \cdots \wedge p_m$ and $\varphi^-(r) = \neg p_{m+1} \wedge \cdots \wedge \neg p_n$. We will denote the set of all atoms in Π by $atoms(\Pi)$ and the set of all rules defining the atom p by $rules(p) = \{r \mid head(r) = p\}$. The *completion* Π_{cc} of a program Π is defined as the formula:

$$\Pi_{cc} = \bigwedge_{p \in atoms(\Pi)} \left(p \leftrightarrow \bigvee_{r \in rules(p)} \left(\varphi^+(r) \wedge \varphi^-(r) \right) \right).$$

Semantics of ASP programs is expressed in terms of *answer sets*. An *interpretation* is a set M of atoms; $p \in M$ (resp. $p \notin M$) denotes that p is true (resp. false). An interpretation is a *model* of a rule r if $head(r) \in M$, or $body^+(r) \backslash M \neq \emptyset$, or $body^-(r) \cap M \neq \emptyset$. M is a model of a program Π if it is a model of each rule in Π. M is an *answer set* of Π if it is the subset-minimal model of the *reduct program* Π^M.

An important connection exists between the answer sets of Π and the minimal models of Π_{cc}. In fact, any answer set of Π is a minimal model of Π_{cc}. The converse is not true, but it can be shown [17] that the answer sets of Π are the minimal models of Π_{cc} satisfying the *loop formulas* of Π. The number of loop formulas can be, in general, exponential in the size of Π. Hence, modern ASP solvers adopt some form of *lazy* approach to generate loop formulas only "when needed". We refer the reader to [13,17] for the details; in what follows we will describe an alternative approach to answer set computation that avoids the generation of loop formulas. The new approach exploits *ASP computations* to avoid the introduction of loop formulas and the need of performing *unfounded set checks* [13] during the search of answer sets.

The notion of ASP computations originates from a computation-based characterization of answer sets [4,18] based on an incremental construction process, where at each step choices determine which rules are actually applied to extend the partial answer set. More specifically, for a program Π let T_Π be the immediate consequence operator of Π. Namely, if I is an interpretation, then

$$T_\Pi(I) = \{head(r) \mid r \in \Pi \wedge body^+(r) \subseteq I \wedge body^+(r) \cap I = \emptyset\}.$$

An *ASP Computation* for Π is a sequence of interpretations $I_0, I_1, I_2, \ldots$ (where I_0 can be any set of atoms that are logical consequences of Π) satisfying these conditions:

PERSISTENCE OF BELIEFS: $I_i \subseteq I_{i+1}$ for all $i \geq 0$
CONVERGENCE: $I_\infty = \bigcup_{i=0}^\infty I_i$ is such that $T_\Pi(I_\infty) = I_\infty$;
REVISION: $I_{i+1} \subseteq T_\Pi(I_i)$ for all $i \geq 0$;
PERSISTENCE OF REASON: if $p \in I_{i+1} \backslash I_i$ then there is $r \in rules(p)$ such that I_j is a model of $body(r)$ for each $j \geq i$.

Following [18], an interpretation I is an answer set of Π if and only if there exists an ASP computation such that $I = \bigcup_{i=0}^\infty I_i$.

GPU-Computing and the CUDA Framework. *Graphical Processing Units (GPUs)* are massively parallel devices, originally developed to efficiently implement the graphics pipeline for the rendering of 2D and 3D scenes. The use of such multicore systems has become pervasive in general-purpose applications that are not directly related to computer graphics, but demand massive computational power. The term *GPU-computing* indicates the use of the modern GPUs for such general-purpose computing. NVIDIA is one of the pioneering manufacturers in promoting GPU-computing, especially through the support to its *Computing Unified Device Architecture (CUDA)* [22]. A GPU contains hundreds or thousands of identical computing units (*cores*) and provides access to both on-chip memory (used for registers and shared memory) and off-chip memory (used for cache and global memory). Cores are grouped in a collection of *Streaming MultiProcessors (SMs)*. In turn, each SM contains fixed number of computing cores (up to 64 in the latest generation of GPUs). The SMs are responsible for creating, scheduling, and executing threads organized in groups of 32 parallel threads called *warps*. Threads in the same warp follow the same program address which means that program branches potentially introduce thread serialization. Whenever two (or more) groups of threads belonging to the same warp fetch/execute different instructions, *thread divergence* occurs. In this case the execution of the different groups is serialized and the overall performance decreases. Hence, the maximum efficiency is achieved when all 32 threads execute the same instruction.

The underlying conceptual parallel model is defined as *Single-Instruction Multiple-Thread (SIMT)*, where the same instruction is executed by different threads that run on cores, while data and operands may differ from thread to thread. A logical view of computations is introduced by CUDA, in order to define abstract parallel work and to schedule it among different hardware configurations. A typical CUDA program is a C/C++ program that includes parts meant for execution on the CPU (referred to as the *host*) and parts meant for parallel execution on the GPU (referred to as the *device*). The CUDA framework supports interaction, synchronization, and communication between host and device. Each device computation is described as a collection of concurrent threads, each executing the same device function (called a *kernel*, in CUDA terminology). These threads are hierarchically organized in *blocks* of threads and

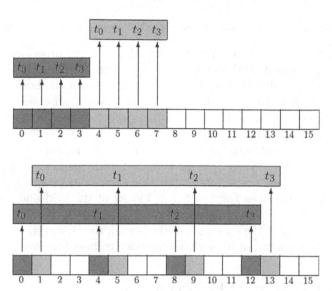

Fig. 1. Different memory-access patterns on an array data-structure by a group of four threads $t_0 - t_3$. Coalesced access pattern (top) and strided access pattern (bottom).

grids of blocks. The host program contains instructions for data initialization, grids/blocks/threads management, and kernel execution. Each thread in a block executes an instance of the kernel, and has a thread ID within its block. A grid is a 3D array of blocks that execute the same kernel, read/write data input from/to the global memory. When a CUDA program on the host launches a kernel, the blocks of the grid are scheduled to the SMs with available execution capacity. The threads in the same block can share data, using high-throughput on-chip shared memory, while threads belonging to different blocks can only share data through the global memory. Thus, the block size allows the programmer to define the granularity of threads cooperation.

It should be noticed that the most efficient access pattern to be adopted by threads in reading/storing data depends on the kind of memory. We briefly mention here two possibilities (see [21] for a comprehensive description). Shared memory is organized in *banks*. In case threads of the same block access locations in the same bank, a *bank conflict* occurs and the accesses are serialized. To avoid bank conflicts, *strided* access pattern has to be adopted. On the contrary, concerning global memory, *coalesced* accesses allows to reach the highest throughput since it minimizes the number of memory transactions. Intuitively, this can be achieved if consecutive threads access contiguous global memory locations. Figure 1 shows a simple example where a group of four threads $t_0 - t_3$ performs two steps (emphasized in different colors) in reading the elements of an array.

A simple CUDA application presents the following basic components:[1]

MEMORY ALLOCATION AND DATA TRANSFER. Before being processed by kernels, data must be copied to the global memory of the device. The CUDA API supports memory allocation and data transfer to/from the host.

KERNELS DEFINITION. Kernels are defined as standard C functions; the annotation used to communicate to the CUDA compiler that a function should be treated as kernel has the form:

    `__global__void kernelName(Formal Arguments).`

KERNELS EXECUTION. A kernel can be launched from the host program using:

    `kernelName <<< GridDim, TPB >>> (Actual Arguments)`

where `GridDim` describes the number of blocks of the grid and `TPB` specifies the number of threads in each block.

DATA RETRIEVAL. After the execution of the kernel, the host retrieves the results with a transfer operation from global memory to host memory.

2   Conflict-Driven ASP-Solving

Conflict-driven nogood learning (CDNL) is one of the techniques successfully used by ASP-solvers, such as the CLINGO system [13]. The first attempt in exploiting GPU parallelism for conflict-driven ASP solving has been made in [7,8]. The approach adopts a conventional architecture of an ASP solver which starts by translating the completion Π_{cc} of a given ground program Π into a collection of *nogoods* (see below). Then, the search for the answer sets of Π is performed by exploring a search space composed of all interpretations for the atoms in Π, organized as a binary tree. Branches of the tree correspond to (partial) assignments of truth values to program atoms (i.e., partial interpretations). The computation of an answer set proceeds by alternating decision steps and propagation phases. Intuitively: (1) A decision consists in selecting an atom and assigning it a truth value. (This step is usually guided by powerful heuristics analogous to those developed for SAT [2].) (2) Propagation extends the current partial assignment by adding all consequences of the decision. The process repeats until a model is found (if any). It may be the case that inconsistent truth values are propagated for the same atom after i decisions (i.e., while visiting a node at depth i in the tree-shaped search space). In such cases a *conflict* arises *at decision level i* testifying that the current partial assignment cannot be extended to a model of the program. Then, a *conflict analysis* procedure is run to detect the reasons of the failure. The analysis identifies which decisions should be undone in order to restore consistency of the assignment. It also produces a new *learned* nogood to be added to the program at hand, so as to exclude repeating the same failing sequence of decisions, in the subsequent part of the computation. Consequently, the program is extended with the learned nogood

---

[1] Notice that, for the sake of simplicity, we are ignoring many aspects of CUDA programming and advanced techniques such as dynamic parallelism, cooperative groups, multi-device programming, etc. We refer the reader to [21] for a detailed treatment.

and the search backjumps to a previous (consistent) point in the search space, at a decision level $j < i$. Whenever a conflict occurs at the top decision level ($i = 1$), the computation ends because no (more) solutions exist.

Following [7,8], let us outline how CDNL can be combined with ASP computation in order to obtain a solver that does not need to use loop formulas. We describe both assignments A and nogoods δ as sets of *signed atoms*—i.e., entities of the form Tp or Fp, denoting that $p \in atoms(\Pi)$ has been assigned true or false, respectively. Plainly, an assignment contains at most one element between Tp and Fp for each atom p. Given an assignment A, let $A^T = \{p \mid Tp \in A\}$. Note that A^T is an interpretation for Π. A *total* assignment A is such that, for every atom p, $\{Tp, Fp\} \cap A \neq \emptyset$. Given a (possibly partial) assignment A and a nogood δ, we say that δ is *violated* if $\delta \subseteq A$. In turn, A is a *solution* for a set of nogoods Δ if no $\delta \in \Delta$ is violated by A. Nogoods can be used to perform deterministic propagation (*unit propagation*) and extend an assignment. Given a nogood δ and a partial assignment A such that $\delta \backslash A = \{Fp\}$ (resp., $\delta \backslash A = \{Tp\}$), then we can infer the need to add Tp (resp., Fp) to A in order to avoid violation of δ.

Given a program Π, a set of *completion nogoods* $\Delta_{\Pi_{cc}}$ is derived from Π_{cc} as follows. For each rule $r \in \Pi$ and each atom $p \in atoms(\Pi)$, we introduce the formulas:

$$b_r \leftrightarrow t_r \wedge n_r \qquad t_r \leftrightarrow \varphi^+(r) \qquad n_r \leftrightarrow \varphi^-(r) \qquad p \leftrightarrow \bigvee_{r \in rules(p)} b_r$$

where b_r, t_r, n_r are new atoms (if $rules(p) = \emptyset$, then the last formula reduces to $\neg p$). The completion nogoods reflect the structure of the implications in these formulas:

- from the first formula we have the nogoods: $\{Fb_r, Tt_r, Tn_r\}, \{Tb_r, Ft_r\}$, and $\{Tb_r, Fn_r\}$.
- From the second and third formulas we have the nogoods: $\{Tt_r, Fp\}$ for each $p \in body^+(r)$; $\{Tn_r, Tq\}$ for each $q \in body^-(r)$; $\{Ft_r\} \cup \{Tp \mid p \in body^+(r)\}$; and $\{Fn_r\} \cup \{Fq \mid q \in body^-(r)\}$.
- From the last formula we have the nogoods: $\{Fp, Tb_r\}$ for each $r \in rules(p)$ and $\{Tp\} \cup \{Fb_r \mid r \in rules(p)\}$.

Moreover, for each constraint $\leftarrow p_1, \ldots, p_m, not\ p_{m+1}, \ldots, not\ p_n$ in Π we introduce a *constraint nogood* of the form $\{Tp_1, \ldots, Tp_m, Fp_{m+1}, \ldots, Fp_n\}$. The set $\Delta_{\Pi_{cc}}$ is the set of all the nogoods so defined.

The basic CDNL procedure described earlier can be easily combined with the notion of ASP computation. Indeed, it suffices to apply a specific heuristic during the selection steps to satisfy the four properties defined in Sect. 1. This can be achieved by assigning true value to a selected atom only if this atom is supported by a rule with true body. More specifically, let A be the current partial assignment, the selection step acts as follows. For each unassigned atom p occurring as head of a rule in the original program, all nogoods reflecting the rule $b_r \leftarrow t_r, n_r$, such that $r \in rules(p)$ are analyzed to check whether $Tt_r \in A$ and $Fn_r \notin A$ (i.e., the rule is *applicable* [18]). One of the rules r that pass this test is selected. Then, Tb_r is added to A. In the subsequent propagation phase Tp and Fn_r are also added to A and Fn_r imposes that all the atoms of $body^-(r)$ are set to false. This, in particular, ensures the *persistence of beliefs* of the ASP computation. (In the real implementation (see Sect. 4) all applicable rules r, and their heads, are evaluated according to a heuristic weight and the rule r with highest ranking is selected.) It might be the case that no selection is possible because no unassigned atom p exists such that there is an applicable $r \in$ $rules(p)$. In this situation the computation ends by assigning false value to all unassigned heads in Π. This completes the assignment, which is validated by a final propagation step in order to check that no constraint nogoods are violated. In the positive case the assignment so obtained is an answer set of Π.

3 ASP as an Irregular Application

The design of GPU-based ASP-solvers poses various challenges due to the structure and intrinsic nature of the satisfiability problem. The same holds for GPU-based approaches to SAT [3]. As a matter of fact, the paralleliza-tion of SAT/ASP-solving shares many aspects with other applications of GPU-computing where problems/instances are characterized by the presence of large, sparse, and unstructured data. Parallel graph algorithms constitute significant examples, that, like SAT/ASP solving, exhibit irregular and low-arithmetic intensity combined with data-dependent control flow and memory access pat-terns. Typically, in these contexts, large instances/graphs have to be mod-eled and represented using sparse data structures (e.g., matrices in *Compressed Sparse Row/Column* formats). The parallelization of such algorithms struggles to achieve scalability due to lack of data locality, irregular access patterns, and unpredictable computation [19]. Although, in the case of some graph algorithms, several techniques have been established in order to improve performance on par-allel architectures [16] and accelerators [1], the different character of the algo-rithms used in SAT/ASP might prevent from obtaining comparable impact on performance by directly applying the same techniques. This is because, first, the time-to-solution of a SAT/ASP problem is dominated by heuristic selection and learning procedures able to cut the exponential search space. In several cases, smart heuristics might be most effective than advanced parallel solutions. Sec-ond, because of intrinsic data-dependencies, procedures like propagation or learn-ing often require to access large parts of the data/graph, sequentially. Similarly to what experienced in other complex graph-based problems [11], the kind of com-putation involved differs from that of traversal-like algorithms (such as, Breadth-First Search) which process a subset of the graph in iterative/incremental man-ners and for which advanced GPU-solutions exist. Furthermore, aspect specific to the underlying architecture enters into play, such as coalesced memory access and CUDA-thread balancing, which are major objectives in parallel algorithm design. In this scenario, our GPU-based proposal to ASP solving also imple-ments:

- efficient parallel propagation able to maximize memory throughput and min-imize thread divergence.

– Fast parallel learning algorithm which avoids the bottleneck represented by the intrinsically sequential resolution-like learning procedures commonly used in CDNL solvers.
– Specific thread-data mapping solutions able to regularize the access to data stored in global, local, and shared memories.

In what follows we will describe how to achieve these requirements in the GPU-based solver for ASP.

4   The CUDA-Based ASP-Solver YASMIN

In this section, we present a solver that exploits ASP computation, nogoods handling, and GPU parallelism. The ground program Π, as produced by the grounder GRINGO [13], is read by the CPU. The CPU also computes the completion nogoods $\Delta_{\Pi_{cc}}$ and transfers them to the device. The rest of the computation is performed completely on the GPU. During this process, the only memory transfers between the host and device involve control-flow flags (e.g., an "exit" flag, used to communicate whether the computation is terminated) and the computed answer-set (from the GPU to the CPU).

As concerns representation and storing of data on the device, each atom a in Π is uniquely identified by an integer $index$, say p (consequently, the signed atom Ta, Fa are represented by p and $-p$, respectively).

Nogoods are stored using Compressed Sparse Row (CSR) format, usually exploited to store sparse matrices. Namely, the (signed) atoms of each nogood are stored contiguously and all nogoods are stored in consecutive locations of an array allocated in global memory. An indexing array contains the offset of each nogood, to enable direct accesses to them. The positions in the indexing array are used as identifiers for the corresponding nogoods. Moreover, nogoods are sorted in increasing order, depending on their length. Figure 2 shows the representation of four nogoods $ng_0, \ldots, ng_3$ (identified by their indices $0-3$) involving the atoms $\{a_1, a_2, a_3, a_4, a_7, a_{11}\}$.

An array A of integers is used to store in global memory the set of assigned atoms (with their truth values) in this manner:

– $A[p] = 0$ if and only if the atom p is unassigned;
– $A[p] = i$, $i > 0$ (resp., $A[p] = -i$) means that atom p has been assigned true (resp., false) at the decision level i.

The basic structure of the YASMIN solver is shown in Algorithm 1. We adopt the following notation: for each signed atom p, let $\bar{p}$ represent the same atom with opposite sign. Moreover, let us refer to the stored set of nogoods simply by the variable Δ. The variable cdl (initialized in line 1) represents the current decision level. As mentioned, cdl acts as a counter that keeps track of the current number of decisions that have been made.

Since the set of input nogoods may include some unitary nogoods, a preliminary parallel computation partially initializes A accordingly (line 2). It may be

---

Algorithm 1: Host code of the ASP-solver YASMIN   (simplified)

```
   procedure YASMIN(Δ: SetOfNogoods, P: GroundProgram)
 1   cdl ← 1 ; reset (A)                    /* set initial decision level and empty assignment */
 2   InitialPropagation<<<b,t>>>(A, Δ, Viol)              /* check input units satisfaction */
 3   if Viol then return no-answer-set
 4   else loop
 5   │   PropagateAndCheck(A, Δ, cdl, Viol)                      /* update A and flag Viol */
 6   │   if Viol ∧ (cdl = 1) then return no-answer-set    /* Violation at first dec.level */
 7   │   else if Viol then                                /* Violation at level cdl>1 */
 8   │   │   Learning<<<b,t>>>(Δ, A, cdl)          /* conflict analysis: update Δ and cdl */
 9   │   │   Backjump<<<b,t>>>(A, cdl)                          /* update A and cdl */
     │   end
10   │   if (A is not total) then
     │   │   /* rank selectable literals and applicable rules. If possible, select Lit,
     │   │      extend A, update cdl. Otherwise, Lit ← nil :                         */
11   │   │   Decision<<<b,t>>>(Δ, A, Lit)
12   │   │   if Lit = nil then                            /* no applicable rules */
13   │   │   │   CompleteAssignment<<<b,t>>>(A)            /* falsify unassigned atoms */
14   │   else return Aᵀ ∩ atom(P)                         /* stable model found */
```

---

the case that inconsistent assignments occur in this phase. In such case a flag *Viol* is set, the given program Π in declared unsatisfiable (line 3) and the computation ends. Notice that the algorithm can be *restarted* several times—typically, this happens when more than one solution is requested or if restart strategy is activated by command-line options. (For simplicity, we did not include the code for restarting the solver in Algorithm 1.) In such cases, `InitialPropagation()` also handles unit nogoods that have been learned in the previous execution. The kernel invocation in line 2 specifies a grid of b blocks each composed of t threads. The mapping is one-to-one between threads and unitary nogood. In particular, if k is the number of unitary nogoods, b=$\lceil k/TPB \rceil$ and t=TPB, where TPB is the number of threads-per-block specified via command-line option. The loop in lines 4–14 computes the answer set, if any. Propagation is performed by the procedure `PropagateAndCheck()` in line 5, which also checks whether nogood violations occur. To better exploit the SIMT parallelism and maximize the number of concurrently active threads, in each device computation the workload has to be divided among the threads of the grid as uniformly as possible. To this aim, `PropagateAndCheck()` launches multiple kernels: one kernel deals with all

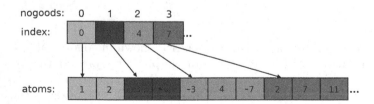

Fig. 2. Representation in memory of the nogoods $ng_0 = \{Ta_1, Ta_2\}$, $ng_1 = \{Ta_3, Fa_4\}$, $ng_2 = \{Fa_3, Ta_4, Fa_7\}$, $ng_3 = \{Ta_2, Ta_7, Ta_{11}\}$,... using the Compressed Sparse Row (CSR) format. Signed atoms are represented by signed integers.

nogoods with exactly two literals; a second one processes the nogoods composed of three literals, and a further kernel processes all remaining nogoods. In this manner, threads of the same grid process a uniform number of atoms, reducing the divergence between them and minimizing the number of inactive threads. Moreover, because, as mentioned, nogoods of the same length are stored contiguously, threads of the same grid are expected to realize coalesced accesses to global memory. A more detailed description of the third of such device functions is given in Sect. 4.1. A similar technique is used in `PropagateAndCheck()` to process those nogoods that are learned at run-time through the conflict analysis step (cf. Sect. 4.2). These nogoods are partitioned depending on their cardinality and processed by different kernels, accordingly. In general, if n is the number of nogoods of one partition, the corresponding kernel has $b = \lceil n/TPB \rceil$ blocks of $t = TPB$ threads each. Each thread processes one learned nogood.

Propagation stops because either a fixpoint is reached (no more propagations are possible) or one or more conflicts occur. In the latter case, if the current decision level is the top one the solver ends: no solution exists (line 6). Otherwise, (lines 7–9) conflict analysis (`Learning()`) is performed and then the solver backjumps to a previous decision point (line 9). The learning procedure is described in Sect. 4.2. A specific kernel `Backjump()` takes care of updating the value of cdl and the array that stores the assignment. A mapping one-to-one between threads and atoms in A is used.

On the other hand, if no conflict occurs and A is not complete, a new `Decision()` is made (line 11). As mentioned, the purpose of this kernel is to determine an unassigned atom p which is head of an applicable rule r. All candidates p and applicable r are evaluated in parallel according to a typical heuristics to rank the atoms. Possible criteria, selectable by command-line options, use the number of positive/negative occurrences of atoms in the program (by either simply counting the occurrences or by applying the Jeroslow-Wang heuristics) or the "activity" of atoms [2]. The first access to global memory to retrieve needed data is done in coalesced manner (a mapping one-to-one between threads and rules is used). Then, a logarithmic parallel reduction scheme, implemented using thread-shuffling to avoid further accesses to global memory, yields the rule r with highest ranking. Its head is selected and set true in the assignment. `Decision()` also communicates to the solver whether no applicable rule exists (line 12). In this case all unassigned heads in Π are assigned false (by the kernel `CompleteAssignment()` in line 13). A successive invocation of `PropagateAndCheck()` validates the answer set and the solver ends in line 14.

4.1 The Propagate-and-Check Procedure

After each assignment of an atom of the current partial assignment A, each nogood δ needs to be analyzed to detect whether: (1) it is violated, or (2) there is exactly one literal p in it that is unassigned in A, in which case an inference step adds $\bar{p}$ to A (cf., Sect. 2). The procedure is repeated until a fixpoint is reached. As seen earlier, this task is performed by the kernels launched by the procedure `PropagateAndCheck()`.

Algorithm 2 shows the device code of the generic kernel dealing with nogoods of length greater than three (the others are simpler). The execution of each iteration is driven by the atoms that have been assigned a truth value in the previous iteration (array *Last* in Algorithm 2). Thus, each kernel involves a number of blocks that is equal to the number of such assigned atoms. The threads in each block process the nogoods that share the same assigned atom. The number of threads of each block is established by considering the number of occurrences of each assigned atom in the input nogoods. Observe that the dimension of the grid may change between two consecutive invocations of the same kernel, and, as such, it is evaluated each time. Specific data structures (initialized once during a pre-processing phase and stored in the sparse matrix *Map*[][] in Algorithm 2) are used in order to determine, after each iteration and for each assigned atom, which are the input nogoods to be considered. A further technique is adopted to improve performance. Namely, the processing of nogoods is realized by implementing a standard technique based on *watched literals* [2]. In this case, each thread accesses the watched literals of a nogood and acts accordingly. The combination of nogood sorting and the use of watched literals, improves the workload balancing among threads and mitigates thread divergence. (Watched literals are exploited also for learned nogoods.)

Concerning Algorithm 2, each thread of the grid first retrieves one of the atoms propagated during the previous step (line 1). Threads of the same block obtain the same atom L. In line 2, threads accesses the data structure *Map*, mentioned earlier, to retrieve the number *ngInBlock* of nogoods to be processed by the block. In line 5 each thread of the block determines which nogood has to be processed and retrieves its watched literals (lines 6–7). In case one or both literals belongs to the current assignment A, suitable substitutes are sought for (lines 10 and 14). Violation might be detected (lines 12 and 19, resp.) or propagation might occur (lines 16–18). Notice that, concurrent threads might try to propagate the same atom (possibly with different sign), originating race conditions. The use of atomic functions (line 16) allows one nondeterministically chosen thread t to perform the propagation. Other threads may discover agreement or detect inconsistency w.r.t. the value set by t (line 19). In line 17 the thread t updates the set *Next* of propagated atoms (to be used in the subsequent iteration) and stores (line 18) information needed in future conflict analysis steps (by means of mk_dl_bitmap(), to be described in Sect. 4.2) and concerning the causes of the propagation.

4.2 The Learning Procedure

As mentioned, the Learning() procedure is used to resolve a conflict detected by PropagateAndCheck() and to identify a decision level the computation should backjump to, in order to remove the violation. The analysis usually performed in ASP solvers such as CLINGO [13] demonstrated rather unsuitable to SIMT parallelism. This is due to the fact that a sequential sequence of resolution-like steps must be encoded.

Algorithm 2: Device code implementing propagation and nogood check   (simplified)

---

   procedure NOGOOD_CHECK(*Last*, *Next*: ArrayOfLits, *Map*: AtomsNogoodsMatrix, *A*:
   Assignment)

```
 1   L ← Last[blockIdx.x]           /* each block processes one of the propagated lits */
 2   ngInBlock ← |Map[L]|           /* get the number of nogoods in which L occurs */
 3   i ← threadIdx.x               /* each nogood in which L occurs is treated by a thread */
 4   if i < ngInBlock then
 5       δ ← Map[L][i]                                /* get the nogood */
 6       w₁ ← watched₁[δ]          /* copy the two watched lits in registers */
 7       w₂ ← watched₂[δ]
 8       if w̄₁ ∈ A ∨ w̄₂ ∈ A then return       /* satisfied nogood, thread exits */
 9       if w₁ ∈ A ∧ w₂ ∈ A then
10           if exists w ∈ δ such that w ∉ A ∧ w̄ ∉ A then
11             │  w₁ ← w
12           else Viol ← true                        /* nogood violation */
13       if w₁ ∉ A ∧ w₂ ∈ A then       /* the case w₂ ∉ A ∧ w₁ ∈ A is analogous (omitted) */
14           if exists u ∈ δ such that w₁ ≠ u ∧ u ∉ A ∧ ū ∉ A then
15             │  w₂ ← u
           else              /* first thread propagates (others may agree or cause violation) */
16             │  if atomicSet(A, w₁, cdl) then   /* returns true if found not disagreeing */
17             │    │  Next ← Next ∪ {w₁}          /* update set of propagated lits */
18             │    │  Deps[w₁] = mk_dl_bitmap(w₁, δ)      /* set dependencies of w₁ */
19             │  else Viol ← true                /* if disagreeing, it is a violation */
20       watched₁[δ] ← w₁ ;   watched₂[δ] ← w₂          /* update the two nogoods */
     end
```

   __inline__   **procedure** MK_DL_BITMAP(*w*: Literal, δ: Nogood)

```
21   reset(res)                                /* empty set = null bitmap */
22   foreach x ∈ δ \ {w, w̄} do         /* collect causes of propagation of w ∈ δ */
23   │  if dl(x) > 1 then  res ← res | Deps[x]    /* if dl(x) > 1, x is not an input unit */
24   return res
```

Algorithm 3: Resolution based learning schema in CLASP [13]

---

   procedure RES-LEARNING(δ: Nogood, Δ: SetOfNogoods, A: Assignment)

```
 1   while exists σ ∈ δ such that δ \ A = {σ} do
         /* get the decision level κ of the last but one assigned literal in δ    */
 2   │  κ ← max({dl(ρ) | ρ ∈ δ \ {σ}} ∪ {0})
 3   │  if κ = dl(σ) then   /* there is another lit in δ decided at level dl(σ) */
 4   │    │  let ε ∈ Δ such that ε \ A = {σ̄} in
 5   │    │  │  δ ← (δ \ {σ}) ∪ (ε \ {σ̄})       /* resolution step between δ and ε */
 6   │  else return(δ, κ)
```

In the case of the parallel solver YASMIN, more than one conflict might be detected by `PropagateAndCheck()`. The solver selects one or more of them (heuristics can be applied to perform such a selection, for instance, priority can be assigned to shorter nogoods.) For each selected conflict, a grid of a single block, to facilitate synchronization, is run to perform a sequence of resolution steps, starting from the conflicting nogood (say, δ), and proceeding backward, by resolving upon the last but one assigned atom σ ∈ δ. The step involves δ and a nogood ε including σ̄. Resolution steps end as soon as the last two assigned atoms in δ correspond to different decision levels. This approach identifies the *first UIP (Unique Implication Point* [2]). Algorithm 3 shows the pseudo-code of such procedure (see also [2,13] for the technical details). The block contains a

---

Algorithm 4: CUDA device code using warp-shuffling for fwd-learning   (simplified)

---

   procedure FWD-LEARNING(δ: Nogood, Δ: SetOfNogoods, A: Assignment, *Deps*:
   ArrayOfBitmaps)

1 $i \leftarrow threadIdx.x$ /* id of the thread (for simplicity in D1 grid) */

2 _shared_ $sh\_bitmap[warpSize]$ /* array of bitmaps shared among threads */

3 $lane \leftarrow i \% warpSize$ /* lane of the thread in its warp */

4 $wid \leftarrow i/warpSize$ /* id of thread's warp */

5 reset ($vbitmap$)   /* each thread resets its private bitmap */

6 _syncthreads ()   /* synchronization barrier */

7 **while** $i < | \delta |$ **do**   /* collect dependencies of all atoms in δ from global memory */

8      $atom \leftarrow$ the i-th atom in δ /* strided access to memory */

9      $vbitmap \leftarrow vbitmap \mid Deps[atom]$ /* bit-a-bit disjunction: collects deps */

10     $i \leftarrow i + blockDim.x$ /* next stride */

11 _syncthreads ()

   /* logarithmic reduction using shuffling within each warp: */

12 **for** ($offset \leftarrow warpSize/2$; $offset > 0$; $offset/ = 2$) **do**

13     $vbitmap \leftarrow vbitmap \mid$ _shfl_down_sync(0xFFFFFFFF, $vbitmap$, $offset$)

14 **if** $lane=0$ **then** $sh\_bitmap[wid] \leftarrow vbitmap$ /* store reduced value in shared memory */

15 _syncthreads ()   /* wait for all partial reductions */

   /* read from shared memory only if that warp participates: */

16 $vbitmap \leftarrow (threadIdx.x < blockDim.x/warpSize) ? sh\_bitmap[lane] : 0$

17 **if** $wid=0$ **then**   /* the first warp performs the final reduction */

18   **for** ($offset \leftarrow warpSize/2$; $offset > 0$; $offset/ = 2$) **do**

19       $vbitmap \leftarrow vbitmap \mid$ _shfl_down_sync(0xFFFFFFFF, $vbitmap$, $offset$)

20 _syncthreads ()

   /* Here $vbitmap$ encodes all dependencies of all literals in $\delta \setminus \{\sigma\}$ */

21 **if** $threadIdx.x = 0$ **then**   /* add deps for $\overline{\sigma}$ in ε (gathered during propagation) */

22     $sh\_bitmap[0] \leftarrow vbitmap \mid Deps[\overline{\sigma}]$

23     $backjump\_dl \leftarrow$ leftmost_set_bit ($sh\_bitmap[0]$)   /* gets the level to backjump to */

24 _syncthreads ()

   /* Store the learned nogood: the threads of the first warp store in global memory, in
   coalesced way, the relevant decision literals   */

25 **if** $threadIdx.x < warpSize$ **then**

26     $i \leftarrow threadIdx.x$

27   **while** $i < max\_dl$ **do**   /* for all decision levels */

28   **if** ($sh\_bitmap[0]$ & 2^{i+1}) **then**   /* if conflict depends on the i-th decision */

29          $new\_nogood \leftarrow new\_nogood \cup$ get_ith_decision(i)

30       $i \leftarrow i + warpSize$

---

fixed number (e.g., 1024) of threads and every thread takes care of one atom (if there are more atoms than threads involved in the learning, atoms are equally partitioned among threads). For each analyzed conflict, a new nogood is learned and added to Δ. In case of multiple learned nogoods involving different "target" decision levels, the lowest level is selected.

In order to remove the computational bottleneck represented by this kind of learning strategy we designed an alternative, parallelizable, technique. The basic idea consists in collecting, during the propagation phase, information useful to speed up conflict analysis, affecting as little as possible, performance of propagation. A bitmap $Deps[p]$ is associated to each atom p. The i-th bit of $Deps[p]$ is set 1 if the assignment of p depends (either directly or transitively) on the atom decided at level i. Hence, when an atom q is decided at level j, $Deps[q]$ is assigned the value 2^{j-1} (by the procedure Decision()). Whenever propagation of an atom w_1 occurs (see Algorithm 2, line 18) the function mk_dl_bitmap() computes the bit-a-bit disjunction of all bitmaps associated to all other atoms in δ. To maximize efficiency this computation is performed by a group of threads, exploiting shuffling, through a logarithmic parallel reduction scheme. Algorithm 4 shows the code of the new learning procedure. The kernel fwd_learning() is run by a grid of a single block, where each thread processes an atom of the conflicting nogood δ. Initially, each thread determines the index of its warp (line 4) and its relative position in the warp (line 3). After a synchronization barrier (line 6) each thread retrieves the bitmaps of one or more atoms of δ. The disjunction of these bitmaps is stored in the private variable *vbitmap*. Then, each warp executes a logarithmic reduction scheme (lines 12–14) to compute a partial result in shared memory (allocated in line 2). At this point, the first warp performs a last logarithmic reduction (lines 17–19) combining all partial results. After a synchronization barrier, thread 0 adds the dependencies relative to $\bar{\sigma}$ in ε (line 22) and determines the decision level to backjump to (line 23). Finally, the learned nogood in built up using the bitmap $sh\_bitmap[0]$ and stored in global memory in coalesced way (lines 25–30).

4.3   Exploiting Stream-Based Parallelism

In a CUDA application, all operations (memory transferts, kernel launches, etc) issued by the host for execution on the device are associated to a *stream*. A default stream is provided by the CUDA framework, but the programmer can create and manage different streams in the same application. The operations within a stream are guaranteed to execute in the order in which they are issued. However, different streams may execute their commands out of order with respect to one another or even concurrently, depending on the way device's control-logic performs their scheduling to the available SMs (see [21] for a detailed treatment). Hence, the host can issue operations in different streams, in order to overlap their execution and, consequently, to better exploit the computing power of the GPU and maximize the usage of all SMs.

In the rest of this section we outline a possible way to extend the ASP solver YASMIN so as to take advantage of the asynchronous concurrent execution enabled by streams. Recall that, roughly speaking, the parallel CUDA-based solver described in the previous sections proceeds by exploring a search space, guided by decision steps and nogoods learned through conflict analysis. We envisage now the introduction of a further level of parallelism, obtained by partitioning the search space and running several copies of the basic solver, each one exploring one portion of the search space.

Algorithm 5 shows the host code of the multi-pthread[2] procedure MULTI_YASMIN which first splits (line 1) the given ASP-program/problem into a number Np of subproblems, possibly, by applying some heuristics and user options. Various alternatives can be considered to generate the collection of subproblems. One of the simplest possibility consists in splitting the search space by

---

[2] For the sake of simplicity, we will refer to host POSIX threads by using the term pthread, so as to distinguish them from device CUDA threads.

assigning in different ways the truth values of a subset of the input atoms. Consequently, the nogoods and the atoms of each subproblem would be obtained by simplifying (using propagation) the input collection of nogoods. In this way the search spaces of the Np subproblems would not overlap and their visits can proceed independently. Different strategies can be used to determine which atoms should be used for splitting. For instance, one might exploit *parallel lookahead* [6] or select atoms using heuristics similar to those used in the selection step (occurrence count, Jeroslow-Wang, etc). Notice that, one might also identify possibly overlapping subproblems, intended to be explored by adopting different search strategies and heuristics for atom decision.

The main procedure MULTI_YASMIN, in lines 2–3 of Algorithm 5, creates a pool of POSIX threads by spawning a number Nt of host pthreads (both Np and Nt can be specified by the user). Each pthread executes the host procedure yasmin_launcher (line 3). Finally, the main procedure waits for the termination of all pthreads (lines 4–5) before terminating (for simplicity, in Algorithm 5 we omitted the code that outputs the results).

Each concurrent instance of the procedure yasmin_launcher iterates until all subproblems have been processed. In particular, each pthread extracts one subproblem, S in (line 8), from the set *Parts*, calls an instance of the CUDA solver described in Algorithm 1 to solve S (line 9), and waits for its termination (line 10). Once the solver ended, the pthread proceeds to process the next available subproblem, if any. When *Parts* becomes empty, the pthread exits (line 11). Notice that, the CUDA framework allows each host pthread to exploit a private CUDA stream. Hence, the computation of each instance of the solver proceeds by issuing commands (memory transfers, kernel launches, etc) in its own stream, concurrently with the other solver instances.

As concerns the data structures described in the previous sections, part of them can be safely shared among pthreads/solvers, both on the host and on the device. In particular, this is true for the collection of input nogoods and all the data that are not modified during the computation (such as the sparse matrix *Map*, see Sect. 4.1). On the other hand, the arrays that stores the assignment, the information needed to manage watched literals, the selected and propagated atoms, etc, have to be replicated, because each solver needs to develop its own computation. Such data structure are private to each solver, hence there is no need to impose mutual exclusion in accesses. As concerns learned nogoods, the corresponding data structure is shared among the solvers, but learned nogoods are added by acting in mutual exclusion on the shared data. This enables a useful form of communication between solvers: each of them benefits from the nogoods inferred by other solvers.

5   Experimental Results

In this section we briefly report on some experiments we run to compare the two learning techniques described in the previous section. Table 1 shows a selection of the instances (taken from [8]) we used. For each instance the table indicates, together with an ID, the number of nogoods and the number of atoms.

Table 1. Some instances used in experiments. The table shows: shorthand IDs, instance names (taken from [8]), the numbers of nogoods/atoms given as input to the solving phase of YASMIN.

ID	Instance	Nogoods	Atoms	ID	Instance	Nogoods	Atoms
I0	0001-visitall	42286	17251	I16	0072-ppm	591542	14679
I1	0003-visitall	40014	16337	I17	0153-ppm	721971	16182
I2	0167-sokoban	68585	29847	I18	0001-stablemarriage	975973	63454
I3	0010-graphcol	37490	15759	I19	0005-stablemarriage	975945	63441
I4	0007-graphcol	37815	15889	I20	0010-stablemarriage	975880	63415
I5	0589-sokoban	76847	33417	I21	0004-stablemarriage	975963	63453
I6	0482-sokoban	84421	36639	I22	0003-stablemarriage	975930	63438
I7	0345-sokoban	119790	51959	I23	0009-stablemarriage	975954	63447
I8	0058-labyrinth	228881	84877	I24	0002-stablemarriage	975907	63430
I9	0039-labyrinth	228202	84633	I25	0006-stablemarriage	975953	63446
I10	0009-labyrinth	228859	84865	I26	0008-stablemarriage	975934	63439
I11	0023-labyrinth	228341	84677	I27	0007-stablemarriage	976047	63486
I12	0008-labyrinth	229788	85189	I28	0061-ppm	1577625	24465
I13	0041-labyrinth	228807	84853	I29	0130-ppm	1569609	24273
I14	0007-labyrinth	229539	85100	I30	0121-ppm	2208048	28776
I15	0128-ppm	589884	14388	I31	0129-ppm	4854372	43164

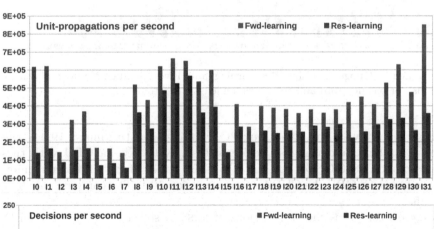

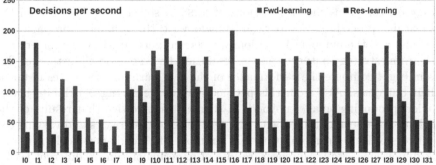

Fig. 3. Performance of the two versions of YASMIN (using Res-learning and Fwd-learning). Number of propagations per second (top) and number of decisions per second (bottom).

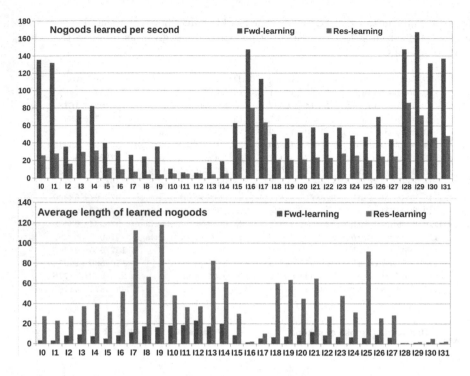

Fig. 4. Learned nogoods using Res-learning and Fwd-learning. Number of learned nogoods per second (top) and their average length (bottom).

Experiments were run on a Linux PC (running Ubuntu Linux v.19.04), used as host machine, and using as device a Tesla K40c Nvidia GPU with these characteristics: 2880 CUDA cores at 0.75 GHz, 12 GB of global device memory. We used on such GPU the CUDA runtime version 10.1. The compute capability was 3.5.

Figure 3 compares the two versions of YASMIN solver, differing only on the used learning procedure. Comparison is made w.r.t. the number of propagations per second and the number of decisions per second performed by the solver. The new learning strategy outperforms the resolution-based one on all instances. The plots in Fig. 4 compare the performance of the two learning procedures in terms of their outcomes. Also from this perspective `fwd_learning()` exhibits better behavior, producing smaller nogoods in shorter time. Notice that results of the same kind have been obtained with different selection heuristics and varying the parameters of kernel configuration (e.g., number of threads-per-block, grid and block dimensions, etc.). Moreover, results of experiment run on different GPUs are in line with those reported.

Algorithm 5: Host code of the pthreaded version of the ASP-solver YASMIN   (simplified)

```
      procedure MULTI_YASMIN(Δ: SetOfNogoods, P: GroundProgram, Np: int, Nt: int)
      /* Generates Np subproblems according to input options/heuristics Opts:        */
   1  Parts ← partition_problem(Δ, Np, Opts)
      /* Creates a pool of Np host POSIX threads (pthreads share host variables Δ, P,
         Parts,...). Each pthread will issue commands in a private CUDA stream:       */
   2  for (pth ← 0; pth < Nt; pth++) do
           /* Spawns a pthread. Each pthread concurrently executes an instance of the host
              procedure yasmin_launcher():                                            */
   3  |    pths[pth] ← pthread_create(yasmin_launcher(pth))
      /* Waits for all pthreads' completion:                                          */
   4  for (pth ← 0; pth < Nt; pth++) do
   5  |    pthread_join(pths[pth])
   6  cudaDeviceSynchronize ()   /* waits for termination of all issued commands before output
      the results */

      procedure YASMIN_LAUNCHER(pth: int)
      /* Code executed by each host pthread to solve a sequence of subproblems        */
   7  while exists  S ∈ Parts do      /* repeat until all Np subproblem has been processed */
   8  |    Parts ← Parts \ {S}                /* selects a subproblem, in mutual exclusion */
   9  |    yasmin(Δ, P, S, pth)      /* calls basic CUDA-solver (Algorithm 1) for subproblem S */
  10  |    cudaStreamSynchronize ()       /* waits for termination of commands in the stream */
  11  pthread_exit()                            /* pthread ends and joins the main pthread */
```

Conclusions

In this paper we described the main traits of a CUDA-based solver for Answer Set Programming. The fact that the algorithms involved in ASP-solving present an irregular and low-arithmetic intensity, usually combined with data-dependent control flows, makes it difficult to achieve high performance without adopting proper sophisticated solutions and fulfilling suitable programming directives. In this paper we dealt with the basic software architecture of a parallel prototypical solver with the main aim of demonstrating that GPU-computing can be exploited in ASP solving. Much is left to do in order to obtain a full-blown parallel solver able to compete with the state-of-the-art existing solvers. First, efforts have to be made in enhancing the parallel solver with the collection of heuristics proficiently used to guide the search in sequential solvers. Indeed, experimental comparisons [8] show that good heuristics might be the most effective component of a solver. Second, the applicability of further techniques and refinements have to be investigated. For instance, techniques such as *parallel lookahead* [6], *multiple learning* [12], should be considered. The development of a parallel solver that operates on multiple GPUs represents an interesting theme of research. In this context, we observe that the multi-pthread approach outlined in Sect. 4.3 can be easily adapted to operate with multiple devices. Indeed, it would suffice to partition/replicate input data, distribute them to the available GPUs, and allow the host pthreads to launch the basic solver on various devices. Also the possibility of implementing a distributed parallel solver that operates on multiple GPUs installed on different hosts represents a challenging theme of research. In this case, message passing frameworks, such as MPI [20], could be proficiently exploited to implement communication among hosts.

References

1. Bernaschi, M., Bisson, M., Mastrostefano, E., Vella, F.: Multilevel parallelism for the exploration of large-scale graphs. IEEE Trans. Multi-Scale Comput. Syst. **4**(3), 204–216 (2018)
2. Biere, A., Heule, M., van Maaren, H., Walsh, T.: Handbook of Satisfiability, Volume 185 of Frontiers in Artificial Intelligence and Applications. IOS Press (2009)
3. Dal Palù, A., Dovier, A., Formisano, A., Pontelli, E.: CUD@SAT: SAT solving on GPUs. J. Exper. Theor. Artif. Intell. (JETAI) **27**(3), 293–316 (2015)
4. Dal Palù, A., Dovier, A., Pontelli, E., Rossi, G.: GASP: answer set programming with lazy grounding. Fundam. Inf. **96**(3), 297–322 (2009)
5. Dovier, A., Formisano, A., Pontelli, E.: An experimental comparison of constraint logic programming and answer set programming. In: Proceedings of the 22nd AAAI Conference on Artificial Intelligence, pp. 1622–1625. AAAI Press (2007)
6. Dovier, A., Formisano, A., Pontelli, E.: Parallel answer set programming. In: Hamadi, Y., Sais, L. (eds.) Handbook of Parallel Constraint Reasoning, pp. 237–282. Springer, Cham (2018). https://doi.org/10.1007/978-3-319-63516-3_7
7. Dovier, A., Formisano, A., Pontelli, E., Vella, F.: Parallel execution of the ASP computation. In: de Vos, M., Eiter, T., Lierler, Y., Toni, F. (eds.) Technical Communications of ICLP 2015, vol. 1433. CEUR-WS.org (2015)
8. Dovier, A., Formisano, A., Pontelli, E., Vella, F.: A GPU implementation of the ASP computation. In: Gavanelli, M., Reppy, J. (eds.) PADL 2016. LNCS, vol. 9585, pp. 30–47. Springer, Cham (2016). https://doi.org/10.1007/978-3-319-28228-2_3
9. Erdem, E., Gelfond, M., Leone, N.: Applications of answer set programming. AI Mag. **37**(3), 53–68 (2016)
10. Falkner, A., Friedrich, G., Schekotihin, K., Taupe, R., Teppan, E.C.: Industrial applications of answer set programming. Künstliche Intelligenz **32**(2), 165–176 (2018)
11. Formisano, A., Gentilini, R., Vella, F.: Accelerating energy games solvers on modern architectures. In: Proceedings of the 7th Workshop on Irregular Applications: Architectures and Algorithms, IA3@SC, pp. 12:1–12:4. ACM (2017)
12. Formisano, A., Vella, F.: On multiple learning schemata in conflict driven solvers. In: Bistarelli, S., Formisano, A. (eds.), Proceedings of ICTCS, vol. 1231. CEUR-WS.org (2014)
13. Gebser, M., Kaminski, R., Kaufmann, B., Schaub, T.: Answer Set Solving in Practice. Morgan & Claypool Publishers, San Rafael (2012)
14. Gelfond, M.: Answer sets. In: van Harmelen, F., Lifschitz, V., Porter, B.W. (eds), Handbook of Knowledge Representation, chap. 7. Elsevier (2008)
15. Gupta, G., Pontelli, E., Ali, K.A.M., Carlsson, M., Hermenegildo, M.V.: Parallel execution of prolog programs: a survey. ACM Trans. Program. Lang. Syst. **23**(4), 472–602 (2001)
16. Hong, S., Oguntebi, T., Olukotun, K.: Efficient parallel graph exploration on multi-core CPU and GPU. In: International Conference on Parallel Architectures and Compilation Techniques, pp. 78–88. IEEE (2011)
17. Lin, F., Zhao, J.: On tight logic programs and yet another translation from normal logic programs to propositional logic. In: Gottlob, G., Walsh, T. (eds.), Proceedings of IJCAI 2003, pp. 853–858. Morgan Kaufmann (2003)
18. Liu, L., Pontelli, E., Son, T.C., Truszczynski, M.: Logic programs with abstract constraint atoms: the role of computations. Artif. Intell. **174**(3–4), 295–315 (2010)

19. Lumsdaine, A., Gregor, D., Hendrickson, B., Berry, J.: Challenges in parallel graph processing. Parallel Process. Lett. **17**(01), 5–20 (2007)
20. MPI Forum. MPIForum site (2019). https://www.mpi-forum.org/
21. NVIDIA. CUDA C: Programming Guide (v.10.1). NVIDIA Press, Santa Clara (2019)
22. NVIDIA Corporation. NVIDIA CUDA Zone (2019). https://developer.nvidia.com/cuda-zone

A Process Calculus for Formally Verifying Blockchain Consensus Protocols

Wolfgang Jeltsch[1,2]([✉]) [iD]

[1] Well-Typed, London, UK
wolfgang@well-typed.com
[2] IOHK, Hong Kong, Hong Kong

Abstract. Blockchains are becoming increasingly relevant in a variety of fields, such as finance, logistics, and real estate. The fundamental task of a blockchain system is to establish data consistency among distributed agents in an open network. Blockchain consensus protocols are central for performing this task.

Since consensus protocols play such a crucial role in blockchain technology, several projects are underway that apply formal methods to these protocols. One such project is carried out by a team of the Formal Methods Group at IOHK. This project, in which the author is involved, aims at a formally verified implementation of the Ouroboros family of consensus protocols, the backbone of the Cardano blockchain. The first outcome of our project is the ♮-calculus (pronounced "natural calculus"), a general-purpose process calculus that serves as our implementation language. The ♮-calculus is a domain-specific language embedded in a functional host language using higher-order abstract syntax.

This paper will be a ramble through the ♮-calculus. First we will look at its language and its operational semantics. The latter is unique in that it uses a stack of two labeled transition systems to treat phenomena like data transfer and the opening and closing of channel scope in a modular fashion. The presence of multiple transition systems calls for a generic treatment of derived concurrency concepts. We will see how such a treatment can be achieved by capturing notions like scope opening and silent transitions abstractly using axiomatically defined algebraic structures based on functors and monads.

Keywords: Blockchain · Distributed computing · Formal verification · Process calculus · Functional programming · Higher-order abstract syntax

1 Introduction

A blockchain is an open, distributed database that stores a growing list, the *ledger*, and achieves security by employing advanced cryptographic methods. Blockchains are used in finance for implementing cryptocurrencies and smart contracts and have applications in other fields too.

A blockchain system establishes data consistency using a *consensus protocol*. There are two main kinds of such protocols:

© Springer Nature Switzerland AG 2020
P. Hofstedt et al. (Eds.): DECLARE 2019, LNAI 12057, pp. 24–39, 2020.
https://doi.org/10.1007/978-3-030-46714-2_2

- *Proof-of-work* protocols require participants to solve computational puzzles in order to contribute data to the blockchain.
- *Proof-of-stake* protocols make the opportunity to contribute data dependent on the stake participants possess, such as money in a cryptocurrency.

Since the correctness of a blockchain system rests on the correctness of its consensus protocol, several projects are underway that apply formal methods to consensus protocols. One such project is carried out by a team of the Formal Methods Group at IOHK. This project, in which the author is involved, aims at a formally verified implementation of the Ouroboros family of consensus protocols [1,7,11], which form the backbone of the Cardano blockchain.

All protocols in the Ouroboros family use the proof-of-stake mechanism and come with rigorous security guarantees. In fact, the original Ouroboros protocol, dubbed Ouroboros Classic, was the first proof-of-stake protocol to have such guarantees. The Cardano blockchain is the basis of the cryptocurrency Ada and the smart contract languages Plutus [6] and Marlowe [12]. Both Plutus and Marlowe are functional languages, but while Plutus is Turing-complete, Marlowe is deliberately restricted in its expressivity to make implementing common contracts easy.

In this paper, we report on the first outcome of our Ouroboros formalization effort: the ♮-*calculus* (pronounced "natural calculus"). The ♮-calculus is a process calculus that serves as our specification and implementation language. We make the following contributions:

- In Sect. 2, we present the language and the operational semantics of the ♮-calculus. The latter is unique in that it uses a stack of two labeled transition systems to treat phenomena like data transfer and the opening and closing of channel scope in a modular fashion
- The presence of multiple transition systems calls for a generic treatment of derived concurrency concepts, such as strong and weak bisimilarity. In Sect. 3, we develop an abstract theory of transition systems to achieve such a generic treatment. Our theory captures notions like scope opening and silent transitions using axiomatically defined algebraic structures. In these structures, functors and monads play a crucial role.

We conclude this paper with Sects. 4 and 5, where we discuss related work and give a summary and an outlook.

To this end, we have formalized [10] large parts of the ♮-calculus and our complete theory of transition systems in Isabelle/HOL. Furthermore, we have produced this paper from documented Isabelle source code [9], which we have checked against our formalization.

2   The ♮-Calculus

The ♮-calculus is a process calculus in the tradition of the π-calculus [14]. It is not tied to blockchains in any way but is a universal language for concurrent and distributed computing.

Unlike the π-calculus, the ♮-calculus is not an isolated language but is embedded into functional host languages. In our application scenario, we use embeddings into both Haskell, for execution, and Isabelle/HOL, for verification. The user is expected to write programs as Haskell-embedded process calculus terms, which can then be turned automatically into Isabelle-embedded process calculus terms to make them available for verification. In this paper, we focus on the Isabelle embedding, leaving the discussion of the Haskell embedding for another time. Whenever we use the term "♮-calculus", we refer to either the calculus in general or its embedding into Isabelle/HOL.

Our embedding technique uses higher-order abstract syntax (HOAS) [15], which means we represent binding of names using functions of the host language. An immediate consequence of this is that the host language deals with all the issues regarding names, like shadowing and α-equivalence, which simplifies the implementation of the calculus. Furthermore, HOAS gives us support for arbitrary data for free, since we can easily represent data by values of the host language. This lifts the restriction of the π-calculus that channels are the only kind of data. Finally, HOAS allows us to move computation, branching, and recursion to the host language level and thus further simplify the implementation of the calculus.

The ♮-calculus is similar to ψ-calculi [3] in that it adds support for arbitrary data to the core features of the π-calculus. However, since the ♮-calculus uses HOAS, we can avoid much of the complexity of ψ-calculi that comes from their need to cope with data-related issues themselves.

2.1 Language

We define a coinductive data type *process* whose values are the terms of the ♮-calculus. We call these terms simply *processes*.

In the following, we list the different kinds of processes. For describing their syntax, we use statements of the form $C\ x_1 \ldots x_n \equiv e$. The left-hand side of such a statement is an application of a data constructor of the *process* type to argument variables; it showcases the ordinary notation for the respective kind of processes. The right-hand side is a term that is equal to the left-hand side but uses convenient notation introduced by us using Isabelle's means for defining custom syntax. The kinds of processes are as follows:

– Do nothing:

$$Stop \equiv \mathbf{0}$$

– Send value x to channel a:

$$Send\ a\ x \equiv a \lhd x$$

– Receive value x from channel a and continue with $P\ x$:

$$Receive\ a\ P \equiv a \rhd x.\ P\ x$$

– Perform processes p and q concurrently:

$$Parallel\ p\ q \equiv p \parallel q$$

– Create a new channel a and continue with P a:

$$NewChannel\ P \equiv \nu\ a.\ P\ a$$

The binders ($\triangleright$ and ν) bind stronger than the infix operator ($\parallel$), which is not what the reader might have expected but is typical for process calculi.

There are a few interesting points to note regarding processes and their notation:

– Our use of HOAS manifests itself in the *Receive* and *NewChannel* cases. In both of them, the respective data constructor takes an argument P that is a continuation which maps a received value or a newly created channel to a remainder process.
– Although dependencies on received values and newly created channels are encoded using functions, we can still use convenient binder notation for *Receive* and *NewChannel* processes. A term e in $a \triangleright x.\ e$ or $\nu\ a.\ e$ does not have to be an application of a function P to the bound variable. Every term that possibly mentions the bound variable is fine. For example, $a \triangleright x.\ (b \triangleleft x \parallel c \triangleleft x)$ is a valid term, which is equal to *Receive* $a\ (\lambda x.\ b \triangleleft x \parallel c \triangleleft x)$.
– HOAS gives us the opportunity to construct processes that include computation and branching, despite the process calculus not having dedicated constructs for these things. For example, the process $a \triangleright y.\ (if\ y \neq x\ then\ b \triangleleft y\ else\ \mathbf{0})$, which performs a kind of conditional forwarding, carries the inequality test and the branching inside the continuation argument of *Receive*.
– *Send* does not have a continuation argument. This is to make communication effectively asynchronous. The operational semantics defines communication in the usual way, making it actually synchronous, but without *Send* continuations, synchrony cannot be observed. This approach is common for asynchronous process calculi and is used, for example, in the asynchronous π-calculus [5]. We use asynchronous communication, because it is sufficient for our use case and easier to implement in common programming languages, like Haskell.
– The $\natural$-calculus does not have a construct for nondeterministic choice, because execution of nondeterministic choice is difficult to implement.
– The $\natural$-calculus does not have a construct for replication. We do not need such a construct, since the *process* type is coinductive and thus allows us to form infinite terms. The replication of a process p can be defined as the infinite term $p \parallel p \parallel \ldots$, that is, the single term p^∞ for which $p^\infty = p \parallel p^\infty$.

2.2 Operational Semantics

We define the operational semantics of the $\natural$-calculus as a labeled transition system. We write $p \to (\!|\xi|\!)\ q$ to say that p can transition to q with label ξ.

We handle isolated sending and receiving as well as communication in the standard manner. We introduce labels $a \lhd x$, $a \rhd x$, and τ, which denote sending of a value x to a channel a, receiving of a value x from a channel a, and internal communication, respectively, and call these labels *actions*. Then we introduce the following rules:

- Sending:
$$a \lhd x \to (\!| a \lhd x |\!) \; \mathbf{0}$$

- Receiving:
$$a \rhd x. \; P \; x \to (\!| a \rhd x |\!) \; P \; x$$

- Communication:
$$[\![p \to (\!| a \lhd x |\!) \; p'; q \to (\!| a \rhd x |\!) \; q']\!] \implies p \parallel q \to (\!| \tau |\!) \; p' \parallel q'$$

- Acting within a subsystem:
$$p \to (\!| \xi |\!) \; p' \implies p \parallel q \to (\!| \xi |\!) \; p' \parallel q$$

The last two of these rules have symmetric versions, which we do not show here for the sake of simplicity.

Channels created by *NewChannel* are initially local. However, such channels can later be made visible by sending them to other subsystems. Let us see how this is captured by the transition system of the π-calculus. Besides ordinary sending labels $a \lhd b$, the π-calculus has labels $a \lhd \nu \, b$. b that additionally bind the variable b. The bound variable denotes a channel not yet known to the outside. Using it as the value being sent thus conveys the information that a local channel is being published by sending it to a. When used as part of a transition statement, the scope of the binder includes the target process, so that the target process can depend on the published channel. Therefore, the general form of a transition statement with local channel publication is $p \to (\!| a \lhd \nu \, b. \; b |\!) \; Q \; b$. The following rules are HOAS versions of the π-calculus rules that deal with local channels:

- Scope opening:
$$(\bigwedge b. \; P \; b \to (\!| a \lhd b |\!) \; Q \; b) \implies \nu \, b. \; P \; b \to (\!| a \lhd \nu \, b. \; b |\!) \; Q \; b$$

- Communication with scope closing:
$$[\![p \to (\!| a \lhd \nu \, b. \; b |\!) \; P \; b; \bigwedge b. \; q \to (\!| a \rhd b |\!) \; Q \; b]\!] \implies p \parallel q \to (\!| \tau |\!) \; \nu \, b. \; (P \; b \parallel Q \; b)$$

- Acting inside scope:
$$(\bigwedge a. \; P \; a \to (\!| \delta |\!) \; Q \; a) \implies \nu \, a. \; P \; a \to (\!| \delta |\!) \; \nu \, a. \; Q \; a$$

For the $\natural$-calculus, these rules are unfortunately not enough. Unlike the π-calculus, the $\natural$-calculus permits arbitrary data to be sent, which includes values that contain several channels, like pairs of channels and lists of channels. As a result, several local channels can be published at once. Variants of the above rules that account for this possibility are complex and hard to get right. The complexity has two reasons:

- Some labels deal with multiple concepts, namely scope opening and sending. In the $\natural$-calculus, these labels are not necessarily of the relatively simple form $a \triangleleft \nu\, b.\, b$ discussed above, but generally of the more complex form $\nu\, b_1 \ldots b_n.\, a \triangleleft f\, b_1 \ldots b_n$, because arbitrary values depending on multiple local channels can be sent.
- Some rules deal with multiple concepts, namely the rule about communication with scope closing, which deals with precisely these two things, and the rule about acting inside scope, which essentially adds scope opening before and scope closing after the given action.

To tame this complexity, we conduct the definition of the transition system in two steps:

1. We define a transition system that uses distinct transitions for opening scopes, so that each label and each rule deals with a single concept only. We call this transition system the *basic transition system* and write a transition in this system $p \to_\flat \{\!| \xi |\!\}\, q$.
2. We define the transition system that describes the actual semantics of the $\natural$-calculus by adding a layer on top of the basic transition system that bundles scope opening and sending transitions. We call this transition system the *proper transition system* and write a transition in this system $p \to_\natural (\!| \xi |\!)\, q$.

The basic transition system has *action labels* $a \triangleleft x$, $a \triangleright x$, and τ as well as *opening labels* $\nu\, a$, the latter binding their variables in any following target process. The rules for sending, receiving, and communication are the ones we have seen at the beginning of Sect. 2.2. For dealing with local channels, the basic transition system contains the following rules:

- Scope opening:
$$\nu\, a.\, P\, a \to_\flat \{\!| \nu\, a |\!\}\, P\, a$$
- Scope closing after acting:
$$[\![p \to_\flat \{\!| \nu\, a |\!\}\, Q\, a; \bigwedge a.\, Q\, a \to_\flat \{\!| \alpha |\!\}\, R\, a]\!] \Longrightarrow p \to_\flat \{\!| \alpha |\!\}\, \nu\, a.\, R\, a$$
- Scope closing after another scope opening:
$$[\![p \to_\flat \{\!| \nu\, a |\!\}\, Q\, a; \bigwedge a.\, Q\, a \to_\flat \{\!| \nu\, b |\!\}\, R\, a\, b]\!] \Longrightarrow p \to_\flat \{\!| \nu\, b |\!\}\, \nu\, a.\, R\, a\, b$$
- Scope opening within a subsystem:
$$p \to_\flat \{\!| \nu\, a |\!\}\, P\, a \Longrightarrow p \parallel q \to_\flat \{\!| \nu\, a |\!\}\, P\, a \parallel q$$

The last rule has a symmetric version, which we do not show here for the sake of simplicity.

The proper transition system has labels $a \triangleright x, \tau$, and $a \triangleleft \nu\, b_1 \ldots b_n.\, f\, b_1 \ldots b_n$, the latter binding their variables also in any following target process. The rules for sending, receiving, and communication just refer to the basic transition system:

– Sending:

$$p \rightarrow_\flat \{\!|a \lhd x|\!\} \; q \Longrightarrow p \rightarrow_\sharp (\!|a \lhd x|\!) \; q$$

– Receiving:

$$p \rightarrow_\flat \{\!|a \rhd x|\!\} \; q \Longrightarrow p \rightarrow_\sharp (\!|a \rhd x|\!) \; q$$

– Communication:

$$p \rightarrow_\flat \{\!|\tau|\!\} \; q \Longrightarrow p \rightarrow_\sharp (\!|\tau|\!) \; q$$

For scope opening, we have a series of facts, one for each number of published channels. The facts for one and two published channels are as follows:

– One channel:

$$[\![p \rightarrow_\flat \{\!|\nu \; b|\!\} \; Q \; b; \; \bigwedge b. \; Q \; b \rightarrow_\sharp (\!|a \lhd f \; b|\!) \; R \; b]\!] \Longrightarrow p \rightarrow_\sharp (\!|a \lhd \nu \; b. \; f \; b|\!) \; R \; b$$

– Two channels:

$$[\![p \rightarrow_\flat \{\!|\nu \; b|\!\} \; Q \; b; \; \bigwedge b. \; Q \; b \rightarrow_\sharp (\!|a \lhd \nu \; c. \; f \; b \; c|\!) \; R \; b \; c]\!] \Longrightarrow$$
$$p \rightarrow_\sharp (\!|a \lhd \nu \; b \; c. \; f \; b \; c|\!) \; R \; b \; c$$

The facts for more published channels are analogous. All of these facts can be captured by a single rule, which we do not show here for the sake of simplicity.

As it stands, the proper transition system has the issue that a scope can also be opened when the respective channel is not published. For example, $\nu \; b. \; a \lhd x \rightarrow_\sharp (\!|a \lhd \nu \; b. \; x|\!) \; \mathbf{0}$ is a possible transition. We are currently investigating ways to fix this issue. That said, this issue is of little relevance for the rest of this paper, where we discuss the effects of transitions involving scope opening in a way that is largely independent of the particularities of concrete transition systems.

A key issue with both the basic and the proper transition system is that, whenever a label contains a binder, the scope of this binder includes any following target process. As a result, we can treat neither of the two transition relations as a ternary relation, where source processes, labels, and target processes are separate entities. As a solution, we consider the combination of a label and an associated target process a single entity, which we call a *residual*. Our transition relations then become binary, relating source processes and residuals. This approach has been taken in the formalization of ψ-calculi [3], for example.

We define an inductive data type whose values are the residuals of the basic transition system. There are two kinds of such residuals:

– Acting:

$$Acting \; \alpha \; p \equiv \{\!|\alpha|\!\} \; p$$

– Opening:

$$Opening \; P \equiv \{\!|\nu \; a|\!\} \; P \; a$$

Note that in the *Opening* case we use HOAS and binder notation again.

Actually we do not just define a single data type for residuals but a type constructor *basic-residual* that is parametrized by the type of the target. As a result, terms $\{\!|\xi|\!\}$ *e* can be formed from terms *e* of any type α, with the resulting type being α *basic-residual*. This permits us to construct *nested residuals*, residuals with two labels, which have type *process basic-residual basic-residual*. Nested residuals will play a role in Subsect. 3.2.

We also introduce an analogous type constructor *proper-residual* for the proper transition system. The definition of *proper-residual* is considerably more complex than the definition of *basic-residual*, which is why we do not show it here. However, its general approach to capturing scope opening is the same.

2.3   Behavioral Equivalence

Ultimately, we are interested in proving that different processes behave in the same way or at least in similar ways. The standard notion of behavioral equivalence is *bisimilarity*. A typical approach to define bisimilarity is the following one:

1. We define the predicate *sim* on binary relations between processes as follows:

$$sim \; \mathcal{X} \longleftrightarrow (\forall p \, q \, \xi \, p'. \, \mathcal{X} \, p \, q \wedge p \to\!(\!|\xi|\!) \, p' \longrightarrow (\exists q'. \, q \to\!(\!|\xi|\!) \, q' \wedge \mathcal{X} \, p' \, q'))$$

A relation $\mathcal{X}$ for which *sim* $\mathcal{X}$ holds is called a *simulation relation*.

2. We define the predicate *bisim* on binary relations between processes as follows:[1]

$$bisim \; \mathcal{X} \longleftrightarrow sim \; \mathcal{X} \wedge sim \; \mathcal{X}^{-1\,-1}$$

A relation $\mathcal{X}$ for which *bisim* $\mathcal{X}$ holds is called a *bisimulation relation*.

3. We define bisimilarity as the greatest bisimulation relation:

$$(\sim) = (GREATEST \; \mathcal{X}. \; bisim \; \mathcal{X})$$

The above definition of *sim* refers to labels and target processes separately and assumes each transition has exactly one target process. This is a problem in the presence of scope opening, where labels and target processes have to be considered together and where a single transition may have different target processes depending on published channels.

Let us see how we can solve this problem for the basic transition system. We develop a definition of the notion of simulation relation that retains the essence of the above definition but is able to deal with the peculiarities of opening residuals. First, we define an operation *basic-lift* that turns a relation between processes into a relation between basic residuals. The general idea is that *basic-lift* $\mathcal{X}$ relates two residuals if and only if their labels are the same and their target processes are in relation $\mathcal{X}$. This idea can be tweaked in an obvious way to work with opening residuals. We define *basic-lift* inductively using the following rules:

---

[1] Note that $\text{-}^{-1\,-1}$ is Isabelle/HOL syntax for conversion of relations that are represented by binary boolean functions.

– Acting case:
$$\mathcal{X}\ p\ q \implies basic\text{-}lift\ \mathcal{X}\ (\{\!\!|\alpha|\!\!\}\ p)\ (\{\!\!|\alpha|\!\!\}\ q)$$

– Opening case:

$$(\bigwedge a.\ \mathcal{X}\ (P\ a)\ (Q\ a)) \implies basic\text{-}lift\ \mathcal{X}\ (\{\!\!|\nu\ a|\!\!\}\ P\ a)\ (\{\!\!|\nu\ a|\!\!\}\ Q\ a)$$

Using *basic-lift*, we define the notion of simulation relation for the basic transition system as follows:

$$basic.sim\ \mathcal{X} \longleftrightarrow (\forall p\ q\ c.\ \mathcal{X}\ p\ q \wedge p \to_\flat c \longrightarrow (\exists d.\ q \to_\flat d \wedge basic\text{-}lift\ \mathcal{X}\ c\ d))$$

For the proper transition system, we can define a lifting operation *proper-lift* in an analogous way. Afterwards we can define the notion of simulation relation for the proper transition system in exactly the same way as for the basic transition system, except that we have to replace *basic-lift* by *proper-lift*.

3   Residuals Axiomatically

As it stands, we have to develop the theory of bisimilarity separately for the basic and the proper transition system. This means, we have to essentially duplicate definitions of concepts like simulation relation, bisimulation relation, and bisimilarity and also proofs of various properties of these concepts. The reason is that these two transition systems use different notions of residual and consequently different lifting operations.

However, we can develop the theory of bisimilarity also generically. We describe axiomatically what a lifting operation is and construct all definitions and proofs of our theory with reference to a lifting operation parameter that fulfills the respective axioms. Whenever we want our theory to support a new notion of residual, we just have to define a concrete lifting operation for it and prove that this lifting operation has the necessary properties.

Note that this approach not only allows for a common treatment of the basic and the proper transition system but also captures transition systems of other process calculi. In particular, it also works with transition systems that do not allow scope opening, like CCS [13], as there is a trivial lifting operation for such systems.

3.1   Residuals in General

As indicated in Subsect. 2.3, a lifting operation *lift* should generally behave such that *lift* $\mathcal{X}$ relates two residuals if and only if their labels are the same and their target processes are in relation $\mathcal{X}$. The axioms for lifting operations should be in line with this behavior and should at the same time be specific enough to allow us to develop the theory of bisimilarity solely based on a lifting operation parameter. It turns out that the following axioms fulfill these requirements:[2]

---

[2] Note that - *OO* - is Isabelle/HOL syntax for composition of relations that are represented by binary boolean functions.

- Equality preservation:
$$lift \; (=) = (=)$$
- Composition preservation:

$$lift \; (\mathcal{X} \; OO \; \mathcal{Y}) = lift \; \mathcal{X} \; OO \; lift \; \mathcal{Y}$$

- Conversion preservation:

$$lift \; \mathcal{X}^{-1-1} = (lift \; \mathcal{X})^{-1-1}$$

The presence of the equality preservation and composition preservation axioms means that lifting operations are functors. However, they are not functors in the Haskell sense. Haskell's functors are specifically endofunctors on the category of types and functions, but lifting operations are endofunctors on the category of types and *relations*.[3]

With the additional conversion preservation axiom, the axioms for lifting operations are precisely the axioms for *relators* [4, Sect. 5.1]. Therefore, we can say that a residual structure is just an endorelator on the category of types and relations – no problem here. Luckily, Isabelle/HOL automatically generates relator-specific constructs for every data type, namely the lifting operation and various facts about it, including the instances of the axioms. As a result, instantiating our theory of bisimilarity to a new notion of residual is extremely simple.

3.2 Weak Residuals

Our axiomatic treatment of lifting operations allows us to handle ordinary bisimilarity, which is also known as *strong bisimilarity*. In practice, however, we are more interested in *weak bisimilarity*. Weak bisimilarity cares only about observable behavior; it treats internal communication as silent and ignores it.

Normally, weak bisimilarity can be elegantly defined as the bisimilarity of the *weak transition relation* ($\Rightarrow$), which is derived from the original transition relation ($\rightarrow$) using the following equivalences:[4]

- Silent:

$$p \Rightarrow\!(\!|\tau|\!) \; q \longleftrightarrow p \rightarrow\!(\!|\tau|\!)^{**} \; q$$

- Observable:

$$\xi \neq \tau \Longrightarrow p \Rightarrow\!(\!|\xi|\!) \; q \longleftrightarrow (\exists s \; t. \; p \Rightarrow\!(\!|\tau|\!) \; s \wedge s \rightarrow\!(\!|\xi|\!) \; t \wedge t \Rightarrow\!(\!|\tau|\!) \; q)$$

Unfortunately, the above definition of ($\Rightarrow$) refers to a dedicated silent label and thus cannot be applied to our setting, where we treat residuals as black boxes. To resolve this issue, we modify the definition of ($\Rightarrow$) such that it is

---

[3] The analogy to functors in the Haskell sense can be seen from the fact that replacing *lift*, $(=)$, and (OO) in the equality preservation and composition preservation axioms by Haskell's `fmap`, `id`, and `(.)` yields Haskell's functor axioms.

[4] The notation - $\rightarrow\!(\!|\tau|\!)^{**}$ - stands for the reflexive and transitive closure of - $\rightarrow\!(\!|\tau|\!)$ -.

based on two relations that together identify silence. We define these relations differently for different notions of residual but specify their general properties by a set of axioms.

The first of the relations that identify silence relates each process with the residual that extends this process with the silent label. For *basic-residual*, we define this relation inductively using the following rule:

$$basic\text{-}silent \; p \; (\{\!|\tau|\!\} \; p)$$

For *proper-residual* and other residual type constructors, we can define the corresponding relation in an analogous way.

The second of the relations that identify silence relates each nested residual that contains the silent label at least once with the ordinary residual that is obtained by dropping this label. For *basic-residual*, we define this relation inductively using the following rules:

– Silent–acting case:
$$basic\text{-}fuse \; (\{\!|\tau|\!\}\{\!|\alpha|\!\} \; p) \; (\{\!|\alpha|\!\} \; p)$$
– Silent–opening case:
$$basic\text{-}fuse \; (\{\!|\tau|\!\}\{\!|\nu \; a|\!\} \; P \; a) \; (\{\!|\nu \; a|\!\} \; P \; a)$$

– Acting–silent case:
$$basic\text{-}fuse \; (\{\!|\alpha|\!\}\{\!|\tau|\!\} \; p) \; (\{\!|\alpha|\!\} \; p)$$
– Opening–silent case:
$$basic\text{-}fuse \; (\{\!|\nu \; a|\!\}\{\!|\tau|\!\} \; P \; a) \; (\{\!|\nu \; a|\!\} \; P \; a)$$

For *proper-residual* and other residual type constructors, we can define the corresponding relation in an analogous way.

We define the weak transition relation ($\Rightarrow$) of a given transition relation ($\rightarrow$) generically based on two parameters *silent* and *fuse*. The definition of ($\Rightarrow$) is inductive, using the following rules:

– Strong transitions:
$$p \rightarrow c \Longrightarrow p \Rightarrow c$$
– Empty transitions:
$$silent \; p \; c \Longrightarrow p \Rightarrow c$$
– Compound transitions:
$$[\![\, p \Rightarrow c; \; lift \; (\Rightarrow) \; c \; z; \; fuse \; z \; d \,]\!] \Longrightarrow p \Rightarrow d$$

As indicated above, the behavior of *silent* and *fuse* should generally be such that *silent* adds a silent label to a process and *fuse* removes a silent label from a nested residual. The following axioms are in line with this behavior and are at the same time specific enough to allow us to develop the theory of weak bisimilarity solely based on the *silent* and *fuse* parameters:

- Silent naturality:
$$\mathcal{X} \; OO \; silent = silent \; OO \; lift \; \mathcal{X}$$

- Fuse naturality:
$$lift \; (lift \; \mathcal{X}) \; OO \; fuse = fuse \; OO \; lift \; \mathcal{X}$$

- Left-neutrality:
$$silent \; OO \; fuse = (=)$$

- Right-neutrality:
$$lift \; silent \; OO \; fuse = (=)$$

- Associativity:
$$fuse \; OO \; fuse = lift \; fuse \; OO \; fuse$$

The above axioms are precisely the axioms for monads.[5] Therefore, we can say that a weak residual structure is just a monad in the category of types and relations – a completely unproblematic specification.

The monadic approach to weak residuals is actually very general. In particular, it makes non-standard notions of silence possible, for example, by allowing multiple silent labels. Despite this generality, typical properties of weak bisimilarity can be proved generically. Concretely, we have developed formal proofs of the following statements:

- Weak bisimilarity is the same as "mixed" bisimilarity, a notion of bisimilarity where ordinary transitions are simulated by weak transitions.
- Strong bisimilarity is a subrelation of weak bisimilarity.

Furthermore, the generic definition of the weak transition relation ($\Rightarrow$) is simpler than the traditional definition shown at the beginning of Sect. 3.2 in that it does not distinguish between silent and observable transitions; this distinction is pushed into the definitions of the *silent* and *fuse* relations of the individual notions of weak residual. The simple structure of the definition of ($\Rightarrow$) encourages a simple structure of generic proofs about weak transitions.

3.3   Normal Weak Residuals

The monadic approach to weak residuals forces us to implement the two relations *silent* and *fuse* and prove their properties for every notion of residual. This usually takes quite some effort, in particular because the definition of the *fuse* relation is typically non-trivial, which also affects the proofs of its properties. The reward is that we can use non-standard notions of silence. However, we rarely need this additional power, because we are usually fine with having *normal*

---

[5] The analogy to monads in the Haskell sense can be seen from the fact that replacing *lift*, *silent*, *fuse*, (=), and (*OO*) in these axioms by Haskell's `fmap`, `return`, `join`, `id`, and (`.`) yields the naturality properties of `return` and `join`, which hold automatically because of parametricity [18], as well as Haskell's `join`-based monad axioms.

weak residuals, weak residuals that use a dedicated label to indicate silence. We introduce a more specific algebraic structure for normal weak residuals, which is much easier to instantiate than the monad structure of arbitrary weak residuals.

We identify silence using just a *silent* relation that has the following properties:

– Naturality:
$$\mathcal{X} \; OO \; silent = silent \; OO \; lift \; \mathcal{X}$$

– Left-uniqueness and left-totality:
$$silent \; OO \; silent^{-1-1} = (=)$$

– Right-uniqueness:
$$silent^{-1-1} \; OO \; silent \leq (=)$$

Note that in fact these axioms ensure that *silent* identifies a single label, our silent label. This shows that, although we do not have first-class labels explicitly, we can nevertheless have first-class representations of those labels that do not involve scope opening.

From a *silent* relation we can derive a relation *fuse* as follows:

$$fuse = silent^{-1-1} \sqcup lift \; silent^{-1-1}$$

This derivation captures exactly the idea that *fuse* removes a silent label from a nested residual: since *silent* adds a silent label, $silent^{-1-1}$ removes a silent label, and consequently $lift \; silent^{-1-1}$ removes a silent label under another label.

A *silent* relation with the above properties and the *fuse* relation derived from it together fulfill the monad axioms, which shows that normal weak residuals are in fact weak residuals.

4   Related Work

We are not the first ones to formalize a process calculus using HOAS. Honsell et al. [8], for example, define a HOAS-version of the π-calculus in Coq and prove considerable parts of its metatheory. Their formalization does not allow the construction of *exotic terms*, that is, processes whose structure depends on data. In our formalization, we use exotic terms deliberately for branching. However, we actually want process structure to depend on ordinary data only; dependence on channels, especially local channels, is something we would like to prevent. The approach of Honsell et al. for ruling out exotic terms is to declare the type of channels as a parameter. Unfortunately, we cannot adopt this approach for our formalization, since the classical nature of Isabelle/HOL makes exotic terms possible even if the channel type is abstract.

Röckl and Hirschkoff [17] develop a HOAS-based implementation of the language of the π-calculus in Isabelle/HOL and show that it is adequate with respect to an ordinary, first-order implementation. They prove several syntactic properties but do not deal with transitions and bisimilarity at all. Their definition of processes includes exotic terms, but they define a separate wellformedness predicate that identifies those processes that are not exotic.

Neither of the two works described uses an abstract theory of transition systems like we do. However, there is also no real demand for that, as these developments only deal with one or even no transition system.

We use HOAS, because we can avoid the difficulties of name handling this way. Another approach is to keep names explicit but use nominal logic [16] to make name handling easier. Bengtson follows this approach in his dissertation [2]. He formalizes several process calculi, namely CCS, the π-calculus, and ψ-calculi, in Isabelle/HOL, making use of its support for nominal logic.

5 Summary and Outlook

We have presented the language and the operational semantics of the $\natural$-calculus, a general-purpose process calculus embedded into functional host languages using HOAS. Since the operational semantics of the $\natural$-calculus is defined using two transition systems, we have developed an abstract theory of transition systems to treat concepts like bisimilarity generically. We have formalized [10] large parts of the $\natural$-calculus and our complete theory of transition systems in Isabelle/HOL.

Because of our use of HOAS, the $\natural$-calculus allows process structure to depend on channels. An important task for the future is the development of techniques that allow us to prevent channel-dependent behavior while continuing to use HOAS for expressing binding of names.

We plan to very soon start using our process calculus for developing a formally verified implementation of the Ouroboros family of consensus protocols. Our hope is to gain valuable feedback about our process calculus work this way, which can potentially lead to improvements of the calculus and its implementation.

Acknowledgements. I want to thank my colleagues at Well-Typed and IOHK for their encouraging and helpful feedback on this work. Special thanks go to Javier Díaz for stress-testing the $\natural$-calculus in his proofs of network equivalences, pointing me to some important related work, and proofreading this paper. Furthermore, I want to particularly thank Duncan Coutts and Philipp Kant for providing guidance and feedback concerning our efforts towards a verified implementation of the Ouroboros family of consensus protocols as well as Edsko de Vries for his help with process calculi and in particular for putting me on the HOAS path.

References

1. Badertscher, C., Gaži, P., Kiayias, A., Russell, A., Zikas, V.: Ouroboros genesis: composable proof-of-stake blockchains with dynamic availability. In: Proceedings of the 2018 ACM SIGSAC Conference on Computer and Communications Security, pp. 913–930. ACM, New York (2018). https://doi.org/10.1145/3243734.3243848. https://iohk.io/en/research/library/papers/ouroboros-genesis composable-proof-of-stake-blockchains-with-dynamic-availability/

2. Bengtson, J.: Formalising process calculi. Ph.D. thesis, Uppsala Universitet, Uppsala, Sweden (2010). http://www.itu.dk/people/jebe/my-phd.html
3. Bengtson, J., Johansson, M., Parrow, J., Victor, B.: Psi-calculi: a framework for mobile processes with nominal data and logic. Log. Methods Comput. Sci. **7**(1), (2011). https://doi.org/10.2168/LMCS-7(1:11)2011. https://arxiv.org/abs/1101.3262
4. Bird, R., de Moor, O.: Algebra of Programming. Prentice Hall International Series in Computer Science. Prentice Hall, Upper Saddle River (1997)
5. Boudol, G.: Asynchrony and the pi-calculus. Technical report RR-1702, INRIA, Rocquencourt, France, May 1992. https://hal.inria.fr/inria-00076939
6. Chakravarty, M., et al.: Functional blockchain contracts, May 2019. https://iohk.io/en/research/library/papers/functional-blockchain-contracts/. Unpublished draft
7. David, B., Gaži, P., Kiayias, A., Russell, A.: Ouroboros praos: an adaptively-secure, semi-synchronous proof-of-stake blockchain. In: Nielsen, J.B., Rijmen, V. (eds.) EUROCRYPT 2018. LNCS, vol. 10821, pp. 66–98. Springer, Cham (2018). https://doi.org/10.1007/978-3-319-78375-8_3. https://iohk.io/en/research/library/papers/ouroboros-praosan-adaptively-securesemi-synchronous-proof-of-stake-protocol/
8. Honsell, F., Miculan, M., Scagnetto, I.: π-calculus in (co)inductive type theory. Theor. Comput. Sci. **253**(2), 239–285 (2001). https://doi.org/10.1016/S0304-3975(00)00095-5. https://users.dimi.uniud.it/ marino.miculan/Papers/TCS99.pdf
9. Jeltsch, W.: A process calculus for formally verifying blockchain consensus protocols, November 2019. https://github.com/jeltsch/wflp-2019. Source code of this paper
10. Jeltsch, W., Díaz, J.: Towards a formalization of the Ouroboros protocol family, November 2019. https://github.com/input-output-hk/fm-ouroboros/tree/bbeec3136ae68e7bb6800680e216b12db6c1113a/Isabelle. Current version of the source code of the formalization
11. Kiayias, A., Russell, A., David, B., Oliynykov, R.: Ouroboros: a provably secure proof-of-stake blockchain protocol. In: Katz, J., Shacham, H. (eds.) CRYPTO 2017. LNCS, vol. 10401, pp. 357–388. Springer, Cham (2017). https://doi.org/10.1007/978-3-319-63688-7_12. https://iohk.io/en/research/library/papers/ouroborosa-provably-secure-proof-of-stake-blockchain-protocol/
12. Lamela Seijas, P., Thompson, S.: Marlowe: financial contracts on blockchain. In: Margaria, T., Steffen, B. (eds.) ISoLA 2018. LNCS, vol. 11247, pp. 356–375. Springer, Cham (2018). https://doi.org/10.1007/978-3-030-03427-6_27. https://iohk.io/en/research/library/papers/marlowefinancial-contracts-on-blockchain/
13. Milner, R.: Communication and Concurrency. Prentice Hall International Series in Computer Science. Prentice HallPrentice Hall, Upper Saddle River (1989)
14. Milner, R.: Communicating and Mobile Systems: The π-Calculus. Cambridge University Press, Cambridge (1999)
15. Pfenning, F., Elliott, C.: Higher-order abstract syntax. In: Proceedings of the ACM SIGPLAN 1988 Conference on Programming Language Design and Implementation, pp. 199–208. ACM, New York (1988). https://doi.org/10.1145/53990.54010
16. Pitts, A.M.: Nominal logic, a first order theory of names and binding. Inf. Comput. **186**(2), 165–193 (2003). https://doi.org/10.1016/S0890-5401(03)00138-X

17. Röckl, C., Hirschkoff, D.: A fully adequate shallow embedding of the π-calculus in Isabelle/HOL with mechanized syntax analysis. J. Funct. Program. **13**(2), 415–451 (2003). https://doi.org/10.1017/S0956796802004653
18. Wadler, P.: Theorems for free! In: Proceedings of the Fourth International Conference on Functional Programming Languages and Computer Architecture, pp. 347–359. ACM, New York (1989). https://doi.org/10.1145/99370.99404

22nd International Conference on Applications of Declarative Programming and Knowledge Management - INAP 2019

Modular Modeling and Optimized Scheduling of Building Energy Systems Based on Mixed Integer Programming

Armin Wolf[✉][iD]

IT4Energy Center, Fraunhofer FOKUS, Kaiserin-Augusta-Allee 31,
10589 Berlin, Germany
armin.wolf@fokus.fraunhofer.de

Abstract. Almost climate neutral buildings are one of the core goals in terms of sustainability. Beside the support of the necessary design decisions for an integrated, interoperable, ecological and economical operation of building energy systems, innovative management solutions for scheduling the operation of decentralized energy systems are of great importance. The challenge is an optimal interaction between energy system components in terms of own consumption, energy efficiency and resource consumption as well as greenhouse gas emissions. To achieve these goals a modular optimization approach based on Mixed Integer Programming is proposed. In detail, and to our knowledge the first time, a MIP model for the dynamic behavior of fuel cell Combined Heat and Power plants is presented. Our approach is evaluated for the operation of heat pumps showing that their energy efficiency can be increased significantly.

Keywords: Building energy systems · Constraint-based scheduling and optimization · Cross-sector coupling · Energy efficiency · Mixed Integer Programming

1 Introduction

In the context of the energy transformation, known as the "Energiewende", and global warming almost climate neutral buildings are one of the core goals. Beside the support of the necessary design decisions for an integrated, interoperable, ecological and economical operation of building energy systems, innovative management solutions for scheduling the operation of decentralized energy systems are of great importance. The challenge is the optimal interaction between energy system components in terms of own consumption, energy efficiency and resource consumption as well as greenhouse gas emissions. To achieve these goals, a Mixed Integer Programming (MIP) based optimization tool for the combination of

The presented work was funded by the German Federal Ministry for Economic Affairs and Energy within the project "WaveSave" (BMWi, funding number 03ET1312A).

© Springer Nature Switzerland AG 2020
P. Hofstedt et al. (Eds.): DECLARE 2019, LNAI 12057, pp. 43–58, 2020.
https://doi.org/10.1007/978-3-030-46714-2_3

energy system components like Combined Heat and Power plants (CHPs) and the operation of integrated energy systems was developed, using real or virtual costs in an overall objective function and taking into account the uncertainties caused by weather, volatility of renewable energies as well as the behavior and spontaneity of residents. This tool prototype was implemented and evaluated using previously defined application scenarios.

The paper is organized as follows. In the next section some related work is presented. In Sect. 3 a modular modeling approach for optimal operation of building energy systems based on MIP is presented. In detail, the linear modeling of the dynamic behavior of fuel cell CHPs (fcCHPs) is shown using some specific "modeling tricks". Then, in Sect. 4 some implementation issues of our "MIP Optimizer" are given. Finally, in Sect. 5 our approach is successfully evaluated: It is shown how the operation of heat pumps can be optimized significantly while reducing electric energy demand and cost without loss of comfort. The last section concludes and points to some future work to be done.

2   Related Work

For scheduling and optimization of decentralized energy systems MIP is an adequate approach [2–4] which we also use when modeling building energy systems. In [2] microCHPs based on combustion engines are used in two different scheduling scenarios: In the Single House Planning Problem (SHPP), the focus is on satisfying the heat demand of residents. The second scenario combines many microCHPs into a Fleet Planning Problem (FPP) in order to satisfy some electric power demands, still considering domestic heat demands. Both problems are modeled as MIP problems. There, the MIP model of the microCHPs is rather simple compared to our MIP model for fcCHPs (cf. Sect. 3.1). However, it is shown that for large fleets the MIP approach is impractical. Therefore a local search method was developed for the FPP, based on a dynamic programming formulation of the SHPP.

For additional flexibility to freely combine components in a modular MIP model of an energy system and to add sub-models of further energy system components we categorized the energy system components and used some conventions in our modular and extendable MIP modeling approach (cf. Sect. 3). This approach was motivated by [9].

In [8] the optimal configuration and operation of combined cooling, heating, and power (CCHP) microgrids are considered. Similar to our approach the uncertainty of cooling, heating, and power load is predicted, however, be aware the energy consumption can still deviate from the predicted values. The components of the microgrid considered in [8] and by us overlap in photovoltaic (PV) systems, (gas) boilers, thermal storage tanks (TSTs), absorption chillers, electric chillers, as well as in cooling, heating, and power loads. In [8] gas turbines and electric chillers are part of the microgrid while we take fcCHPs, batteries and heat or cold pumps into account, too. However, for optimization in [8] a nonlinear programming model is proposed, which aims to minimize the total costs of the CCHP system.

3   Developing Extendible, Modular Optimization Models

In order to realize the optimizing component of an energy management system, we carried out an extendible, modular modeling approach of building energy systems. Therefore combinable MIP sub-models of the energetic behavior of plant components (cf. Sect. 2) are developed. The optimization component generates corresponding mathematical optimization problems from problem-specific descriptions of building energy systems. Their solutions result in timetables resp. operation schedules for the components of the respective building energy system, where the supply, use and conversion of the various forms of energy is determined. Real or fictitious costs (e.g., for CO_2 emissions) can be minimized by this component.

A modular modeling approach is chosen where each component is characterized by whether it is an electrical, warming, cooling or financial source, sink or reservoir.[1] For example, energetic sources provide power, energetic sinks draw it. Energetic reservoirs have an energy level and can both draw and deliver power within minimum and maximum levels. With this knowledge, it is then determined for each time unit in the scheduling horizon that the sum of power supplies and demands must be balanced, i.e., zero, for electricity, heat and cold. The sum of the yields and costs of the financial sources and sinks form the objective function for the optimization. With these conditions, the specific sub-models of the energy system components are combined to form an overall model. The sub-models, which are to be defined for each component under consideration of these conventions, describe the plant-specific energetic behavior as well as the associated financial effects. This approach was motivated by [9]. Within this approach energy storage devices such as batteries or TSTs are reservoirs. Energy converters such as heat pumps are both electrical sinks and thermal sources (either cold or heat, depending on the operating mode). In order to join the sub-models of the energy system components into an overall model of the energy system, a naming convention is used for decision variables that define the consumption or production of the respective energy type in a discrete unit of time. For example, any electrical source p has a variable "electricOutputPower$_p(t)$" specifying the (average) electric power supply (output) during time unit t. The integration of all electrical sinks and sources in an energy system model then takes place depending on the relevant system components with the help of the equation

$$\forall t: \sum_{p \in \text{ElectricalSource}} \text{electricOutputPower}_p(t) = \sum_{c \in \text{ElectricalSink}} \text{electricInputPower}_c(t),$$

which states that the sum of electrical energy consumption and production must be balanced at all times. Similar equations are used to integrate system components via other types of energy. Since components are included in several equations, a quasi-automatic cross-sector coupling occurs across the considered energy types.

---

[1] In this context "modular" means that the MIP sub-models can be combined in accordance to any building energy system specification – not in the sense of [11].

Since costs but also yields were used to optimize energy system operations, we have supplemented the chosen approach with financial sources and sinks. Their outputs (yields) and inputs (costs) are added together over the scheduling horizon

$$\sum_{t \in \text{horizon}} \left(\sum_{p \in \text{FinancialSource}} \text{financialOutput}_p(t) + \sum_{c \in \text{FinancialSink}} \text{financialInput}_c(t) \right),$$

such that the optimization of an energy system is done either by minimizing the total costs or by maximizing the total yields, depending on whether the costs are represented by positive values and the yields by negative values or vice versa.

Taking these characterizations and conventions into account, a set of extendible and connectable MIP sub-models were created for the following energy system components:

- User behavior with time-variable electricity, heat/cooling and hot water requirements,
- Mains connections with power limitations, time-variable electricity prices and refunds,
- Mechanical block-type CHPs with switchable peak load boilers with efficiency factors,
- Heat/cooling pumps with variable (outdoor temperature-dependent) Coefficients of Performance (COP),
- Heat/cold storages with charging losses and efficiency factors,
- Battery storages with charging losses and efficiency factors,
- Absorption chillers with efficiency factors,
- Heating rods and burners with efficiency factors,
- Photovoltaic (PV) systems with predicted power supply,
- fcCHPs with their special characteristics.

In this context efficiency factors ($\in [0, 1]$) are reflecting energy conversion losses. Modeling approaches from [3] and useful suggestions for MIP modeling coming from [1] are adopted. In addition to the characteristic energetic behavior, cost factors such as (variable) primary energy costs or costs for emissions as well as wear and tear costs during start-up and shut-down of plants, i.e., operating and maintenance costs, were also taken into account. The most challenging part was the modeling of fcCHPs with their special characteristics. With the help of a fcCHP manufacturer, we created a mathematical model to describe the energetic relationships in fcCHPs. This will be presented in detail in the next section.

3.1   A MIP Model for Fuel Cell Combined Heat and Power Plants

FcCHPs have characteristic physical parameters (constant values) and characteristic curves for broad electrical energy, thermal energy and primary energy supply on the basis of monitoring data from practical tests. For fcCHPs their processing phases such as cold start, warm start etc. as well as their power modulation opportunities are typical. The individual phases within downtime and

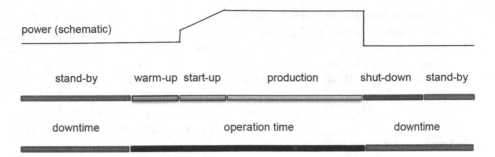

Fig. 1. Schematic power profile and according state phases of a fcCHP.

operating time are shown in Fig. 1. For example, the provision of thermal and electrical energy is delayed by a warm-up phase with a duration depending on the length of the immediately preceding downtime. Furthermore, typical consumption data for primary energy (e.g., natural gas) and electric energy were given by the manufacturer on the basis of measurements during the individual phases. On the basis of characteristic parameters and curves of fcCHPs as well as explanations of the corresponding energetic correlations, we developed a general mathematical model which formally describes the relationship between primary energy demand as well as thermal and electrical energy supply. Therefore, the model distinguishes between different phases and explains the temporal dependencies between these phases. Within our model of a fcCHP we used the following physical parameters (constant values) of such power plants:

- A *thermal efficiency factor* $0 < \eta_{th} < 1$ and an *electric efficiency factor* $0 < \eta_{el} < 1$ (with respect to the primary energy source) such that $\eta_{th} + \eta_{el} < 1$.
- A *maximal power output (thermal/electric) within the production phase* $P_{th_{max}}$ resp. $P_{el_{max}}$ where $\eta_{el} \cdot P_{th_{max}} = \eta_{th} \cdot P_{el_{max}}$ because in general it applies that $P_{th}/\eta_{th} = P_{prim} = P_{el}/\eta_{el}$ where P_{prim} is the power of the primary energy carrier.
- A *minimal power output (thermal/electric) within the production phase* $P_{th_{min}}$ resp. $P_{el_{min}}$ where $\eta_{el} \cdot P_{th_{min}} = \eta_{th} \cdot P_{el_{min}}$.
- A *minimal and maximal operation time* $D_{on_{min}}$ resp. $D_{on_{max}}$ as well as a *minimal off-time* $D_{off_{min}}$.
- a *bounded, monotonically increasing function* $f : \mathbb{N}^+ \to \mathbb{N}^+$ *to determine the warm-up time* d_{warmUp} depending on its recent *off-time* d_{off}, i.e., $d_{warmUp} = f(d_{off})$.
- A *constant electric power input during stand-by phases*: $P_{el_{standBy}}$.
- Some *constant primary and electric power inputs* during the warm-up phase: $P_{pr_{warmUp}}$ and $P_{el_{warmUp}}$. There, a cold-start requires additional input power: $P_{pr_{coldStart}}$ and $P_{el_{coldStart}}$.
- An *additional constant electric power input during shut-down*: $P_{el_{addShutDown}}$ during the short shut-down interval D_{down}. This means that electric power input from the production phase to the stand-by phase has the power peak $P_{el_{standBy}} + P_{el_{addShutDown}}$.

– A *constant thermal and electric output power "peak"* at the beginning of the start-up phase from zero to $P_{th_{init}}$ resp. to $P_{el_{init}}$ within a (short) constant time interval D_{init} where $\eta_{el} \cdot P_{th_{init}} = \eta_{th} \cdot P_{el_{init}}$ applies.
– A *constant power enhancement within a constant start-up phase to a final power value*: It is assumed that the total duration of the start-up phase $D_{startUp}$ as well as the final power value $P_{th_{startUp}}$ are given such that $P_{th_{init}} \leq P_{th_{min}} < P_{th_{startUP}} \leq P_{th_{max}}$ applies. Thus, the constant power enhancement is $(P_{th_{startUp}} - P_{th_{init}})/(D_{startUp} - D_{init})$. Consequently, the electric power enhancement results from $P_{el_{startUp}} = \eta_{el}/\eta_{th} \cdot P_{th_{startUp}}$.
– A *maximal gradient for power modulation in the production phase*: $\Delta P_{th_{prod}}/1h$ resp. $\Delta P_{el_{prod}} = \eta_{el}/\eta_{th} \cdot \Delta P_{th_{prod}}$.

The chosen MIP model of fcCHPs uses discrete time units. Therefore, the considered scheduling horizon $[0, T]$ is divided into N equidistant time intervals of equal duration – typically of 15 min[2], however, other time unit durations are possible, too. It is assumed that a fcCHP is either in operation or down within one time unit. Discretization of time is a common approach in mathematical modeling of dynamic processes. Further, it is compatible with the time units used in short-term energy markets. This means that a scheduling horizon $[0, T]$ is divided into N time units/intervals $[t_{i-1}, t_i)(i = 1, \ldots, n)$ of the same duration, namely T/N.

The minimum and maximum operating durations (in time units) are therefore $On_{min} = \lceil D_{on_{min}} \cdot N/T \rceil$ and $On_{max} = \lfloor D_{on_{max}} \cdot N/T \rfloor$ and the minimum downtime is $Off_{min} = \lceil D_{off_{min}} \cdot N/T \rceil$ time units.

The decision whether a fcCHP is switched on or off (operation time vs. downtime) is always made for a complete time unit i (i.e., for a time interval $[t_{i-1}, t_i)$). For this purpose, Boolean decision variables $x_0, \ldots, x_N$ are introduced and $x_i = 1$ applies if the fcCHP is *on* at time unit i and $x_i = 0$ if it is *off* at time unit i, where x_0 indicates the on/off state at the beginning of the scheduling horizon which is known in advance. Furthermore, for $i = 2 - On_{min}, \ldots, N$ the *start variables* $start_i$ are Boolean decision variables which determine whether the fcCHP starts in time unit i (start of the operating phase) or not, i.e., $x_i = 1$ and $x_{i-1} = 0$ applies or not. There, for $j = 2 - On_{min}, \ldots, 0$ $start_i$ indicates any potentially interesting start event in the past which is known in advance. Similarly, the *stop variables* $stop_i$ are Boolean decision variables which determine whether the fcCHP is switched off in time unit i (begin of the down phase) or not, i.e., $x_i = 0$ and $x_{i-1} = 1$ applies or not.

In order to ensure that the start and stop variables are compatible with the on/off variables, the following conditions must be met (cf. [2]). There, the status of the fcCHP immediately before the start of the scheduling horizon, namely x_0, is relevant:

$$
\begin{aligned}
start_i &\geq x_i - x_{i-1} & stop_i &\geq x_{i-1} - x_i \\
start_i &\leq x_i & stop_i &\leq x_{i-1} & \text{for } i = 1, \ldots, N. \\
start_i &\leq 1 - x_{i-1} & stop_i &\leq 1 - x_i
\end{aligned}
$$

---

[2] A one-day scheduling horizon is subdivided into 96 time units.

In order to further ensure that neither the minimum operating times nor down-times are undercut, the following conditions must also be fulfilled:

$$x_i \geq \sum_{k=i-\text{On}_{\min}+1}^{i-1} \text{start}_k \ \wedge \ x_i \leq 1 - \sum_{k=i-\text{Off}_{\min}+1}^{i-1} \text{stop}_k \qquad \text{for } i = 1,\ldots,N.$$

Example 1. Let a fcCHP with a minimal operation time $\text{On}_{\min} = 5$ time units be given. Further let $\text{start}_{-3} = 1$ and $\text{start}_{-2} = \text{start}_{-1} = \text{start}_0 = 0$. Then for any admissible schedule $x_1 = 1$ must apply, i.e., the fcCHP must be operative ("on") at time unit 1, otherwise its minimal operation time is undercut.

In order to limit the operating time, further auxiliary integer variables $l_1,\ldots,l_N$ are required, such that the difference $l_i - l_{i-1}$ corresponds to the dura-tion (in time units) from the last stop or start when starting or stopping at time unit i assuming that a stop follows a start and vice versa. For this purpose let $l_0 \leq 0$ be the non-positive time unit at the *last* start or stop just before the beginning of the considered scheduling horizon. For any time unit $i \in \{1,\ldots,N\}$ the last start/stop time unit is kept if the on/off status of the fcCHP does not change: If $x_i = x_{i-1}$ applies, then let $l_i = l_{i-1}$. Otherwise, if there is change of the status the last start/stop time unit is updated: If $x_i \neq x_{i-1}$ applies, then let $l_i = i$. Combining both cases results in:

$$l_i = (1 - |x_i - x_{i-1}|) \cdot l_{i-1} + |x_i - x_{i-1}| \cdot i \qquad \text{for } i = 1,\ldots,N. \tag{1}$$

Example 2. Let a fcCHP be given which runs from time unit -3 (already running at the beginning of the scheduling horizon) to time unit 13. Consequently $l_0 = -3$, $x_0 = x_1 = \cdots = x_{13} = 1$ and $x_{14} = 0$ apply. Thus, $l_1 = \cdots = l_{13} = -3$ but $l_{14} = 14$ apply due to the fact that $x_{13} = 1$ and $x_{14} = 0$. Then the difference $l_{14} - l_{13} = 14 - (-3) = 17$ defines the recent operation time of the fcCHP in time units.

In general, Eq. (1) cannot be processed directly by a MIP Solver, because it contains products of Boolean terms and decision variables. Therefore any such product $\alpha \cdot U$ with $\alpha \in \{0,1\}$ and $U \in [u_{\min}, u_{\max}]$ has to be replaced by a new auxiliary decision variable $V \in [\min(0, u_{\min}), u_{\max}]$ and the additional linear inequalities

$$u_{\min} \cdot \alpha \leq V \wedge V \leq u_{\max} \cdot \alpha \ \wedge$$
$$U - u_{\max} \cdot (1 - \alpha) \leq V \wedge V \leq U - u_{\min} \cdot (1 - \alpha).$$

The replacement is correct: On the one hand it follows from $\alpha = 0$ that $U - u_{\max} \leq 0 \leq V \leq 0 \leq U - u_{\min}$ applies and therefore $V = 0$. On the other hand if follows from $\alpha = 1$ that $u_{\min} \leq U \leq V \leq U \leq u_{\max}$ applies and therefore $V = U$. In summary, $V = \alpha \cdot U$ applies.

Furthermore, Eq. (1) contains the absolute amount of a difference. However, any equation $X = |B - A|$ can be modeled by means of a new auxiliary Boolean variable $\beta \in \{0, 1\}$ and some additional linear constraints

$$X \geq 0 \quad \wedge$$
$$X = \beta \cdot (B - A) + (1 - \beta) \cdot (A - B).$$

Consequently, either $X = A - B$ or $X = B - A$ applies depending on the value of β. Since X must not be negative, $X = |B - A| = |A - B|$ applies.

In order to ensure that the maximum operating time is not exceeded, the following condition must therefore apply:[3]

$$\mathsf{stop}_i \cdot (l_i - l_{i-1}) \leq \mathsf{On}_{\max} \qquad \text{for } i = 1, \ldots, N.$$

These auxiliary variables are also useful to determine the duration of downtimes, which will be $\mathsf{start}_i \cdot (l_i - l_{i-1})$ and thus the duration of warm-up times, which will be $f(\mathsf{start}_i \cdot (l_i - l_{i-1}))$.[4]

If the downtime is greater than a specified value $L > 0$, this is referred to as a *cold start*. Auxiliary Boolean variables $k_1, \ldots, k_N$ are given, such that the value of k_i in the warm-up phase indicates whether this occurred after a cold start, i.e., $k_i = 1$ is implied:

$$\mathsf{start}_i \cdot (i - l_{i-1}) - L \leq M \cdot k_i \wedge k_{i-1} \cdot (i - l_i) \leq M \cdot k_i$$

for $i = 1, \ldots, N$, a sufficiently large value M and a corresponding value k_0, e.g., known from a previous scheduling horizon. If the modeled fcCHP is starting at time unit i then $\mathsf{start}_i = 1$ and $l_i = i$ apply. If this start event is a cold start, i.e., if $(i - l_{i-1}) > L$ applies, then $\mathsf{start}_i \cdot (l_i - l_{i-1}) - L > 0$ applies, too. If follows that $k_i = 1$ applies, otherwise there is a violation. If $k_{i-1} = 1$ indicates that a downtime will require a cold-start and there is not any start event at time t_i then $k_i = 1$ is implied further indicating a cold-start, because $(i - l_i) > 0$ applies, otherwise there is violation.

The determination of the warm-up times requires additional auxiliary integer variables $w_1, \ldots, w_N$, such that the value of w_i corresponds to the last *warm-up* time. To do this, let w_0 be the warm-up time from the previous scheduling horizon. If $\mathsf{start}_i = 1$ applies, let $w_i = f(l_i - l_{i-1})$. Otherwise, if $\mathsf{start}_i = 0$ applies, let $w_i = w_{i-1}$. Combining both cases results in

$$w_i = \mathsf{start}_i \cdot f(i - l_{i-1}) + (1 - \mathsf{start}_i) \cdot w_{i-1} \qquad \text{for } i = 1, \ldots, N.$$

Due to the fact that the argument of the function f is variable, i.e., not known in advance, the computation of $f(x)$ for a variable $x \in \{1, \ldots, N\}$ (assuming that the maximum downtime is shorter than the scheduling horizon) requires additional auxiliary Boolean variables $\lambda_1, \ldots, \lambda_N$. Then the condition

$$\forall i \in \{1, \ldots, N\} : \lambda_i \cdot (x - i) = 0 \wedge \sum_{i=1}^{N} \lambda_i = 1$$

---

[3] Here and in the following there are products of Boolean terms and decision variables, too.

[4] Remember that the function f maps downtimes to warm-up times, see above.

ensures that $x = i \Leftrightarrow \lambda_i = 1$ applies for $i = 1, \ldots, N$. Consequently, it applies

$$f(x) = \sum_{i=1}^{N} \lambda_i \cdot F_i \qquad \text{for any } x \in \{1, \ldots, N\},$$

where the supporting values $F_1 = f(1), \ldots, F_n = f(N)$ are technical parameters of the fcCHP which are known in advance.[5]

Furthermore, Boolean decision variables $y_1, \ldots, y_N$ are introduced such that $y_i = 1$ applies if and only if the modeled fcCHP warms up in time unit i. In particular it applies that $x_i \geq y_i$. Additionally, stopWarmUp$_i$ are Boolean decision variables that determine whether the fcCHP has completed the end of the warm-up phase in time unit i (i.e., the start of the production phase) or not, i.e., $y_{i-1} = 1$ and $y_i = 0$ apply. In order to ensure that these "stop of warm-up" variables are compatible with the "warm-up" variables, the following conditions must be met, whereby the "warm-up" state of the fcCHP immediately before the start of the scheduling horizon – determined by y_0 – is relevant:

$$\begin{aligned}
\text{start}_i &\geq y_i - y_{i-1} & \text{stopWarmUp}_i &\geq y_{i-1} - y_i \\
\text{start}_i &\leq y_i & \text{stopWarmUp}_i &\leq y_{i-1} & \text{for } i = 1, \ldots, N. \\
\text{start}_i &\leq 1 - y_{i-1} & \text{stopWarmUp}_i &\leq 1 - y_i
\end{aligned}$$

A minimal duration of the warm-up phase has to be guaranteed. Therefore for each time unit $i = 1, \ldots, N$ and for each possible warm-up duration $j = F_1, \ldots, F_n$ an auxiliary Boolean variable $\sigma_{i,j}$ is defined such that $\sigma_{i,j} = 1$ if and only if a start occured no longer than j time units before time unit i:

$$\sigma_{i,j} \cdot M \geq \sum_{k=i-j+1}^{i-1} \text{start}_k \wedge \sigma_{i,j} \leq \sum_{k=i-j+1}^{i-1} \text{start}_k$$

Then the minimal warm-up time is satisfied, if

$$(F_n - F_1 + 1) \cdot y_i \geq (w_i - j + 1) \cdot \sigma_{i,j}$$

applies for $i = 1, \ldots, N$ and $j = F_1, \ldots, F_n$. This means that if $w_i - j + 1$ is positive and the start is no longer than w_i time units ago, i.e., $\sigma_{i,j} = 1$, then the fcCHP is in the warm-up phase, i.e., $y_i = 1$ must apply.[6]

For an upper boundary of the warm-up time, additional auxiliary integer variables are necessary. Let $r_1, \ldots, r_N$ be given such that r_i represents the index of the last (i.e., most recent) start. Therefore let $r_0 \leq 0$ be the time unit of the latest start before the scheduling horizon. Now if start$_i = 1$ then $r_i = i$ will apply, otherwise $r_i = r_{i-1}$:

$$r_i = \text{start}_i \cdot i + (1 - \text{start}_i) \cdot r_{i-1} \tag{2}$$

---

[5] $F_1 \leq \cdots \leq F_n$ applies due to the fact that f is monotonically increasing, see above.
[6] N.B.: $(F_n - F_1 + 1) \geq (w_i - j + 1)$ always applies, see above.

Then the maximal warm-up time is satisfied, if

$$y_i \cdot i - r_i \leq w_i. \tag{3}$$

This means that if the fcCHP warms up at time unit i, then the latest start is no longer than the warm-up time ago.

At the end of the warm-up phase, the start-up phase begins, the duration of which is known in advance from the fcCHP characteristics. The same applies to the thermal and electrical power available in the start-up phase. In detail, there are $\mathsf{LowerInit} = \lfloor D_{\mathsf{init}} \cdot N/T \rfloor$ time units with power jump, in general one time unit at $\mathsf{UpperInit} = \lceil D_{\mathsf{init}} \cdot N/T \rceil$ with parts of the power jump and gradual starting (if $\mathsf{LowerInit} < \mathsf{UpperInit}$ and then $\mathsf{StartUp} - \mathsf{UpperInit}$ time units in which the power increases constantly up to a given target value with $\mathsf{StartUp} = \lceil D_{\mathsf{startUp}} \cdot N/T \rceil$. The end of the start-up phase is thus after further $\mathsf{StartUp}$ time units reached. This means that discrete power levels can be determined for primary energy and electricity consumption as well as for thermal and electric output power (abstract $P_{x\mathsf{Up}}$). One type is sufficient, the others behave proportionally according to their efficiency factors:

$$(P_{x\mathsf{Up}_1}, \ldots, P_{x\mathsf{Up}_{\mathsf{StartUp}}}).$$

Analogously to these power steps and due to the discretization there result electric power steps from $P_{\mathsf{el}_{\mathsf{addShutDown}}}$ during the shut-down phase (mostly one time unit because the duration D_{Down} of the shut-down phase is in general short):

$$(P_{\mathsf{el}_{\mathsf{Down}_1}}, \ldots, P_{\mathsf{el}_{\mathsf{Down}_{\mathsf{ShutDown}}}}),$$

where $\mathsf{ShutDown} = \lceil D_{\mathsf{Down}} \cdot N/T \rceil$ is the duration of the shut-down phase in time units.

The time units of the "jump" phases are characterized by Boolean decision variables $s_1, \ldots, s_N$ where $s_i = 1$, if the fcCHP makes a performance jump in time unit i and $s_i = 0$, if it is not the case in this time unit i:

$$s_i = \sum_{j=1}^{\mathsf{LowerInit}} \mathsf{stopWarmUp}_{i-j+1}.$$

Boolean decision variables $z_1, \ldots, z_N$ are introduced for the following production phase. $z_i = 1$ will apply, if the fcCHP is productive in time unit i, i.e., delivering thermal and electrical power and $z_i = 0$ will apply, if it is not in the production phase in time unit i, i.e., in particular, it applies that $x_i \geq z_i$. In order to ensure that these "productive" variables are compatible with the corresponding start/stop variables, the following conditions must be met, whereby the status of the fcCHP directly before the start of the scheduling horizon – determined by z_0 – is relevant:

$$
\begin{array}{lll}
\mathsf{stopWarmUp}_{i-\mathsf{StartUp}} \geq z_i - z_{i-1} & \mathsf{stop}_i \geq z_{i-1} - z_i & \\
\mathsf{stopWarmUp}_{i-\mathsf{StartUp}} \leq z_i & \mathsf{stop}_i \leq z_{i-1} & \text{for } i = 1, \ldots, N. \\
\mathsf{stopWarmUp}_{i-\mathsf{StartUp}} \leq 1 - z_{i-1} & \mathsf{stop}_i \leq 1 - z_i &
\end{array}
$$

Summarizing, the *thermal power supply (output)* of a fcCHP at time unit i is characterized by the following equation:

$$\text{thermalOutputPower}_{\text{fcCHP}_i} = \sum_{j=1}^{\text{StartUp}} \text{stopWarmUp}_{i-j+1} \cdot P_{\text{th}_{\text{Up}_j}} + z_i \cdot u_{\text{th}_i}$$

where the values of the variable u_{th_i} must lie within a specified performance band in the production phase, i.e., $P_{\text{th}_{\text{min}}} \leq u_{\text{th}_i} \leq P_{\text{th}_{\text{max}}}$ and the gradient of the value change is limited:[7]

$$|u_{\text{th}_i} - u_{\text{th}_{i-1}}| \leq \Delta P_{\text{th}_{\text{prod}}}/[h] \cdot T/N[h].$$

The electrical power supply (output) results directly from the thermal power supply:

$$\text{electricOutputPower}_{\text{fcCHP}_i} = \frac{\eta_{\text{el}}}{\eta_{\text{th}}} \cdot \text{thermalOutputPower}_{\text{fcCHP}_i}$$

The *electrical power demand (input)* of a fcCHP depends on whether there is a cold-start or a warm-start:

$$\text{electricInputPower}_{\text{fcCHP}_i} = y_i \cdot P_{\text{el}_{\text{WarmUp}}} + (y_i \wedge k_i) \cdot P_{\text{el}_{\text{ColdStart}}}$$
$$+ \sum_{j=1}^{\text{ShutDown}} \text{stop}_{i-j+1} \cdot P_{\text{el}_{\text{Down}_j}} + (1 - x_i) \cdot P_{\text{el}_{\text{standBy}}}.$$

There, the conjunction of two Boolean variables $(y_i \wedge k_i)$ will be represented by an auxiliary Boolean variable γ_i satisfying $\gamma_i \geq y_i + k_i - 1 \wedge \gamma_i \leq y_i \wedge \gamma_i \leq k_i$ for $i = 1, \ldots, N$.

Analogously, the *primary power demand (input)* of a fcCHP over the production phases depends also on whether there is a cold-start or a warm-start:

$$\text{primaryInputPower}_{\text{fcCHP}_i} = y_i \cdot P_{\text{pr}_{\text{WarmUp}}} + \gamma_i \cdot P_{\text{pr}_{\text{ColdStart}}}$$
$$+ \sum_{j=1}^{\text{StartUp}} \text{stopWarmUp}_{i-j+1} \cdot P_{\text{pr}_{\text{WarmUp}_j}} + z_i \cdot \frac{u_{\text{th}_i}}{\eta_{\text{th}}}.$$

In Fig. 2, typical thermal and electric power profiles of a fcCHP are shown according to the presented MIP model. These profiles are matching the profiles measured by the fcCHP manufacturer giving some evidence that the energetic behavior of fcCHP is modeled adequately. Assuming that the costs K_{pr_i} for primary energy at time unit i, as well as the costs for switching on K_{on} and for switching off K_{off} a fcCHP, as well as the costs for the wear and tear per time unit during heating up K_{warmUp}, during cold start $K\text{coldStart}$ and during productive operation K_{prod} are known, then the costs for the operation of a fcCHP in time unit i result directly:

---

[7] How to model the absolute amount of a difference has already been explained. Time values must be of the same dimension which is emphasized by the explicit use of the dimension $[h]$ (hour).

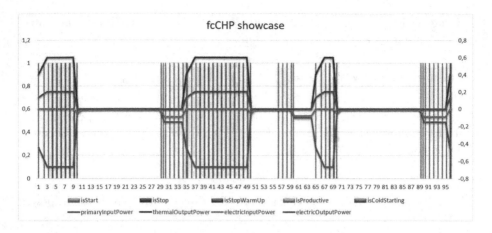

Fig. 2. Typical operation of a fcCHP.

$$\text{financialInput}_{\text{fcCHP}_i}$$

$$= K_{\text{pr}_i} \cdot \text{primaryInputPower}_{\text{fcCHP}_i} \cdot \frac{T}{N} + K_{\text{on}} \cdot \text{start}_i$$

$$+ K_{\text{off}} \cdot \text{stop}_i + K_{\text{warmUp}} \cdot y_i + K_{\text{coldStart}} \cdot (y_i \wedge k_i) + K_{\text{prod}} \cdot z_i.$$

This is only a simplified approach for the consideration of wear and tear costs of a fcCHP. For instance, aging effects are not taken into account. Although an aging approach can be converted into a linearly approximated model, initial runtime investigations result in very long computation times for cost optimization. However, the resulting operational plans hardly differ qualitatively from those with simplified models.

4   Implementing a MIP-Based Optimizing Tool

A software named "MIP Optimizer" is realized to transfer specifications of building energy systems into MIP models and then based on these models to determine cost-minimal operation schedules for the specified energy system components, so that predicted energy requirements for heating or cooling, domestic hot water and electricity over a given scheduling horizon are covered. In detail, the MIP Optimizer generates a MIP optimization problem from a formal description of the energy system components, i.e., the *configuration* of the energy system and from a formal description of the demand and the environmental and operational *situation* over the scheduling period. For this purpose, both formal descriptions determining the general *configuration* and the current *situation* are to be specified in XML files (cf. [13]) and must comply with a fixed XML schema (XSD) [14]. Energy demand profiles and other time series predicting the environmental situation (e.g., fluctuating primary energy prices or volatile PV power) shall be provided in files in Hierarchical Data Format (HDF5) [5,7], referred to in the

XML descriptions. Examples of the XML configuration and situation files are presented in Sect. 5.

Then, the MIP Optimizer uses the <Coliop|Coin> Mathematical Programming Language (CMPL) [12] to generate and solve the optimization problem, since various MIP problem solvers can be used, such as the freely available Cbc [6] or the commercial CPLEX [10]. The operation schedules of the components of the building energy system are then extracted from the solution and stored in the form of time series in an HDF5 file, such that these data can be further used by a building management system to control the energy components.

The MIP Optimizer is implemented in Java and has a modular structure. Due to the modular modeling approach (cf. Sect. 3) and its object-oriented implementation, flexible extensions including further energy systems components are supported by design.

5   Evaluation on a Heat Pump Scenario

In order to prove the usefulness of our MIP-based optimization approach, generated operational schedules for building energy systems are considered. For this purpose, we considered a residential building, i.e., a single family detached house, according to the EnEV standard 2014 with 172 m^2 usable area (Berlin site), an air-to-water heat pump with thermal storage tank for heat supply.

It was investigated, how an efficient operation can be planned/scheduled with the help of the MIP Optimizer as cost- and energy-efficient as possible by predicting the Coefficients of Performance (COP) of the heat pump dependent on the outside temperature and the residential heat demand. The building energy system consists of a heat pump and a heat storage. The heat demand and COP of the heat pump changing with the outside temperature were determined and provided by our project partners at Berlin University of the Arts, Institute for Architecture and Urban Planning, Department of Building Physics and Building Technology. These partners used weather forecasts and Modelica to model and simulate the thermal behavior of the selected building.

In the subsequent operational scheduling, partial models of a heat pump with a constant electrical power consumption of 1.8 kW in operation (cf. the XML element <HeatPump> below) and of a 2 m^3 thermal storage tank with a charging capacity of 20.82 kWh (cf. the XML element <HeatBuffer> below) were combined at an ambient temperature of 20 °C to form an overall model of the energy system. Electricity prices, the heat demand profiles determined by simulation and time-dependent COP as well as the system status data (e.g., state of charge of the thermal storage tank) were added. The description of the building energy system was specified in XML as a *configuration* with characteristic physical parameters, which were further processed by the MIP Optimizer:

```xml
<BuildingConfiguration
    xmlns="http://www.fokus.fraunhofer.de/WaveSave"
    xmlns:xsi="http://www.w3.org/2001/XMLSchema-instance"
    xsi:schemaLocation="http://www.fokus.fraunhofer.de/WaveSave_BuildingSystem.xsd"
    id="UDKHeatPumpScenario" powerUnit="kW" energyUnit="kWh" priceUnit="ct"
    energyPriceUnit="ct/kWh">
```

```
<Usage id="generalUsage" maxElectricPowerUse="32.0" maxHeatingPowerUse="32.0"
    maxCoolingPowerUse="0.0" powerUnit="kW"/>
<Grid id="GridConnection" maxFeedInPower="0.0" maxSupplyPower="32.0"
    powerUnit="kW"/>
<HeatBuffer id="HotWaterBuffer" minThermalEnergyLevel="0"
    maxThermalEnergyLevel="20.82" thermalLossPerHourFactor="0.000"
    maxThermalChargingPower="10.0" maxThermalDischargingPower="10.0"
    powerUnit="kW" energyUnit="kWh"/>
<HeatPump id="HeatPump" electricPower="1.8" powerUnit="kW"
    minOffTimeInHours="0.25" minRunTimeInHours="0.25"/>
</BuildingConfiguration>
```

Actual and predicted data were also transferred to the MIP Optimizer with the help of a *situation* description, also in XML, whereby the time series for heat demand, COP, electricity prices etc. were to be found in separate HDF5 files to which references are made:

```
<BuildingSituation
        xmlns="http://www.fokus.fraunhofer.de/WaveSave"
        id="UDKHeatPumpScenario" nbsOfTimeUnits="96" hoursPerTimeUnit="0.25"
        start="2016-08-17T00:00:00" fileNameHDF5="UDKHeatPumpScenario.h5">
    <Usage id="generalUsage" maxInitialHeatingEnergy="0.0"
        maxInitialCoolingEnergy="0.0" energyUnit="kWh">
        <ElectricPowerUsage fileName="UDK_Heat_Pump_Scenario-2017-05.h5"
            dataSetPath="/ENull" powerUnit="kW"/>
        <HotWaterPowerUsage fileName="UDK_Heat_Pump_Scenario-2017-05.h5"
            dataSetPath="/DHWNull" powerUnit="kW"/>
        <MinHeatingPowerUsage fileName="UDK_Heat_Pump_Scenario-2017-05.h5"
            dataSetPath="/MinHeating" powerUnit="W"/>
        <MaxHeatingPowerUsage fileName="UDK_heat_pump_scenario-2017-05.h5"
            dataSetPath="/MaxHeating" powerUnit="W"/>
        <MinCoolingPowerUsage fileName="UDK_Heat_Pump_Scenario-2017-05.h5"
            dataSetPath="/MinCoolingNull" powerUnit="kW"/>
        <MaxCoolingPowerUsage fileName="UDK_Heat_Pump_Scenario-2017-05.h5"
            dataSetPath="/MaxCoolingNull" powerUnit="kW"/>
    </Usage>
    <Grid id="GridConnection">
        <ElectricEnergyPrice fileName="UDK_Heat_Pump_Scenario-2017-05.h5"
            dataSetPath="/ECostFix" energyPriceUnit="ct/kWh"/>
        <ElectricEnergyRefund fileName="UDK_Heat_Pump_Scenario-2017-05.h5"
            dataSetPath="/ERefundFix" energyPriceUnit="ct/kWh"/>
    </Grid>
    <HeatBuffer id="HotWaterBuffer" initialThermalEnergyLevel="0.0"
        energyUnit="kWh"/>
    <HeatPump id="HeatPump" isOnAtBegin="false" lastStartStopChangeInHours="0.5"
        priceUnit="ct">
        <CoefficientOfPerformance fileName="UDK_Heat_Pump_Scenario-2017-05.h5"
            dataSetPath="/COP"/>
    </HeatPump>
</BuildingSituation>
```

In detail, usage profiles are stored in HDF5 files (with file extension ".h5"), which are referenced in the respective XML elements (e.g., <ElectricPowerUsage>). The name of the file containing the operation schedules must be entered as the value of the attribute fileNameHDF5 in the XML root element <BuildingSituation>. After processing the models the optimized schedule of the heat pump is stored in this file.

The resulting cost-minimized schedule of the operation of the building energy system (cf. Fig. 3) shows that, in contrast to charging the thermal storage tank during the night hours (blue), an extensive operation of the heat pump at low outside temperatures and low COP can be avoided, if the heat demand and COP is known in advance and the heat pump is operated accordingly (red). Covering the currently predicted heat demand only enables a saving of 25% electric energy, provided that the forecasts correspond to reality. Due to the general uncertainty of forecasts for energy supply and demand it is strongly recommended for practical applications to use some energy reservoirs, e.g., thermal storage tanks or batteries, and parts of their charging/discharging capacities as buffers to balance deviations.

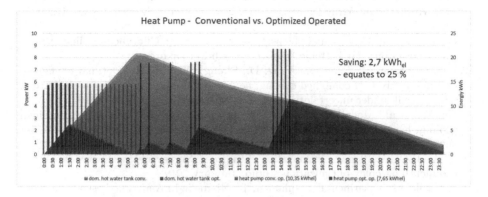

Fig. 3. Heat pump conventional operation versus optimized operation. (Color figure online)

6   Conclusion and Future Work

In this paper a MIP-based approach is presented to model and optimize the operation of building energy systems. In detail the modeling of the energetic behavior of fcCHPs is presented and it is shown how sub-models of different energy component can be combined reflecting their integration into building energy systems. By example it is shown that the approach can be applied successfully. However, a comprehensive analysis on the accuracy and adequacy of the MIP models and the impact of imperfect forecasts for energy demand/production and energy prices has the be performed in the future, maybe in a follow-up research and development project.

References

1. Beasley, J.E.: OR Notes - Separable Programming. http://people.brunel.ac.uk/%7Emastjjb/jeb/or/sep.html
2. Bosman, M.G.C., Bakker, V., Molderink, A., Hurink, J.L., Smit, G.J.M.: Planning the production of a fleet of domestic combined heat and power generators. Eur. J. Oper. Res. **216**(1), 140–151 (2012)

3. Bozchalui, M.C., Sharma, R.: Optimal operation of commercial building microgrids using multi-objective optimization to achieve emissions and efficiency targets. In: Power and Energy Society General Meeting, 2012, pp. 1–8. IEEE (2012)
4. Brahman, F., Honarmand, M., Jadid, S.: Optimal electrical and thermal energy management of a residential energy hub, integrating demand response and energy storage system. Energy Build. **90**, 65–75 (2015)
5. Folk, M., Heber, G., Koziol, Q., Pourmal, E., Robinson, D.: An overview of the HDF5 technology suite and its applications. In: Proceedings of the EDBT/ICDT 2011 Workshop on Array Databases - AD 2011 Uppsala, Sweden, pp. 36–47. ACM Press (2011)
6. Forrest, J.: CBC User Guide. https://www.coin-or.org/Cbc/cbcuserguide.html
7. The HDF Group. HDF Home. https://www.hdfgroup.org/
8. Wei, G., Tang, Y., Peng, S., Wang, D., Sheng, W., Liu, K.: Optimal configuration and analysis of combined cooling, heating, and power microgrid with thermal storage tank under uncertainty. J. Renew. Sustain. Energy **7**(1), 013104 (2015)
9. Gu, W., et al.: Modeling, planning and optimal energy management of combined cooling, heating and power microgrid: a review. Electr. Power Energy Syst. **54**, 26–37 (2014)
10. IBM. ILOG CPLEX Optimization Studio - Survey. https://www.ibm.com/products/ilog-cplex-optimization-studio, January 2019
11. Järvisalo, M., Oikarinen, E., Janhunen, T., Niemelä, I.: A module-based framework for multi-language constraint modeling. In: Erdem, E., Lin, F., Schaub, T. (eds.) LPNMR 2009. LNCS (LNAI), vol. 5753, pp. 155–168. Springer, Heidelberg (2009). https://doi.org/10.1007/978-3-642-04238-6_15
12. Steglich, M., Schleiff, T.: CMPL: Coliop Mathematical Programming Language - Version 1.12 - March 2018 (2018)
13. W3C. Extensible Markup Language (XML). https://www.w3.org/XML/
14. W3C. XML Schema. https://www.w3.org/XML/Schema

Finding Maximal Non-redundant Association Rules in Tennis Data

Daniel Weidner[1]([✉]), Martin Atzmueller[2], and Dietmar Seipel[1]

[1] Department of Computer Science, University of Würzburg,
Am Hubland, 97074 Würzburg, Germany
{daniel.weidner,dietmar.seipel}@uni-wuerzburg.de

[2] Department of Cognitive Science and Artificial Intelligence,
Tilburg University, Warandelaan 2, 5037 AB Tilburg, The Netherlands
m.atzmuller@uvt.nl

Abstract. The concept of association rules is well-known in data mining. But often redundancy and subsumption are not considered, and standard approaches produce thousands or even millions of resulting association rules. Without further information or post-mining approaches, this huge number of rules is typically useless for the domain specialist – which is an instance of the infamous pattern explosion problem. In this work, we present a new definition of redundancy and subsumption based on the confidence and the support of the rules and propose post-mining to prune a set of association rules.

In a case study, we apply our method to association rules mined from spatio-temporal data. The data represent the trajectories of the ball in tennis matches – more precisely, the points/times the tennis ball hits the ground. The goal is to analyze the strategies of the players and to try to improve their performance by looking at the resulting association rules. Here, the domain specialist was able to select useful rules during post-mining. The proposed approach is general and could also be applied to other spatio-temporal data with a similar structure.

Keywords: Association rule mining · Pattern mining · Post-mining · Declarative data mining · Prolog · Spatio-temporal data

1 Introduction

The field of artificial intelligence (AI) can be divided into symbolic and subsymbolic approaches, e.g., [7,19,27,33]. *Symbolic, knowledge- or rule-based AI* models central cognitive abilities of humans like *logic*, deduction and planning in computers; mathematically exact operations can be defined. *Subsymbolic or statistical AI* tries to learn a model of a process (e.g., an optimal action of a robot or the classification of sensor data) from the data.

Association rules declaratively and symbolically describe logical relations with probabilities in the form of if-then-rules, thus incorporating aspects from

© Springer Nature Switzerland AG 2020
P. Hofstedt et al. (Eds.): DECLARE 2019, LNAI 12057, pp. 59–78, 2020.
https://doi.org/10.1007/978-3-030-46714-2_4

both symbolic and statistical approaches. Then, using declarative specifications, e.g., using domain knowledge, specific (inductive) biases, and post-mining
approaches, the learning and mining can be supported [5,7], and post-mining on
the set of association rules – for improving their interestingness and relevancy –
can be conveniently implemented. In general, data mining aims to obtain a set of
novel, potentially useful and ultimately interesting patterns from a given (large)
data set [15]. Here, one prominent method is association rule mining. However,
many standard approaches for mining association rules – like the approaches
based on the well-known Apriori algorithm – do not consider redundancy or
subsumption.

In this paper, we tackle this problem, and demonstrate its application in the
spatio-temporal domain of tennis data. Our contributions are summarized as
follows: We introduce a new definition of redundant and subsumed association
rules to prune the set of rules we obtain from the Apriori algorithm. Furthermore,
we present a general post-mining approach for finding maximal non-redundant
association rules. Based on the results of previous mining steps, unimportant
attributes are excluded in further steps.

Fig. 1. One picture from the video of a tennis match.

From an application perspective, analyzing real-world tennis data and pruning the result effectively can lead to individual training methods for the observed
players. Furthermore, using data from a video in real-time, a coach could change
the player's strategy during a tennis match. Some pre-research had been made
in the diploma/master theses [8,35] and the technical report [31]; by getting
information directly from media-data like video-sequences (a screenshot can be
seen in Fig. 1), essentially the complete (tennis) data mining process can be
automated.

The rest of this paper is structured as follows: Sect. 2 discusses related work on association rule mining, and Sect. 3 gives the necessary definitions of association rules and explains association rule mining in the well-known tool Weka. Next, we present the proposed data mining process including the new definition of subsumption and maximality in Sect. 4. The case study about tennis data shows its usefulness in Sect. 5; this section ends with some directions for future work. Finally, Sect. 6 concludes with a summary.

2 Related Work

This section discusses related work on association rule mining, condensed representations, and finally post-mining approaches on sets of association rules.

2.1 Association Rule Mining

Association rule mining [1,2] has been established as a prominent approach in data mining and knowledge discovery in databases, cf. [22] for a survey. Several efficient algorithms have been proposed, including, e.g., the Apriori [2] and the FP-Growth [20] algorithms.

In the research on association rules and finding the most relevant ones, many approaches have been discussed. In [23], the authors present a method to extract rules on user-defined templates or time constraints. In [21], association rules are ranked. This happens with different interestingness measures. Different formats or properties of association rules are discussed in [12]. Finally, the pruning of redundant rules is presented in [14]. Constraint-based data mining also tackles the problem of redundancy in association rule mining. For example, the approach presented in [9] presents an approach for constraint-based rule mining in large, dense databases, focusing on the interestingness of specializations of rules relative to their parent generalization with specific thresholds.

In contrast to the approaches discussed above, we employ a standard method for association rule mining (e.g., Apriori) which is customized using logic programming, such that the mining step can be re-iterated in a declarative way.

2.2 Condensed Representations and Post-mining Methods

Condensed representations of association rules for reducing redundancy mainly focus on closed itemsets, e.g., [6,39]. Furthermore, also research in the domain of formal concept analysis has resulted in several algorithms, e.g., [28,34]; also cf. [10] for a survey on condensed representations. Furthermore, [16] presents a mining approach for finding the top-k non-redundant association rules using an approximation algorithm.

Considering *post-mining methods*, [40] discusses several techniques for effective knowledge extraction from association rules, while [24–26] apply ontologies to facilitate the post-processing of a set of association rules, also including interaction with a domain expert. Logic-based post-mining approaches include a technique where patterns are filtered using constraints formulated with answer set programming (ASP) [18].

Similar to the approaches described above, we also apply post-mining but using declarative techniques. We apply formalizations of subsumption and redundancy for declaratively shaping the association rules. However, specifically in contrast to the existing logic-based approaches, the presented approach is not restricted to work on the set of association rules directly, but can further refine the mechanism of how to discover association rules, by e.g., refining the data representation, the parameters of the mining process, and its subsequent results at the same time in incremental fashion.

3   Association Rules and the Apriori Algorithm

In this section, we provide an overview on the relevant background on association rules, before briefly summarizing the Apriori algorithm.

3.1   Definitions for Association Rules

We consider a set $\mathcal{T}$ of transactions, where each transaction is a set of items, called an itemset. For an itemset I, let $\mathcal{T}_I$ be the subset of transactions containing I, i.e.

$$\mathcal{T}_I = \{ t \in \mathcal{T} \mid I \subseteq t \},$$

and let the frequency be the number of these transactions, i.e. $freq(I) = |\mathcal{T}_I|$. Given a lower bound f for the frequency, an itemset I is called $frequent$, if $freq(I) \geq f$.

An $association\ rule$ $r = L \Rightarrow R$ is an if-then-rule, where the antecedent L and the conclusion R are itemsets; without loss of generality, we can assume $L \cap R = \emptyset$. For a transaction $t \in \mathcal{T}$, the association rule means that $L \subseteq t$ suggests $R \subseteq t$. The $support$ of an association rule is the number of the transactions containing both sides divided by the number of all transactions. The $confidence$ of an association rule expresses the likelihood that R occurs in a transaction, if L occurs in the transaction. It is defined as the percentage of transactions containing $L \cup R$ among the transactions containing L. We write $sup(r)$ and $conf(r)$ for the support and confidence, respectively:

$$sup(r) = \frac{|\mathcal{T}_{L \cup R}|}{|\mathcal{T}|} \quad \text{and} \quad conf(r) = \frac{|\mathcal{T}_{L \cup R}|}{|\mathcal{T}_L|}.$$

Note, that support and confidence do not depend on each other, and both definitions are necessary for association rule mining. There can be rules with a large support but a small confidence, and vise versa.

Obviously, for a frequent itemset I, the support of all association rules $r = L \Rightarrow R$, such that $L \cup R \subseteq I$, exceeds $f/|\mathcal{T}|$, since

$$sup(r) = freq(L \cup R)/|\mathcal{T}| \geq freq(I)/|\mathcal{T}| \geq f/|\mathcal{T}|.$$

3.2   Mining Association Rules with Weka

The main goal of association rule mining is to find rules having a minimum confidence c and support s. These rules may be obvious for an expert, but we will show in a case study for tennis data that they can also reveal new, unknown relations.

A basic step in standard association rule mining is the Apriori algorithm for finding frequent itemsets I first. This algorithm incrementally searches for frequent itemsets for $f = s \cdot |T|$: it starts with frequent itemsets of size 1, and iteratively extends frequent k-itemsets by frequent 1-itemsets to obtain $(k + 1)$-itemsets (iteration k), and then it selects the frequent ones for the next iteration. The algorithm stops after k_{max} iterations, if there are no frequent $(k_{max} + 1)$-itemsets. It returns all computed frequent k-itemsets ($1 \leq k \leq k_{max}$), that could not be extended to a frequent $(k + 1)$-itemset; these itemsets are called maximal frequent itemsets. From all maximal frequent itemsets I, the mining algorithms create association rules $r = L \Rightarrow R$, such that $L \cup R \subseteq I$ and the confidence exceeds c, i.e. $conf(r) \geq c$.

In the context of this paper, we apply the algorithm of the well-known data mining tool Weka [37] for association rule mining, which is based on the Apriori algorithm. In Sect. 5.2, we will see, that Weka can be used with a parameter which stands for a required number of rules. In the Apriori algorithm implemented in Weka, the support is reduced until this number of rules is reached.

Depending on the size and characteristics of the data set, potentially be a very large number of association rules exceeding a given minimal confidence can be produced. Depending on the size of the table, this number of rules can be unusably high, so that users lose track of these rules. At this point, the process has to be run again with other parameters, or some expert needs to filter important rules, which ends in looking for a needle in a haystack.

Since both of these methods are very time-consuming and expensive, we will propose a new approach by pruning rules effectively. For this, we employ the idea of redundancy and subsumption, which we define in the next section in detail.

4   Data Mining Process

The proposed declarative data mining process, which will be discussed in this section, is implemented within the software package Declare [29] for knowledge-based intelligent systems that is developed using Swi-Prolog [36]. We introduce a (semi-) automatic data mining process that consists of the steps outlined below. By repeating these steps with different parameters or transformations, we achieve different results in each iteration, until some result is convincing enough according to the assessment of a domain expert. Thus, the evaluation of the results has to be supported by a domain expert or some knowledge structure like a knowledge graph. In the latter case, the process can then also be potentially automatized, which we plan to do in the future; so far the process workflow is semi-automatic. The process workflow is presented in Fig. 2. In the following, we will present the steps of an iteration.

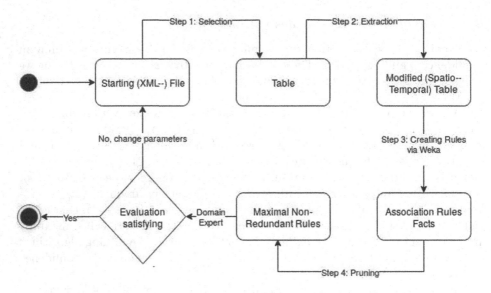

Fig. 2. Flowchart of the data mining process.

Step 1: Selecting Attributes from the Input Data

Given an XML-file with data to be analyzed, we want to create a structured table. For this, some aspects should be discussed. First of all, we have to think about which attributes of the XML-file should be included in the table and the data mining process. In our test data we skip some unimportant attributes by projecting the table. By now, the selection step is not automatic at all. We use a domain expert, who chooses attributes, which may lead to interesting association rules. Surely, this selection can be automatized by selecting all attributes or by selecting different pairs of attributes in every iteration. But these two extremes would either lead to many rules with unimportant information or to many different iterations and also many evaluation failures. So we depend on a domain expert or need to include knowledge such as a knowledge graph.

Step 2: The Spatio-Temporal Data Table

As it can be seen in Sect. 5.2, we did not only select attributes of the XML-file, we also transformed some selected attributes. More precisely, we applied two extraction methods. First we generalized attributes, which occur with support nearly zero. Such attributes are values, that are stored as exact values, i.e. time-points and/or coordinates. These exact values appear only once in the whole table and so their support is the reciprocal to the size of the table; the greater the file and so the table, the smaller the support and therefore the probability that this item will be observed in the Apriori algorithm. To avoid this, we create intervals and store the interval numbers instead of the exact values.

Since all entries of exact values are different, the domain size of this attribute is equal to the size of the table. With this information an automatized algorithm can compare all domains with the table size to detect the exact values. With minimum and maximum, default intervals can be created.

Another transformation is done to create a spatio-temporal data scheme. In our tennis-data, we have sequences of the same event in the whole table, i.e. tennis hits. Instead of considering one event in each row, we combine pairs of events in each row. It is also possible to consider more than two events, namely three of more hits and re-hits for tennis data.

Both transformations may be applicable to other XML-files, but it is impossible to guide this full automatically. Nevertheless, if users are familiar with the used file, they should think about such transformations, since attributes with a probability near to zero will only reach a small support and confidence, and a spatio-temporal data table allows other data mining methods too, see [3].

Step 3: From a Table to Association Rules (via Weka)

As discussed in Sect. 3.2, we use the tool Weka to compute association rules based on the Apriori algorithm. This step includes two thresholds that can be modified in each iteration: first the number of required rules can be increased, and second the value of the minimum confidence can be decreased. This may lead to a greater number of rules: so the bigger the search space of rules, the higher is the chance to find very interesting rules. But on the other hand, every iteration is very time consuming for itself and will be slower when considering more rules. In total, finding the optimal parameters is very complicated.

In Listing 2, we can see how to call Weka from the command line of a shell. It is getting even more complicated when we consider optional parameters of Weka, e.g. a starting value -U and a stopping value -M for the minimum support of frequent itemsets. Also metrics different from the confidence can be used to sort rules. In our tennis data, we focus only on the number of required rules and the minimum confidence. We discuss the Weka call and the output in detail in Subsect. 5.2.

Step 4: Pruning Non-maximal Redundant Association Rules

After all computed association rules are loaded into the system, we want to get rid of redundant and non-maximal association rules. For this, we need a new definition of redundancy, where an association rule $r_1 = L_1 \Rightarrow R_1$ is called *redundant*, if there is another association rule $r_2 = L_2 \Rightarrow R_2$, such that

$$L_2 \subseteq L_1, \ R_1 \subseteq R_2 \ \text{and} \ conf(r_2) = 1.$$

Note that, if a rule r_1 is redundant, then its confidence does not have to be 1 in general; e.g., for a redundant rule $r_1 = L_1 \Rightarrow R_1$ and a rule $r_2 = L_2 \Rightarrow R_2$ with $conf(r_2) = 1$, such that $L_2 = L_1$ and $R_1 \subsetneq R_2$, we have $\emptyset = L_2 \cap R_2 = L_1 \cap R_2$, and we get

$$1 = conf(r_2) = \frac{|L_2 \cup R_2|}{|L_2|} = \frac{|L_1 \cup R_2|}{|L_1|} > \frac{|L_1 \cup R_1|}{|L_1|} = conf(r_1).$$

Our definition of redundancy is different from related literature [16,17,23].

We say that an association rule $r_1 = L_1 \Rightarrow R_1$ *subsumes* another association rule $r_2 = L_2 \Rightarrow R_2$, if

$$L_1 \subseteq L_2, \ R_2 \subseteq R_1 \ \text{and} \ sup(r_1) \geq sup(r_2), \ conf(r_1) \geq conf(r_2).$$

A rule r is called *maximal*, if it is not subsumed by any other rule $r' \neq r$. Both definitions have first appeared in the lecture on Advanced Databases [32]; As we have seen in Subsect. 3.1, redundancy implies subsumption but not vice versa. After applying these definitions, we hope to finally obtain a small number of maximal non-redundant rules.

The case study, which will be presented in Sect. 5, will motivate that these definitions are useful for finding interesting association rules. This is shown in Fig. 3, where we ran Weka with the initial table of Fig. 4, but searching for all possible association rules. This means the minimum confidence is increased by 0.1, and we count the number of all association rules found by Weka. For the tennis data, which will be presented in detail in Sect. 5, we found about 22 000 rules, even if we required a minimum confidence of 1. And with a standard minimum confidence of 0.50 or 0.75, we reach 70 000 or 40 000 rules. As said before, detecting the most interesting rules in this large rule set is nearly impossible; but it is reasonable to work with a small number of maximal non-redundant rules to obtain unknown relations.

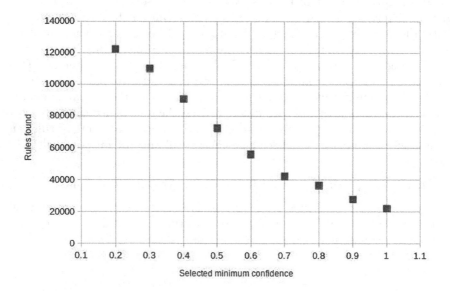

Fig. 3. Relation between minimum confidence and number of computed association rules in the tested tennis data set.

Step 5: Iterating the Process with New Parameters

After one iteration, some evaluation of the result has to be done. Depending on the quality of the evaluation, the system should repeat the process with different parameters, starting with those for Weka. This is because these thresholds need no information about the initial data. It can be increased and decreased, respectively, to create more association rules. If all these iterations fail the evaluation, then some modification of the starting table and attributes should be done. For this, the user needs information or knowledge about the data to guide the data mining process, i.e., in- and excluding the right attributes and changing the right parameters correctly.

Another way to create a successful evaluation is creating queries to the maximal non-redundant association rules. For this some searching items are needed. As said before, a domain expert can guide the analysis. This time-consuming effort is also discussed in Subsect. 5.4.

5 Case Study: Analysis of Tennis Data

A system for the management and analysis of tennis data had been started in SWI-Prolog in the diploma thesis [35], where an XML representation had been developed (see Listing 1 below), and some simple analysis had been done. Later, this analysis had been extended with a functionality to query the data [31] using the Prolog-based XML processing utilities of [30]. Prolog is very useful here, since knowledge bases with semi-structured, symbolic data, such as relational, deductive, XML or semantic web data can be handled nicely with Prolog [11,13].

In the following subsections, we are *refining* the proposed *data mining process* for deriving suitable association rules. First, the XML file with the tennis data is transformed into a relational table. Columns are created from the attributes of the file; attributes can be omitted, if they should not be involved in the data mining process. This initial table is transformed into a modified, temporal table; some of these modifications are not universally applicable, but key ideas may be portable to other types of data. First, we create a *spatial tessellation* for the tennis court, see Fig. 5, since exact coordinates will be repeated with a probability near to zero. Second, we duplicate a part of the table in order to model the data in a special way, such that traditional data mining is lifted to *temporal* data mining.

Then, the association rules are computed using the Apriori algorithm for frequent itemsets of the tool Weka. After wrapping the Weka output text file of the rules into Prolog facts and consulting them, the interesting association rules could be selected by suitable queries from the *maximal non-redundant rules*.

5.1 Preparing the Data: Creating and Duplicating the Table

We start with a given XML-file in the format of [35]; an example is given in Listing 1. Here the main information is saved in the (sub-) elements set, game, point and hit. These attributes will mostly form the columns of our table. For a different file, a similar approach is conceivable.

Listing 1. XML File of a Tennis Match.

```xml
<?xml version='1.0' encoding='ISO-8859-1' ?>
<match>
  <player id="A" name="Sampras"/>
  <player id="B" name="Agassi"/>
  <result>
    <score set="1" player_A="6" player_B="3"/> ...
  </result>
  <match_facts>
    <tournament>US Open 2002</tournament> ...
  </match_facts>
  <set id="1" score_A="5" score_B="3">
    <game id="1" service="A" score_A="0" score_B="0">
      <point id="1" top="B" service="A" score_A="0"
          score_B="0" winner="A" error="0">
        <hit id="1" hand="forehand" type="ground"
            time="00:00:42" x="0.17" y="-12.07"/>
        <hit id="2" hand="backhand" type="ground"
            time="00:00:44" x="-0.49" y="5.89"/>
        <hit id="3" hand="backhand" type="ground"
            time="00:00:46" x="-3.92" y="-3.42"/>
        <hit id="4" hand="forehand" type="ground"
            time="00:00:48" x="3.56" y="2.06"/>
      </point> ...
    </game> ...
  </set> ...
</match>
```

This file is transformed into a relational table, see Fig. 4.

hit:1	set:'1'	game:'1'	point:'1'	top:'B'	service:'A'	score_A:'0'	score_B:'0'	winner:'A'	error:'0'	hand:forehand	type:ground	time:'00:00:42'	x:'0.17' y:'-12.07'
hit:2	set:'1'	game:'1'	point:'1'	top:'B'	service:'A'	score_A:'0'	score_B:'0'	winner:'A'	error:'0'	hand:backhand	type:ground	time:'00:00:44'	x:'-0.49' y:'5.89'
hit:3	set:'1'	game:'1'	point:'1'	top:'B'	service:'A'	score_A:'0'	score_B:'0'	winner:'A'	error:'0'	hand:backhand	type:ground	time:'00:00:46'	x:'-3.92' y:'-3.42'
hit:4	set:'1'	game:'1'	point:'1'	top:'B'	service:'A'	score_A:'0'	score_B:'0'	winner:'A'	error:'0'	hand:forehand	type:ground	time:'00:00:48'	x:'3.56' y:'2.06'
hit:1	set:'1'	game:'1'	point:'2'	top:'B'	service:'A'	score_A:'0'	score_B:'0'	winner:'A'	error:'0'	hand:forehand	type:ground	time:'00:01:19'	x:'-0.27' y:'-12.03'
hit:2	set:'1'	game:'1'	point:'2'	top:'B'	service:'A'	score_A:'1'	score_B:'0'	winner:'A'	error:'0'	hand:forehand	type:ground	time:'00:01:21'	x:'0.08' y:'6.06'
hit:1	set:'1'	game:'1'	point:'3'	top:'B'	service:'A'	score_A:'2'	score_B:'0'	winner:'A'	error:'0'	hand:forehand	type:ground	time:'00:01:42'	x:'0.51' y:'-12.03'
hit:2	set:'1'	game:'1'	point:'3'	top:'B'	service:'A'	score_A:'2'	score_B:'0'	winner:'A'	error:'0'	hand:forehand	type:ground	time:'00:01:45'	x:'-3.92' y:'2.97'

Fig. 4. Part of the initial relational table for the tennis data.

As said in Sect. 4, we do not consider exact values. In our tennis data we saved coordinates where the ball hits the ground. At this point we transform this information and create a *tessellation* of the court in $N \times M$ tiles (regions), since an exact spot will not be hit twice and so the probability of this coordinates are nearly zero. It can both be useful to combine x- and y-coordinates to one attribute or to consider them separately. In Fig. 5, we illustrate the regions: for

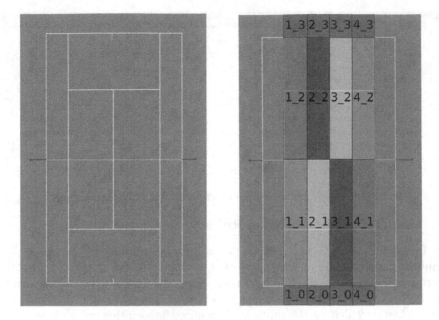

Fig. 5. Tessellation of a tennis court.

example the green tiles 1_1 and 4_2 inside the court or the red tile 0_1 outside the court, where a service can be take place. Figure 6 shows a spatio-temporal table, where the derived attributes Ix_1, Iy_1, Ix_2 and Iy_2 give the values for the tiles. Another issue is the optimal number of intervals in both x- and y-directions. This is also discussed in Subsect. 5.4.

Next, we create the spatio-temporal table, by duplicating part of the table of Fig. 4. Here, we save the information for a hit and the next hit, if there is one for this point. This means, that if a point has a hit order 1-2-3, then we have the rows of hit pairs $(1, 2)$ and $(2, 3)$. In the resulting rows, all attributes are saved. But, since not all information is useful, we omit some which might not be interesting for the data mining process; from Listing 1: we omit **set**, **game**, **top**, **service**, **score_A**, **score_B**; also attributes for the spatio-temporal data, namely **type_{1,2}**, **time_{1,2}**, **x_{1,2}**, **y_{1,2}**, are omitted, too. Thus, we obtain the table of Fig. 6. Here the red boxes show the spatio-temporal data. Note that the first attribute **hit** stands for hit pairs; for example in the fourth point with the hits 1-2-3-4-5, we get the four hit pairs $(1, 2)$, $(2, 3)$, $(3, 4)$ and $(4, 5)$ (see the blue boxes).

This transformation could be modified, such that we combine triples of hit. Also different tessellations with different x- and y- intervals lead to different association rules. The modification of the table may be supported by a domain expert. In future work, we plan to involve some knowledge at this point.

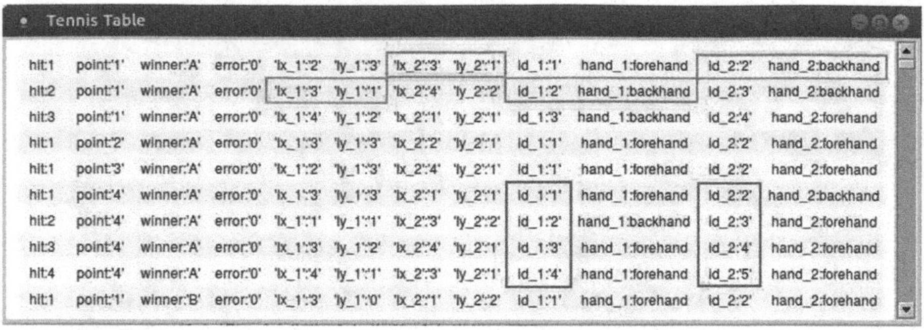

Tennis Table

hit:1	point:'1'	winner:'A'	error:'0'	'lx_1':'2'	'ly_1':'3'	'lx_2':'3'	'ly_2':'1'	id_1:'1'	hand_1:forehand	id_2:'2'	hand_2:backhand
hit:2	point:'1'	winner:'A'	error:'0'	'lx_1':'3'	'ly_1':'1'	'lx_2':'4'	'ly_2':'2'	id_1:'2'	hand_1:backhand	id_2:'3'	hand_2:backhand
hit:3	point:'1'	winner:'A'	error:'0'	'lx_1':'4'	'ly_1':'2'	'lx_2':'1'	'ly_2':'1'	id_1:'3'	hand_1:backhand	id_2:'4'	hand_2:forehand
hit:1	point:'2'	winner:'A'	error:'0'	'lx_1':'3'	'ly_1':'3'	'lx_2':'2'	'ly_2':'1'	id_1:'1'	hand_1:forehand	id_2:'2'	hand_2:forehand
hit:1	point:'3'	winner:'A'	error:'0'	'lx_1':'2'	'ly_1':'3'	'lx_2':'4'	'ly_2':'1'	id_1:'1'	hand_1:forehand	id_2:'2'	hand_2:forehand
hit:1	point:'4'	winner:'A'	error:'0'	'lx_1':'3'	'ly_1':'3'	'lx_2':'1'	'ly_2':'1'	id_1:'1'	hand_1:forehand	id_2:'2'	hand_2:backhand
hit:2	point:'4'	winner:'A'	error:'0'	'lx_1':'1'	'ly_1':'1'	'lx_2':'3'	'ly_2':'2'	id_1:'2'	hand_1:backhand	id_2:'3'	hand_2:forehand
hit:3	point:'4'	winner:'A'	error:'0'	'lx_1':'3'	'ly_1':'2'	'lx_2':'4'	'ly_2':'1'	id_1:'3'	hand_1:forehand	id_2:'4'	hand_2:forehand
hit:4	point:'4'	winner:'A'	error:'0'	'lx_1':'4'	'ly_1':'1'	'lx_2':'3'	'ly_2':'1'	id_1:'4'	hand_1:forehand	id_2:'5'	hand_2:forehand
hit:1	point:'1'	winner:'B'	error:'0'	'lx_1':'3'	'ly_1':'0'	'lx_2':'1'	'ly_2':'2'	id_1:'1'	hand_1:forehand	id_2:'2'	hand_2:forehand

Fig. 6. Part of the spatio-temporal tennis data. (Color figure online)

5.2 From Table to Association Rules

The input file `tennis.arff` of the data mining tool Weka describes the attributes, their domain and the rows of the table. This file is created after the selection and extraction step, i.e. the spatio-temporal database is transformed to this file. The other additional parameters `-N 4000` and `-C 0.5` in the Weka call given in Listing 2 denote the number of required association rules (here 4000) and the minimum confidence (here 0.5), respectively; their default values would be 10 and 0.9.

Listing 2. Shell Command to Call Weka.

```
java -cp ./weka.jar weka.associations.Apriori -t
   tennis.arff -N 4000 -C 0.5 -M 0.05 > rules
```

We call this shell command via the built-in predicate `unix/1` of SWI-Prolog to create the output text file `rules` shown in Listing 3. Weka sorts the association rules r by the confidence $conf(r)$ and stops once the number N of required rules is reached. Behind the antecedent of a rule $L \Rightarrow R$, $freq(L)$ is given, and behind the consequent, $freq(L \cup R)$ is given.

Listing 3. Fragment of the Output File from Weka.

```
Apriori
=======
Minimum support: 0.02 (18 instances)
Minimum metric <confidence>: 0.05
Number of cycles performed: 20
Generated sets of large itemsets:
Size of set of large itemsets L(1): 20
Size of set of large itemsets L(2): 16
Best rules found:

  1. Txy_1=2_0  61 ==> Txy_2=4_2 44   conf:(0.72)
  2. Txy_1=3_0  64 ==> Txy_2=2_2 38   conf:(0.59)
```

```
11. Txy_1=3_0   64 ==> Txy_2=1_2 25   conf:(0.39)

 3. Txy_1=2_3   76 ==> Txy_2=3_1 38   conf:(0.5)
 4. Txy_1=3_3   75 ==> Txy_2=2_1 36   conf:(0.48)
 5. Txy_1=2_3   76 ==> Txy_2=4_1 35   conf:(0.46)
 6. Txy_1=3_3   75 ==> Txy_2=1_1 34   conf:(0.45)

14. Txy_1=1_1  106 ==> Txy_2=4_2 37   conf:(0.35)
18. Txy_1=2_1   65 ==> Txy_2=4_2 20   conf:(0.31)
28. Txy_1=1_1  106 ==> Txy_2=1_2 20   conf:(0.19)

10. Txy_1=4_2  116 ==> Txy_2=1_1 46   conf:(0.4)
12. Txy_1=1_2   68 ==> Txy_2=4_1 25   conf:(0.37)
16. Txy_1=3_2   66 ==> Txy_2=1_1 21   conf:(0.32)
19. Txy_1=3_2   66 ==> Txy_2=4_1 20   conf:(0.3)
21. Txy_1=2_2   73 ==> Txy_2=2_1 21   conf:(0.29)
24. Txy_1=2_2   73 ==> Txy_2=1_1 19   conf:(0.26)

...
```

The players in the file `tennis.arff` are Sampras (top) and Agassi (bottom). From the 4000 best rules found, we show the fragment of the 16 rules that were interesting for us, namely the rules with `Txy_1` in the body and `Txy_2` in the head; the derived attributes `Txy_1` and `Txy_2` refer to the combination of the derived tile attributes:`Txy_i = A_B` means `Ix_i = A` and `Iy_i = B`.

Services (Groups 1 and 2): The rules 1, 2 and 11 refer to services of Agassi (`Txy_1`: left side 2_0; right side 3_0) to Sampras (`Txy_2`: backhand 4_2 and 2_2; forehand 1_2), while the rules 3–6 refer to services of Sampras (`Txy_1`: right side 2_3; left side 3_3) to Agassi (`Txy_2`: backhand 3_1 and 1_1; forehand 2_1 and 4_1).

Ground Hits (Groups 3 and 4): The rules 14, 18 and 28 describe how Agassi plays his backhand balls (`Txy_1`: 1_1 and 2_1): he plays 35% cross to the extreme backhand of Sampras (`Txy_2=4_2` in rule 14), 31% cross to the extreme backhand of Sampras (`Txy_2=4_2` in rule 18), and 19% longline to the forehand of Sampras (`Txy_2=1_2` in rule 28). The rules for Sampras are 10, 12, 16, 19, 21 and 24. It turns out that Sampras plays fewer longline balls, since the association rules `Txy_1=1_2 ==> Txy_2=1_1` and `Txy_1=4_2 ==> Txy_2=4_1` are not produced.

From the output file obtained by Weka, we create corresponding Prolog facts for the computed association rules. Since an association rule has four characteristic attributes, namely antecedent, consequent, support and the confidence, we save them in addition to a unique identifier. In particular we get facts of the form

`association_rule(Id, Ant, Cons, Sup, Conf),`

where Ant and Cons are lists that represent the itemsets. These facts are obtained using the Prolog-based parsing and XML processing utilities of Declare. After loading them into the system, the user can query them in Prolog. Currently, we are also experimenting with other programming languages like Python for working with strings and text files.

5.3   From Facts to Maximal Non-redundant Rules

From the facts for the association rules, we compute the redundancy and subsumption in Declare. Listing 4 defines in Prolog when the rule with the identifier Id_1 is redundant because of the rule Id_2, and when the rule with Id_1 is subsumed by the rule Id_2:

Listing 4. Definition of Redundant and Subsumed Rules in Declare.

```
redundant_association_rule(Id_1, Id_2) :-
    association_rule(Id_1, Ant_1, Cons_1, _, _),
    association_rule(Id_2, Ant_2, Cons_2, _, 1),
    Id_1 =\= Id_2,
    subset(Ant_2, Ant_1), subset(Cons_1, Cons_2).

subsumed_association_rule(Id_1, Id_2) :-
    association_rule(Id_1, Ant_1, Cons_1, Sup_1, Conf_1),
    association_rule(Id_2, Ant_2, Cons_2, Sup_2, Conf_2),
    Id_1 =\= Id_2, Sup_2 > Sup_1, Conf_2 > Conf_1,
    subset(Ant_2, Ant_1), subset(Cons_1, Cons_2).
```

In Subect. 5.5, we test many parameters and compare them with the number of maximal non-redundant association rules, for example, whether it has an impact on the number of maximal non-redundant association rules if we choose a dense or coarse tessellation. Nevertheless it is an advanced task for the domain expert to select the rules, which are useful for trainers or players. Here, domain knowledge has to be included.

5.4   Manual Workflow for Domain Experts

The domain expert had to experiment with different sets of attributes and different tessellations. Unfortunately, the interesting association rules were not the ones with a high confidence or support.

If too few association rules were required in the call to Weka, then no interesting results were obtained, since only rules with a high confidence or support were produced. If more association rules were required, then the user was overwhelmed by the result, and interesting association rules had to be selected suitably with queries; e.g. only the association rules with the derived attribute Txy_1 in the head and Txy_2 in the body were selected in Declare, c.f. Listing 5. These derived attributes Txy_1 and Txy_2 had been added to denote the tiles of a pair of successive hits.

Listing 5. Selection of Suitable Association Rules in Declare.

```
tennis_association_rules_filter(Rules_1, Rules_2) :-
  findall( Rule,
    ( member(Rule, Rules_1),
      Rule = association_rule(_, Ant, Cons, _, _),
      member('Txy_1':_, Ant),
      member('Txy_2':_, Cons) ),
    Rules ),
  sort(Rules, Rules_2).
```

Although `Txy_i = A_B` is equivalent to the combination of `Ix_i = A` and `Iy_i = B`, no interesting results had been produced, when `Ix_i` and `Iy_i` were in the set of input attributes (for `i=1,2`). Only after introducing the new, derived attributes `Txy_i` and excluding `Ix_i` and `Iy_i` from the input attributes, interesting association rules could be found.

After many attempts without interesting results, the parameters $N = 4$ and $M = 2$ were detected to produce a tessellation resulting in useful association rules. If `Txy_i`, `Ix_i` and `Iy_i` were in the set of input attributes and in the selected association rules, then further *subsumption* rules could be used to reflect the equivalence of `Txy_i = A_B` and `Ix_i = A`, `Iy_i = B`. E.g., in an association rule, the conjunction `Txy_i = A_B`, `Ix_i = A` could be reduced to `Txy_i = A_B`.

During the case study, which included a domain expert that was also a Prolog expert, a collection of useful Prolog operations for transforming the input relation with the tennis data (selecting attributes, adding additional derived attributes) and for selecting suitable produced association rules has been developed and implemented in Declare. In the future, we are planning to automatize the iterative process of searching for suitable transformations of the input relation, applying useful tessellations and selecting a subset of the produced association rules; thus, we would like to refine our currently presented manual workflow to an iterative and *automatic workflow* for declarative data mining.

5.5 Experimental Results

In the following, some experiments and their results are discussed. Concerning the *subsumption* and the *redundancy* of association rules, we first compare the number of maximal non-redundant rules with the maximal number of rules and the minimum confidence in the Apriori algorithm of Weka. Then, we take a look at the time the process costs us. As a last example, we check whether different *tessellations* lead to different association rules or not.

Table 1 shows that the 4 × 2-tessellation leads to a small (and so manageable) number of rules together with our definitions of redundancy and subsumption. In the case of 7500 or 10000 rules, we had to reduce the minimum confidence to 0.4 and 0.2, respectively, because otherwise we would not find 7500 or 10000 rules at all. Our definition of pruning decreases the number of association rules massively. Despite of the 10000 required rules and 0.2 minimum confidence case, in all other cases the percentage of maximal non-redundant rules among all rules is less than 10%.

Table 1. Number of required association rules, minimum confidence, Number of maximal non-redundant association rules (MNR rules)

Required rules	Minimum confidence	MNR rules
1000	0.5	**61**
5000	0.5	**354**
7500	0.4	**640**
10000	0.2	**1297**
1000	1.0	**11**
5000	1.0	**12**
7500	1.0	**12**
10000	1.0	**12**

In a second test, we have compared how much time it costs to create maximal non-redundant rules, see Table 2, where MNR Rules, stands for maximal non-redundant association rules. Here we can see that creating maximal non-redundant rules – and so the whole iteration – is very fast, and the main problem is the evaluation.

Table 2. Time experimental results.

Required rules	MNR rules	Time
25	**7**	0.4 s
50	**10**	0.4 s
100	**10**	0.5 s
200	**54**	0.5 s
1.000	**61**	1 s
2.000	**19**	1.2 s
10.000	**457**	9.6 s

For testing the effect of the tessellation on the number of maximal non-redundant rules – i.e. for finding parameters leading to a lower number of rules – we choose a maximal number of required rules of 5000 and a minimum confidence of 0.5. Then we get the result of Table 3. We can see, that the number of rules varies only a little bit. This shows that a domain expert is very helpful to evaluate the result, since the final number of maximal non-redundant association rules is not really effected by the tessellation; a computer scientist does not know the right parameters in the first place.

Table 3. Relationship of tessellation and maximal non-redundant association rules. N and M is the number of x and y intervals, respectively.

N	M	MNR rules
2	4	**354**
2	6	**202**
4	4	**298**
4	6	**308**
4	8	**267**
6	8	**238**

Summarizing, we have manually tested many different parameters for required rules, minimum confidence and the tessellations. We have also seen that the process is very fast, such that evaluation is the main issue to automatize to create a fast framework. In the future, we would like to automatize the whole process of searching for suitable parameters for convincing association rules, which can be used as initial parameters in further experiments. This will increase our experience about parameters leading to good results.

5.6 Future Work on Data Mining for Tennis Data

In the following, we will give an overview about some ideas which we want to explore in the future in the *tennis domain*; these ideas may then confirm the results of Subsect. 5.5. There are many different interesting questions which we want to analyze and solve in the future with our data mining workflow.

Temporal Data Analysis of Different Matches. It will be very interesting to find out if and how a player changes his playing style; we can consider many different matches in different seasons. Then we can create a spatio-temporal database to explore the players' way of playing. Maybe different dates in the season will give different association rules, and therefore we conclude information we do not get by looking at one game per data mining workflow. Then, we can make predictions of how the next game will look like, and a tennis trainer could prepare his player to prevail against his opponent.

As a special case, it is very interesting how one tennis player performs in different matches against the same opponent. In this case we take a look on a sequence of tennis matches of the same two players.

Influence of the Court Surface on the Players. During a tennis season, the players compete on different types of surfaces; four main of them are clay, grass, hard and carpet courts. All of them have their own characteristics and properties, that playing on different surfaces lead to different styles of playing. The international tennis federation (ITF) classifies the courts into the one of five pace settings. For analyzing how different surfaces effect the players, we need different matches from a player, which are close together. So matches only have to differ in the surface to make a statement.

Classification of the Players by their Style of Playing. This last new approach can be seen as a classification by association rules. On the basis of the resulting association rules, we want to classify a player's style: if an association rule $L_1 \Rightarrow R_1$ appears, then we have a player of style 1, and if there is in addition an association rule $L_2 \Rightarrow R_2$, then it is a player of style 2. This approach is very interesting, because it uses two data mining methods in one process. First, we need association rules, and then we classify the players due to this rules into classes of styles.

6 Conclusions

In this paper, we have introduced new definitions of redundant and subsumed association rules, respectively. With these definitions, we have discussed a data mining process. In a case study with *spatio-temporal* tennis data, the definitions have proven useful and led to results, which improve the results based on association rule mining with the standard Apriori algorithm.

In the future, we are considering to use logic programming (e.g. Prolog, Datalog and answer set programming) for guiding an automatized data mining process. The handling of the symbolic data (relations, deduction or association rules) can be done nicely in logic programming. In particular, we are planning to automatize parts of the *data mining workflow* given in Fig. 2 to decide on suitable parameters for the next iteration based on an analysis of the previously derived association rules.

We will also consider other pattern mining approaches, such as, e.g., subgroup discovery [4, 38].

Finally, we might extend the subsumption and redundancy theory for association rules, e.g., by combining computed rules to new rules.

References

1. Agrawal, R., Imieliński, T., Swami, A.: Mining association rules between sets of items in large databases. In: Proceedings of the 1993 ACM SIGMOD Conference on Management of Data, Washington D.C., vol. 22, pp. 207–216. ACM (1993)
2. Agrawal, R., Srikant, R.: Fast algorithms for mining association rules. In: Proceedings of the 20th VLDB Conference, Santiago de Chile, pp. 487–499 (1994)
3. Antunes, C.M., Oliveira, A.L.: Temporal data mining: an overview. In: KDD Workshop on Temporal Data Mining, vol. 1, pp. 1–13 (2001)
4. Atzmueller, M.: Subgroup discovery. WIREs DMKD 5(1), 35–49 (2015)

5. Atzmueller, M., Seipel, D.: Declarative specification of ontological domain knowledge for descriptive data mining. In: Proceedings of the International Conference on Applications of Declarative Programming and Knowledge Management (INAP), pp. 158–170 (2007)
6. Bastide, Y., Pasquier, N., Taouil, R., Stumme, G., Lakhal, L.: Mining minimal non-redundant association rules using frequent closed itemsets. In: Lloyd, J., et al. (eds.) CL 2000. LNCS (LNAI), vol. 1861, pp. 972–986. Springer, Heidelberg (2000). https://doi.org/10.1007/3-540-44957-4_65
7. Battaglia, P.W., et al.: Relational Inductive Biases, Deep Learning, and Graph Networks. arXiv preprint arXiv:1806.01261 (2018)
8. Baumgart, M.: Erkennung von Spielstand, Schlagposition und Spielertrajektorien beim Tennis. Master Thesis, University of Würzburg (2019)
9. Bayardo Jr., R.J., Agrawal, R., Gunopulos, D.: Constraint-based rule mining in large, dense databases. Data Min. Knowl. Discov. **4**(2–3), 217–240 (2000). https://doi.org/10.1023/A:1009895914772
10. Boulicaut, J.-F.: Condensed representations for data mining. In: Encyclopedia of Data Warehousing and Mining, pp. 207–211. Idea Group (2005)
11. Bratko, I.: Prolog Programming for Artificial Intelligence, 4th edn. Addison-Wesley Longman, Boston (2011)
12. Brin, S., Motwani, R., Silverstein, C.: Beyond market baskets: generalizing association rules to correlations. In: Proceedings of the ACM Conference on Management of Data (SIGMOD), pp. 265–276 (1997)
13. Clocksin, W., Mellish, C.S.: Programming in Prolog. Springer, Heidelberg (2003). https://doi.org/10.1007/978-3-642-55481-0
14. Cristofor, L., Simovici, D.: Generating an informative cover for association rules. In: Proceedings of the 2002 IEEE International Conference on Data Mining, pp. 597–613 (2002)
15. Fayyad, U., Piatetsky-Shapiro, G., Smyth, P.: From data mining to knowledge discovery in databases. AI Mag. **17**(3), 37–54 (1996)
16. Fournier-Viger, P., Tseng, V.S.: Mining top-k non-redundant association rules. In: Chen, L., Felfernig, A., Liu, J., Raś, Z.W. (eds.) ISMIS 2012. LNCS (LNAI), vol. 7661, pp. 31–40. Springer, Heidelberg (2012). https://doi.org/10.1007/978-3-642-34624-8_4
17. Fournier-Viger, P., Tseng, V.S.: TNS: mining top-k non-redundant sequential rules. In: Proceedings of the 28th Annual ACM Symposium on Applied Computing, pp. 164–166. ACM (2013)
18. Gebser, M., Guyet, T., Quiniou, R., Romero, J., Schaub, T.: Knowledge-based sequence mining with ASP. In: 5th International Joint Conference on Artificial Intelligence (IJCAI), pp. 8–15 (2016)
19. Goertzel, B.: Perception processing for general intelligence: bridging the symbolic/subsymbolic gap. In: Bach, J., Goertzel, B., Iklé, M. (eds.) AGI 2012. LNCS (LNAI), vol. 7716, pp. 79–88. Springer, Heidelberg (2012). https://doi.org/10.1007/978-3-642-35506-6_9
20. Han, J., Pei, J., Yin, Y.: Mining frequent patterns without candidate generation. In: Proceedings of ACM SIGMOD International Conference on Management of Data, pp. 1–12. ACM Press (2000)
21. Hilderman, R.J., Hamilton, H.J.: Knowledge Discovery and Measures of Interest, vol. 638. Springer (1999)
22. Hipp, J., Güntzer, U., Nakhaeizadeh, G.: Algorithms for association rule mining - a general survey and comparison. SIGKDD Explor. **2**(1), 58–64 (2000)

23. Kotsiantis, S., Kanellopoulos, D.: Association rules mining: a recent overview. GESTS Int. Trans. Comput. Sci. Eng. **32**(1), 71–82 (2006)
24. Mansingh, G., Osei-Bryson, K.-M., Reichgelt, H.: Using ontologies to facilitate post-processing of association rules by domain experts. Inf. Sci. **181**(3), 419–434 (2011)
25. Marinica, C., Guillet, F.: Knowledge-based interactive postmining of association rules using ontologies. IEEE Trans. Knowl. Data Eng. **22**(6), 784–797 (2010)
26. Marinica, C., Guillet, F., Briand, H.: Post-processing of discovered association rules using ontologies. In: 2008 IEEE International Conference on Data Mining Workshops, pp. 126–133. IEEE (2008)
27. McMillan, C., Mozer, M.C., Smolensky, P.: Rule induction through integrated symbolic and subsymbolic processing. In: Advances in Neural Information Processing Systems, vol. 4, pp. 969–976 (1992)
28. Pasquier, N., Bastide, Y., Taouil, R., Lakhal, L.: Discovering frequent closed itemsets for association rules. In: Beeri, C., Buneman, P. (eds.) ICDT 1999. LNCS, vol. 1540, pp. 398–416. Springer, Heidelberg (1999). https://doi.org/10.1007/3-540-49257-7_25
29. Seipel, D.: Declare - A Declarative Toolkit for Knowledge-Based Systems and Logic Programming. http://www1.pub.informatik.uni-wuerzburg.de/databases/research.html
30. Seipel, D.: Processing XML-documents in Prolog. In: Workshop on Logic Programming, WLP 2002 (2002)
31. Seipel, D.: Analyse von Tennismatches am Beispiel des Finales der US Open 2002: Pete Sampras - Andre Agassi (2004)
32. Seipel, D.: Advanced Databases. Lecture Notes of a Course at the University of Würzburg (since 2015)
33. Smolensky, P.: Connectionist AI, symbolic AI, and the brain. Artif. Intell. Rev. **1**(2), 95–109 (1987). https://doi.org/10.1007/BF00130011
34. Stumme, G., Taouil, R., Bastide, Y., Pasquier, N., Lakhal, L.: Computing iceberg concept lattices with Titanic. Data Knowl. Eng. **42**(2), 189–222 (2002)
35. Wehner, J.: Verwaltung und Analyse von Zeitreihen zu Videosequenzen. Diploma Thesis, University of Würzburg (2003)
36. Wielemaker, J.: SWI-Prolog Reference Manual 7.6. Technical report (2017)
37. Witten, I.H., Frank, E.: Data Mining: Practical Machine Learning Tools with Java Implementations. Morgan Kaufmann, Burlington (2000)
38. Wrobel, S.: An algorithm for multi-relational discovery of subgroups. In: Komorowski, J., Zytkow, J. (eds.) PKDD 1997. LNCS, vol. 1263, pp. 78–87. Springer, Heidelberg (1997). https://doi.org/10.1007/3-540-63223-9_108
39. Zaki, M.J.: Generating non-redundant association rules. In: 6th ACM SIGKDD International Conference on Knowledge Discovery and Data Mining, pp. 34–43 (2000)
40. Zhao, H.: Post-Mining of Association Rules: Techniques for Effective Knowledge Extraction. Information Science Reference, Hershey (2009)

From Textual Information Sources
to Linked Data in the Agatha Project

Paulo Quaresma⬛, Vitor Beires Nogueira⁽⬛⁾⬛, Kashyap Raiyani⬛,
Roy Bayot⬛, and Teresa Gonçalves⬛

LISP - Laboratory of Informatics, Systems and Parallelism,
Universidade de Évora, Evora, Portugal
{pq,vbn,kshyp,rkbayot,tcg}@uevora.pt

Abstract. Automatic reasoning about textual information is a challenging task in modern Natural Language Processing (NLP) systems. In this work we describe our proposal for representing and reasoning about Portuguese documents by means of Linked Data like ontologies and thesauri. Our approach resorts to a specialized pipeline of natural language processing (part-of-speech tagger, named entity recognition, semantic role labeling) to populate an ontology for the domain of criminal investigations. The provided architecture and ontology are language independent. Although some of the NLP modules are language dependent, they can be built using adequate AI methodologies.

Keywords: Linked data · Ontology · Natural Language Processing · Events

1 Introduction

The automatic identification, extraction and representation of the information conveyed in texts is a key task nowadays. In fact, this research topic is increasing its relevance with the exponential growth of social networks and the need to have tools that are able to automatically process them [10].

Some of the domains where it is more important to be able to perform this kind of action are the juridical and legal ones. Effectively, it is crucial to have the capability to analyse open access text sources, like social nets (Twitter and Facebook, for instance), blogs, online newspapers, and to be able to extract the relevant information and represent it in a knowledge base, allowing posterior inferences and reasoning.

In the context of this work, we will present results of the R&D project Agatha[1], where we developed a pipeline of processes that analyses texts (in Portuguese, Spanish, or English) and is able to populate a specialized ontology [16] (related to criminal law) for the representation of events, depicted in such

---

[1] http://www.agatha-osi.com/en/.

P. Hofstedt et al. (Eds.): DECLARE 2019, LNAI 12057, pp. 79–88, 2020.
https://doi.org/10.1007/978-3-030-46714-2_5

texts. Events are represented by objects having associated actions, agents, elements, places and time. After having populated the event ontology, we have an automatic process linking the identified entities to external referents, creating, this way, a linked data knowledge base.

It is important to point out that, having the text information represented in an ontology allows us to perform complex queries and inferences, which can detect patterns of typical criminal actions.

Another axe of innovation in this research is the development, for the Portuguese language, of a pipeline of Natural Language Processing (NLP) processes, that allows us to fully process sentences and represent their content in an ontology. Although there are several tools for the processing of the Portuguese language, the combination of all these steps in a integrated tool is a new contribution.

Moreover, we have already explored other related research path, namely author profiling [18], aggression identification [17] and hate-speech detection [20] over social media, plus statute law retrieval and entailment for Japanese [21].

The remainder of this paper is organized as follows: Sect. 2 describes our proposed architecture together with the Portuguese modules for its computational processing. Section 3 discusses different design options and Sect. 4 provides our conclusions together with some pointers for future work.

2   Framework for Processing Portuguese Text

The framework for processing Portuguese texts is depicted in Fig. 1, which illustrates how relevant pieces of information are extracted from the text. Namely, input files (Portuguese texts) go through a series of modules: part-of-speech tagging, named entity recognition, dependency parsing, semantic role labeling, subject-verb-object triple extraction, and lexicon matching.

The main goal of all the modules except lexicon matching is to identify events given in the text. These events are then used to populate an ontology.

The lexicon matching, on the other hand, was created to link words that are found in the text source with the data available not only on the Eurovoc [2] thesaurus but also on the EU's terminology database IATE [6] (see Sect. 2.7 for details).

Most of these modules are deeply related and are detailed in the subsequent subsections.

2.1   Part-Of-Speech Tagging

Part-of-speech tagging happens after language detection. It labels each word with a tag that indicates its syntactic role in the sentence. For instance, a word could be a noun, verb, adjective or adverb (or other syntactic tag). We used the Freeling [13] library to provide the tags. This library resorts to a Hidden Markov Model as described by Brants [11]. The end result is a tag for each word as described by the EAGLES tagset[2].

---

[2] https://talp-upc.gitbook.io/freeling-4-0-user-manual/tagsets/tagset-pt.

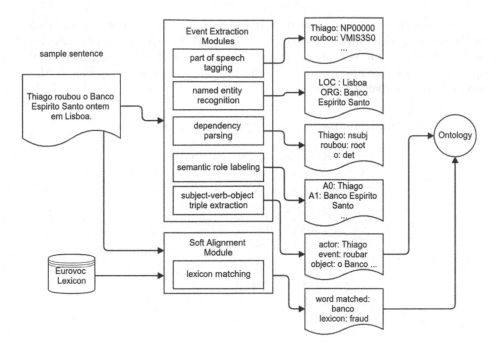

Fig. 1. System overview.

2.2   Named Entity Recognition

We use the named entity recognition module after part-of-speech tagging. This module labels each part of the sentence into different categories such as "PERSON", "LOCATION", "ORGANIZATION". We also used the Freeling to label the named entities and the details of the algorithm are shown in the paper by Carreras *et al.* [14]. Aside from the three aforementioned categories, we also extracted "DATE/TIME" and "CURRENCY" values by looking at the part-of-speech tags: date/time words have a tag of "W", while currencies have "Zm".

2.3   Dependency Parsing

Dependency parsing involves tagging a word based on different features to indicate if it is dependent on another word. The Freeling library also has dependency parsing models for Portuguese. Since we wanted to build a SRL (Semantic Role Labeling) module on top of the dependency parser and the current released version of the Freeling does not have an SRL module for Portuguese, we trained a different Portuguese dependency parsing model that was compatible (in terms of used tags) with the available annotated.

We used the dataset from System-T [7], which has SRL tags, as well as, the other preceding tags. It was necessary to do some pre-processing and tag mapping in order to make it viable to train a Portuguese model.

We made 589 tag conversions over 14 different categories. The breakdown of tag conversions per category is given by Table 1. These rules can be further seen in the corresponding Github repository [1]. The modified training and development datasets are also available on another Github repository [9] for further research and comparison purposes.

Table 1. Training and development - tag set details.

Category	Number of tags
NOUN	20
VERB	101
PROPN	39
PRON	121
ADJ	70
DET	62
AUX	149
ADP	3
NUM	1
PUNCT	18
CCONJ	1
SCONJ	1
INTJ	1
ADV	2

2.4 Semantic Role Labeling

We execute the SRL (Semantic Role Labeling) module after obtaining the word dependencies. This module aims at giving a semantic role to a syntactic constituent of a sentence. The semantic role is always in relation to a verb and these roles could either be an actor, object, time, or location, which are then tagged as A0, A1, AM-TMP, AM-LOC, respectively. We trained a model for this module on top of the dependency parser described in the previous subsection using the modified dataset from System-T. The module also needs co-reference resolution to work and, to achieve this, we adapted the Spanish co-reference modules for Portuguese, changing the words that are equivalent (in total, we changed 253 words).

2.5 SVO Extraction

From the yield of the SRL (Semantic Role Labeling) module, our framework can distinguish actors, actions, places, time and objects from the sentences. Utilizing this extracted data, we can distinguish subject-verb-object (SVO) triples using the SVO extraction algorithm [19]. The algorithm finds, for each sentence, the verb and the tuples related to that verb using Semantic Role Labeling (Subsect. 2.4). After the extraction of SVOs from texts, they are inserted into a specific event ontology (see Sect. 2.7 for the creation of a knowledge base).

2.6   Lexicon Matching

The sole purpose of this module is to find important terms and/or concepts from the extracted text. To do this, we use the Eurovoc [2], a multilingual thesaurus that was developed for and by the European Union. The Euvovoc has 21 fields and each field is further divided into a variable number of micro-thesauri. Here, due to the application of this work in the Agatha project (mentioned in Sect. 1), we use the terms of the criminal law [3] micro-thesaurus. Further, we classified each term of the criminal law micro-thesaurus into four categories namely, actor, event, place and object. The term classification can be seen in Table 2.

Table 2. Eurovoc criminal law - term classification.

Classification	# Terms
Actor	9
Event	133
Place	22
Object	3

After the classification of these terms, we implemented two different matching algorithms between the extracted words and the criminal law micro-thesaurus terms. The first is an exact string match wherein lowercase equivalents of the words of the input sentences are matched exactly with lower case equivalents of the predefined terms. The second matching algorithm uses Levenshtein distance, allowing some near-matches that are close enough to the target term.

2.7   Linked Data: Ontology, Thesaurus and Terminology

In the computer science field, an ontology can be defined has:

- a formal specification of a conceptualization;
- shared vocabulary and taxonomy which models a domain with the definition of objects and/or concepts and their properties and relations;
- the representation of entities, ideas, and events, along with their properties and relations, according to a system of categories.

A knowledge base is one kind of repository typically used to store answers to questions or solutions to problems enabling rapid search, retrieval, and reuse, either by an ontology or directly by those requesting support. For a more detailed description of ontologies and knowledge bases, see for instance [15].

For designing the ontology adequate for our goals, we referred to the Simple Event Model (SEM) [22] as a baseline model. A pictorial representation of this ontology is given in Fig. 2.

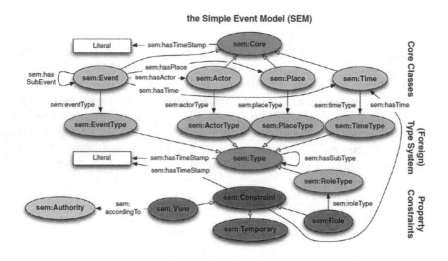

Fig. 2. The Simple Event Model [22]

Considering the criminal law domain case study, we made a few changes to the original Simple Event Model ontology. The entities of the model are:

- Actor: person involved with event
- Place: location of the event
- Time: time of the event
- Object: that actor act upon
- Organization: organization involved with event
- Currency: money involved with event

The proposed ontology was designed in such a manner that it can incorporate information extracted from multiple documents. In this context, suppose that the source of documents is a police department, where each document is under the hood of a particular case/crime; furthermore, a single case can have documents from multiple languages. Now, considering case 1 has 100 documents and case 2 has 100 documents then there is not only a connection among the documents of a single case but rather among all the cases with all the combined 200 documents. In this way, the proposed method is able to produce a detailed and well-connected knowledge base.

Figure 3 shows the proposed ontology, which, in our evaluation procedure, was populated with 3121 events entries from 51 documents.

Protege [8] tool was used for creating the ontology and GraphDB [5] for populating & querying the data. GraphDB is an enterprise-ready Semantic Graph

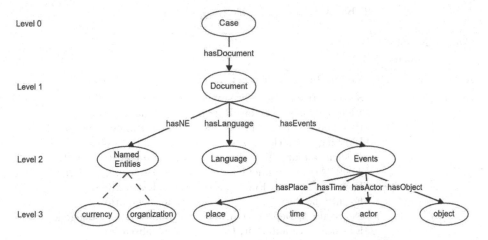

Fig. 3. Ontology diagram.

Database, compliant with W3C Standards. Semantic Graph Databases (also called RDF triplestores) provide the core infrastructure for solutions where modeling agility, data integration, relationship exploration, and cross-enterprise data publishing and consumption are important. GraphDB has a SPARQL (SQL-like query language) interface for RDF graph databases with the following types:

- SELECT: returns tabular results
- CONSTRUCT: creates a new RDF graph based on query results
- ASK: returns "YES", if the query has a solution, otherwise "NO"
- DESCRIBE: returns RDF data about a resource. This is useful when the RDF data structure in the data source is not known
- INSERT: inserts triples into a graph
- DELETE: deletes triples from a graph

Furthermore, we have extended the ontology [4] to connect the extracted terms with the Eurovoc criminal law (discussed in Subsect. 2.6) and IATE [6] terms. IATE (**I**nteractive **T**erminology for **E**urope) is the EU's general terminology database and its aim is to provide a web-based infrastructure for all EU terminology resources, enhancing the availability and standardization of the information. The extended ontology has a number of sub-classes for Actor, Event, Object and Place classes detailed in Table 3. This extension could be regarded has an extra Level (4) of Fig. 3 where Level 3 classes are mapped to Level 4 sub-classes.

Table 3. Extended ontology [4] - sub-classes.

Class	No. of sub-classes	Terms
Actor	6	Victim, Inmate, Prisoner, Hostage, Hijacker, Accomplice
Event	64	Slavery, Trade, Tax, Evasion, Spoofing, Slander, Shady, Violence, Sexual, Scam, Repentance, Rehabilitation, Refoulement, Rape, Punishment, Ponzi, Piracy, Aggression, Phishing, Trafficking, Pardon, Harassment, Mobbing, Misdemeanour, Libel, Trading, Imprisonment, Restraint, Theft, Arrest, Homicide, Hit-and-run, Hijacking, Forgery, Forfeiture, Fraud, Fight, Falsification, Extradition, Expulsion, Elimination, Offence, Drug, Detention, Deprivation, Deportation, Defamation, Penalty, Negligence, Execution, Counterfeit, Corruption, Confiscation, Conditional, Con, Order, Complicity, Campaign, Bully, Breach, Banish, Aggravate, Crime, Abduction
Object	3	Fine, Invoice, Bill
Place	11	Facility, Institution, Center, Confinement, Reformatory Penitentiary, Penal, Prison, Jail, Isolation, Banco

3   Discussion

We have defined a major design principle for our architecture: it should be modular and not rely on human made rules allowing, as much as possible, its independence from a specific language. In this way, its potential application to another language would be easier, simply by changing the modules or the models of specific modules. In fact, we have explored the use of already existing modules and adopted and integrated several of these tools into our pipeline.

It is important to point out that, as far as we know, there is no integrated architecture supporting the full processing pipeline for the Portuguese language. We evaluated several systems like Rembrandt [12] or LinguaKit: the former only has the initial steps of our proposal (until NER) and the later performed worse than our system.

This framework, developed within the context of the Agatha project (described in Sect. 1) has the full processing pipeline for Portuguese texts: it receives sentences as input and outputs ontological information: (a) first performs all NLP typical tasks until semantic role labelling; (b) then, it extracts subject-verb-object triples; (c) and, then, it performs ontology matching procedures. As a final result, the obtained output is inserted into a specialized ontology.

We are aware that each of the architecture modules can, and should, be improved but our main goal was the creation of a full working text processing pipeline for the Portuguese language.

4   Conclusions and Future Work

Besides the end–to–end NLP pipeline for the Portuguese language, the other main contributions of this work can be summarized as follows:

- Development of an ontology for the criminal law domain;
- Alignment of the Eurovoc thesaurus and IATE terminology with the ontology created;
- Representation of the extracted events from texts in the linked knowledge base defined.

The obtained results support our claim that the proposed system can be used as a base tool for information extraction for the Portuguese language. Being composed by several modules, each of them with a high level of complexity, it is certain that our approach can be improved and an overall better performance can be achieved.

As future work we intend, not only to continue improving the individual modules, but also plan to extend this work to the:

- automatic creation of event timelines;
- incorporation in the knowledge base of information obtained from videos or pictures describing scenes relevant to criminal investigations.

Acknowledgments. The authors would like to thank COMPETE 2020, PORTUGAL 2020 Program, the European Union, and ALENTEJO 2020 for supporting this research as part of Agatha Project SI & IDT number 18022 (Intelligent analysis system of open of sources information for surveillance/crime control). The authors would also like to thank LISP - Laboratory of Informatics, Systems and Parallelism.

References

1. Automated event extraction model for multiple linked portuguese documents. https://github.com/kraiyani/Automated-Event-Extraction-Model-for-Multiple-Linked-Portuguese-Documents/blob/master/Universal_to_eagle_tagset.xlsx. Accessed 06 May 2019
2. Eu vocabularies. https://publications.europa.eu/en/web/eu-vocabularies. Accessed 06 May 2019
3. Eu vocabularies, thesauri, 1216 criminal law. https://publications.europa.eu/en/web/eu-vocabularies/th-concept-scheme/-/resource/eurovoc/100180?target=Browse. Accessed 06 May 2019
4. Extended ontology. http://owlgred.lumii.lv/online_visualization/e9fh. Accessed 25 June 2019
5. Graphdb. http://graphdb.ontotext.com/. Accessed 06 May 2019
6. Iate (interactive terminology for Europe). https://iate.europa.eu/home. Accessed 06 May 2019
7. Portuguese universal propositions. https://github.com/System-T/UniversalPropositions/tree/master/UP_Portuguese-Bosque. Accessed 06 May 2019
8. Protege. https://protege.stanford.edu/. Accessed 06 May 2019

9. Training and development dataset for automated event extraction model for multiple linked portuguese documents. https://github.com/kraiyani/Automated-Event-Extraction-Model-for-Multiple-Linked-Portuguese-Documents. Accessed 06 May 2019
10. Amato, F., Moscato, V., Picariello, A., Sperlì, G.: Extreme events management using multimedia social networks. Future Gener. Comp. Syst. **94**, 444–452 (2019). https://doi.org/10.1016/j.future.2018.11.035
11. Brants, T.: TnT: a statistical part-of-speech tagger. In: Proceedings of the Sixth Conference on Applied Natural Language Processing, pp. 224–231. Association for Computational Linguistics (2000)
12. Cardoso, N.: Rembrandt - a named-entity recognition framework. In: Proceedings of the Eighth International Conference on Language Resources and Evaluation (LREC-2012), pp. 1240–1243. European Language Resources Association (ELRA), Istanbul, May 2012. http://www.lrec-conf.org/proceedings/lrec2012/pdf/409_Paper.pdf
13. Carreras, X., Chao, I., Padró, L., Padro, M.: Freeling: an open-source suite of language analyzers. In: Proceedings of the 4th International Conference on Language Resources and Evaluation (LREC 2004) (2004)
14. Carreras, X., Màrquez, L., Padró, L.: A simple named entity extractor using AdaBoost. In: Proceedings of the Seventh Conference on Natural Language Learning at HLT-NAACL 2003 (2003)
15. Guarino, N., Giaretta, P.: Ontologies and knowledge bases: towards a terminological clarification. In: Towards Very Large Knowledge Bases: Knowledge Building and Knowledge Sharing, pp. 25–32. IOS Press (1995)
16. Guarino, N., Oberle, D., Staab, S.: What Is an Ontology?, pp. 1–17, May 2009
17. Raiyani, K., Gonçalves, T., Quaresma, P., Nogueira, V.B.: Fully connected neural network with advance preprocessor to identify aggression over Facebook and Twitter. In: Proceedings of the First Workshop on Trolling, Aggression and Cyberbullying (TRAC-2018), pp. 28–41. Association for Computational Linguistics (2018). http://aclweb.org/anthology/W18-4404
18. Raiyani, K., Gonçalves, T., Quaresma, P., Nogueira, V.B.: Multi-language neural network model with advance preprocessor for gender classification over social media: notebook for PAN at CLEF 2018. In: Working Notes of CLEF 2018 - Conference and Labs of the Evaluation Forum, Avignon, France, September 10–14, 2018. (2018). http://ceur-ws.org/Vol-2125/paper_105.pdf
19. Raiyani, K., Gonçalves, T., Quaresma, P., Nogueira, V.B.: Automated event extraction model for linked Portuguese documents. In: Proceedings of Text2Story – Second Workshop on Narrative Extraction from Texts Co-located with 41th European Conference on Information Retrieval (ECIR 2019), Cologne, Germany, 14 April (2019). http://ceur-ws.org/Vol-2342/paper2.pdf
20. Raiyani, K., Gonçalves, T., Quaresma, P., Nogueira, V.B.: Vista.ue at semeval-2019 task 5: single multilingual hate speech detection model. In: Proceedings of the 13th International Workshop on Semantic Evaluation (SemEval-2019), pp. 520–524. Association for Computational Linguistics (2019)
21. Raiyani, K., Quaresma, P.: Keyword & machine learning based Japanese statute law retrieval and entailment task at COLIEE-2019. In: Proceedings of Competition on Legal Information Retrieval and Entailment Workshop (COLIEE 2019) in Association with the 17th International Conference on Artificial Intelligence and Law 2019 (ICAIL 2019). Easychair (2019)
22. Van Hage, W.R., Malaisé, V., Segers, R., Hollink, L., Schreiber, G.: Design and use of the simple event model (SEM). Web Semant. Sci. Serv. Agents World Wide Web **9**(2), 128–136 (2011)

Allen's Interval Algebra
Makes the Difference

Tomi Janhunen[1,2](✉)[iD] and Michael Sioutis[1][iD]

[1] Department of Computer Science, Aalto University, Espoo, Finland
{tomi.janhunen,michael.sioutis}@aalto.fi
[2] Computing Sciences Unit, Tampere University, Tampere, Finland

Abstract. Allen's Interval Algebra constitutes a framework for reasoning about temporal information in a qualitative manner. In particular, it uses intervals, i.e., pairs of endpoints, on the timeline to represent entities corresponding to actions, events, or tasks, and binary relations such as *precedes* and *overlaps* to encode the possible configurations between those entities. Allen's calculus has found its way in many academic and industrial applications that involve, most commonly, planning and scheduling, temporal databases, and healthcare. In this paper, we present a novel encoding of Interval Algebra using answer-set programming (ASP) extended by difference constraints, i.e., the fragment abbreviated as ASP(DL), and demonstrate its performance via a preliminary experimental evaluation. Although our ASP encoding is presented in the case of Allen's calculus for the sake of clarity, we suggest that analogous encodings can be devised for other point-based calculi, too.

Keywords: Answer set programming · Difference constraints · Qualitative constraints · Spatial and Temporal Reasoning · Symbolic AI

1 Introduction

Qualitative Spatial and Temporal Reasoning (QSTR) is a Symbolic AI approach that deals with the fundamental cognitive concepts of space and time in a qualitative, human-like, manner [10,20]. As an illustration, the first constraint language to deal with time on a qualitative level was proposed by Allen in [1], called Interval Algebra. Allen wanted to define a framework for reasoning about time in the context of natural language processing that would be reliable and efficient enough for reasoning about temporal information in a qualitative manner. In particular, Interval Algebra uses intervals on the timeline to represent entities corresponding to actions, events, or tasks, and relations such as *precedes* and *overlaps* to encode the possible configurations between those entities. Interval Algebra has become one of the most well-known qualitative constraint languages, due to its use for representing and reasoning about temporal information in various applications. More specifically, typical applications

© Springer Nature Switzerland AG 2020
P. Hofstedt et al. (Eds.): DECLARE 2019, LNAI 12057, pp. 89–98, 2020.
https://doi.org/10.1007/978-3-030-46714-2_6

of Interval Algebra involve planning and scheduling [2,3,9,26,29], natural language processing [8,33], temporal databases [7,32], multimedia databases [22], molecular biology [13] (e.g., arrangement of DNA segments/intervals along a linear chain involves particular temporal-like problems [4]), workflow [23], and healthcare [18,25,30].

Answer-set programming (ASP) is a declarative programming paradigm [6,17] designed for solving computationally hard search and optimization problems from the first two levels of polynomial hierarchy. Typically, one *encodes* the solutions of a given problem as a logic program and then uses an answer-set solver for their computation. The idea of representing Allen's Interval Algebra in terms of rules is not new; existing encodings can be found in [5,19]. However, these encodings do not scale well when the number of intervals is increased beyond 20 [5, Section 6]. The likely culprit for decreasing performance is the explicit representation of compositions of base relations, which tends to cause cubic blow-ups when instantiating the encoding for a particular problem instance. In this paper, we circumvent such negative effects by using an appropriate extension of ASP to encode the underlying constraints of Allen's calculus. The crucial primitive is provided by difference logic (DL) [28] featuring *difference constraints* of form $x - y \leq k$. The respective fragment of ASP is known as ASP(DL) [16] and it has been efficiently implemented within the CLINGO solver family. When encoding Allen's calculus in ASP(DL), the transitive effects of relation composition can be delegated to propagators implementing difference constraints. Hence, no blow-ups result when instantiating the ASP rules for a particular constraint network and the resulting ground logic program remains linear in network size.

The rest of this article is organized as follows. The basic notions of qualitative constraint networks (QCNs) and, in particular, Allen's Interval Algebra are first recalled in Sect. 2. Then, difference constrains are introduced in Sect. 3 and we also show how they are available in ASP, i.e., the fragment abbreviated as ASP(DL). The actual encodings of QCNs in ASP(DL) are presented in Sect. 4. The preliminary experimental evaluation of the resulting encodings takes place in Sect. 5. Finally, we present our conclusions and future directions in Sect. 6.

2   Preliminaries

A binary qualitative constraint language is based on a finite set B of *jointly exhaustive and pairwise disjoint* relations, called the set of *base relations* [21], that is defined over an infinite domain D. These base relations represent definite knowledge between two entities with respect to the level of granularity provided by the domain D; indefinite knowledge can be specified by a union of possible base relations, and is represented by the set containing them. The set B contains the identity relation Id, and is closed under the *converse* operation ($^{-1}$). The total set of relations 2^B is equipped with the usual set-theoretic operations of union and intersection, the converse operation, and the *weak composition* operation denoted by $\diamond$ [21]. For all $r \in 2^B$, $r^{-1} = \bigcup \{b^{-1} \mid b \in r\}$. The weak composition ($\diamond$) of two base relations $b, b' \in B$ is defined as the smallest (i.e., strongest) relation

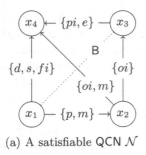

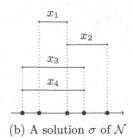

(a) A satisfiable QCN $\mathcal{N}$ (b) A solution σ of $\mathcal{N}$

Fig. 1. Examples of QCN terminology using Interval Algebra; symbols p, e, m, o, d, s, and f correspond to the base relations *precedes*, *equals*, *meets*, *overlaps*, *during*, *starts*, and *finishes* respectively, with $\cdot i$ denoting the converse of $\cdot$ (note that $ei = e$)

$r \in 2^B$ that includes $b \circ b'$, or, formally, $b \diamond b' = \{b'' \in B \mid b'' \cap (b \circ b') \neq \emptyset\}$, where $b \circ b' = \{(x, y) \in D \times D \mid \exists z \in D \text{ such that } (x, z) \in b \land (z, y) \in b'\}$ is the (true) composition of b and b'. For all $r, r' \in 2^B$, $r \diamond r' = \bigcup \{b \diamond b' \mid b \in r, b' \in r'\}$.

As an illustration, consider the well-known qualitative temporal constraint language of Interval Algebra (IA), introduced by Allen in [1]. The domain D of Interval Algebra is defined to be the set of intervals on the line of rational numbers, i.e., $D = \{x = (x^-, x^+) \in \mathbb{Q} \times \mathbb{Q} \mid x^- < x^+\}$. Each base relation can be defined by appropriately constraining the endpoints of the two intervals at hand, which yields a total of 13 base relations comprising the set $B = \{e, p, pi, m, mi, o, oi, s, si, d, di, f, fi\}$; these symbols are explained in the caption of Fig. 1. For example, d is defined as $d = \{(x, y) \in D \times D \mid x^- > y^- \text{ and } x^+ < y^+\}$. The identity relation Id of Interval Algebra is e and its converse is again e.

Definition 1. *A* qualitative constraint network (QCN) *is a tuple* (V, C) *where:*

- *$V = \{v_1, \ldots, v_n\}$ is a non-empty finite set of variables, each representing an entity of an infinite domain D;*
- *and C is a mapping $C : V \times V \to 2^B$ such that $C(v, v) = \{\text{Id}\}$ for all $v \in V$ and $C(v, v') = (C(v', v))^{-1}$ for all $v, v' \in V$.*

An example of a QCN of IA is shown in Fig. 1a; for clarity, neither converse relations nor Id loops are mentioned or shown in the figure.

Given a QCN $\mathcal{N} = (V, C)$, a *solution* of $\mathcal{N}$ is a mapping $\sigma : V \to D$ such that $\forall (u, v) \in V \times V$, $\exists b \in C(u, v)$ so that $(\sigma(u), \sigma(v)) \in b$ (see Fig. 1b).

3 Difference Constraints for Answer-Set Programming

We assume that the reader is already familiar with the basics of ASP (cf. [6,17]) and merely concentrate on extending ASP in terms of *difference constraints*. Such a constraint is an expression of the form $x - y \leq k$ where x and y are variables and k is a constant. Intuitively, the *difference* of x and y should be less than or equal to k. Potential domains for x and y are integers and reals, for instance. The domain is usually determined by the application and, for the purposes of this paper, the set of integers is assumed in the sequel. The given form of difference constraints can be taken as a normal form for such constraints. However, with a little bit of elaboration some other and very natural constraints concerning x and y become expressible. While $x \leq y$ is equivalent to $x - y \leq 0$, the strict difference $x < y$ translates into $x - y \leq -1$. To state the equality $x = y$, two difference constraints emerge, since $x = y \iff x - y \leq 0$ and $y - x \leq 0$.

Difference constraints can be implemented very efficiently, since they enable a linear-time check for unsatisfiability. Given a set S of such constraints, one can use the Bellman-Ford algorithm to check if S has a *loop* of variables $x_1, \ldots, x_n$ where $x_n = x_1$ along with difference constraints $x_2 - x_1 \leq d_1, \ldots, x_n - x_{n-1} \leq d_{n-1}$ such that $\sum_{i=1}^{n-1} d_i < 0$. When carrying out the check for satisfiability, it is not necessary to find concrete values for the variables in S. This is in perfect line with the idea of reasoning about QCNs on a qualitative, symbolic, level.

Example 1. The set of difference constraints $S_1 = \{y - x \leq 1, z - y \leq 1, x - z \leq -3\}$ is unsatisfiable, since $1 + 1 - 3 < 0$. However, if the second difference constraint is revised to $z - y \leq 2$, the resulting set of difference constraints S_2 is satisfiable, as witnessed by an assignment with $x = 0$, $y = 1$, and $z = 3$. ∎

More formally, an *assignment* τ is a mapping from variables to integers and a difference constraint $x - y \leq k$ is *satisfied* by τ, denoted $\tau \models x - y \leq k$, if $\tau(x) - \tau(y) \leq k$. Also, we write $\tau \models S$ for a set of difference constraints S, if $\tau \models x - y \leq k$ for every constraint $x - y \leq k$ in S. If $\tau \models S$, we also say that S is *satisfiable* and that τ is a *solution* to S. Moreover, it is worth pointing out that if $\tau \models S$ then also $\tau' \models S$ where $\tau'(x) = \tau(x) + k$ for some integer k. Thus S has infinitely many solutions if it has at least one solution. If S is satisfiable, it is easy to compute one concrete solution by using a particular variable z as a point of reference via the intuitive assignment $\tau(z) = 0$.[1]

Difference logic (DL) extends classical propositional logic in the *satisfiability modulo theories* (SMT) framework [28]. A propositional formula ϕ in DL is formed in terms of usual atomic propositions a and difference constraints $x - y \leq k$. A *model* of ϕ is a pair $\langle \nu, \tau \rangle$ such that (i) $\nu, \tau \models a$ iff $\nu(a) = \top$, (ii) $\nu, \tau \models x - y \leq k$ iff $\tau \models x - y \leq k$, and (iii) $\nu, \tau \models \phi$ by the recursive rules of propositional logic. Difference logic lends itself for applications where integer variables are needed in addition to Boolean ones. Thus, it serves as a potential target formalism when it comes to implementing ASP via translations [14,15].

The rule-based language of ASP can be generalized in an analogous way by using difference constraints as additional conditions in rules. The required theory extension of the CLINGO solver is documented in [12]. For instance, a difference constraint $x - y \leq 5$ can be expressed as &diff{x-y} <= 5 where x and y are constants in the syntax of ASP but understood as integer variables of difference logic. However, using such fixed names for variables is often too restrictive from

---

[1] This distinguished variable z can be used as a name for 0 in other difference constraints. Then, e.g., $x - z \leq k$ and $z - x \leq -k$ express together that $x = k$.

Listing 1.1. Choice of Base Relations

```
1  % Domains
2  var(X)   :- brel(X,Y,R).
3  var(Y)   :- brel(X,Y,R).
4  arc(X,Y) :- brel(X,Y,R).
5
6  % Intervals for every variable X: sp(X) <= ep(X)
7  &diff{ sp(X)-ep(X) } <= 0 :- var(X).
8
9  % Choose base relations
10 { chosen(X,Y,R): brel(X,Y,R) } = 1 :- arc(X,Y).
```

Listing 1.2. Difference Constraints Expressing Base Relations

```
1  % Relation eq(X,Y): sp(X) = sp(Y) and ep(X) = ep(Y)
2  &diff{ sp(X)-sp(Y) } <= 0 :- chosen(X,Y,eq).
3  &diff{ sp(Y)-sp(X) } <= 0 :- chosen(X,Y,eq).
4  &diff{ ep(X)-ep(Y) } <= 0 :- chosen(X,Y,eq).
5  &diff{ ep(Y)-ep(X) } <= 0 :- chosen(X,Y,eq).
6
7  % Relation during(X,Y): sp(Y) < sp(X) and ep(X) < ep(Y)
8  &diff{ sp(Y)-sp(X) } <= -1 :- chosen(X,Y,d).
9  &diff{ ep(X)-ep(Y) } <= -1 :- chosen(X,Y,d).
```

application perspective. It is possible to use function symbols to introduce collections of integer variables for a particular application. For instance, if the arcs of a digraph are represented by the predicate arc/2, we could introduce a variable w(X,Y) for the *weight* for each pair of first-order variables X and Y satisfying arc(X,Y). Recall that free variables in rules are universally quantified in ASP. More details about the theory extension corresponding to difference logic can be found in [16] whereas its implementation is known as the CLINGO-DL solver.[2]

4   Encoding Temporal Networks in ASP(DL)

In what follows, we present our novel encoding of temporal networks using ASP extended by difference constraints. To encode base relations from B in a systematic fashion, we introduce constants eq, p, pi, m, mi, o, oi, s, si, d, di, f, and fi as names for the base relations (see again Sect. 2). The structure of networks themselves is described in terms of predicate brel/3 whose first two arguments are variables from the network and the third argument is one possible base relation for the pair of variables in question. Then, for instance, the base relations associated with variables x_1 and x_2 in Fig. 1a could be encoded in terms of facts

---

[2] https://potassco.org/labs/clingodl/.

`brel(1,2,p)` and `brel(1,2,m)`. Given any such collection of facts, some basic inferences are made using the ASP rules in Listing 1.1. First, the rules in lines 2–3 extract the identities of variables for later reference. Secondly, the rule in line 4 defines the arc relation for the underlying digraph of the network. Given these pieces of information, we are ready to formalize the solutions of the temporal network. For each interval X, we introduce integer variables `sp(X)` and `ep(X)` to capture the respective *starting* and *ending* points of the interval. The relative order of theses points is then determined using the difference constraint expressed by the rule in line 7. Interestingly, there is no need to constrain the domain of time points otherwise, e.g., by specifying lower and upper bounds; arbitrary integer values are assumed. In addition, the choice rule in line 10 picks exactly one base relation for each arc of the constraint network.

The satisfaction of the chosen base relations is enforced by further difference constraints, which are going to be detailed next. Rather than covering all 13, we picked two representatives for more detailed discussion (see Listing 1.2). In case of equality, the starting and ending points of intervals X and Y must coincide. The difference constraints introduced in lines 2–3, whenever activated by the satisfaction of `chosen(X,Y,eq)`, enforce the equality of the starting points and those of lines 4–5 cover the respective ending points. The case of the *during* relation is simpler since the relationships of starting/ending points are strict and only two rules are needed for a pair of intervals X and Y. The rule in line 8 orders the starting points. The rule in line 9 puts the ending points in the opposite order. The encodings for the remaining base relations are obtained similarly.

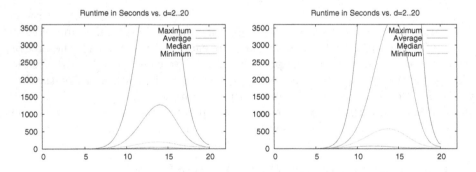

Fig. 2. Runtime scaling: checking *satisfiability* vs computing *intersection of solutions*

5   Experimental Evaluation

We generated QCN instances using model $A(n = 100, 2 \leq d \leq 20, s = 6.5)$ [27], where n denotes the number of variables, d the average degree, and s the average size (number of base relations) of a constraint of a given instance. For each $d \in \{2, \ldots, 20\}$, we report runtimes based on 10 random instances because the runtime distribution is *heavy tailed*, i.e., the severity of outliers encountered increases along the number of instances generated. As a consequence, the maximum and average runtimes tend to infinity as can be seen from the plots in Fig. 2. The graphs have been smoothened using GNUPLOT's option *bezier*.

Table 1. Median runtimes for IA instances with 100 variables

d	9	10	11	12	13	14	15	16	17	18	19
Satisfiability	4.7	34.9	60.9	163.0	180.7	543.8	157.3	38.0	32.5	86.5	56.4
Backbone	24.7	67.8	210.0	483.5	658.8	1488.4	223.0	382.9	64.6	44.1	55.2

The graph on the left shows the runtime scaling for checking the existence of a solution, and the graph on the right concerns the computation of the intersection of solutions, which amounts to the identification of *backbones* for QCNs [31]. The CLINGO-DL solver supports the computation of the intersection as one of its command-line options. It is also worth noting a phase transition around the value $d = 14$ where instances turn from satisfiable to unsatisfiable, which affects the complexity of reasoning. Moreover, due to outliers, it is perhaps more informative to check the median runtimes as given in Table 1. It is clear that intersection of solutions computation is more demanding, but the difference is not tremendous. Moreover, to contrast the performance of our encoding with respect to [5], we note that only 10% of 190 instances exceeded the timeout of 300 s (this same timeout was used in that work). In addition, the experiments of [5] covered instances from 20 to 50 variables only and the encodings were already performing poorly by the time 50 variables were considered. On the other hand, our encoding still underperforms with respect to native QSTR tools and, at least as far as satisfiability checking is concerned, the state-of-the-art qualitative reasoner GQR [11] tackles each of the 190 instances in a few seconds on average. To the best of our knowledge, there is no native QSTR tool for calculating intersection of solutions and in this way the advanced reasoning modes of the CLINGO-DL solver enable new kinds of inference and for free, since the same encoding can be used and no further implementation work is incurred.

Our second experiment studies the scalability of our ASP(DL) encoding when the number of variables is gradually increased from 50 to 90. The results are illustrated in Fig. 3. The plots on the left illustrate the scaling of the backbone computation, i.e., the intersection of solutions. It turned out that this kind of reasoning is easier than computing the union of solutions, also known as the *minimum labeling problem* [24], as depicted by the graphs on the right. The random instances used so far are relatively easy, and for that reason we take into consideration a modified scheme $H(n, 2 \leq d \leq 20)$ [27] that yields much harder network instances. The difference with respect to model A used above is that constraints are picked from a set of relations expressible in 3-CNF when transformed into first-order formulae. As a consequence, we are only able to analyze instances up to $n = 50$ variables in reasonable time. Table 2 shows the performance difference when computing the intersection and the union of solutions. In most cases, the intersection of solutions can be computed faster.

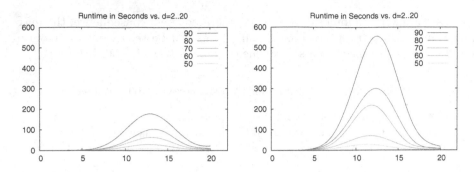

Fig. 3. Runtime scaling (median): computing intersection of solutions vs computing union of solutions

Although $d = 15$ is kind of an exception, its significance is diminished by the most demanding instances encountered: 8 477 vs 24 199 s spent on computing the intersection and the union, respectively.

Table 2. Median runtimes for IA instances with 50 variables

d	9	10	11	12	13	14	15	16	17	18	19
Intersection	**4.8**	**8.7**	**19.8**	**50.8**	**122.3**	**940.7**	1738.0	**758.5**	**384.4**	258.0	**155.9**
Union		25.6	46.9	105.5	298.5	7226.3	5636.5	**749.8**	1585.5	438.9	**93.8**	169.3

6   Conclusion and Future Work

In this paper, we encoded qualitative constraint networks (QCNs) based on Allen's Interval Algebra in ASP(DL), which is an extension of answer set programming (ASP) by difference constraints. Due to native implementation of such constraints as propagators in the CLINGO-DL solver, the transitive effects of relation composition are avoided when it comes to the space complexity of representing QCN instances. This contrasts with existing encodings in pure ASP [5,19] and favors computational performance, which rises to a new level due to our ASP(DL) encoding. As regards other positive signs, it seems that the presented encoding scales for other reasoning modes as well. Since ASP encodings are highly elaboration tolerant, we expect that it is relatively easy to modify and extend our basic encodings for other reasoning tasks as well. As regards future work, we aim to investigate more thoroughly the performance characteristics of our ASP(DL) encoding, and to use it for establishing collaborative frameworks among ASP-based and native QSTR tools.

Acknowledgments. This research was partially supported by the project *Ethical AI for the Governance of Society* (ETAIROS, grant #327352) funded by the Academy of Finland.

References

1. Allen, J.F.: Maintaining knowledge about temporal intervals. Commun. ACM **26**, 832–843 (1983)
2. Allen, J.F.: Planning as temporal reasoning. In: KR (1991)
3. Allen, J.F., Koomen, J.A.G.M.: Planning using a temporal world model. In: IJCAI (1983)
4. Benzer, S.: On the topology of the genetic fine structure. Proc. Natl. Acad. Sci. U.S.A. **45**, 1607–1620 (1959)
5. Brenton, C., Faber, W., Batsakis, S.: Answer set programming for qualitative spatio-temporal reasoning: methods and experiments. In: ICLP (Technical Communications) (2016)
6. Brewka, G., Eiter, T., Truszczynski, M.: Answer set programming at a glance. Commun. ACM **54**, 92–103 (2011)
7. Chen, C.X., Zaniolo, C.: Universal temporal data languages. In: DDLP (1998)
8. Denis, P., Muller, P.: Predicting globally-coherent temporal structures from texts via endpoint inference and graph decomposition. In: IJCAI (2011)
9. Dorn, J.: Dependable reactive event-oriented planning. Data Knowl. Eng. **16**, 27–49 (1995)
10. Dylla, F., et al.: A survey of qualitative spatial and temporal calculi: algebraic and computational properties. ACM Comput. Surv. **50**, 7:1–7:39 (2017)
11. Gantner, Z., Westphal, M., Wölfl, S.: GQR-A fast reasoner for binary qualitative constraint calculi. In: AAAI Workshop on Spatial and Temporal Reasoning (2008)
12. Gebser, M., Kaminski, R., Kaufmann, B., Ostrowski, M., Schaub, T., Wanko, P.: Theory solving made easy with clingo 5. In: ICLP (Technical Communications) (2016)
13. Golumbic, M.C., Shamir, R.: Complexity and algorithms for reasoning about time: a graph-theoretic approach. J. ACM **40**, 1108–1133 (1993)
14. Janhunen, T.: Cross-translating answer set programs using the ASPTOOLS collection. Künstliche Intelligenz **32**, 183–184 (2018)
15. Janhunen, T., Niemelä, I., Sevalnev, M.: Computing stable models via reductions to difference logic. In: LPNMR (2009)
16. Janhunen, T., Kaminski, R., Ostrowski, M., Schellhorn, S., Wanko, P., Schaub, T.: Clingo goes linear constraints over reals and integers. TPLP **17**, 872–888 (2017)
17. Janhunen, T., Niemelä, I.: The answer set programming paradigm. AI Mag. **37**, 13–24 (2016)
18. Kostakis, O., Papapetrou, P.: On searching and indexing sequences of temporal intervals. Data Min. Knowl. Disc. **31**(3), 809–850 (2017). https://doi.org/10.1007/s10618-016-0489-3
19. Li, J.J.: Qualitative spatial and temporal reasoning with answer set programming. In: ICTAI (2012)
20. Ligozat, G.: Qualitative Spatial and Temporal Reasoning. Wiley, Hoboken (2013)
21. Ligozat, G., Renz, J.: What is a qualitative calculus? A general framework. In: PRICAI (2004)
22. Little, T.D.C., Ghafoor, A.: Interval-based conceptual models for time-dependent multimedia data. IEEE Trans. Knowl. Data Eng. **5**, 551–563 (1993)
23. Lu, R., Sadiq, S.W., Padmanabhan, V., Governatori, G.: Using a temporal constraint network for business process execution. In: ADC (2006)
24. Montanari, U.: Networks of constraints: fundamental properties and applications to picture processing. Inf. Sci. **7**, 95–132 (1974)

25. Moskovitch, R., Shahar, Y.: Classification of multivariate time series via temporal abstraction and time intervals mining. Knowl. Inf. Syst. **45**(1), 35–74 (2014). https://doi.org/10.1007/s10115-014-0784-5
26. Mudrová, L., Hawes, N.: Task scheduling for mobile robots using interval algebra. In: ICRA (2015)
27. Nebel, B.: Solving hard qualitative temporal reasoning problems: evaluating the efficiency of using the ORD-Horn class. Constraints **1**, 175–190 (1997)
28. Nieuwenhuis, R., Oliveras, A.: DPLL(T) with exhaustive theory propagation and its application to difference logic. In: CAV (2005)
29. Pelavin, R.N., Allen, J.F.: A model for concurrent actions having temporal extent. In: AAAI (1987)
30. Sioutis, M., Alirezaie, M., Renoux, J., Loutfi, A.: Towards a synergy of qualitative spatio-temporal reasoning and smart environments for assisting the elderly at home. In: IJCAI Workshop on Qualitative Reasoning (2017)
31. Sioutis, M., Janhunen, T.: Towards leveraging backdoors in qualitative constraint networks. In: KI, pp. 308–315 (2019)
32. Snodgrass, R.T.: The temporal query language TQuel. ACM Trans. Database Syst. **12**, 247–298 (1987)
33. Song, F., Cohen, R.: The interpretation of temporal relations in narrative. In: IJCAI (1988)

Exploring Properties of Icosoku by Constraint Satisfaction Approach

Ke Liu$^{(\boxtimes)}$ⓘ, Sven Löffler, and Petra Hofstedt

Department of Mathematics and Computer Science, MINT,
Brandenburg University of Technology Cottbus-Senftenberg,
Konrad-Wachsmann-Allee 5, 03044 Cottbus, Germany
{liuke,sven.loeffler,hofstedt}@b-tu.de

Abstract. Icosoku is a challenging and interesting puzzle that exhibits highly symmetrical and combinatorial nature. In this paper, we pose the questions derived from the puzzle, but with more difficulty and generality. In addition, we also present a constraint programming model for the proposed questions, which can provide the answers to our first two questions. The purpose of this paper is to share our preliminary result and problems to encourage researchers in both group theory and constraint communities to consider this topic further.

Keywords: Constraint programming · Group theory · Constraint modelling · Icosoku

1 Introduction

Icosoku is a three-dimensional puzzle on a regular icosahedron block consisting of 20 tiles and 12 pegs (see Fig. 1), where every vertex of a triangular tile has four possible number of black dots $\{0, \dots, 3\}$ and each peg takes on distinct values from $\{1, \dots, 12\}$. To solve the puzzle, one needs to arrange the pegs and place the tiles. A feasible solution of the puzzle is that the value of any peg on the icosahedron is equal to the number of black dots surrounding itself. For example, the numeral 12 is surrounded by 12 black dots in Fig. 1.

Fig. 1. An icosoku (Figure reproduced from Amazon.com.)

© Springer Nature Switzerland AG 2020
P. Hofstedt et al. (Eds.): DECLARE 2019, LNAI 12057, pp. 99–105, 2020.
https://doi.org/10.1007/978-3-030-46714-2_7

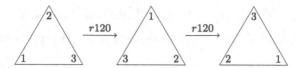

Fig. 2. The three symmetries of a triangular tile with values {1, 2, 3}. Here, we use numbers to replace the black dots.

There exists 4^3 possible triangular tiles since each of the three vertices of a triangle has four choices. However, because of the rotational symmetry, three assignments for the vertices of a triangle might represent the same triangular tile. For instance, we can rotate a tile about the triangle center by 120 and 240° in a clockwise direction, as shown in Fig. 2. Therefore, there are only 24 different types of triangular tiles after breaking these symmetries. The original icosoku puzzle only uses 14 different types of triangular tiles and claims that any arrangement of 12 pegs on the 12 vertices of the icosahedron can lead to a feasible solution. But the questions raised by the icosoku are far more than solving the puzzle itself. We believe that the icosoku is a proper research object for both constraint programming and group theory because of its combinatorial and symmetrical nature. And, thus, the following questions deserve to be explored:

1. Does there exist a feasible solution that the triangular tiles placed on the faces of the icosahedron are pairwise distinct? That is to say, the value at each vertex of the icosahedron is equal to the sum of values of the five vertices of the five faces that meet at this vertex of the icosahedron. And moreover, the 20 faces of the icosahedron are all different because of the values assigned to the vertices of triangular faces. In this paper, we call this kind of feasible solution *all different triangular solution* (ADTS).
2. Can any permutation of {1, ..., 12} assigned to the 12 vertices of the icosahedron lead to at least one ADTS?
3. Can any 20-combination from the 24 different types of triangular tiles lead to an ADTS?
4. Is it possible to find a 20-combination from the 24 triangular tiles that can produce a set of feasible solutions (ADTSs) which contains all the permutations of the set {1, ..., 12} arranged on the 12 vertices of the icosahedron?
5. If the answer to the previous question is affirmative, how many such 20-combinations are there?
6. How many non-isomorphic ADTSs are there if the ADTS exists?

In this paper, we present a constraint model that can answer the first two questions and discuss the difficulty encountered when solving the other problems. The rest of the paper is organized as follows. In Sect. 2, we give a brief introduction to the constraint programming. Afterward, in Sect. 3, we describe our constraint model. Then, we present the experimental results in Sect. 4. Finally, we conclude in Sect. 5.

2   Preliminaries

In this section, we give some basic definitions and concepts of constraint programming (CP) and the constraints relevant to the model of the icosoku puzzle.

The CP is a powerful technique to tackle combinatorial problems, generally NP-complete or NP-hard. A constraint satisfaction problem (CSP) can be expressed as a triple $\langle X, D, C \rangle$, where $X = \{x_1, \ldots, x_n\}$ is a set of decision variables, $D = \{D_{(x_1)}, \ldots, D_{(x_n)}\}$ contains associated finite domains for each variable in X, and $C = \{c_1, \ldots, c_t\}$ is a collection of constraints. Each constraint c_i is a relation defined over a subset of X, and restricts the values that can be simultaneously assigned to these variables. A solution of a CSP P is a complete instantiation satisfying all constraints of the CSP P.

The **allDifferent** constraint is the most influential global constraint in constraint programming and widely implemented in almost every constraint solver, such as Choco solver [7], Gecode [10], and JaCoP [4]. Formally, let X_a denote a subset of variables of X, the **allDifferent** constraint, which acts on X_a, can be defined as:

$$\forall x_i \in X_a \forall x_j \in X_a (x_i \neq x_j)$$

The **table** constraint is another one of the most frequently-used constraints in practice. For an ordered subset of variables $X_o = \{x_i, \ldots, x_j\} \subseteq X$, a positive (negative) **table** constraint defines that any solution of the CSP P must (not) be explicitly assigned to a tuple in the tuples that consists of the allowed (disallowed) combinations of values for X_o. For a given list of tuples T, we can state the positive **table** constraint as:

$$\big\{(x_i, \ldots, x_j) \mid x_i \in D_{(x_i)}, \ldots, x_j \in D_{(x_j)}\big\} \subseteq T$$

The **scalar** constraint[1] is also a common global constraint, which is defined as follows:

$$c_1 * x_i + c_2 * x_j + \ldots + c_n * x_k \, \Re \, sum$$

where $(c_1, c_2, \ldots, c_n)$ is a collection of integer coefficients, $(x_i, x_j, \ldots, x_k)$ and sum are the variables on which the constraint restricts the relationship. The $\Re$ is an operator in $\{=, <, >, \neq, \leq, \geq\}$. Besides, the **arith** constraint is used to enforce relations between integer variables or between integer variables and integer values. For example, an integer value can be assigned to an integer variable by using the **arith** constraint. We refer to [1,5,9] for more comprehensive and profound introduction to the CP.

3   The Constraint Programming Model

To solve the problem, we first should identify the decision variables for the CSP model. Then we impose constraints on these variables based on the problem

---

[1] This paper follows the naming convention of Choco solver. The other solvers might use a different name for the same constraint. For instance, the **scalar** constraint is called the **linear** and **LinearInt** constraint in Geode and JaCoP, respectively.

definition. Focusing on the Icosoku since it has 12 vertices, a list of 12 integer variables $V = (v_1, v_2, \ldots, v_{12})$ is used to represent these vertices, each of which has domain 1..12. Since the set of values $\{1, \ldots, 12\}$ has to be assigned to the 12 vertices in an ADTS, the 12 integer variables must all take distinct values. Therefore, $(v_1, v_2, \ldots, v_{12})$ must satisfy the **allDifferent** constraint, given by:

$$allDifferent(v_1, v_2, \ldots, v_{12}) \tag{1}$$

Similarly, since there are 20 faces on a regular icosahedron, we can define a 20×4 matrix F with integer variables for the 20 faces, where the first three elements of each row represent the three vertices of a triangular face; and the last element of each row stands for the corresponding type of the triangular tile determined by values of the first three elements of that row. For this reason, the domains of the first three columns and the last column of the matrix F are 0..3 and 1..24, respectively. The first question posed in the Introduction (Sect. 1) asks whether or not a feasible solution with 20 different types of triangular tiles exist. Hence, we can also introduce the **allDifferent** constraint to restrict that the values taken by the last column of the matrix F are pairwise different, which can be expressed by:

$$allDifferent(F[0, 3], F[1, 3], \ldots, F[19, 3]) \tag{2}$$

As mentioned before, only 24 distinct types of triangular tiles exist after eliminating the symmetries. However, all combinations of values that can be assigned to every row of the matrix F are 64 4-tuples, each of which consists of the first three values for a triangular face and the last value which indicates the type of that face. For example, as we have shown in Fig. 2, assigning the following values $[(1, 2, 3), (3, 1, 2), (2, 3, 1)]$ to the three vertexes of a triangle in turn results in the same triangular tile. Thus, the tuples $[(1, 2, 3, 23), (3, 1, 2, 23), (2, 3, 1, 23)]$ contain the same type value (Table 1). Because every Platonic solid has a different number of faces, we do not present the algorithm that generates all 64 tuples. Let T_{faces} denote the 64 tuples. We utilize the **table** constraint

Table 1. A partial list of tuples. We do not list all 64 tuples due to the limited space.

$$
\begin{vmatrix} 0\ 0\ 0\ 1 \\ 1\ 1\ 1\ 2 \\ 2\ 2\ 2\ 3 \end{vmatrix} \cdots
\begin{vmatrix} 0\ 0\ 2\ 7 \\ 0\ 2\ 0\ 7 \\ 2\ 0\ 0\ 7 \end{vmatrix} \cdots
\begin{vmatrix} 0\ 3\ 3\ 10 \\ 3\ 0\ 3\ 10 \\ 3\ 3\ 0\ 10 \end{vmatrix} \cdots
\begin{vmatrix} 1\ 2\ 3\ 23 \\ 3\ 1\ 2\ 23 \\ 2\ 3\ 1\ 23 \end{vmatrix}
\begin{vmatrix} 3\ 2\ 1\ 24 \\ 2\ 1\ 3\ 24 \\ 1\ 3\ 2\ 24 \end{vmatrix}
$$

specified with T_{faces} to limit possible combinations of values for each row of the matrix F, which can be stated as:

$$I = \{i \in \mathbb{Z} \mid 0 \leq i \leq 19\}, \ \forall i \in I(table(F[i, *], T_{faces})) \tag{3}$$

where $F[i, *]$ stands for a row in the matrix F. By using these 20 table constraints, we can associate the values at the vertices of a triangular face with its corresponding type so that the Constraint (2) can restrict the number of triangular types to be exactly 20.

The last property that an ADTS must satisfy is that the value assigned to any vertex of the icosahedron must be equal to the sum of values assigned to the vertices of the triangle surrounding this vertex of the icosahedron. To ensure this property, we can impose the **scalar** constraints on the CP model, given by:

$$I = \{i \in \mathbb{Z} | \ 0 \le i \le 11\}, \ \forall i \in I(scalar(F_{subset}, coefficients, =, v_i)) \quad (4)$$

where F_{subset} is a subset of the matrix F with cardinality five, *coefficients* is an array with 5 ones, and v_i denotes the decision variable for the vertices of the icosahedron. Obviously, the Constraint (4) guarantees that $\sum F_{subset} = v_i$ where F_{subset} consists of the five vertices of the five triangular faces meeting at v_i. Please note that we do not explicitly specify the five elements in the F_{subset} because they depend on how the triangular faces and the variables representing their vertices on the icosahedron are labelled in practice.

To partially break *value symmetry* [8], which preserves the solution with regard to the permutation of values, we can set the first vertex in V to one. Thus, we have the constraint:

$$arithm(v_0, =, 1) \quad (5)$$

In summary, Constraints (1), (2), (3), (4), and (5) form the model used to answer the question 1 in the Introduction (Sect. 1). It is easy to calculate that the total number of constraints and variables are 35 and 92, respectively.

4 Experiments

In this section, we present the experimental results that can answer the first two questions posed in the Introduction. We implemented the model in the Java library Choco 4.10.0 [7] running on JVM 11.0.2. All the experiments were executed on a Linux laptop with Intel i7-3720QM 2.60 GHz CPU and 8 GB DDR3 memory. The results of our first experiment for obtaining the first ADTS is summarized in Table 2. Besides, we specified the filtering algorithms FC and $GAC3rm+$ for all the **allDifferent** and **table** constraints; and the search strategy was set to the *minDomLBSearch*.

Table 2. Result for obtaining the first ADTS

Visited nodes	Backtracks	CPU time (ms)
48	1	32

In order to answer the second question in the Introduction (Sect. 1), we conducted the experiment that exhaustively tests the possible permutations of the set $\{1, \ldots, 12\}$ for the 12 vertices of the icosahedron by fixing the values of the V in each iteration. Moreover, to reduce the computational effort, we avoid evaluating the symmetries that are generated by rotating about the vertex v_0 of the icosahedron (see Fig. 3). Consequently, $\frac{(12-1)!}{5}$ permutations of the set $\{1,\ldots,12\}$ were tested since Constraint (5) fixes the value of v_0 and four-fifths of the symmetries are removed. The total CPU time is 7.03e5 s (8.13 days). Thus, all permutations of $\{1,\ldots,12\}$ arranged on the 12 vertices of the icosahedron can lead to at least one ADTS.

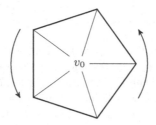

Fig. 3. The view from the top of the vertex v_0 of the icosahedron

5   Conclusions and Future Work

By means of constraint programming approach, we have proved the existence of the ADTS, and any permutation of $\{1\ldots12\}$ for the vertices of the icosahedron can produce at least one ADTS. But the rest of questions posed in the Intro-duction (Sect. 1) remain open to us. Even the third question requires non-trivial efforts. Because when we enforce a set of 20 types of triangular, which is chosen from the 24 triangular tiles, on the model, the upper bound of traversing the entire search tree is 4^{60} if we do not take account of constraint propagation. Hence, to find the 20 different tiles whose corresponding ADTSs cover all the permutations of $\{1\ldots12\}$ arranged on the vertices of the icosahedron (Question 4) is even more difficult.

As future work, we plan to employ parallel constraint solving to seek to answer the rest of the questions. Furthermore, we believe that Question 4 (Sect. 1) requires a well-designed nogood recording mechanism to avoid explor-ing the search space including the permutations of $\{1\ldots12\}$ already visited. Finally, we propose that the icosoku problem can be a standard benchmark for CSPLib [3], which is a library of test problems for constraint solvers. Because we believe it has the advantages as an excellent CSP benchmark should have, which are summarized as follows: (1) The constraints required by the CSP model of the benchmark are widely implemented in the state-of-art constraint solvers. (2) The benchmark can be readily generalized and scaled from easy instance to difficult instances, e.g., increasing the number of golfers from 15 to 18 results in the Social Golfer Problem [2] more difficult to be solved [6]. Indeed, the regu-lar icosahedron has the highest number of faces among the five Platonic solids, which limits its scalability to increase the difficulty of the problem. But the prob-lem can be expanded to other polyhedra such as Kepler–Poinsot polyhedron or higher dimensions (e.g., four-dimensional Platonic Solids). (3) The benchmark does not rely on third party data (e.g., the Travelling Salesman Problem needs maps of instances), which is more convenient to make comparisons.

Acknowledgment. We should like to thank our colleague Ekkehard Köhler for drawing our attention to the icosoku problem.

References

1. Dechter, R.: Constraint Processing. Elsevier Morgan Kaufmann (2003). http://www.elsevier.com/wps/find/bookdescription.agents/678024/description
2. Harvey, W.: CSPLib problem 010: social golfers problem (2002). http://www.csplib.org/Problems/prob010. Accessed 28 Apr 2019
3. Jefferson, C., Akgün, Ö.: CSPLib: a problem library for constraints (1999). http://www.csplib.org/. Accessed 28 Apr 2019
4. Kuchcinski, K., Szymanek, R.: JaCoP Documentation. Lund University (2017). https://osolpro.atlassian.net/wiki/spaces/JACOP/pages/24248322/JaCoP+Overview
5. Lecoutre, C.: Constraint Networks: Techniques and Algorithms. Wiley, London (2009)
6. Liu., K., Löffler., S., Hofstedt., P.: Solving the social golfers problems by constraint programming in sequential and parallel. In: Proceedings of the 11th International Conference on Agents and Artificial Intelligence - Volume 2: ICAART. INSTICC, pp. 29–39. SciTePress (2019). https://doi.org/10.5220/0007252300290039
7. Prud'homme, C., Fages, J.G., Lorca, X.: Choco Documentation. TASC - LS2N CNRS UMR 6241, COSLING S.A.S. (2017). http://www.choco-solver.org
8. Puget, J.: Symmetry breaking revisited. Constraints **10**(1), 23–46 (2005). https://doi.org/10.1007/s10601-004-5306-8
9. Rossi, F., van Beek, P., Walsh, T. (eds.): Handbook of Constraint Programming, Foundations of Artificial Intelligence, vol. 2. Elsevier (2006). http://www.sciencedirect.com/science/bookseries/15746526/2
10. Schulte, C., Tack, G., Lagerkvist, M.Z.: Modeling and programming with Gecode. Gecode Team (2017). https://www.gecode.org/

The Regularization of Small Sub-Constraint Satisfaction Problems

Sven Löffler[(✉)], Ke Liu, and Petra Hofstedt

Department of Mathematics and Computer Science,
MINT, Programming Languages and Compiler Construction Group,
Brandenburg University of Technology Cottbus-Senftenberg,
Konrad-Wachsmann-Allee 5, 03044 Cottbus, Germany
{sven.loeffler,liuke,hofstedt}@b-tu.de

Abstract. This paper describes a new approach on optimization of constraint satisfaction problems (CSPs) by means of substituting sub-CSPs with locally consistent regular membership constraints. The purpose of this approach is to reduce the number of fails in the resolution process, to improve the inferences made during search by the constraint solver by strengthening constraint propagation, and to maintain the level of propagation while reducing the cost of propagating the constraints. Our experimental results show improvements in terms of the resolution speed compared to the original CSPs and a competitiveness to the recent tabulation approach [1, 15]. Besides, our approach can be realized in a preprocessing step, and therefore wouldn't collide with redundancy constraints or parallel computing if implemented.

Keywords: Constraint programming · CSP · Refinement ·
Optimizations · Regular membership constraint · Regular CSPs

1 Introduction

A CSP can be often described in several ways, each of which might consist of different types and combinations of constraints, which leads to various statistical results of the resolution, including the execution time, the number of fails, the number of backtracks, the number of nodes etc. The reason for this is, that the combination of constraints and their propagators have a significant impact on the shape and the size of the search tree. Therefore, the diversity of models and constraints for a given CSP offers us an opportunity to improve the resolution process by using another model in which fewer fails occur during the resolution process. Based on this idea, previous works show that the performance of a constraint problem often can be improved by converting a sub-problem into a single constraint [1–4, 15].

In this paper, we propose an algorithm which substitutes parts of CSPs by singleton, locally consistent constraints. In contrast to [15], the replacement is based on the regular membership constraint instead of the table constraint. Since

© Springer Nature Switzerland AG 2020
P. Hofstedt et al. (Eds.): DECLARE 2019, LNAI 12057, pp. 106–115, 2020.
https://doi.org/10.1007/978-3-030-46714-2_8

our algorithm can be applied at the pre-processing stage, other approaches which accelerate the resolution process such as redundant modeling [6], parallel search [21], or parallel consistency [12] can be used in combination with ours.

The rest of this paper is organized as follows. In Sect. 2, we introduce the necessary notions for the approach. In Sect. 3, the substitution of small sub-CSPs with the regular membership constraint is explained. In Sect. 4, the benefit of our regularization approach is shown in two case studies based on the Solitaire Battleships Problem [9] and the Black Hole Problem [17]. Furthermore, we compare our results with the tabulation approach presented in [15]. Finally, Sect. 5 concludes and proposes research directions for the future.

Remark 1. In this paper we will use the notion of a *"regular constraint"* synonym for *"regular membership constraint"*.

2   Preliminaries

In this section, we introduce necessary definitions and methods for our regularization approach. We consider CSPs which are defined in the following way:

CSP [7]. A constraint satisfaction problem (CSP) is defined as a 3-tuple $P = (X, D, C)$ with $X = \{x_1, x_2, \ldots, x_n\}$ is a set of variables, $D = \{D_1, D_2, \ldots, D_n\}$ is a set of finite domains where D_i is the domain of x_i and $C = \{c_1, c_2, \ldots, c_m\}$ is a set of primitive or global constraints covering between one and all variables in X.

Additionally, we define a sub-CSP P_{sub} as a part of a CSP $P = (X, D, C)$ which covers only a part of the constraints and their variables.

Sub-CSP. Let $P = (X, D, C)$ be a CSP. For $C' \subseteq C$ we define $P_{sub} = (X', D', C')$ such that $X' = \bigcup_{c \in C'} scope(c)$ with corresponding domains $D' = \{D_i \mid x_i \in X'\} \subseteq D$, where the *scope* of a constraint c is defined as the set of variables which are part of the constraint c [7].

After we defined CSPs and sub-CSPs, we need a measure for the size of such a CSP or sub-CSP.

size(P). We define the maximal size $size(P)$ of a CSP $P = (X, D, C)$ as the product of the cardinalities of the domains of the CSP P, see Eq. 1.

$$size(P) = \prod_{i=1}^{|X|} |D_i| \tag{1}$$

The regular constraint, its propagation [13,18,19] and deterministic finite automatons (DFAs) [14] provide the basis of our approach. We briefly review the notion of a deterministic finite automaton (DFA) and of the regular constraint.

DFA [14]. A deterministic finite automaton (DFA) is a quintuple $M = (Q, \Sigma, \delta, q_0, F)$, where Q is a finite set of states, Σ is the finite input alphabet, δ is a transformation function $Q \times \Sigma \to Q$, $q_0 \in Q$ is the initial state, and $F \subseteq Q$

is the set of final or accepting states. A word $w \in \Sigma^*$ is accepted by M, i.e. $w \in L(M)$, if the corresponding DFA M with the input w stops in a final state $f \in F$.

Regular Constraint [19]. Let $M = (Q, \Sigma, \delta, q_0, F)$ be a DFA and let $X = \{x_1, x_2, ..., x_n\}$ be a set of variables with $D(x_i) \subseteq \Sigma$ for $1 \leq i \leq n$. Then

$$regular(X, M) = \{(d_1, ..., d_n) | \forall i \ d_i \in D_i, d_1 \circ d_2 \circ ... \circ d_n \in L(M)\}, \quad (2)$$

i.e. every sequence $d_1...d_n$ of values for $x_1, ..., x_n$ must be a word of the regular language recognized by the DFA M, where $\circ$ is the concatenation of two words.

3   Substitution of Constraints by Regular Constraints

Previous work [4] has shown that each CSP can be transformed into an equivalent one with only one regular constraint (rCSP), theoretically. In this section, we present a practical algorithm to transform the constraints of a sub-CSP P_{sub} of a given CSP P into a regular constraint. For the reason of effectiveness the sub-CSP P_{sub} should be much smaller than the original CSP P (size(P_{sub}) $\ll$ size(P)).

It is the aim to detect and substitute such sub-CSPs, which are preferably as big as possible but can be represented by a DFA which is as small as possible at the same time. An algorithm to detect such sub-CSPs must be developed in the future. Currently, we use the heuristics to find sub-CSPs given in [1]. Alternatively, an algorithm like Gottlobs hypertree decomposition [11] or Ke Lius det-k-CP [16] can be used.

Our transformation algorithm obtains a sub-CSP $P_{sub} = (X', D', C')$ from CSP $P = (X, D, C)$ as input, where $C' \subset C$, $X' = \{x_1, \dots, x_n\} = \bigcup_{c \in C'} scope(c) \subset X$, $|X'| \ll |X|$ and $D' = \{D_1, \dots, D_n\} \subset D$, where D_i is the domain of variable x_i, $\forall i \in \{1, 2, \dots, n\}$, and returns a regular constraint which is equivalent to the constraints in C'. Our regularization algorithm has two phases:

1. Solve the detected/given sub CSP P_{sub}.
2. Transform all solutions $S = \{s_1, s_2, \dots, s_k\}$ of the sub-CSP P_{sub} into a regular constraint.

The first phase is obvious. Notice that the sub-CSP P_{sub} should be much smaller than the original CSP P, otherwise the solving step would be too time consuming.

We continue with a description of the second phase. Let $S = \{s_1, s_2, \dots, s_k\}$ be the set of all solutions of P_{sub} calculated in step one. Every solution s_j, $j \in \{1, 2, \dots, k\}$ consists of n values $s_{i,j}$, $i \in \{1, 2, \dots, n\}$, cf. Table 1.

To define a deterministic finite automaton as the basis for the regular constraint, we need the set $T = \{T_1, \dots, T_n\}$ of prefix sets of all solutions of P_{sub}, where all elements in T_i are concatenations of the i first values of a solution $s \in S$ (see Eq. 3):

$$T_i = \bigcup_{l=1}^{k} \{s_{1,l} \circ s_{2,l} \circ \dots \circ s_{i,l} \mid \forall i \in \{1, \dots, n\}\} \quad (3)$$

Table 1. The solutions $s_1, ..., s_k$ of the sub-CSP P_{sub}

S	s_1	s_2	$\cdots$	s_k
x_1	$s_{1,1}$	$s_{1,2}$	$\cdots$	$s_{1,k}$
x_2	$s_{2,1}$	$s_{2,2}$	$\cdots$	$s_{2,k}$
$\vdots$	$\vdots$	$\vdots$	$\ddots$	$\vdots$
x_n	$s_{n,1}$	$s_{n,2}$	$\cdots$	$s_{n,k}$

This results in e.g. $T_1 = \{s_{1,1}, s_{1,2}, \ldots, s_{1,k}\}$, $T_2 = \{s_{1,1} \circ s_{2,1}, s_{1,2} \circ s_{2,2}, \ldots, s_{1,k} \circ s_{2,k}\}$, $T_n = S$. Note that we enumerate the elements in each T_i from 1 to k but actually they mostly have fewer elements then k for the reason that multiple occurrences of elements do not occur in sets. It follows $|T_1| \leq |T_2| \leq \ldots \leq |T_n| = k$.

For each element t of each set T_i, $i \in \{1, \ldots, n-1\}$ a state q_t for the DFA is created, which represents the solution prefix t. Furthermore, the initial state q_{start} and the final state q_{end} (representing all solutions $S = T_n$ of P_{sub}) are added to Q. Thus, the *set of states Q of the DFA* is

$$Q = \{q_t \mid t \in T_i, i \in \{1, 2, \ldots, n-1\}\} \cup \{q_{start}, q_{end}\}.$$

The *initial state* is q_{start} and $F = \{q_{end}\}$ is the *set of final states*.

The alphabet Σ of the DFA is the union of all domains of the variables of X':

$$\Sigma = \bigcup_{D_i \in D'} D_i \tag{4}$$

Finally, we define the *transition function δ* as follows:

- Let $t \in T_1$. Then it holds
$$\delta(q_{start}, t) = q_t \tag{5}$$
- Let t_{i-1} be an element in T_{i-1}, t_i be an element in T_i, $i \in \{2, \ldots, n-1\}$ and $w \in D_i$ with $t_i = t_{i-1} \circ w$. Then it holds

$$\delta(q_{t_{i-1}}, w) = q_{t_i} \tag{6}$$

- Let t_{n-1} be an element in T_{n-1}, t_n be an element in $T_n = S$ and $w \in D_n$ with $t_n = t_{n-1} \circ w$. Then it holds

$$\delta(q_{t_{n-1}}, w) = q_{end} \tag{7}$$

This altogether provides the DFA $M = (Q, \Sigma, \delta, q_{start}, \{q_{end}\})$. The constraint $regular(X', M)$ can be used as a replacement for the constraints of C' in the original CSP P.

Remark 2. This algorithm is only useful for sub-CSPs P_{sub} which are proper subsets of the original CSP P ($size(P_{sub}) \ll size(P)$). Solving a sub-problem P_{sub} and finding all solutions is also an NP-hard problem. Nevertheless, due to the exponential growth of constraint problems, sub-problems with smaller size than the original problem can be solved significantly faster.

4   Examples and Experimental Results

After presenting our approach to transform the constraints of small sub-CPSs into a regular constraint, we want to show two case studies to underline its benefits. For this, we use the Black Hole Problem [17] and the Solitaire Battleships Problem [9] from the CSPlib.

All the experiments are set up on a DELL laptop with an Intel i7-4610M CPU, 3.00 GHz, with 16 GB 1600 MHz DDR3 and running under Windows 7 professional with service pack 1. The algorithms are implemented in Java under JDK version 1.8.0_191 and Choco Solver [20]. We used the *DowOverWDeg* search strategy which is explained in [5] and is used as default search strategy in the Choco Solver [20].

4.1   The Black Hole Problem

Black Hole is a common card game, where all 52 cards are played one after the other from seventeen face-up fans of three cards into a discard pile named 'black hole', which contains at the beginning only the card $A\spadesuit$. All cards are visible at all times. A card can be played into the 'black hole' if it is adjacent in rank to the previous card (colors are not important). The goal is to play all cards into the Black Hole.

Black Hole was modelled for a variety of solvers by Gent et al. [10]. We use the simplest and most declarative model of Dekker et al. [8], where two variables a and b represent adjacent cards if $|a - b| \bmod 13 \in \{1, 12\}$.

The heuristic *Weak Propagation*, presented in [1], detects the adjacency constraints as replaceable[1]. For our benchmark suite we computed 50 different instances of the Black Hole Problem, where 49 instances are randomly created (so the position of every card in the 17 fans is random) and the remaining instance has an enumerated card distribution ($1\spadesuit$, $2\spadesuit$, ..., $K\spadesuit$, $A\clubsuit$, $1\clubsuit$,..., $K\clubsuit$, $A\heartsuit$, $1\heartsuit$, ..., $K\heartsuit$, $A\diamondsuit$, $1\diamondsuit$, ..., $K\diamondsuit$).

For all instances, we limited the solution time to 10 min and each problem was solved in 4 ways:

1. *Original*: The problem was modelled as described in [8].
2. *Table*: The detected adjacency constraints were substituted by table constraints.
3. *Regular*: The detected adjacency constraints were substituted by regular constraints.
4. *RegularIntersected*: The detected adjacency constraints were substituted by only one regular constraint. The single regular constraint was created by the intersection of the underlying automatons of the substituted regular constraints from item (3) *Regular* as given above.

---

[1] In [1], the detected constraints are substituted by table constraints, in contrast to the here presented approach; we will substitute them with regular constraints.

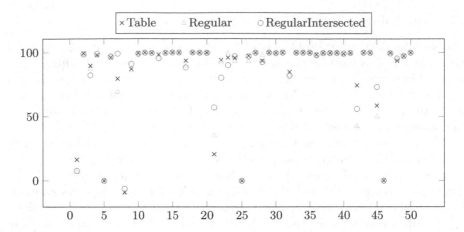

Fig. 1. The time improvements (in %) of the *Table*, *Regular* and *RegularIntersected* models for finding the first solution of each instance of the Black Hole Problem in comparison to the *Original* model (0%).

Table 2. Overview of the Black Hole benchmark.

	Ave. solution time	Ave. imp. in %	# Fastest	# Sol. instances
Original	516.432 s	–	1	7
Table	58.796 s	83.413%	25	47
Regular	63.679 s	82.054%	2	47
RegularIntersected	54.883 s	84.165%	19	47

Figure 1 shows the time improvements (in %) of the three substituted models (*Table*, *Regular* and *RegularIntersected*) in comparison to the *Original* model when the first solution is searched. In 49 of 50 cases all modified models are better than the original. The only exception is sample case 8, where the original approach is 62–95% faster than the substituted ones[2]. Table 2 shows that the *Table* approach was 25 times, the *RegularIntersected* approach was 19 times, the *Regular* approach was two times and the *Original* approach was one time the fastest. In average we could reach the first solution 83.413%, 82.054% or 84.165% faster than the *Original* approach and we could solve many more problem instances with the substitution approaches in the time limit in comparison to the *Original* model (47 instead of 7).

---

[2] For case 8 exists a deterioration of 65% (90%, 95%) for the *RegularIntersected* (*Table* and *Regular*) approach. To keep the graphic small the negative values were drawn in $\frac{1}{10}$ of the real distance. In cases 5, 25 and 46 none of the four models found a solution in the time bounds of 10 min.

4.2   The Solitaire Battleships Problem

The Solitaire Battleships Problem is a famous symbol puzzle, where several ships with different sizes must be placed on a two-dimensional grid. The ships may be oriented horizontally or vertically, and no two ships will occupy adjacent grid squares, not even diagonally. Numerical values along the right hand side of and below the grid indicate the number of grid squares in the corresponding rows and columns that are occupied by vessels (see more details in [9]).

We created an equivalent Choco version of the *MiniZinc* model given in [9] and tested the introductory example and the 35 instances given in the "sb_Mini-Zinc_Benchmarks.zip" from [9]. We indicated the "spacing constraints", the "ship shape constraints" and the "count number of bigger ships constraints" as potential good candidates for a substitution by regular (or table) constraints.

For all instances we limited the solution time to 30 min and each problem was solved in five ways:

1. *Original*: The problem was modelled as described in [9].
2. *Table*: With reference to [9], the single lines 75 to 80 of the "spacing constraints", the single lines 86 to 89 and the three lines 91 to 93 together of the "ship shape constraints" and each two lines 117 to 118 and 122 to 123 together of the "count number of bigger ships constraints" were each substituted by singleton table constraints.
3. *Regular*: The lines enumerated in *Table* were substituted with regular constraints.
4. *RegularIntersected*: Equivalently to *Regular*, except the partial constraints in "count number of bigger ships constraints" which count the number of ships of size s in a row, respectively in a column, were combined each to one regular constraint.
5. *TableRegularIntersected*: There, we have the same combined regular constraints (for representing the "count number of bigger ships constraints") as described in *RegularIntersected*, but, apart from that, use the table constraints described in *Table* (for representing the "spacing constraints" and "ship shape constraints").

Figure 2 shows that the results for the Solitaire Battleships Problem are not that clear as the results for the Black Hole Problem. A look into Table 3 reveals that the improvements for finding a first solution are very streaky. The *Table* approach was the best approach, if using only one substitution style (tabulation or regularization). It found the first solution in 9 cases as fastest and was in average 37% faster than the original approach. The *Regular* approach slows the solution process down here but the *RegularIntersected* approach leads again to a speed up (2 times fastest approach, 29.701% better as the *Original* approach), which is not much worse than the speed up from the *Table* approach.

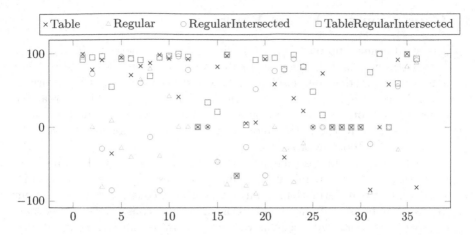

Fig. 2. The time improvements (in %) of the *Table, Regular, RegularIntersected* and *TableRegularIntersected* models for finding the first solution of each instance of the Solitaire Battleships Problem in comparison to the *Original* model (0%).

Table 3. Overview of the Black Hole benchmark.

	Ave. sol. time	Ave. imp. in %	# Fastest	# Sol. instances
Original	935.168	–	1	23
Table	632.955	37.303%	9	28
Regular	1120.421	−11.551%	0	17
RegularIntersected	677.923	29.701%	2	26
TableRegularIntersected	507.820	60.763%	19	30

The *TableRegularIntersected* approach shows that a combination of regularization and tabulation can lead to a significant improvement. Here it was the best approach. It could solve the most problems (30), could find most often as fastest the first solution (19) and had in average the biggest time improvement (60.763%).

Remark 3. The *TableRegularIntersected* approach was not calculated fully automatically here, but it shows the potential of both approaches in combination. Future work has to be done automate the combination of both approaches.

Remark 4. In the evaluation, we did not present the needed time for the transformations. Depending on the specific CSPs, we observed big differences in the necessary transformation times. In our case, the total transformation time needed for all transformations were in all Black Hole instances less than three and in all Solitaire Battleship instances less than four seconds. Because the transformation time can be neglected in comparison to the solution time (less than three respectively four seconds vs. 10 respectively 30 min) we did not figure out them explicitly.

5   Conclusion and Future Work

We presented a new approach for the optimization of general CSPs using the regular constraint. For this a suitable sub-set of constraints are detected (for example with heuristics presented in [1]), solved separately and transformed into a regular constraint. Two benchmarks stress the benefit of this approach in comparison to the original problems and the competitiveness to the tabulation approach presented in [15]. Furthermore, our benchmarks indicate the potential of a combination of both approaches.

In the future we will research heuristics, for finding sub-CSPs which are especially suitable for the regularization approach. Besides, we want to consider the idea of direct transformations from several global constraints to equivalent regular constraints [4] and the combination of regular constraints transformed from global constraints with regular constraints transformed from sub-CSPs. We expect that this combination approach can be applied more often than the tabulation approach [15], because big sub-CSPs can be represented by a small DFA often; in contrast to this a table constraint always needs to store all solution tuples. Therefore, the regularization approach looks more promising for big problems.

The most obvious next step is a detailed comparison of the regularization approach with the tabulation approach and the formulation of heuristics which suggest when which approach is more advantageous.

References

1. Akgün, Ö., Gent, I.P., Jefferson, C., Miguel, I., Nightingale, P., Salamon, A.Z.: Automatic discovery and exploitation of promising subproblems for tabulation. In: Hooker, J. (ed.) CP 2018. LNCS, vol. 11008, pp. 3–12. Springer, Cham (2018). https://doi.org/10.1007/978-3-319-98334-9_1
2. Löffler, S., Liu, K., Hofstedt, P.: The power of regular constraints in CSPs. In: 47. Jahrestagung der Gesellschaft für Informatik, Informatik 2017, Chemnitz, Germany, 25–29 September 2017, pp. 603–614 (2017). https://doi.org/10.18420/in2017_57
3. Löffler, S., Liu, K., Hofstedt, P.: The regularization of CSPs for rostering, planning and resource management problems. In: Iliadis, L., Maglogiannis, I., Plagianakos, V. (eds.) AIAI 2018. IAICT, vol. 519, pp. 209–218. Springer, Cham (2018). https://doi.org/10.1007/978-3-319-92007-8_18
4. Löffler, S., Liu, K., Hofstedt, P.: A meta constraint satisfaction optimization problem for the optimization of regular constraint satisfaction problems. In: Rocha, A.P., Steels, L., van den Herik, J. (eds.) Proceedings of the 11th International Conference on Agents and Artificial Intelligence, ICAART 2019, Prague, Czech Republic, 19–21 February 2019, vol. 2, pp. 435–442. SciTePress (2019). https://doi.org/10.5220/0007260204350442
5. Boussemart, F., Hemery, F., Lecoutre, C., Sais, L.: Boosting systematic search by weighting constraints. In: de Mántaras, R.L., Saitta, L. (eds.) Proceedings of the 16th Eureopean Conference on Artificial Intelligence, ECAI 2004, including Prestigious Applicants of Intelligent Systems, PAIS 2004, Valencia, Spain, 22–27 August 2004, pp. 146–150. IOS Press (2004)

6. Cheng, B.M.W., Lee, J.H.M., Wu, J.C.K.: Speeding up constraint propagation by redundant modeling. In: Freuder, E.C. (ed.) CP 1996. LNCS, vol. 1118, pp. 91–103. Springer, Heidelberg (1996). https://doi.org/10.1007/3-540-61551-2_68
7. Dechter, R.: Constraint Processing. Elsevier Morgan Kaufmann, Burlington (2003)
8. Dekker, J.J., Björdal, G., Carlsson, M., Flener, P., Monette, J.: Auto-tabling for subproblem presolving in MiniZinc. Constraints **22**(4), 512–529 (2017). https://doi.org/10.1007/s10601-017-9270-5
9. Gent, I.: CSPLib problem 014: Solitaire battleships. http://www.csplib.org/Problems/prob014. Accessed 07 May 2019
10. Gent, I.P., et al.: Search in the patience game 'black hole'. AI Commun. **20**(3), 211–226 (2007). http://content.iospress.com/articles/ai-communications/aic405
11. Gottlob, G., Samer, M.: A backtracking-based algorithm for hypertree decomposition. J. Exp. Algorithmics (JEA) **13**, 1 (2008)
12. Hamadi, Y.: Optimal distributed arc-consistency. Constraints **7**(3–4), 367–385 (2002). https://doi.org/10.1023/A:1020594125144
13. Hellsten, L., Pesant, G., van Beek, P.: A domain consistency algorithm for the stretch constraint. In: Wallace, M. (ed.) CP 2004. LNCS, vol. 3258, pp. 290–304. Springer, Heidelberg (2004). https://doi.org/10.1007/978-3-540-30201-8_23
14. Hopcroft, J.E., Ullman, J.D.: Introduction to Automata Theory, Languages and Computation. Addison-Wesley, Boston (1979)
15. Lecoutre, C.: STR2: optimized simple tabular reduction for table constraints. Constraints **16**(4), 341–371 (2011). https://doi.org/10.1007/s10601-011-9107-6
16. Liu, K., Löffler, S., Hofstedt, P.: Hypertree decomposition: the first step towards parallel constraint solving. In: Seipel, D., Hanus, M., Abreu, S. (eds.) WFLP/WLP/INAP -2017. LNCS (LNAI), vol. 10997, pp. 81–94. Springer, Cham (2018). https://doi.org/10.1007/978-3-030-00801-7_6
17. Nightingale, P.: CSPLib problem 081: Black hole. http://www.csplib.org/Problems/prob081. Accessed 07 May 2019
18. Pesant, G.: A filtering algorithm for the stretch constraint. In: Walsh, T. (ed.) CP 2001. LNCS, vol. 2239, pp. 183–195. Springer, Heidelberg (2001). https://doi.org/10.1007/3-540-45578-7_13
19. Pesant, G.: A regular language membership constraint for finite sequences of variables. In: Wallace, M. (ed.) CP 2004. LNCS, vol. 3258, pp. 482–495. Springer, Heidelberg (2004). https://doi.org/10.1007/978-3-540-30201-8_36
20. Prud'homme, C., Fages, J.G., Lorca, X.: Choco Documentation. TASC, INRIA Rennes, LINA CNRS UMR 6241, COSLING S.A.S. (2016). http://www.choco-solver.org/. Accessed 07 May 2019
21. Régin, J.-C., Rezgui, M., Malapert, A.: Embarrassingly parallel search. In: Schulte, C. (ed.) CP 2013. LNCS, vol. 8124, pp. 596–610. Springer, Heidelberg (2013). https://doi.org/10.1007/978-3-642-40627-0_45

**33rd Workshop on (Constraint) Logic
Programming - WLP 2019**

Declarative Programming
for Microcontrollers - Datalog on Arduino

Mario Wenzel$^{(\boxtimes)}$ and Stefan Brass

Institut für Informatik, Martin-Luther-Universität Halle-Wittenberg,
Von-Seckendorff-Platz 1, 06099 Halle (Saale), Germany
{mario.wenzel,brass}@informatik.uni-halle.de

Abstract. In this paper we describe a novel approach to programming microcontrollers based on the Arduino platform using Datalog as a clear and concise description language for system behaviors.

The application areas of cheap and easily programmable microcontroller platforms, like robotics, home automation, and IoT devices hold mainstream appeal and are often used as motivation in natural science and technology teaching. The choice of programming languages for microcontrollers is severely limited, especially with regard to rule-based declarative languages.

We use an approach that is based on the Dedalus language augmented with operations that allow for side-effects and we also take the limited resources of a microcontroller into account.

Our compiler and runtime environment allow to run Datalog programs on Arduino-based systems.

1 Introduction

Logic and declarative programming is successfully used for parts of desktop and server applications. We value the declarative techniques because it is easier to write programs that relate closely to the specification (or even write compilable specifications) and show their correctness. Furthermore they can be more easily optimized by a compiler to make use of new hardware developments and new ideas in algorithms and data structures. Declarative programming has found its place in most computer science curricula in some form (often SQL, Haskell, and Prolog) as well. But especially in logic programming the applications often are theoretical or only used as part of a larger system. The parts that interact with the outside world are usually written in an imperative fashion. For embedded systems, where rule-based interaction with the outside world is often the majority of the application, declarative programming is an avenue not well explored.

With the advent of really cheaply produced microchips that allow for direct hardware interaction, small and easily programmable systems have found a place in STEM education (Science, Technology, Engineering, Math) and are used to teach electrical engineering, signal processing, mechanical engineering, robotics, and of course, programming in all levels of school and academia [1,13,14]. Systems like these are ubiquitous in the hobbyist realm and are most often used

© Springer Nature Switzerland AG 2020
P. Hofstedt et al. (Eds.): DECLARE 2019, LNAI 12057, pp. 119–138, 2020.
https://doi.org/10.1007/978-3-030-46714-2_9

in IoT (Internet of Things) devices and home automation. We can categorize systems based on cheap microchips and the manner in which they can be programmed the following way:

- **Single Board Computers** (SBC) like the Raspberry Pi can, in principle, be programmed using any software a traditional desktop computer can be programmed with. While the available resources of SBCs are limited, the available main memory is in the dozens or hundreds of megabyte and even the slowest devices have CPUs with at least 300 MHz while the faster ones use multicore architectures with operating frequencies in the gigahertz range. Those CPUs are often found in phones, tablets, TVs, and other multimedia devices as well. And since the SBCs usually also have a standard-compliant Linux distribution installed, any programming interface suitable to work with the GPIO (General Purpose Input Output) can be used for the described tasks. There is hardly any mainstream programming language that can not be used to program a Raspberry Pi or similar SBCs. Even the LEGO Mindstorms EV3 platform falls into this category and students can engage with this platform using (among others) Python, Java, Go, C, Ruby, Perl, and even Prolog [15] as their programming language of choice. Almost any technology stack for declarative logic programming can be used on these devices.
- In contrast the ways in which **microcontrollers** can be programmed is very limited. Microcontrollers often use 8-bit CPUs with operating frequencies range from 16 to 40 MHz and an operating memory of 0.5 to 8 KB. For this kind of embedded programming there have traditionally been only two options. The approachable method that is often used in teaching beginner and intermediate courses is a graphical block-based programming language like scratch that uses an approach of translating code templates that fit like puzzle-pieces to actual C source code. The second approach that is taken on academic or advanced level is to program C code directly. Both approaches limit the user with regards to available programming paradigms. Imperative programming seems to have no real alternatives, even though such systems that can be equipped with sensors, buttons, lights, displays, etc. are, in principle, well-suited to be programmed using other paradigms. Especially in interactive applications like environmental sensing and robotics, event-driven or rule-based declarative approaches are desirable.
  For larger microcontrollers from the ESP-family – with 32-bit CPUs, operating frequencies of up to 240 MHz, and 520 KB of memory – there are firmwares available for programming in MicroPython (a Python subset) Lua, Lisp, and a few more. While there are embedded operating systems for ESP-based systems that even include network stacks for wired and wireless connections, these devices are not powerful enough to support a modern Linux. Without Linux kernel and userspace, they can not make use of the usual declarative stacks.

There have been many attempts to bring declarative programming to embedded systems. Some declarative approaches, like LUSTRE [9] from the early '90s, aim at reactive and dataflow oriented programming. Comparative experiments with implementations of embedded applications using abstract declarative languages (Prolog, OCaml) showed that while the abstract code is shorter, the overhead for the runtime environments is significant [16].

In the recent past there have been advances in bringing event-driven programming in the form of functional reactive programming (FRP) to the Arduino platform. The Juniper programming language [10] is such a language that leverages the functional reactive style. The `frp-arduino` project[1] provides a domain-specific language that is embedded into Haskell in order to create and compile FRP programs for the Arduino.

A similar approach to leave the imperative programming behind is taken by Haskino [8], a Haskell library where code in a specific monad for remote IO is evaluated on a driving computer and controls an attached Arduino microcontroller via the serial interface. By embedding control flow statements directly into this monad a standalone program can be compiled.

There are other declarative programming approaches for the Arduino-based microcontroller platform like Microscheme[2], a Scheme subset for the Arduino platform. In the home automation context there have been projects that allow to declaratively configure microcontroller systems with common sensor setups (like ESPHome[3]) but this approach is limited to this specific domain and a small number of targeted devices and peripherals.

But in terms of logic programming the Arduino platform is sorely lacking. Logic programming languages like Datalog allow concise and clear descriptions of system behaviors. To use rule-based systems in the domain of robotics and home automation is very appealing.

In this paper we propose a specific dialect of Datalog closely related to the Dedalus language [2] (Sect. 3) that includes IO operations. We define an evaluation order for the different types of rules (Sect. 4) and give a scheme to compile the Datalog code to C code (Sect. 7). This scheme can be used to program Arduino-based microcontrollers in an expressive and declarative fashion which we show by providing some example programs (Sects. 5 and 6).

2   Target Platform

As our target platform we have chosen microcontrollers with the ATmega328 8-bit processor, like the Arduino Nano, Arduino UNO[4], or similar devices (see Fig. 1). The ATmega328 is comparatively cheap and widely used. This target platform comes with a set of limitations and design challenges:

- There is only 2 KB of SRAM available that is used for both heap and stack data. This means we are limited in operational memory for storing derived facts and in algorithm design with regards to function call depth.

---

[1] https://github.com/frp-arduino/frp-arduino
[2] https://github.com/ryansuchocki/microscheme
[3] https://esphome.io/
[4] https://www.arduino.cc

Fig. 1. Arduino Nano and UNO compatible boards with 1 euro cent for size comparison

- 32 KB of Flash memory can be used to store the program. This might seem a lot in comparison but this is also used to store additional libraries for peripheral access that are wanted by the user. This is also quite limiting considering the algorithm design and the amount of source code we are allowed to generate. The `Arduino.h` header files with pin input and output and writing to the serial port already use 2 KB of that memory, when compiled with size optimization enabled.
- A boot loader of about 2 KB is used for the firmware.
- The ATmega328 processor has an operational speed of 20 MHz which is a lot compared to the amount of data we have to operate on.
- There is an additional EEPROM non-volatile storage of 1 KB. This storage is slow and is limited in the amount of write cycles. The EEPROM is specified to handle 100.000 write/erase cycles for each byte with one cycle taking over three milliseconds. If the user chooses to write to or read from this storage as an effectful operation (i.e. IO predicate, see Sect. 3), they can do so.

The chosen target platform gives us restrictions with regards to the resource usage to aim at. Since we generate C-code and our approach to interfacing with the rest of the system is generic our approach works for other embedded systems and processors as well. The generic approach is also useful since there already is a huge ecosystem for embedded development. The "PlatformIO" platform[5] (self-proclaimed "open source ecosystem for IoT development") has well over 700 different supported boards and over 6.800 libraries in its registry[6]. There is no reason why this effort should be duplicated.

3   Extension to Dedalus Language

We base our work on the Dedalus$_0$ language (from here on just Dedalus). Dedalus is a special variant of Datalog with negation where the **final attribute of every predicate** is a "timestamp" from the domain of the whole numbers. We call this attribute the "time suffix". This permits us to treat a time-dependent (changing)

---

[5] https://platformio.org/
[6] As of November 2019.

state in a declarative way: In principle, a model contains the entire information which facts hold at which point in time. The language is restricted in such a way that in order to do deductions it suffices to access only two states: the current and the next state. We give a quick overview over the Dedalus language [2]:

- Every subgoal of a rule that is a literal must use the same variable $\mathcal{T}$ as time suffix.
- Every rule head has the variable $\mathcal{S}$ as a time suffix.
- A rule is **deductive** if $\mathcal{S}$ is bound to $\mathcal{T}$, i.e. $\mathcal{S} = \mathcal{T}$ is a subgoal of this rule.
  Example: $p(X, \mathcal{S}) \leftarrow q(X, Y, \mathcal{T}), p(Y, \mathcal{T}), \mathcal{S} = \mathcal{T}$.
  We allow for stratified negation in the deductive rules.
- A rule is **inductive** if $\mathcal{S}$ is bound to the successor of $\mathcal{T}$, i.e. $successor(\mathcal{T}, \mathcal{S})$ is a subgoal of this rule. The successor function is not allowed in any other context.
  Example: $p(X, \mathcal{S}) \leftarrow q(X, Y, \mathcal{T}), p(Y, \mathcal{T}), successor(\mathcal{T}, \mathcal{S})$.
  We allow arbitrary negated body literals in inductive rules, because the program is always dynamically stratified with regards to the last argument.
- All variables other than the time suffix are range restricted, i.e. appear in a positive literal.

In Dedalus every rule is either deductive or inductive and the time suffix can not be accessed (i.e. bound to a variable) explicitly. To make it easier to work with those restrictions some syntactic sugar is added:

- For deductive rules the time argument is left out in the head of the rule and every subgoal.
  Example: $p(X) \leftarrow q(X, Y), p(Y)$.
- For inductive rules the suffix "@next" is added to rule head and the time argument is left out in the head of the rule and every subgoal.
  Example: $p(X)@next \leftarrow q(X, Y), p(Y)$.
- For facts any timestamp of the domain is allowed as $\mathcal{S}$ (written using the @-notation). To keep the memory footprint low we only allow facts for the timestamp 0 in this notation.
  Example: $p(5)@0$.

If a fact is not transported from one timestamp to the next we have a notion of deletion. This can be used to "table" relations that can be updated in a stateful fashion. Consider a Dedalus program with the following rules:

$$table(X)@next \leftarrow add(X).$$
$$table(X)@next \leftarrow table(X), \neg delete(X).$$

An execution with some derived *add* and *delete* facts at specific timestamps might look like this:

Time	add	delete	table
101	add(1)		
102			table(1)
103	add(27)		table(1)
104			table(1), table(27)
...			table(1), table(27)
300		delete(1)	table(1), table(27)
301			table(27)

But Dedalus is more than just Datalog with updates. With this extension our Datalog program now has a notion of time where not everything happens at once but the facts with some timestamp n can be seen as "happening earlier" than the facts with timestamp m with $n < m$. Depending on the evaluation strategy, any fact with an earlier timestamp may be deduced before those with a later timestamp as derived facts can only depend on facts with the same or an earlier timestamp. The timestamp also captures a notion of state, similar to the Statelog language [12]. This is useful for interactions with the environment.

To facilitate this interaction we add a predicate type and two types of rules that are used to manage effectful functions of the system (IO):

- An **IO predicate** is a predicate that is used with a fixed binding pattern and that corresponds to a system function which may have effectful behavior with regards to the environment. IO predicates do not correspond to members of the minimal model of our program. An IO predicate can be interpreted as an EDB relation that is a partial function from the timestamp and the bound variables to a binding for the free variables, i.e. the timestamp, together with the bound variables, is a superkey of this relation and the corresponding subgoal generates exactly one ground substitution.
- An **IO literal** is a literal from an IO predicate.
- An **input rule** is a **inductive rule** that has exactly one subgoal that is a positive IO literal corresponding to a system function that reads a value from the environment, like the current time or a sensor value. The system function is executed when its result is needed to derive a fact for the next state, so that the partial function corresponding to the IO literal is defined wherever it can be sampled. This is a concept similar to external atoms from Answer Set Programming [5]. We require that input rules are inductive so that the result of the input can be observed only in the next state. This is necessary to prevent infinite derivation chains from fresh constants. The concrete syntax for our language has the restriction, that the IO literal is the last literal of the body. This is no restriction on the expressiveness of our language.
- An **output rule** is a **deductive rule** that has an IO literal as the head. The literal corresponds to a system function that changes the environment, like setting the output current of a pin. The system function is executed when the literal can be derived, so that the corresponding partial function is defined

wherever its arguments are derived. This is a concept similar to action atoms from Answer Set Programming [6].

- A rule has at most one IO literal in either head or body, as a rule can not be both deductive and inductive at the same time.
- For all timestamps T and T' with $T < T'$ all effects corresponding to T must happen before all effects corresponding to T'.
- Besides the IO predicates there is no dynamic database for EDB facts. Static facts can be added through rules without antecedents. If a configuration or parameterization of our program is achieved through facts, the program needs to be recompiled when the configuration changes. A static configuration that is compiled into the program is common practice for microcontroller applications anyway.
- We also allow arithmetic comparison of bound variables and arbitrary arithmetic expressions within the operands of the comparison.

We call this language "Microlog", a Datalog for microcontroller applications.

4   Program Evaluation

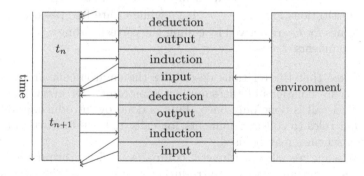

Fig. 2. Fact deduction order

Deduction of facts for the state T, the following state T_{+1}, and scheduling and execution of effectful functions happens in 4 phases (see Fig. 2):

1. In the **deduction phase** all facts for the current timestamp T are derived. During this phase only the deductive rules (i.e. the rules that derive facts for the current timestamp) that ore not output rules are used. In our case we use a naive evaluation strategy (taking the strata into account) that uses the least amount of additional memory (see Sect. 7) but any Datalog evaluation strategy that computes the fixpoint can be used to derive the facts for the current timestamp.

2. In the **output phase** IO functions that write data or affect the environment can be executed. Output rules of the form $B \leftarrow A_1 \wedge \cdots \wedge A_n$ where B is the single IO literal are evaluated. The function $\mathcal{B}$ corresponding to every unique $B\theta$ is evaluated for every ground substitution θ for A_1 to A_n where $A_1\theta \ldots A_n\theta$ is in the minimal model for that state. This means that iff $B(\vec{X}, \mathcal{T})$ would be in the minimal model (i.e. can be derived), then the corresponding system function is called with arguments $\vec{X}$.

3. In the **induction phase** all facts for the next timestamp are derived. During this phase only the inductive rules (i.e. the rules that derive facts for the next timestamp $\mathcal{T}_{+1}$) that are not input rules are used. Since facts derived through inductive rules may only depend on facts from the current timestamp $\mathcal{T}$, all necessary facts are known after one execution of each rule. Therefore all inductive rules are evaluated once (and in any order) for this timestamp.

4. In the **input phase** IO functions that read data from the environment can be executed. Input rules of the form $B@next \leftarrow A_1 \wedge \cdots \wedge A_n$, where A_n is the single IO literal, are evaluated. The function $\mathcal{A}$ corresponding to every unique $A_n\theta$ is evaluated for every ground substitution θ for A_1 to A_{n-1} where $A_1\theta \ldots A_{n-1}\theta$ is in the minimal model of the current state, then derived $B\theta$ is in the minimal model for the following state.

   Let the binding pattern for A_n be as such that the variables $\vec{I}$ in $A_n(\vec{I}, \vec{O})$ are bound in that context (used as input) by constants in that literal or ground substitutions for $A_1 \wedge \cdots \wedge A_{n-1}$ while $\vec{O}$ are free (used as output). Then bindings for $\vec{O}$ are derived by calling the corresponding system function with the arguments $\vec{I}$.

To guarantee that the relations describing the environment are functional (i.e. there are no violations of the superkey constraint), for every state every system function call is done only once. This is done by introducing additional predicates and rules to collect arguments for calls and call-contexts, but other deduplication schemes may be used.

Note that while we allow arithmetic comparison with arbitrary arithmetic expressions, new constants can only introduced by input rules. Since the number of facts for a specific timestamp generated by input rules is limited, the number of new constants introduced is finite as well. While termination does not hold for the whole program (and we do not want it to), the minimal model for any specific state is always finite. We say that our program is locally terminating, meaning that every following timestamp is reached eventually, if every call to system functions returns eventually.

5   IO Literals and Example Programs

Our application is statically typed and we only allow primitive types for our data values. This is why all predicates need to be declared beforehand with the static types of their arguments. To define the datatypes of relations we use a syntax similar to what the Soufflé system [11] uses: `.decl r(unsigned long,` byte) declares the predicate r with two arguments and their respective types. Since we have no general mechanism for textual output of relations, we do not need to define names for the arguments.

Before we can show example programs we want to give some IO predicates for the Arduino interface. Users can write their own IO predicates to interface with any number of existing libraries for their system. On a most basic level, an embedded board communicates with the outside world by means of GPIO-pins (general purpose input/output) that are attached to sensors, actors, or other mechanical or electrical components. Basic interface functions[7] for the pins in an Arduino-based systems (see Fig. 3) are the functions pinMode that sets whether a pin is in input or output mode, digitalWrite that sets the output voltage (usually one of the constants HIGH and LOW) of a pin (both persistent until the next call), and digitalRead that reads the voltage on a pin and gives either a LOW or HIGH value.

```
void pinMode(uint8_t pin, uint8_t mode);
void digitalWrite(uint8_t pin, uint8_t val);
int digitalRead(uint8_t pin);
unsigned long millis(void);
```

Fig. 3. Extract from Arduino.h header files

The computations that are modeled with IO predicates, as per our definition from Sect. 3, are computations that return a single variable assignment. Computations that return sets or lists of variable assignments, or computations that might fail and do not return any variable assignment, do not fit in this model. This is a limitation, but in the microcontroller context there is no best practice to encode these kinds of computations with regards to types or data-structures, that is also adhered to by a majority of external libraries. We chose this restricted model to keep our runtime environment and the "plumbing code" for the external libraries simple. For any timestamp this restriction is stronger than usual for Datalog-based models, where the external database is only assumed to be finite.

We define an IO predicate, which always starts with an # to denote that it is an IO predicate, with its arguments (left side) by arbitrary C statements (right side). Every IO predicate may only have one definition. Within the defining C-statements variables from the predicate arguments can be used (prepended with # as to not overlap with constants like HIGH and LOW). Constants from the outside C-code may also be used as constants in the Datalog-code using # as a prefix. The hash sign can be seen as a context-switch for values between the C-context and the Microlog context. These base functions are part of our standard library but since there are many different community-created libraries, we allow arbitrary C-code for interaction with our Datalog system (Fig. 4).

---

[7] github.com/arduino/ArduinoCore-avr/blob/master/cores/arduino/Arduino.h

```
#pinIn(P)   = {pinMode(#P, INPUT);}
#pinOut(P)  = {pinMode(#P, OUTPUT);}
#digitalWrite(P, Val) = {digitalWrite(#P, #Val);}
#digitalRead(P, Val)  = {int Val = digitalRead(#P);}
#millis(T) = {unsigned long T = millis();}
```

Fig. 4. Defined IO predicates from the standard library

IO predicates are defined with a fixed binding pattern. Consider the IO predicate defined as

```
#digitalRead(P, Val) = {int Val = digitalRead(#P);}.
```

We say that the variable P is read in the definition (as its value is used in a function call) and the variable Val is set in the definition. This corresponds to binding pattern bf (bound for every read variable, free for every set variable). Every variable that is not read in the definition is considered set in the definition. The variables in bound positions have to appear positive in other body literals. The variables only appearing in free positions may not appear negative in other body literals. It is not syntactically checked, whether a variable that is considered set is actually assigned a value by the C-Code, only the appearance of values to be read is checked.

We want to insert the IO predicate definition code "as is" into the source code (when evaluating the body from left to right) while keeping to the Datalog semantics with the presented extensions. We define a normalized Microlog program with the following properties:

- All IO literals are used with their specific binding pattern.
- The variable names used in the definition are distinct from the variable names in the rules (there are no conflicts in the C-scopes).
- The variables used in the free-positions of IO literals are the only variables in the rule (there are no duplicates).
- Every IO literal only appears in a single input rule or output rule or both (system function calls are collected).

We generate a normalized program from the original program through the following transformations:

- All variables of the rules are renamed if necessary.
- Every input needed to derive facts for the next state should only lead to the corresponding function call once per timestamp as calling the same system function at the same timestamp with the same arguments could have different results and therefore would violate they key constraint of that relation. To achieve this, each input rule is replaced by an inductive rule that collects the call contexts, a deductive rule that collects the IO calls, the simplified input rule, and a deductive rule that brings contexts and call results together again. Let $B(\vec{V})@next \leftarrow A_1 \wedge \cdots \wedge A_n(\vec{X}, \vec{Y})$ where A_n is the single IO literal with

the variables $\vec{X}$ being in the bound positions of the IO literal and $\vec{Y}$ in the free positions and $\vec{V}$ being the variables in the rule head. The replacing rules are the following:

- $A'(\vec{X}) \leftarrow A_1 \wedge \cdots \wedge A_{n-1}$ to deduplicate the input arguments. This is the same A' for all literals of the same IO predicate.
- $A''(\vec{X}, \vec{Y})@next \leftarrow A'(\vec{X}) \wedge A_n(\vec{X}, \vec{Y})$ as new input rule with the deduplicated arguments. This is the same A'' for all literals of the same IO predicate.
- $B'(\vec{V}, \vec{X}, \vec{Y})@next \leftarrow A_1 \wedge \cdots \wedge A_{n-1}$ to capture all call contexts. If any Y_n or V_n is not range restricted, it is left out of B' in this and the following rule.
- $B(\vec{V}) \leftarrow B'(\vec{V}, \vec{X}, \vec{Y}) \wedge A'(\vec{X}, \vec{Y})$ to recombine the call contexts with the deduplicated IO.

– If the IO literal is used in an input rule, all variables read in the definition must be bound by the other literals in the query. If some variable is set in the definition and bound by other literals, we compile the use of $p(A)$ with A bound but set in the definition as $p(A'), A' = A$. When the rule is rewritten this way, the variable set in the definition is free again and we use a later comparison to check whether the values are equal. This allows the original program to use IO literals with more bound arguments than is specified in the predicate definition.

– Every derived output should only lead to the corresponding function call once per timestamp. While this would not violate key constraints, as we do not generate variable bindings, we want to prevent side-effects happening multiple times. Therefore any output rule $B \leftarrow A_1 \wedge \cdots \wedge A_n$ is replaced by deduplication rules before compilation. Let $\vec{X}$ be the variables used and constants in the head of the rule, then a new deductive rule $B'(\vec{X}) \leftarrow A_1 \wedge \cdots \wedge A_n$ is introduced for deduplication of results and the original rule is replaced by the output rule $B(\vec{X}) \leftarrow B'(\vec{X})$. This is the same B' for all literals of the same IO predicate.

```
% Predicates              % Input
.decl setup               pressed@next :- #digitalRead(2, #HIGH).
.decl pressed

% Setup and Initialization % Output
setup@0.                  #digitalWrite(13, #HIGH) :- pressed.
#pinIn(2) :- setup.       #digitalWrite(13, #LOW) :- !pressed.
#pinOut(13) :- setup.
```

Fig. 5. Program that changes the led when a connected button is pressed

We give an example program "touch" that switches an LED (the internal LED on this example board is connected to pin 13) on when the button connected to pin 2 (external component) is pressed, and off when it is released (see Fig. 5). This program only has input and output rules and defines a minimal behavior that can easily be adapted to arbitrary connected sensors (temperature, distance) and actors (relays, motors).

We give an assignment for the partial functions corresponding to the IO predicates (i.e. the environment) of an example run. The functions used as output are defined (map to unit) and their code executed wherever their arguments can be derived and the functions used as input are defined (mapping from bound to free values) wherever they are sampled:

Time	digitalRead	digitalWrite	pinIn	pinOut
0	$\emptyset$	$\{(13, \texttt{LOW}) \mapsto ()\}$	$\{2 \mapsto ()\}$	$\{13 \mapsto ()\}$
1	$\{2 \mapsto \texttt{LOW}\}$	$\{(13, \texttt{LOW}) \mapsto ()\}$	$\emptyset$	$\emptyset$
2	$\{2 \mapsto \texttt{LOW}\}$	$\{(13, \texttt{LOW}) \mapsto ()\}$	$\emptyset$	$\emptyset$
3	$\{2 \mapsto \texttt{HIGH}\}$	$\{(13, \texttt{LOW}) \mapsto ()\}$	$\emptyset$	$\emptyset$
4	$\{2 \mapsto \texttt{HIGH}\}$	$\{(13, \texttt{HIGH}) \mapsto ()\}$	$\emptyset$	$\emptyset$
5	$\{2 \mapsto \texttt{LOW}\}$	$\{(13, \texttt{HIGH}) \mapsto ()\}$	$\emptyset$	$\emptyset$
6	$\{2 \mapsto \texttt{LOW}\}$	$\{(13, \texttt{LOW}) \mapsto ()\}$	$\emptyset$	$\emptyset$
...	$\{2 \mapsto ...\}$	$\{(13, ...) \mapsto ()\}$	$\emptyset$	$\emptyset$

In the same manner as the "touch"-program we define the "blink"-program (see Fig. 6) that toggles the LED every second using the system function `millis` that returns the number of milliseconds since the microcontroller has been turned on. In this example we use the deduction phase to deduce actions and depending on those actions we both affect the environment and change the following state. The switching action (`turn_on` and `turn_off`) is deduced explicitly and the current state (`on_since` and `off_since`) is passed into the following state through the inductive rules until the decision to toggle is reached.

Of course, these are just very simple example programs and in the home automation context these kinds of conditions and programs are usually expressible within the existing configuration languages. Using our fixpoint semantics we can also write a program that calculates all rooms in a house that are connected via open doors and force the heating off in all connected rooms, if a window is open in any of them. A model train control unit could calculate all track segments that are reachable from a segment (that has a train on it) with the current switch positions and force a crossing barrier down.

6   Macro Expansion

In the context of home automation and IoT some tasks are quite common and need to be accomplished in many projects. Examples of these tasks are initialization of sensors or delayed deduction of facts. To facilitate this, we allow for macro

```
% Declarations                      % Deduction
.decl setup                         turnOff :- onSince(P), now(T), P+1000<T.
.decl now(unsigned long)            turnOn :- offSince(P), now(T), P+1000<T.
.decl offSince(unsigned long)       % Induction
.decl onSince(unsigned long)        onSince(P)@next :- !turnOff, onSince(P).
.decl turnOff                       onSince(T)@next :- turnOn, now(T).
.decl turnOn                        offSince(P)@next:- !turnOn, offSince(P).
                                    offSince(T)@next:- turnOff, now(T).
% Setup and Initialization          % Input
setup@0.                            now(T)@next :- #millis(T).
#pinOut(13) :- setup.               % Output
offSince(0)@0.                      #digitalWrite(13, #HIGH) :- turnOn.
now(0)@0.                           #digitalWrite(13, #LOW) :- turnOff.
```

Fig. 6. Blink-program

expansion in our programming language. Macros are written in square brackets and are placed in front of a rule. The rule is then rewritten on a syntactic level to accomplish the task. We give a few macros as an example:

- The setup-macro rewrites a rule [setup]head. to head :- setup. and adds the fact setup@0 that marks the first state T_0 with the fact setup. This can be used for initialization of pins and sensors as well as initial state.
- The [delay:1000] macro (with any integer number) adds rules that deduces the fact in the future (as many milliseconds in the future). The rule [delay:X]head(Args) :- body(Args) is replaced by the following rules:
  - Initial time fact: now(0)@0.
  - Reading current time: now(T)@next :- #millis(T).
  - Deriving the fact that is to be delayed:
    delayed_head(Args, Curr) :- body(Args), now(Curr).
  - Deriving the delayed fact when the delay time is reached:
    head(Args) :- delayed_head(Args, Await),
                  now(Curr), Await+X <= Curr.
  - Transporting the delay forward if the time is not yet reached:
    delayed_head(Args, Await)@next :- delayed_head(Args, Await),
                                      now(Curr), Await+X>Curr.
  - New predicate declarations: .decl now(unsigned long)
    .decl delayed_head(<former arguments>, unsigned long)
- The persist-macro (as proposed by Alvaro et al. [2]) creates two predicates that allow for formulation of state updates as shown in the initial Dedalus example (see Sect. 3). The macro replaces [persist]head(Args). with the following rules:
  - head(Args)@next :- add_head(Args). to add facts to the "tabled" relation.
  - head(Args)@next :- head(Args), !del_head(Args). to allow deletion of tabled facts.

- New predicate declarations for add_head and del_head:
  ```
  .decl add_head(<former arguments>)
  .decl del_head(<former arguments>)
  ```

Macros decrease the program size (but not the compiled code size) and allow us to write programs on a higher level. Using the presented macros we can now show the final and very concise version (without the declarations) of our blink-program. Note that the expanded version is slightly different to the hand-crafted version of the blink-program but behaves the same (Fig. 7).

```
[setup]#pinOut(13).                    [setup]turnOff.
[delay:1000]turnOn :- turnOff.         [delay:1000]turnOff :- turnOn.
#digitalWrite(13, #HIGH) :- turnOn.    #digitalWrite(13, #LOW) :- turnOff.
```

Fig. 7. Concise blink-program using macros

7   Runtime Environment and Compilation

7.1   Memory Management

Our runtime environment uses two buffers to store deduced facts. One buffer is for the facts in the current state and the other buffer is for the facts in the following state. Since we discard facts from previous states and do not dynamically allocate memory, this scheme allows us to not store timestamp data. For the state transition the buffers are switched and the buffer for the next state is reset. The buffer size is given by the user during compilation as some unknown amount of memory might be needed for the other libraries and their data structures. Our facts are stored in the buffers in a simple manner (Fig. 8):

- Predicates are numbered (from 1) and we use the first byte to store the predicate (up to 255 different predicates).
- Subsequent bytes are used for the arguments.
- Facts are stored one after the other in the buffer.
- The start of the empty tail of the buffers are stored.

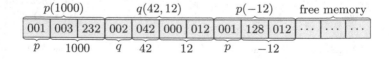

Fig. 8. Mapping example with declarations .decl p(int), .decl q(byte, int)

This memory management scheme is very simple and compact. Fact access time is linear in the number of stored facts. This is a reasonable compromise since we can not store many facts anyways. Consider predicates with lengths of 8 Bytes. If we want to use 800 Bytes of our RAM for fact storage we would allocate 400 Bytes per Buffer with 50 facts until the buffer is full. Saving memory on facts, pointers, and call stack by not using more complex data structures is reasonable.

7.2 Target Code

The following functions are generated from the predicate definitions in the program:

- Inserting a fact into a buffer.
- Retrieving a fact position from a buffer according to the used binding patterns with the first argument for the start of the memory area to search in and one additional argument for every bound value. At least the pattern where every value is bound is used since we use it for duplicate checking on insertion of facts. These functions return 0 if there is no matching fact in the buffer.
- Reading an argument value from a fact given the fact position in a buffer.

Additionally we compile the size and memory locations of the buffers (`curr_buff`, `next_buff`), the size of the facts depending on the predicate, and the mapping from predicates to numbers as constants into the code, effectively storing them in the program memory.

- For every rule we generate a function without arguments that tries to execute the rule and returns whether facts have been inserted.
- The generated function contains a nested-loop-join for every literal in the body with variables bound in order of appearance in the rule.
- The generated function contains an if-statement for every arithmetic comparison.
- Additionally we generate a duplicate check for the fact that is to be inserted, and an insertion statement.

The code that we compile the rule $p(A) \leftarrow q(A), p(B), A < B$ to, where all arguments are integers, is shown in Fig. 9.

For inductive rules instead of writing the fact to the buffer corresponding to the current timestamp, it is written into the buffer corresponding to the following (next) timestamp. IO literals are compiled "as is" according to the rules from Sect. 5 with their usage replaced by the C-statements they are defined with.

7.3 Compiled Source File

The end result of the compilation process is a C source file that can be compiled to machine code using the Arduino toolchain (for example PlatformIO or the Arduino IDE[8]) and has the following general format (see Fig. 10):

---

[8] https://www.arduino.cc/en/Main/Software

```
         bool deductive_rule_1() {
           bool inserted_facts = false;
 q(A)     size_t q1 = curr_buff;
           while ((q1 = q_f(q1)) != 0) {        // find next q-fact
             int A = q_arg1(q1);                // read first argument
 p(B)       size_t p1 = curr_buff;
             while ((p1 = p_f(p1)) != 0) {      // find next p-fact
               int B = p_arg1(p1);              // read first argument
 A<B           if (A < B) {
 p(A)            if (p_b(curr_buff, A) == 0) {  // duplicate check
                   insert_p(curr_buff, A);      // insertion
                   inserted_facts = true;
 p(A)           }
 A<B           }
 p(B)           p1 += size_of_p; // advance pointer past seen fact
             }
 q(A)         q1 += size_of_q;   // advance pointer past seen fact
           }
           return inserted_facts;
         }
```

Fig. 9. Compiled Rule $p(A) \leftarrow q(A), p(B), A < B$. (Color figure online)

- Including headerfiles and defining the buffers for the states.
- Definition of constants for the types and sizes of facts.
- Defining functions to write facts to buffers and find and access facts and their arguments from buffers, corresponding to the used binding patterns.
- setup() function that initializes the buffers and writes the facts for the initial state.
- loop() function that executes the deductive rules according to their strata, then it executes the output rules, the inductive rules and then the input rules, and in the end clears the buffer for the current state and swaps the buffers around so that the cleared buffer is now the one for the following state.

The setup and loop functions are the entrypoints for the processor. The setup function is called once when the microcontroller is started and the loop-function is called repeatedly once the setup has finished. The loop function executes all the derivation steps in the proper order (see Fig. 10).

7.4 Program Sizes and Speeds

To see whether this approach is very taxing on the resource usage we measured the size if the compiled and uploaded program code for some example programs and compared them to equivalently behaving programs that we have crafted by hand. The handcrafted version of the "touch" program (excluding setup) was just digitalWrite(13, digitalRead(2));.

```
// includes
#include "Arduino.h"
// Buffer Declarations
static byte buffer0[bufsize];  static byte buffer1[bufsize];
// Functions for Buffer Access
...
// Reading and Writing Facts
...
void setup() {
  // Buffer initialization
  // Facts for timestamp 0
}
void loop() {
  // deductive phase
  do { added_facts = false; // stratum 1
    added_facts |= deductive_rule_1();
    ...
    added_facts |= deductive_rule_i();
  } while (added_facts);
  do { // stratum 2
    ...
  } while (added_facts);
  ... // other strata

  // output phase
  output_rule_1();    ... output_rule_j();

  // inductive phase
  inductive_rule_1(); ... inductive_rule_n();

  // input phase
  input_rule_1();    ... input_rule_m();
  switch_buffers();
}
```

Fig. 10. Simplified outline of compiled source file

program	size		time per 1k loop calls	
	handcrafted	generated	handcrafted	generated
touch	996 Bytes	1304 Bytes	8 ms	30 ms
blink	1090 Bytes	2132 Bytes	9 ms	130 ms
blink w. macro		2294 Bytes		136 ms

Fig. 11. Comparison between hand-crafted C-programs and generated programs

For the speed comparison we measured the elapsed milliseconds (by the internal clock) after 1,000 calls of the `loop` function and sent the timing over the serial interface to a computer. Adding the serial library increases code size so we have done those measurements separately.

As we can see from Fig. 11, while the runtime increased drastically, at least for our small example programs, the "reaction time" (i.e. the time to reach the next state) was in the realm of 130 microseconds for the "blink" program but only 30 ms for the "touch" program. The handcrafted programs were much faster, with less than 10 microseconds per loop. The program memory used by our compilation scheme did not increase by the same factor. While our program code is twice the size as the handcrafted ones, at least for this example code, the included mandatory library code dominates the compilation.

8   Conclusion

We have shown that programs for Arduino and similar microcontroller systems can be written in a declarative logic language with few restrictions using a slightly altered version of the Datalog dialect Dedalus that we call "Microlog". The environment is modeled in terms of partial functions that are interpreted as an extensional database. Interaction with the environment through effectful operations is facilitated by defining an evaluation scheme where local termination still holds.

The Dedalus approach seems useful as it not only captures a notion of state-changes during the execution in an interactive environment, the captured notion of time allows us to use IO functions depending on facts corresponding to the state we consider as "now".

Then we have presented a straightforward translation scheme from our program code to Arduino-C that integrates well with existing library functions. While the generated code corresponds to a naive evaluation scheme, it is not algorithmically complex and does not use too much of the available program memory.

Additionally we have shown a method for code expansion that extends the usefulness of our language by autogenerating boilerplate code. This means that introductory examples of Arduino programs written in Microlog are as easy, if not easier, than the equivalent C program.

There are still a few open questions and areas for further research: Is it useful to apply transformations like magic sets, SLDmagic [3], or our Push method [4] with the IO rules as query goals? How well do other Datalog optimization and compilation schemes work with the limited operating memory? With a focus on the physical aspects of specific boards, can we analyze the program to find pins that are used as input but defined as output and vice versa? Can we identify otherwise incorrectly used system resources like pins that might be set differently multiple times in the same state, or facts that may not co-occur in the same state (like `led_on` and `led_off`)?

The initial state of the program is known beforehand (there is no dynamic database for EDB facts) and fresh constants are only introduced through input rules. Can a set of possible states for the application, parameterized in the arguments of the facts, be calculated beforehand and used as program state instead of a general purpose fact storage, creating a state machine where possible? Optimizations of this kind will help decrease program size and state duration. For example, the touch program (see Sect. 5) does not store any facts with arguments. So for every timestamp the corresponding subset of the minimal model must be a combination of the predicates (only **setup** and **pressed**), meaning that the program is, after any timestamp, in one of (at most) four states. On the other hand, a program that uses the persist macro (see Sect. 6) and derives more **add**-facts with fresh constants than it deletes, will use up all its available memory eventually.

Since the memory on the chip is severely limited, can we give an upper bound on the number of facts deduced for every timestamp (e.g. the amount of memory needed for the runtime system) using functional dependency analysis for derived predicates [7]? If the maximum number of facts was known during compilation, the buffers can be appropriately sized automatically. How quickly can the minimal model for a state be deduced and can we give upper and lower bounds for the duration of one timestamp? The last two questions are especially interesting with regards to real-time applications and safety and liveness properties of embedded systems.

References

1. Agatolio, F., Moro, M.: A workshop to promote Arduino-based robots as wide spectrum learning support tools. In: Merdan, M., Lepuschitz, W., Koppensteiner, G., Balogh, R. (eds.) Robotics in Education - Research and Practices for Robotics in STEM Education. AISC, vol. 457, pp. 113–125. Springer, Cham (2017). https://doi.org/10.1007/978-3-319-42975-5_11
2. Alvaro, P., Marczak, W.R., Conway, N., Hellerstein, J.M., Maier, D., Sears, R.: DEDALUS: datalog in time and space. In: de Moor, O., Gottlob, G., Furche, T., Sellers, A. (eds.) Datalog 2.0 2010. LNCS, vol. 6702, pp. 262–281. Springer, Heidelberg (2011). https://doi.org/10.1007/978-3-642-24206-9_16
3. Brass, S.: SLDMagic — the real magic (with applications to web queries). In: Lloyd, J., et al. (eds.) CL 2000. LNCS (LNAI), vol. 1861, pp. 1063–1077. Springer, Heidelberg (2000). https://doi.org/10.1007/3-540-44957-4_71
4. Brass, S., Stephan, H.: Pipelined bottom-up evaluation of datalog programs: the push method. In: Petrenko, A.K., Voronkov, A. (eds.) PSI 2017. LNCS, vol. 10742, pp. 43–58. Springer, Cham (2018). https://doi.org/10.1007/978-3-319-74313-4_4
5. Eiter, T., Ianni, G., Schindlauer, R., Tompits, H.: A uniform integration of higher-order reasoning and external evaluations in answer-set programming. In: Kaelbling, L.P., Saffiotti, A. (eds.) IJCAI-05, Proceedings of the Nineteenth International Joint Conference on Artificial Intelligence, Edinburgh, Scotland, UK, 30 July–5 August 2005, pp. 90–96. Professional Book Center (2005). http://ijcai.org/Proceedings/05/Papers/1353.pdf
6. Eiter, T., Subrahmanian, V.S., Pick, G.: Heterogeneous active agents, I: semantics. Artif. Intell. **108**(1–2), 179–255 (1999). https://doi.org/10.1016/S0004-3702(99)00005-3

7. Engels, C., Behrend, A., Brass, S.: A rule-based approach to analyzing database schema objects with datalog. In: Fioravanti, F., Gallagher, J.P. (eds.) LOPSTR 2017. LNCS, vol. 10855, pp. 20–36. Springer, Cham (2018). https://doi.org/10.1007/978-3-319-94460-9_2

8. Grebe, M., Gill, A.: Haskino: a remote monad for programming the arduino. In: Gavanelli, M., Reppy, J. (eds.) PADL 2016. LNCS, vol. 9585, pp. 153–168. Springer, Cham (2016). https://doi.org/10.1007/978-3-319-28228-2_10

9. Halbwachs, N., Caspi, P., Raymond, P., Pilaud, D.: The synchronous dataflow programming language LUSTRE. In: Proceedings of the IEEE, pp. 1305–1320 (1991)

10. Helbling, C., Guyer, S.Z.: Juniper: a functional reactive programming language for the Arduino. In: Janin, D., Sperber, M. (eds.) Proceedings of the 4th International Workshop on Functional Art, Music, Modelling, and Design, FARM@ICFP 2016, Nara, Japan, 24 September 2016, pp. 8–16. ACM (2016). https://doi.org/10.1145/2975980.2975982

11. Jordan, H., Scholz, B., Subotić, P.: SOUFFLÉ: on synthesis of program analyzers. In: Chaudhuri, S., Farzan, A. (eds.) CAV 2016. LNCS, vol. 9780, pp. 422–430. Springer, Cham (2016). https://doi.org/10.1007/978-3-319-41540-6_23

12. Lausen, G., Ludäscher, B., May, W.: On active deductive databases: the statelog approach. In: Freitag, B., Decker, H., Kifer, M., Voronkov, A. (eds.) DYNAMICS 1997. LNCS, vol. 1472, pp. 69–106. Springer, Heidelberg (1998). https://doi.org/10.1007/BFb0055496

13. Martín-Ramos, P., da Silva, M.M.L., Lopes, M.J., Silva, M.R.: Student2student: Arduino project-based learning. In: García-Peñalvo, F.J. (ed.) Proceedings of the Fourth International Conference on Technological Ecosystems for Enhancing Multiculturality, Salamanca, Spain, 02–04 November 2016, pp. 79–84. ACM (2016). http://dl.acm.org/citation.cfm?id=3012500

14. Russell, I., Jin, K.H., Sabin, M.: Make and learn: A CS principles course based on the arduino platform. In: Clear, A., Cuadros-Vargas, E., Carter, J., Túpac, Y. (eds.) Proceedings of the 2016 ACM Conference on Innovation and Technology in Computer Science Education, ITiCSE 2016, Arequipa, Peru, 9–13 July 2016, p. 366. ACM (2016). https://doi.org/10.1145/2899415.2925490

15. Schwarz, S., Wenzel, M.: Controlling Lego EV3 robots with Prolog. In: Seipel, D., Hanus, M., Abreu, S. (eds.) Declare 2017 - Conference on Declarative Programming, 31st Workshop on Logic Programming (WLP 2017) (2017). https://www.uni-wuerzburg.de/fileadmin/10030100/Publications/TR_Declare17.pdf

16. Specht, E., et al.: Analysis of the use of declarative languages for enhanced embedded system software development. In: Petraglia, A., Pedroni, V.A., Cauwenberghs, G. (eds.) Proceedings of the 20th Annual Symposium on Integrated Circuits and Systems Design, SBCCI 2007, Copacabana, Rio de Janeiro, Brazil, 3–6 September 2007, pp. 324–329. ACM (2007). https://doi.org/10.1145/1284480.1284565

Towards Constraint Logic Programming over Strings for Test Data Generation

Sebastian Krings[1(✉)], Joshua Schmidt[2], Patrick Skowronek[3],
Jannik Dunkelau[2], and Dierk Ehmke[3]

[1] Niederrhein University of Applied Sciences, Mönchengladbach, Germany
sebastian@krin.gs
[2] Institut für Informatik, Heinrich-Heine-Universität, Düsseldorf, Germany
[3] periplus instruments GmbH & Co. KG, Darmstadt, Germany

Abstract. In order to properly test software, test data of a certain quality is needed. However, useful test data is often unavailable because existing or hand-crafted data might not be diverse enough to enable desired test cases. Furthermore, using production data might be prohibited due to security or privacy concerns or other regulations. At the same time, existing tools for test data generation are often limited.

In this paper, we evaluate to what extent constraint logic programming can be used to generate test data, focusing on strings in particular. To do so, we introduce a prototypical CLP solver over string constraints. As case studies, we use it to generate valid IBAN numbers, calendar dates and specific data in JSON.

1 Introduction

Gaining test data for software tests is notoriously hard. Typical limitations include lack of properly formulated requirements or the combinatorial blowup causing an impractically large amount of test cases needed to cover the system under test (SUT). When testing applications such as data warehouses, difficulties stem from the amount and quality of test data available and the volume of data needed for realistic testing scenarios [9]. Artificial test data might not be diverse enough to enable desired test cases [15], whereas the use of real data might be prohibited due to security or privacy concerns or other regulations [18], e.g., the ISO/IEC 27001 [17]. Further challenges have been identified by Khan and ElMadi [20].

In consequence, to properly test applications one often has to resort to artificial test data generation [18]. However, existing tools are limited as they

- generate data that does not cover the desired scenarios [15],
- are specialized and lack options for configuration and adaptation [16], and
- generate an amount of data that is unrealistic for the SUT [29].

In this paper, we evaluate to what extent constraint logic programming could be used for test data generation, in particular for generating strings. We are not concerned with software testing itself.

P. Hofstedt et al. (Eds.): DECLARE 2019, LNAI 12057, pp. 139–159, 2020.
https://doi.org/10.1007/978-3-030-46714-2_10

2   Test Data

The International Software Testing Qualifications Board (ISTQB) describes test data as data created or selected to satisfy the preconditions and inputs to execute one or more test cases [30]. Test data may belong to the following categories:

- status data, files or surrounding systems required for a reusable start state,
- input data transferred to a test object during test execution,
- output data returned by a test object after execution,
- production data, which is deducted from the production system.

Production data is often used for testing as it provides obvious test cases and can be gathered easily. However, using production data does not lead to thorough testing, e.g., it never contains dates in the future. While production data can be anonymized, it is hard to guarantee that de-anonymization is impossible. Furthermore, production data may be biased.

Those problems can be solved by generating synthetic data. The implementation of a test data generator for each specific problem is cumbersome. One just wants to describe the problem at hand without implementing the actual data generation. We therefore consider constraint programming to be appropriate for implementing general test data generators. In particular, relying on constraint programming provides a number of further benefits common to declarative languages: specification of data and generating programs are more closely related and maintainability is increased. Furthermore, constraint-based and logic programming allows to easily extend given specifications by further constraints and thus increases extensibility and combinability.

However, generating synthetic data remains a complex task as it involves thoroughly specifying constraints the data needs to fulfill in order to derive high quality test data.

2.1   Test Data Generators

The generation of synthetic test data can be supported by different test data generators [30]: database-based generators synthesize data according to database schemata or create partial copies of database contents, i.e., they rely on production data. Interface-based generators analyze the test object's API and determine the definition areas of input parameters to derive test data from. In this context, test oracles cannot be derived.

Code-based generators take the source code of the SUT into account, which has disadvantages. For instance, it prevents oracle generation and is unable to work with source code that is not available (e.g., for foreign libraries). Furthermore, code-based generators are a weak test base, especially lacking the intellectual redundancy necessary for testing (four-eyes principle) [27], i.e., the understanding of how a system is supposed to work and how it is implemented are necessarily identical if tests are generated purely based on code.

Specification-based generators generate test data and oracles based on specifications written in a formal notation. A specification-based generator could thus generate data that replaces production data. The quality of the test data is ensured by the model and the correctness of the solver. This includes quality aspects such as conformity and accuracy. To build such a generator, constraint solving over all needed data types is required.

2.2 Requirements Towards Solvers

To gain a sensible set of requirements for a string constraint solver for test data generation, we decided to look at the feature set of Oracle SQL. The reasoning behind this is as follows: SQL was designed for the description of complex data flows and is therefore suited as a modeling language for test data generation [22]. It is widely used by developers, test data specialists and technical testers, i.e., they would be able to use it as a possible input language for generation tools. Additionally, SQL statements can easily be extracted from source code and can thus be used to automatically generate test data for given applications. Furthermore, SQL is declarative and offers a good level of abstraction.

There are several types of strings in Oracle SQL[1], in particular, unbounded unicode strings. In addition, other data types are required for practical test data: integers, fixed point numbers, reals and dates. There are no booleans in SQL, however, booleans ease encoding complex SQL conditions into constraints. Regarding BLOBs (e.g., images stored inside the database), we are so far not interested in supporting them, since SQL does not provide operations on them and their semantics are usually invisible to the applications.

Oracle SQL lists 54 functions on strings[2]. The ones we are interested in are

- CONCAT: concatenation of strings,
- LENGTH: returns the length of a string,
- REGEXP: tests, whether a string matches a given regular expression or not,
- SUBSTRING: returns a substring with given start position and length,
- TO_NUMBER: convert a string to number and vice versa.

Other operations can often be implemented with these functions or are not of interest for test data generation. REGEXP requires the solver to process regular expressions. The constraint handlers for all types must interwork since dependencies can exist between variables of different types. While we expect correctness, we cannot expect (refutation) completeness, since once all desired operations are added the problem becomes undecidable [7].

3   Related Work and Alternative Approaches

In the following, we will briefly present alternative approaches to constraint logic programming. For a selection of alternative solvers, we will discuss their implementation paradigms, in order to later compare to constraint logic programming.

---

[1] https://docs.oracle.com/en/database/oracle/oracle-database/19/cncpt/tables-and-table-clusters.html#GUID-A8F3420D-093C-449F-87E4-6C3DDFA8BCFF.

[2] https://docs.oracle.com/en/database/oracle/oracle-database/19/sqlrf/Functions.html#GUID-D079EFD3-C683-441F-977E-2C9503089982.

3.1   Autogen

Autogen [10] is a specification-based test data generator. autogen is able to directly use SQL as an input language. In order to generate test data from it, SQL is considered as specification of the SUT and is converted into constraints. autogen uses an independently developed string constraint solver called CLPQS, which handles all requirements stated in Sect. 2.2. To support the data types of SQL, autogen interacts with a set of different solvers. In particular, it relies on CLP(Q) and CLP(R) for rationals and reals, which have some limitations when it comes to completeness. CLPQS represents domains as regular expressions. One motivation for this paper is to experiment with different representations and propagation algorithms.

3.2   MiniZinc

MiniZinc is a solver-independent modeling language for constraint satisfaction and optimization problems. A MiniZinc model is compiled into a FlatZinc instance which can be solved by a multitude of constraint solvers. An extension of the MiniZinc modeling language with string variables and a set of built-in constraints has been suggested by Amadini et al. [3]. String variables are defined as words over the alphabet of ASCII characters and have a fixed, bounded or unbounded length. Yet, strings are represented as bounded length arrays of integers when translating to FlatZinc. The MiniZinc model itself does allow strings of unbounded length though. MiniZinc enables optimization over constraints rather than just satisfiability and allows mixing constraints over different domains. However, there are no direct conversions from other types to strings.

3.3   SMT Solvers

SMT solvers such as CVC4 [5] and Z3 [8] have been used for test case generation in the context of programming languages [31]. Both solvers support constraints over strings and regular expressions and are able to handle operations such as concatenation, containment, replacement and constraining the length of strings.

In Z3's original string solver, strings are represented as sequences over bitvectors. The solver itself is incomplete and relies on heuristics. In contrast, Z3-str [39] introduces strings as primitive types. Z3-str leverages the incremental solving approach of Z3 and can be combined with boolean and integer constraints. There have been several improvements of Z3-str in recent years [6,33,38].

CVC4's string solver [24,25] allows mixing constraints over strings and the integers. The authors present a set of algebraic techniques to solve constraints over unbounded strings, usable for arbitrary SMT solvers.

Another SMT solver for string constraints is TRAU [1], which, in contrast to CVC4 and Z3, supports context-free membership queries and transducer constraints by using pushdown automata. TRAU implements a Counter-Example Guided Abstraction Refinement (CEGAR) framework, computing over- and under-approximations to improve performance. Key idea in TRAU is a technique called flattening [2], leveraging that (un)satisfiability can be shown using witnesses of simple patterns expressable as finite automata.

3.4 Other Solvers

Kiezun et al. presented HAMPI [21], a constraint solver over strings of fixed length featuring a set of built-in constraints. HAMPI is able to reason over regular languages. String constraints are encoded in bit-vector logic which are then solved by the STP [13] bit-vector solver. At the expense of expressiveness, limiting the length of strings enables a more restricted encoding, increasing the performance by several orders of magnitude. However, a bit-vector encoding has a larger memory consumption than using finite automata.

G-STRINGS [4] is an extension of the GECODE constraint solver [28]. Both solvers accept strings of bounded but possibly unknown length. In contrast to GECODE, strings are not represented using integer arrays but as a restricted language of finite regular expressions. This prevents the static allocation of possibly large integer arrays and thus improves performance.

Fu et al. introduced Simple Linear String Equations (SISE) [12], a formalism for specifying constraints on strings of unbounded length, and presented the constraint solver SUSHI using finite automata to represent domains.

3.5 Summary

In summary, several approaches have been suggested for string constraints. However, no single approach is able to satisfactorily handle the requirements posed for test data generators described in Sect. 2.2. A comparison of different solvers considering the features described in Sect. 2.2 is shown in Table 1. The requirement of a combined solver states that a direct conversion between strings and other types is provided. As CONSTRING has been developed specifically for this problem domain, it naturally supports the most requirements.

4 Constraint Logic Programming over Strings

We implement a constraint logic programming system for strings using Constraint Handling Rules (CHR) [11] on top of SWI-Prolog [37] called CONSTRING. We use classic constraint propagation to reduce variable domains. The system supports strings of unbounded length and is coupled with CLP(FD), CLP(R) and CLP(B) to handle the integers, reals and booleans respectively. While not all SQL string operations are implemented yet, we plan to do so in the future. One goal is to employ different techniques than CLPQS to compare and possibly improve both solvers. We think CLP is adequate since there are many other solvers to build up upon and since it provides access to all solutions using backtracking.

In the following, we present our encoding of string domains and discuss its advantages and drawbacks, followed by the currently featured constraints, selected constraint handling rules and solver integrations.

Table 1. Features of constraint solvers. (✓) indicates partial support or workaround.

Solver	Strings			Combined solver		
	Unbounded	Unicode	SQL operations	Integer	Boolean	Real
CLPQS	✓	✓	✓	✓	✓	(✓)
MiniZinc	✗	✗	(✓)	✗	✗	✗
CVC4	✓	✗	✓	✓	✗	✗
Z3-str3	✓	✗	(✓)	✓	✗	✗
S3	✓	✗	✓	✓	✓	✗
Hampi	✗	✗	(✓)	✗	✗	✗
Sushi	✓	✓	✓	✗	✗	✗
G-Strings	✗	✗	(✓)	✗	✗	✗
Trau	✓	✗	✓	✓	✗	✗

4.1   Domain Definition

To fulfill the requirements posed in Sect. 2.2, we decided not to enforce a fixed length of strings and to use regular expressions as input. The employed alphabet consists of ASCII characters and some special characters like umlauts and accented characters. Dynamic character matching is possible by specifying ranges (e.g., [0-9a-f]), or by using the dot operator. We match a whitespace in regular expressions by \s while actual whitespace characters can be used to structure regular expressions without being part of the accepted language.

Further, we support the usual regular expression operators on characters, i.e., quantity operators (*, + and ?) and the alternative choice operator (|). For convenience, our regular expressions offer more strict repetition definitions noted by {n} (exactly n times), {m,n} (m to n times) and {m,+} (at least m times).

4.2   Domain Representation

Since ConString is supposed to handle strings of unbounded length, we represent domains as finite automata as done by Golden et al. [14]. First, this allows for a concise specification of regular languages with low memory consumption. Second, finite automata support basic operations such as union, intersection, concatenation or iteration and are closed under each of these operations. In particular, we use non-deterministic finite automata with ϵ-transitions.

Since SWI-Prolog does not have a native library for handling finite automata, we encode them as a self-contained term automaton_dom/4 consisting of a set of states, a transition relation as well as a set of initial and final states. The states are a coherent list of the integers $1 \ldots n$, $n \in \mathbb{N}$. The transition relation is implemented as a list of triples containing a state s_1, a range of characters (might contain a single character only) and a target state s_2 reached after processing a character from the range of characters in s_1, e.g., (0, a, 1).

We implement the common operations on finite automata used for regular languages as well as basic uninformed search algorithms used to label automata, i.e., to find a word having an accepting run. The search is backtrackable providing access to an automaton's complete language.

Efficiency. The chosen representation of finite automata has several drawbacks. We use lists to store states and transitions providing linear time concatenation and element access leading to a loss of performance, especially when labeling automata. It would be desirable to use a data structure such as hashsets, which provide amortized constant time performance for basic operations. However, such a data structure is currently unavailable in SWI-Prolog[3].

Another drawback is that we have to rename states when performing basic operations on automata. For instance, the concatenation $\mathcal{A}_1.\mathcal{A}_2$ is implemented by using the final states of $\mathcal{A}_2$ for the resulting automaton and adding an ϵ-transition from all final states of $\mathcal{A}_1$ to all initial states of $\mathcal{A}_2$. In order to avoid ambiguities, the states of $\mathcal{A}_2$ have to be renamed by shifting their identifier names by the number of states in $\mathcal{A}_1$. This renaming is one of the main issues for efficiency as it adds a linear time complexity component with respect to the size of the second automaton to all the basic operations.

4.3   Constraint Handling Rules

We use CHR on top of SWI-Prolog providing the constraint store and propagation unit to reduce variable domains. Moreover, CHR serves as user interface.

The CHR language is committed-choice, i.e., once a rule is applied it cannot be revoked by backtracking. Rules consist of three parts: a head, a guard and a body. A rule is triggered as soon as the head matches constraints in the constraint store. Guards allow imposing restrictions on rule execution. Finally, the body consists of Prolog predicates and CHR constraints. Predicates are called as usual while constraints are added to the constraint store, possibly triggering further propagation. All available constraints are propagated until the constraint store reaches a fix point. Solving fails if an empty string domain is discovered.

CHR provides three different kinds of rules: First, propagation rules of the form `head ==> guard | body`, where the body is called if the guard is true. The head constraints are kept. Simplification rules of the form `head <=> guard | body` update the constraint store by replacing the head constraints by those derived from the body. Simpagation rules of the form `head1 \ head2 <=> guard | body` are combined rules, retaining the constraints of the first part of the head while discarding those of the second part.

Our implementation currently supports several basic operations on regular languages such as intersection, concatenation or iteration as well as a membership constraint, arithmetic length constraints (fixed or upper bound), string

---

[3] While SWI-Prolog has built-in support for dictionaries, element access is logarithmic and updates are linear in size.

Listing 1. CHR rules for the membership constraint `str_in/2`.

```
1  str_in(S1, S2) <=>
2      string(S2) | gen_dom(S2, D), str_in(S1, D).
3  str_in(_, D) ==> is_empty(D) | fail.
4  str_in(Var,D) ==> D = string_dom(Cst) | Var = Cst.
5  str_in(S, D1), str_in(S, D2) <=>
6      D1 \= D2 | intersection(D1, D2, D3), str_in(S, D3).
7  str_in(S, D1)\ str_in(S, D2) <=>  D1 == D2 | true.
```

Listing 2. CHR rules for the concatenation constraint `str_concat/3`.

```
1  str_in(S1, D1), str_in(S2, D2), str_concat(S1, S2, S3) ==>
2      concat(D1, D2, D3), str_in(S3, D3).
3  str_in(S1, D1), str_concat(S1, S1, S3) ==>
4      concat(D1, D1, D3), str_in(S3, D3).
```

to integer conversion, prefix, suffix and infix constraints and case sensitivity constraints. For now, we ensure arc- and path-consistency of our constraints. Variables can be labeled using `str_label(+Vars)` or `str_labeling(+Options, +Vars)`. As options, we currently support selecting the search strategy for automata (`dfs`, `idfs`, `bfs`) and any option on integer domains provided by SWI-Prolog's CLP(FD) library. In the following, we will describe selected constraint handling rules in more detail.

The membership constraint is defined as shown in Listing 1. The first rule is applied in case membership is called with a string or regular expression. Then, a finite automaton representing the input domain is generated and the same constraint is applied to this automaton domain. The second rule states that whenever a domain is empty constraint solving should fail as no solution exists. Third, in case the string domain becomes constant, we propagate the value to the variable. The fourth rule joins two non-equal membership constraints for the same variable by intersecting both domains and replacing the two constraints by a single membership constraint. A final rule is used to remove one of two identical membership constraints. Note that `gen_dom/2` and `intersection/3` are called for internal domain computation and not added to the constraint store.

Concatenation is defined using two rules as shown in Listing 2. It relies on the membership constraint by assuming that two `str_in/2` refer to different variables. The first rule defines the concatenation of two different string variables by concatenating their automata domains and adding a new membership constraint for the result. Analogously, the second rule defines the concatenation of the same string variable onto itself. In order to efficiently propagate a constant string result to the first two arguments, we add a third rule using SWI-Prolog's string concatenation, e.g., `string_concat(A, B, "test")`, providing all solutions on backtracking. If a candidate has been found, it is checked upon labeling

Listing 3. CHR rules for the infix constraint `str_infix/2`.

```
1  str_infix(S, IStr) <=>
2      string(IStr) | gen_dom(IStr, IDom), str_infix(S, IDom).
3  str_infix(S, IDom) <=>
4      any_char_dom(A), repeat(A, AStar),
5      concat(IDom, AStar, T), concat(AStar, T, ResDom),
6      str_in(S, ResDom).
```

whether the candidate is accepted by the corresponding domains. If so, membership constraints are propagated assigning constant values to all arguments.

The iteration operation `str_repeat/[2,3,4]` is defined as repeated concatenation. Case sensitivity operations are defined by setting up membership constraints to generated domains accepting only upper or lower case characters.

The infix operation `str_infix/2` for two string variables s_1 and s_2 is defined by adding a membership constraint for s_1 to be an element of the regular language $\mathcal{L}(.^*).\mathcal{L}(s_2).\mathcal{L}(.^*)$ as shown in Listing 3. Again, the first rule is a wrapper generating a finite automaton domain from a string or regular expression. Prefix and suffix operations are defined in the same manner.

4.4   Integration of CLP(FD), CLP(R) and CLP(B)

In order to enable the generation of richer test data and allow for a greater coverage of test scenarios, we extend CONSTRING to support combining constraints over different domains. In particular, we support constraints over finite domain integers using CLP(FD) [34], constraints over reals using CLP(R) and constraints over booleans using CLP(B) [35,36]. As an interface, we provide the bidirectional constraints `str_to_int/2`, `str_to_real/2` and `str_to_bool/2`.

The implementation of `str_to_int/2` consists of four rules as shown in Listing 4. In order to detect failure early we check for inequality if both arguments are constants. If only the integer variable is a constant, we convert and assign the value to the string. In the third rule, a constant string is assigned to the integer variable. Note that `number_string/2` removes leading zeros by default. Besides that, we provide a rule to fail for constant strings not representing integers.

We additionally provide a second implementation `str_to_int1/2` allowing leading zeros in order for constraints such as `str_to_int("00", 0)` to hold. This is achieved by additionally concatenating the domain of 0* to IDom in line 6 of Listing 4.

The integration of CLP(R) and CLP(B) is implemented analogously propagating membership constraints to a specific backend if variables are constant values. Again, alternative implementations are provided allowing an arbitrary amount of leading zeros when converting from string to boolean or real.

Listing 4. Basic rules for the integration of CLP(FD) propagating constant values.

```
1  str_to_int(S,I) ==>
2     string(S), integer(I), number_string(SInt, S), I \== SInt |
3     fail.
4  str_to_int(S,I) ==>
5     integer(I), number_string(I, IString) |
6     cst_str_dom(IString, IDom), str_in(S, IDom).
7  str_to_int(S,I), str_in(S,D) ==>
8     D = string_dom(CstString),
9     number_string(CstInteger, CstString) | I #= CstInteger.
10 str_to_int(S,_), str_in(S,D) ==>
11    D = string_dom(CstString), \+ number_string(_, CstString) |
12    fail.
```

5   Case Studies

In this section, we will present three case studies of using CONSTRING: a genera-tion of IBANs, calendar dates and data tables in JSON. Finally, we will conclude this section with a discussion of the benefits from constraint logic programming compared to typical test data generators.

5.1   Generation of IBAN Numbers

As a case study, we specify the computation of valid International Bank Account Numbers (IBANs) as a constraint system as done by Friske and Ehmke [10]. This example is of interest as it yields a relatively large search space and requires the conversion between the integers and strings. Generated data can, for instance, be used to initialize unit tests of components validating IBANs. This example is an excerpt of a project where an interface between a SEPA credit transfer and a micro-service managing financial push notifications has been tested.

A German IBAN consists of 22 characters which are characterized as follows: The first two characters represent the country code (here, the constant "DE") while the third and fourth characters are a checksum. The remaining 18 digits represent the Basic Bank Account Number (BBAN).

We can compute valid IBANs using a given country code as follows: Represent the country code as a digit where "A" equals 10, "B" equals 11, etc. The German country code "DE" is hence encoded as 1314. Concatenate two zeros to the encoded country code (i.e., 131400) and prepend the BBAN. This forms a 24 digit number, σ_b. In order to compute the valid checksum σ_c, the constraint $98 - (\sigma_b \bmod 97) = \sigma_c$ must hold. Finding a solution binds the BBAN to a value in its domain and provides its corresponding checksum σ_c. To derive the actual BBAN, remove the suffix "131400". Finally, concatenate the computed checksum σ_c with the BBAN and prepend the country code "DE" as a string.

Listing 5. Constraint system to compute all valid german IBANs.

```
1   iban(IBAN) :-
2       SigmaC in 0..96,
3       BBAN in 10000000000000000..99999999999999999,
4       SigmaB #= BBAN * 1000000 + 131400,
5       SigmaB mod 97 #= SigmaC,
6       str_label([SigmaB, SigmaC]),
7       str_to_int(BBANStr, BBAN),
8       CheckSum #= 98 - SigmaC,
9       str_to_intl(CheckSumStr, CheckSum),
10      str_size(CheckSumStr, 2),
11      str_in(DE, "DE"),
12      str_concat(DE, CheckSumStr, IBANPrefix),
13      str_concat(IBANPrefix, BBANStr, IBAN),
14      str_label([IBAN]).
```

Table 2. Benchmarks for generating IBANs. Walltime in seconds.

Amount	1	10	100	1,000	10,000	100,000	250,000
CLPQS	0.006	0.024	0.240	2.029	32.163	1525.457	9261.204
CONSTRING	0.007	0.038	0.105	1.066	26.573	1342.597	9841.225

The complete constraint system is shown in Listing 5. Lines 3 and 4 define the BBAN and the 24 digits number σ_b respectively. The constraint for computing σ_c is set in line 5. The remaining specification is straightforward as described above. Note that we allow leading zeros for the checksum's string.

For benchmarking, we generate sets of IBANs of varying sizes, using an Intel Core i7-6700K with 16 GiB RAM. We used SWI-Prolog's predicate `statistics/2` to measure the walltime. Table 2 shows the median time of five independent runs and compares our solver with CLPQS. As can be seen, CONSTRING performs overall slightly better than CLPQS with the exception of the generation of 250,000 IBANs. Up to one thousand samples both solvers appear to scale linearly. Notable exception is the jump from 10,000 to 100,000 generated samples. Here, both solvers scale worse: CLPQS scales with a factor of 47, whereas CONSTRING takes 50 times as long as for generating 10,000 IBANs instead of the expected factor of 10. At least for CONSTRING, experimental results have shown that this non-linear growth is caused by SWI-Prolog's CLP(FD) library.

We also encoded the example in SMT-LIB to compare CONSTRING and CLPQS with Z3-str3 and CVC4. Unfortunately, CVC4 did not return a result but timed out after 600 s. Z3-str3 found a single solution in around 0.2 s. We

Listing 6. Constraint system to compute diverse calendar date expressions.

```
1   date(Date) :-
2     WeekDay str_in "Monday|Tuesday|...|Sunday",
3     Month str_in "January|February|...|December",
4     Day str_in "[1-9]|[1-2][0-9]|3[0-1]",
5     Year str_in "[1-9][0-9]{0,3}",
6     MonthDay match Month + "_" + Day,
7     MonthDayYear match MonthDay + ",_" + Year \/ MonthDay,
8     FullDate match WeekDay + ",_" + MonthDayYear,
9     Date match MonthDayYear \/ FullDate \/ WeekDay,
10    str_label([Date]).
```

Table 3. Benchmarks for generating date expressions. Walltime in seconds.

Amount	1	10	100	1,000	10,000	100,000
CLPQS	0.000	0.000	0.000	0.000	0.000	0.010
CONSTRING	0.010	0.010	0.010	0.011	0.080	0.965

were unable to compute multiple solutions using Z3-str3 as the solver timed out searching for further ones.

5.2   Generation of Calendar Dates

Another example is the generation of various date expressions, which is of interest for testing for many tools which need to parse valid dates and reject invalid ones. The accepted expressions are of either of the forms "Tuesday", "August 30", "Tuesday, August 30", "August 30, 2016" or "Tuesday, August 30, 2016". Listing 6 shows the corresponding constraints taken from Karttunen et al. [19, Section 3]. The constraint system consists of defining the basic building blocks first: the weekdays, the months and valid year numbers. Thus, only the years 1 to 9999 are accepted. Further, the more complex parts are constructed each consisting of a combination of operations on variables constrained before. This leads up to the final definition of Date as a union of all possible notations.

Note that we employ a shorthand notation for the setup of constraints. MonthDayYear for example has to match the language defined by the union of the MonthDay domain and the concatenation of MonthDay, a separator and the Year. This notation enables a more readable definition of constraint systems.

Table 3 shows a brief performance evaluation as done in Sect. 5.1. As can be seen, CLPQS is notably faster than CONSTRING. The automata created by CONSTRING are probably large due to the alternative choice operator and the union operator leading to a lack of performance when labeling data. Reducing the size of automata, e.g., by removing ϵ-transitions, will likely increase performance.

Listing 7. An exemplary dataset in JSON containing the colors black and white.

```
1  { "colors": [
2     { "color": "black",
3       "code": { "rgb": [0,0,0], "hex": "#000000" } },
4     { "color": "white",
5       "code": { "rgb": [255,255,255], "hex": "#FFFFFF" } } ] }
```

We also encoded the example in SMT-LIB to compare CONSTRING and CLPQS with Z3-str3 and CVC4. Z3 found a single solution in around 0.070 s while CVC4 took around 0.084 s. Again, we were unable to compute multiple solutions with both solvers as they timed out.

5.3   Generation of Data in JSON

As a further and more involved example, we want to generate data describing different colors in JavaScript Object Notation (JSON). A color should be described by a name, a six byte hexadecimal code and a corresponding RGB color code. An exemplary dataset in JSON containing the colors black and white is shown in Listing 7.

For the given example, we want to ensure that the hexadecimal and RGB code of a color match each other. Further, each color in the set of colors should be unique. The latter requirement entails the need of two further constraints not mentioned in this paper yet: First, we need to be able to state the difference between two string variables (str_diff/2). This is achieved by a propagation rule which is triggered if both string variables have been labeled, i.e., they hold constant values, and checks for exact inequality (\==/2) between both values. If both values are equal, CONSTRING backtracks and searches for different values effectively restarting the computation from the last choicepoint. Second, we need to be able to state the difference of strings in between a list of string variables (str_all_diff/2). This is achieved by a simplification rule propagating pairwise inequality constraints for each pair of elements.

The constraint system used to generate datasets in JSON as described above is shown in Listing 8. First, we generate a given amount of hexadecimal color codes which have to be all different (lines 20 and 21). After labeling all hexadecimal color codes, we generate the corresponding RGB color codes using SWI-Prolog's predicate hex_bytes/2. We then use the labeled hexadecimal and RGB color codes to generate the strings describing a dataset entry, which is achieved by the predicate get_color_entry/3, and join all strings by concatenation (list_of_colors_concat/3). Finally, we further concatenate strings to the generated string concatenation describing single dataset entries (line 24) to obtain the desired data format in JSON. This last step shows the difference

Listing 8. The constraint system to generate datasets in JSON containing colors.

```
1   get_color_entry(Hex, RgbList, Color) :-
2       term_string(RgbList, Rgb1),
3       escape_special_characters(Rgb1, Rgb),
4       Prefix = "\\{\"color\":\"test\",\"code\":\\{\"rgb\":",
5       Color match Prefix + Rgb + ",\"hex\":#" + Hex + "\\}\\}".
6   list_of_colors_concat_acc([], [], Acc, Acc).
7   list_of_colors_concat_acc([Hex|HT], [Rgb|RT], Acc, Concat) :-
8       get_color_entry(Hex, Rgb, Color),
9       NewAcc = '+'(Acc, '+'(",", Color)),
10      list_of_colors_concat_acc(HT, RT, NewAcc, Concat).
11  list_of_colors_concat([], [], "").
12  list_of_colors_concat([Hex|HT], [Rgb|RT], Concat) :-
13      get_color_entry(Hex, Rgb, Color),
14      list_of_colors_concat_acc(HT, RT, Color, Concat).
15  list_of_hex_codes(0, []) :- !.
16  list_of_hex_codes(C, [HexCode|T]) :-
17      str_in(HexCode, "([A-F]|[0-9]){6}"),
18      C1 is C-1, list_of_hex_codes(C1, T).
19  json_colors(Amount, JSON) :-
20      list_of_hex_codes(Amount, LHex),
21      str_all_diff(LHex), str_label(LHex),
22      maplist(hex_bytes, LHex, RgbList),
23      list_of_colors_concat(LHex, RgbList, ColorsConcat),
24      JSON match "\\{\"colors\":\\[" + ColorsConcat + "\\]\\}",
25      str_label([JSON]).
```

between test data generation and data structure generation. In theory, only the first is needed to gain sensible test data, as the results can easily be stored in various data structures depending on the requirements for the SUT. However, integrating data structure generation into the constraint problem would render data generation more self-contained and could thus be desirable for users. Both data generation and data structure generation are strictly split inside the constraint system, i.e., there are two distinct blocks of constraints which are labeled individually (see labelings in line 21 and 25 of Listing 8).

To evaluate the performance of CONSTRING as done for the other case studies, we generate one dataset for varying amounts of dataset entries, i.e., colors. We noticed several performance bottlenecks in both, CONSTRING and CLPQS, when trying to benchmark the JSON generation. CONSTRING displayed a quadratic increase in runtime with respect to the number of dataset entries. autogen's runtime was somewhat erratic, i.e., it was sometimes faster for a higher (even) number of colors. Overall, autogen's runtime was less predictable than the one of CONSTRING. We will discuss performance bottlenecks of both solvers and how they can be coped with in the following three paragraphs.

Listing 9. An example showing a possible bottleneck for performance when implementing `str_all_diff/2`.

```
1  str_in(X, "1|2"), str_in(Y, "1|2"),
2  str_in(Z, "[0-9]{0,1000}"),
3  str_all_diff([X,Y,Z]), str_label([X,Y,Z]).
```

Order of Constraints. Although constraint systems are declarative, the order of constraints influences performance. For instance, in the given example, we have to ensure that the hexadecimal and RGB color codes are constant values (lines 21 and 22) before setting up the concatenation constraints. Otherwise, performance drops drastically since large automata domains have to be created holding variable references. As soon as such a variable reference is labeled, concatenation constraints are triggered and automata have to be intersected with their prior automata domains (see Sect. 4.3, Listing 1) containing the unlabeled variable references, ultimately leading to bad performance. Note that within our framework, the intersection operation on finite automata is usually the most complex operation when solving string constraints. If we evaluate the concatenations after all necessary variables have been labeled (lines 23 and 24), no intersections have to be computed on automata domains.

Performance of String Difference. Currently, `str_diff/2` is only triggered if both arguments are constant strings and does not propagate any knowledge to an unlabeled domain of a string variable. This is a bottleneck for performance when using the `str_all_diff/1` constraint. Since we only support a linear enumeration order by now, the solver has to backtrack a lot for large lists of variables between labeling a string and checking for inequality. If all variables have the same domain (e.g., as shown in Listing 8), the domain gets enumerated linearly for each variable in the list until finding a new value that is different to the ones labeled so far. For ConString, this leads to a runtime that grows quadratic with the size of the list of variables. As future work, we want to investigate propagating knowledge to domains instead of only checking inequality between constant strings. In SWI-Prolog's CLP(FD) library this corresponds to the constraints `all_different/1`, which behaves similar to our implementation, and `all_distinct/1`, which propagates knowledge to unlabeled domains.

In order to improve upon simple pairwise difference computation, it is essential to propagate `str_diff/2` as soon as the two involved variables are constant values instead of waiting for all variables to be labeled. For instance, consider Listing 9 with X and Y sharing a domain and Z whose domain is considerably larger. When labeling the variables using a linear enumeration order, the first assignment of X and Y is the same, i.e., the string "1". If the pairwise difference constraints are triggered after labeling, the equality of the first two variables is only identified after labeling all three variables, with the last choicepoint being

Listing 10. Pseudocode of an IBAN test data generator.

```
1  bban = 100000000000000000
2  while bban <= 999999999999999999:
3      bban_country = bban * 1000000 + 131400
4      checksum = 98 - (bban_country mod 97 )
5      iban = concat("DE", checksum, bban)
6      bban += 1
7      yield iban
```

in the labeling of Z although the variable is not involved in the conflict at all. The solver would enumerate the domain of Z exhaustively, before detecting the conflict. To counter this behaviour, one has to ensure that str_diff/2 is triggered as soon as X and Y are labeled, possibly suspending an ongoing labeling of variables.

Data Generation vs. Data Structure Generation. Generating a full data structure in JSON representation drastically increased the strain put on the constraint solvers. Within a single labeling operation, the combined generation of data and JSON representation caused a lot of unneeded backtracking through the two problems. With the two labeling operations split up, performance was increased while decreasing the declarativeness of the problem statement.

Overall, including the data structure generation in the constraint satisfaction problem lead to a severe performance decline. In consequence, we suggest splitting the generation of test data from storing it inside an appropriate data structure for testing. While this reduces self-containment of the encoding, it has several benefits as well:

- Constraints are considerably simpler, in particular, many concatenation constraints are avoided at all.
- Variables are less intertwined which reduces the evaluation time of consistency and propagation algorithms.
- Flexibility in the enumeration order is increased which could open the way for optimization.

5.4 Comparison to Test Data Generators

In the following we will give a brief comparison between data generation tools based on constraint solving, such as autogen and CONSTRING, and typical test data generators, i.e., imperative implementations of enumeration algorithms. In this section we have seen three case studies in which we applied our approach of constraint logic programming to test data generation. While the IBAN example in Sect. 5.1 is motivated by a real world application (cf. Friske and Ehmke [10]), it can easily be replicated by a typical test data generator not using a declarative approach, as shown examplary in Listing 10. Such an IBAN generator would probably also keep a linear runtime depending on the number of generated IBANs, whereas we observed in Table 2 that CONSTRING exhibits a non-linear growth. However, if one is in need of generating IBANs with a certain checksum for testing purposes, the test data generator in Listing 10 would need to be modified to account for the requirement. In contrast, with constraint programming, e.g., as used by CONSTRING and autogen, additional requirements can be realized by simply adding a constraint, e.g., `CheckSum #= DesiredChecksum`.

The date example serves as data source to a common problem in programming, that of parsing date inputs (e.g., by the user via a text field). Although the generation itself can be done easily with a test data generator which randomly chooses a style, a weekday and a calendar day, the implementation in Listing 6 can easily be improved to generate only valid dates (e.g., a correct weekday or matching calendar day per month) by adding some further specifications into the constraint system.

In our third example, the color database in JSON, we generate a more strictly defined data set. While the hexadecimal and the RGB color code in a single dataset entry must match, all colors in a generated dataset need to be exclusive. In contrast to a classical imperative test data generator, in which one needs to keep track of generated colors explicitly, our constraint-based approach enables a more declarative implementation using difference constraints and backtracking.

In conclusion, traditional test data generators might run faster and can, depending on the use case, be more suitable than a constraint solver. For highly intertwined test data or requirements that are likely to change, a more declarative approach based on constraint solving leads to a clearer specification of the test data to be generated and allows for simple adaptation to requirement changes. As seen in the calendar date example, using a declarative approach allows constructing complex structures from simple building blocks. No further control structures or instructions are required besides describing the data format.

Due to the intended use for test data generation, we have the strong belief that such data driven development resonates more with the problem domain than using, e.g., imperative programming languages. Thanks to Prolog's off-the-shelf backtracking capabilities, exhaustively traversing a search space is provided by default and one does not depend on explicit loop constructs or caching of results: each solution is found exactly once. Another benefit is the separation of the definition of data and the search for solutions. Consider again the pseudocode example shown in Listing 10. The enumeration order of calculated IBANs will always be the same. To reach another order, the code again needs to be adapted. On the other hand, the implementation for CONSTRING shown in Listing 5 is independent of any enumeration order. The order can easily be changed by passing a corresponding argument to `str_labeling/2` as outlined in Sect. 4.3.

6   Way Forward and Future Work

6.1   An Efficient Backend

For classic domain propagation to work on strings, an efficient representation of possible values is needed. So far, we represent automata as outlined in Sect. 4.2. As discussed, this is not the most efficient approach, as certain algorithms need to traverse the list of states or transitions to find a particular one.

Other known automaton libraries such as dk.brics.automaton [26] feature more efficient representations and algorithms. However, these are usually based on using pointers or objects and cannot easily be ported to Prolog for obvious reasons. At the same time, connecting the Java or C ports of the library to our Prolog system leads to all kinds of difficulties when it comes to proper handling of backtracking. Moreover, Prolog programs are no longer declarative when using stateful data structures without cloning data after each operation.

As future work, we want to experiment with porting dk.brics.automaton or a comparable library to Prolog while retaining its efficiency. So far, we have different approaches in mind. First, we could implement low-level data structures outside of Prolog (e.g., in C) and render them backtrackable using a thin Prolog layer. Second, we could mimic the internal workings of the library, e.g., using attributed variables to store (mutable) class variables and links to other "objects". While this would avoid possible backtracking issues, it would not be as idiomatic. Furthermore, we want to evaluate whether it is more efficient to use deterministic finite automata or, in general, ϵ-free automata. Additionally, we do not provide options for labeling, e.g., concerning the enumeration order. Additional options like enumerating a string domain in alphabetical, reversed alphabetical or a randomized order will most likely improve performance for some constraint satisfaction problems. This would also enable to provide different distributions of test data for a given domain. Especially a randomized enumeration order enables the generation of more diverse test data. Yet, labeling options of integrated solvers like CLP(FD) can already be used.

6.2   Combining Solvers

Of course, a solver like the one we outlined above would still be too weak to efficiently support the constraints we discussed in Sect. 1. In consequence, we envision an integration of a CLP-based solver and the other solvers discussed in Sect. 3 into a combined solving procedure. This could be done following the approach we used for first-order logic in prior work [23].

A more simple strategy would be to use multiple solvers at once and returning the first result computed. This will have a performance benefit, given that the solvers described in Sect. 3 have diverse approaches and mixed performances in certain situations. Implementing such a portfolio is somewhat complicated, since there is no standardized interface for constraint solvers [25], leading to a large overhead translating constraints in between solvers. However, a promising draft for an interface [32] has been proposed recently.

7 Conclusion

In this paper, we discussed how synthetic test data can be generated and what the common pitfalls are. We discussed currently available solvers over strings and outlined that string constraint solving has made considerable progress recently. However, hurdles remain and generation of artificial test data remains complicated at least.

We implemented a simple prototype of a string constraint solver based on constraint logic programming and classical domain propagation. While it does not yet offer all features desired, our prototype shows that our approach is feasible and promising.

However, we believe that no single solver will be able to handle all requirements sufficiently and that reimplementing features commonly found in other solvers might not be worthwhile. In consequence, we think that an integration of solvers such as the one discussed in Sect. 6.2 is very promising and we hope to be able to lift our results for first-order-logic to string domains in the future.

References

1. Abdulla, P.A., et al.: Trau: SMT solver for string constraints. In: 2018 Formal Methods in Computer Aided Design, FMCAD 2018, Austin, TX, USA, 30 October–2 November 2018, pp. 1–5 (2018)
2. Abdulla, P.A., et al.: Flatten and conquer: a framework for efficient analysis of string constraints. In: Proceedings of PLDI 2017, pp. 602–617. ACM (2017)
3. Amadini, R., Flener, P., Pearson, J., Scott, J.D., Stuckey, P.J., Tack, G.: MiniZinc with Strings. CoRR, abs/1608.03650 (2016)
4. Amadini, R., Gange, G., Stuckey, P.J., Tack, G.: A novel approach to string constraint solving. In: Beck, J.C. (ed.) CP 2017. LNCS, vol. 10416, pp. 3–20. Springer, Cham (2017). https://doi.org/10.1007/978-3-319-66158-2_1
5. Barrett, C., et al.: CVC4. In: Gopalakrishnan, G., Qadeer, S. (eds.) CAV 2011. LNCS, vol. 6806, pp. 171–177. Springer, Heidelberg (2011). https://doi.org/10.1007/978-3-642-22110-1_14
6. Berzish, M., Ganesh, V., Zheng, Y.: Z3str3: a string solver with theory-aware heuristics. In: FMCAD, pp. 55–59. IEEE (2017)
7. Chen, T., Chen, Y., Hague, M., Lin, A.W., Wu, Z.: What is decidable about string constraints with the ReplaceAll function. CoRR, abs/1711.03363 (2017)
8. de Moura, L., Bjørner, N.: Z3: an efficient SMT solver. In: Ramakrishnan, C.R., Rehof, J. (eds.) TACAS 2008. LNCS, vol. 4963, pp. 337–340. Springer, Heidelberg (2008). https://doi.org/10.1007/978-3-540-78800-3_24
9. ElGamal, N., ElBastawissy, A., Galal-Edeen, G.: Data warehouse testing. In: Proceedings of EDBT/ICDT, EDBT 2013, pp. 1–8. ACM (2013)
10. Friske, M., Ehmke, D.: Modellbasierte Testdatenspezifikation und -generierung mittels Äquivalenzklassen und SQL. In: Proceedings of TAV, February 2019
11. Frühwirth, T.: Theory and practice of constraint handling rules. J. Logic Program. 37(1–3), 95–138 (1998)
12. Fu, X., Li, C.-C.: A string constraint solver for detecting web application vulnerability, pp. 535–542, January 2010

13. Ganesh, V., Dill, D.L.: A decision procedure for bit-vectors and arrays. In: Damm, W., Hermanns, H. (eds.) CAV 2007. LNCS, vol. 4590, pp. 519–531. Springer, Heidelberg (2007). https://doi.org/10.1007/978-3-540-73368-3_52

14. Golden, K., Pang, W.: Constraint reasoning over strings. In: Rossi, F. (ed.) CP 2003. LNCS, vol. 2833, pp. 377–391. Springer, Heidelberg (2003). https://doi.org/10.1007/978-3-540-45193-8_26

15. Haftmann, F., Kossmann, D., Lo, E.: A framework for efficient regression tests on database applications. VLDB J. **16**(1), 145–164 (2007)

16. Houkjær, K., Torp, K., Wind, R.: Simple and realistic data generation. In: VLDB (2006)

17. Information technology – Security techniques – Information security management systems – Requirements. Standard, International Organization for Standardization, Geneva, CH, June 2017

18. Jeske, D.R., Lin, P.J., Rendon, C., Xiao, R., Samadi, B.: Synthetic data generation capabilties for testing data mining tools. In: Proceedings of MILCOM, pp. 1–6, October 2006

19. Karttunen, L., Chanod, J.-P., Grefenstette, G., Schille, A.: Regular expressions for language engineering. Nat. Lang. Eng. **2**(4), 305–328 (1996)

20. Khan, M.S.A., ElMadi, A.: Data warehouse testing an exploratory study. Master's thesis, School of Computing, Blekinge Institute of Technology, Karlskrona, Sweden (2011)

21. Kieżun, A., Ganesh, V., Guo, P.J., Hooimeijer, P., Ernst, M.D.: HAMPI: a solver for string constraints. Proceedings of ISSTA 2009, 21–23 July 2009

22. Klaus Franz, E.K., Tremmel, T.: Basiswissen Testdatenmanagement: Aus- und Weiterbildung zum Test Data Specialist – Certified Tester Foundation Level nach GTB. dpunkt (2018)

23. Krings, S., Leuschel, M.: SMT solvers for validation of B and Event-B models. In: Ábrahám, E., Huisman, M. (eds.) IFM 2016. LNCS, vol. 9681, pp. 361–375. Springer, Cham (2016). https://doi.org/10.1007/978-3-319-33693-0_23

24. Liang, T., Reynolds, A., Tinelli, C., Barrett, C., Deters, M.: A DPLL(T) theory solver for a theory of strings and regular expressions. In: Biere, A., Bloem, R. (eds.) CAV 2014. LNCS, vol. 8559, pp. 646–662. Springer, Cham (2014). https://doi.org/10.1007/978-3-319-08867-9_43

25. Liang, T., Reynolds, A., Tsiskaridze, N., Tinelli, C., Barrett, C., Deters, M.: An efficient SMT solver for string constraints. Form. Methods Syst. Des. **48**(3), 206–234 (2016)

26. Møller, A.: dk.brics.automaton – finite-state automata and regular expressions for Java (2017). http://www.brics.dk/automaton/

27. Pretschner, A.: Zum modellbasierten funktionalen Test reaktiver Systeme (2003). http://mediatum.ub.tum.de/doc/601738/000006bb.pdf

28. Schulte, C., Tack, G., Lagerkvist, M.Z.: Modeling and programming with Gecode. Schulte, Christian and Tack, Guido and Lagerkvist, Mikael, 2015 (2010)

29. Singh, J., Singh, K.: Statistically analyzing the impact of automated ETL testing on the data quality of a data warehouse. IJCEE **1**(4), 488–495 (2009)

30. Spillner, A., Linz, T.: Basiswissen Softwaretest: Aus- und Weiterbildung zum Certified Tester – Foundation Level nach ISTQB-Standard, 3 edn. dpunkt (2005)

31. Tillmann, N., de Halleux, J.: Pex–white box test generation for .NET. In: Beckert, B., Hähnle, R. (eds.) TAP 2008. LNCS, vol. 4966, pp. 134–153. Springer, Heidelberg (2008). https://doi.org/10.1007/978-3-540-79124-9_10

32. Tinelli, C., Barret, C., Fontaine, P.: Unicode Strings (Draft 2.0) (2019). http://smtlib.cs.uiowa.edu/theories-UnicodeStrings.shtml

33. Trinh, M.-T., Chu, D.-H., Jaffar, J.: S3: a symbolic string solver for vulnerability detection in web applications. In: Proceedings of CCS, CCS 2014, pp. 1232–1243. ACM (2014)
34. Triska, M.: The finite domain constraint solver of SWI-Prolog. In: Schrijvers, T., Thiemann, P. (eds.) FLOPS 2012. LNCS, vol. 7294, pp. 307–316. Springer, Heidelberg (2012). https://doi.org/10.1007/978-3-642-29822-6_24
35. Triska, M.: The boolean constraint solver of SWI-Prolog (system description). In: Kiselyov, O., King, A. (eds.) FLOPS 2016. LNCS, vol. 9613, pp. 45–61. Springer, Cham (2016). https://doi.org/10.1007/978-3-319-29604-3_4
36. Triska, M.: Boolean constraints in SWI-Prolog: a comprehensive system description. Sci. Comput. Program. **164**, 98–115 (2018)
37. Wielemaker, J., Schrijvers, T., Triska, M., Lager, T.: SWI-Prolog. CoRR, abs/1011.5332 (2010)
38. Zheng, Y., et al.: Z3str2: an efficient solver for strings, regular expressions, and length constraints. Formal Methods Syst. Des. **50**(2–3), 249–288 (2017)
39. Zheng, Y., Zhang, X., Ganesh, V.: Z3-str: a Z3-based string solver for web application analysis. In: Proceedings of ESEC/FSE, ESEC/FSE 2013, pp. 114–124. ACM (2013)

Facets of the *PIE* Environment
for Proving, Interpolating and Eliminating
on the Basis of First-Order Logic

Christoph Wernhard(✉)

Berlin, Germany

Abstract. *PIE* is a Prolog-embedded environment for automated reasoning on the basis of first-order logic. Its main focus is on formulas, as constituents of complex formalizations that are structured through formula macros, and as outputs of reasoning tasks such as second-order quantifier elimination and Craig interpolation. It supports a workflow based on documents that intersperse macro definitions, invocations of reasoners, and LATEX-formatted natural language text. Starting from various examples, the paper discusses features and application possibilities of *PIE* along with current limitations and issues for future research.

1 Introduction

First-order logic is used widely and in many roles in philosophy, mathematics, and artificial intelligence as well as other branches of computer science. Many practically successful reasoning approaches can be viewed as derived from reasoning in first-order logic, for example, SAT solving, logic programming, database query processing and reasoning in description logics. The overall aim of the *PIE* environment is to support the *practical mechanized reasoning in first-order logic*. Approaching this aim consequently leads from first-order theorem proving in the strict sense to tasks that *compute first-order formulas*, in particular second-order quantifier elimination and Craig interpolation, whose integrated support characterizes *PIE*. The system is written and embedded in *SWI-Prolog* [58] and provides, essentially as a library of Prolog predicates, a number of functionalities:

- Support for a Prolog-readable syntax of first-order logic formulas.
- Formula pretty-printing in Prolog syntax and in LATEX.
- A versatile formula macro processor.
- Support for processing documents that intersperse formula macro definitions, reasoner invocations and LATEX-formatted natural language text.
- Interfaces to external first-order and propositional reasoners.
- A built-in Prolog-based first-order theorem prover.
- Implemented reasoning techniques that compute formulas:
  • Second-order quantifier elimination on the basis of first-order logic.

© Springer Nature Switzerland AG 2020
P. Hofstedt et al. (Eds.): DECLARE 2019, LNAI 12057, pp. 160–177, 2020.
https://doi.org/10.1007/978-3-030-46714-2_11

- Computation of first-order Craig interpolants.
- Formula conversions for use in preprocessing, inprocessing and output presentation.

The system is available as free software from its homepage

http://cs.christophwernhard.com/pie.

The distribution includes several example documents whose source files as well as rendered LaTeX presentations can also be accessed directly from the system Web page. *Inspecting Gödel's Ontological Proof* is there an advanced application, where the interplay of elimination and modal axioms is applied in several contexts. The system was first presented at the 2016 workshop *Practical Aspects of Automated Reasoning* [55]. Here we show various application possibilities, features and also issues for further research that become apparent with the system by starting from a number of examples. The paper is itself written as a *PIE* document and thus includes fragments generated by *PIE* and the included or integrated reasoners.

The rest of this paper is structured as follows: After introducing in Sect. 2 the document-oriented workflow supported by *PIE*, we show in Sect. 3 how it applies to the invocation of second-order quantifier elimination in the system. Section 4 provides an application example of elimination, a certain form of abduction, which is shown together with basic features of the *PIE* macro system. We proceed in Sect. 5 to outline how systems for theorem proving in the strict sense are embedded into *PIE*. In Sect. 6 the computation of circumscription is discussed as another example of second-order quantifier elimination with *PIE*, along with further features of the macro system and the general issue of finding good presentations of computed formulas that are essentially just characterized semantically. Section 7 sketches a further application of second-order quantifier elimination: a potential way of logic programming with second-order formulas as used for theoretical considerations in descriptive complexity. Further features of *PIE* are summarized in Sect. 9, and Sect. 10 concludes the paper.

Related work is discussed in the respective contexts. The bibliography is somewhat extensive, reflecting that the system relates to methods as well as implementation and application aspects in a number of areas, including first-order theorem proving, Craig interpolation, second-order quantifier elimination and knowledge representation.

2   *PIE* Documents

The main way to interact with *PIE* is by developing or modifying a *PIE document*, a file that intersperses definitions of formula macros, specifications of reasoning tasks, and LaTeX-formatted natural language text in the fashion of literate programming [28]. Such a document can be *loaded* into the Prolog environment like a source code file. Reasoner invocations, where the defined macros are available, can then be submitted as inputs on the Prolog console. The document can also be *processed*, which results in a generated L4TEX document: Macro definitions are pretty-printed in L4TEX, specified reasoner invocations are executed and a pretty-printed L4TEX result presentation is inserted, and L4TEX fragments are inserted directly. The generated L4TEX document can then be displayed in PDF format.

Aside of indentation, the L4TEX pretty-printer can apply certain symbol conversions to subscripted or primed symbols. Also a compact syntax where parentheses to separate arguments from functors and commas between arguments are omitted is available as an option for both Prolog and L4TEX forms.

PIE source documents can be re-loaded into the Prolog environment such that mechanized formalizations can be developed in a workflow similar to programming in AI languages like Prolog and Lisp.

First-order reasoners are often heavily dependent on configuration settings. A *PIE document* specifies all information needed to reproduce the results of reasoner invocations in a convenient way. Effective configuration parameters are combined from system defaults, defaults declared in the document and options supplied with particular specifications of reasoner invocations.

3   Second-Order Quantifier Elimination in *PIE*

Second-order quantifier elimination is the task of computing for a given formula with second-order quantifiers, that is, quantifiers upon predicate or function symbols, an equivalent first-order formula. *PIE* so far just supports second-order quantification upon predicate symbols, or *predicate quantification*. Here is an example of *PIE*'s L4TEX representation of the invocation of a reasoner that performs second-order quantifier elimination:

Input: $\exists p\,(\forall x\,(\mathsf{q}(x) \rightarrow p(x)) \wedge \forall x\,(p(x) \rightarrow \mathsf{r}(x)))$.
Result of elimination:
$$\forall x\,(\mathsf{q}(x) \rightarrow \mathsf{r}(x)).$$

The source code in the *PIE* document that effects this output is:

```
:- ppl_printtime(ppl_elim(ex2(p, (all(x, (q(x) -> p(x))),
                          all(x, (p(x) -> r(x))))))).
```

The directive `ppl_printtime` effects that its argument is evaluated at "print time", that is, at *processing*, when the L4TEX presentation is generated.[1] The argument is an invocation of the elimination reasoner with the predicate `ppl_elim`. It has a formula as argument, possibly with predicate quantifiers. If called at "print time" it prints inputs and outputs formatted in L4TEX, as shown above for the example. It can also be invoked in the context of plain Prolog processing, where it just effects that the output is pretty printed in Prolog syntax. The following interaction would, for example, be possible in the Prolog console:

---

[1] The prefix `ppl_` of this and related predicates should suggest *pretty-print in L4TEX format*.

```
?- ppl_elim(ex2(p, (all(x, (q(x) -> p(x))), all(x, (p(x) -> r(x))))))).
all(x, (q(x)->r(x)))
true.
```

Printing the output is performed there as a side effect. *SWI-Prolog* afterwards prints `true.` to indicate that the invocation of `ppl_elim` was successful. To access the output formula from a program, *PIE* provides two alternate means: With an option list `[printing=false, r=Result]` as second argument, `ppl_elim` does not effect that the elimination result is printed, but instead bound to the Prolog variable `Result` for further processing. The second way to access the result formula of the last reasoner invocation is with the supplied predicate `last_ppl_result(Result)`. This predicate may itself be used in macro definitions.

Let us take a brief look at the syntax of the argument formula of `ppl_elim` in the example. It represents a second-order formula as a Prolog ground term. Conjunction is represented as in Prolog by `,/2` and implication by `->/2`, with standard operator settings from Prolog. The universal first-order quantifier is expressed by `all/2` and the existential second-order quantifier by `ex2/2`.

PIE performs second-order quantifier elimination by an included Prolog implementation of the *DLS* algorithm [14], a method based on formula rewriting until second-order subformulas have a certain shape that allows elimination in one step by rewriting with Ackermann's lemma, an equivalence due to [1]. Implementing *DLS* brings about many subtle and interesting issues [10,23,54], for example, incorporation of non-deterministic alternative courses, dealing with un-Skolemization, simplification of formulas in non-clausal form and ensuring success of the method for certain input classes. The current implementation in *PIE* is far from optimum solutions of these issues, but can nevertheless be used in nontrivial applications and might contribute to improvements by making experiments possible.

Of course, second-order quantifier elimination on the basis of first-order logic does not succeed in general. Nevertheless, along with variants termed *forgetting*, *uniform interpolation* or *projection*, it has many applications, including deciding fragments of first-order logic [3,36], computation of frame correspondence properties from modal axioms [14,19,43], computation of circumscription [14], embedding nonmonotonic semantics in a classical setting [50,51], abduction with respect to classical and to nonmonotonic semantics [15,32,52], forgetting in knowledge bases [13,29,33,34,49], and approaches to modularization of knowledge bases derived from the notion of conservative extension [21,22,35]. Further applications of second-order quantifier elimination are described in the monograph [20].

For second-order quantifier elimination and similar operations there are several implementations based on modal and description logics, but very few on first-order logic: A Web service[2] invokes an implementation [17] of the *SCAN* algorithm [19]. *DLSForgetter* [2] is a recent system that implements the *DLS* algorithm [14]. An earlier implementation [23] of *DLS* seems to be no longer available.

---

[2] Available at http://www.mettel-prover.org/scan/.

4   Abduction with Second-Order Quantifier Elimination – Basic Use of *PIE* Macros

In the simplest case, a *PIE* formula macro serves as a formula label that may be used in subformula position in other formulas and is expanded into its definiens. Here is an example of such a *PIE* macro definition in the L^AT_EX presentation:

---

kb_1

Defined as

$$(\text{sprinkler\_was\_on} \rightarrow \text{wet(grass)}) \qquad \wedge$$
$$(\text{rained\_last\_night} \rightarrow \text{wet(grass)}) \qquad \wedge$$
$$(\text{wet(grass)} \rightarrow \text{wet(shoes)}).$$

The corresponding source is:

```
def(kb1) ::
(sprinkler_was_on -> wet(grass)),
(rained_last_night -> wet(grass)),
(wet(grass) -> wet(shoes)).
```

The source statement has the form def(*MacroName*) :: *ExpansionFormula*., where :: is an infix operator with lower precedence than the operators used as connectives for logical formulas. Formula kb_1 is now defined as a small knowledge base that expresses a variant of a scenario often used to illustrate abduction. Actually, we use it now to show how a certain form of computing abductive explanations can be considered as second-order quantifier elimination. It is based on the notion of *weakest sufficient condition* [15,32,51], which is basically a second-order formula that expresses the weakest formula in a given vocabulary that needs to be conjoined to given axioms to make a given theorem candidate an actual theorem. This second-order formula as such is not very informative as it contains the axioms and the theorem as constituents, with disallowed symbols bound by quantifiers and possibly renamed but still present. However, the result of applying elimination to that second-order formula provides the weakest sufficient condition in the proper sense, or, considered with respect to abduction, the weakest explanation.

PIE allows to specify macros with parameters that are represented by Prolog variables. We utilize this to specify schematically the weakest explanation (or weakest sufficient condition) of observation *Obs* on the complement of *Na* as assumables (*Na* should suggest *non-assumables*) within knowledge base *Kb*:

---

explanation(*Kb*, *Na*, *Obs*)

Defined as

$$\forall Na\,(Kb \rightarrow Obs).$$

The corresponding source code is:

```
def(explanation(Kb, Na, Ob)) ::
all2(Na, (Kb -> Ob)).
```

all2/2 represents the universal second-order quantifier in *PIE*'s input formula syntax. The first argument of all2 specifies the quantified predicates, either as a single Prolog atom or as list of atoms. In the example, there is the macro parameter *Na* that needs to be instantiated correspondingly when the macro is expanded. The expression *explanation*(kb_1, [wet], wet(shoes)) expands into the following "non-informative" version of the weakest sufficient condition:

$$\forall p \, ((\text{sprinkler\_was\_on} \rightarrow p(\text{grass})) \quad \wedge$$
$$(\text{rained\_last\_night} \rightarrow p(\text{grass})) \quad \wedge$$
$$(p(\text{grass}) \rightarrow p(\text{shoes})) \quad\quad\quad \rightarrow$$
$$p(\text{shoes})).$$

Second-order quantifier elimination applied to this formula yields the proper weakest explanation for the observation wet(shoes) in which the predicate wet itself does not occur, with respect to the background knowledge base kb_1:

Input: *explanation*(kb_1, [wet], wet(shoes)).
Result of elimination:

$$\text{rained\_last\_night} \vee \text{sprinkler\_was\_on}.$$

It was obtained by the following directive in the source document:

```
:- ppl_printtime(ppl_elim(explanation(kb1,[wet],wet(shoes)))).
```

In [52] this approach to abduction has been generalized to non-monotonic semantics of logic programming, including the three-valued partial stable models semantics.

5 Invoking Theorem Provers from *PIE*

The abductive explanation computed in the previous section can be validated with a theorem prover. The presentation of the prover invocation and the result is in *PIE* as follows:

This formula is valid: $kb_1 \wedge (\text{rained\_last\_night} \vee \text{sprinkler\_was\_on}) \rightarrow \text{wet(shoes)}$.

The corresponding source directive is

```
:- ppl_printtime(ppl_valid((kb1, (rained_last_night ; sprinkler_was_on)
                            -> wet(shoes)))).
```

The semicolon ;/2 represents disjunction, as in Prolog. The reasoner invocation predicate ppl_valid by default first calls the model searcher *Mace4* with a short timeout, and, if it can not find a "counter"-model of the negated formula, calls the prover *Prover9*, again with a short timeout.[3] Correspondingly, ppl_valid

---

[3] *Prover9* and *Mace4* were developed between 2005 and 2010 by William McCune. Their homepage is https://www.cs.unm.edu/~mccune/prover9/.

prints a representation of one of three result values: *valid, not valid* or *failed to validate* and in LATEX "print time" mode also the input formula, as shown above.

Like `ppl_elim`, also `ppl_valid` can be called with a list of options as second argument. This allows to obtain Prolog term representations of *Prover9*'s resolution proof or *Mace4*'s model, to skip the call to *Mace4*, modify the configuration of *Mace4* and *Prover9*, or to specify another theorem prover to be called.

Other provers can be incorporated through a generic interface to the *TPTP* [47] syntax for proving problems, supported by most current first-order provers. In addition, *DIMACS* and *QDIMACS*, the common formats of SAT and QBF solvers, respectively, are supported by *PIE*. Large propositional formulas are handled there efficiently with an internal representation implemented with destructive term operations. Most of the support of propositional formulas is inherited from the precursor system *ToyElim* [53].

PIE also includes a Prolog-based first-order prover, *CM,* whose calculus can be understood as model elimination, clausal tableau construction [31], or the connection method [6], similar to provers of the *leanCoP* family [26,27,40]. Its implementation follows the compilation-based *Prolog Technology Theorem Prover (PTTP)* paradigm [46]. It computes proofs that are represented by Prolog terms and can be used to compute Craig interpolants (Sect. 8). Details and evaluation results are available at http://cs.christophwernhard.com/pie/cmprover.

6   Computing Circumscription as Second-Order Quantifier Elimination – *PIE* Macros with Prolog Bodies, Result Simplifications

The circumscription of a predicate P in a formula F is a formula whose models are the models I of F that are minimal with respect to P. That is, there is no model I' of F that is like I except that the extension of P in I' is a strict subset of the extension of P in I. Predicate circumscription can be expressed by a second-order schema such that the *computation* of circumscription is second-order quantifier elimination [14]. The second-order circumscription of predicate P in formula F can thus be defined as a *PIE* macro as follows:

$circ(P, F)$

Defined as

$$F \wedge \neg \exists P' \, (F' \wedge T_1 \wedge \neg T_2),$$

where

$$F' := F[P \mapsto P'],$$
$$A := \text{arity of } P \text{ in } F,$$
$$T_1 := \text{transfer clauses } [P/A\text{-n}] \rightarrow [P'],$$
$$T_2 := \text{transfer clauses } [P'] \rightarrow [P/A\text{-n}].$$

This definition utilizes that *PIE* macro definitions may contain a Prolog body that permits expansions involving arbitrary computations. Utility predicates with pretty-printing templates for use in these bodies are provided for common tasks. The source of the above definition reads:

```
def(circ(P, F)) ::
F, ~ex2(P_p, (F_p, T1, ~T2)) ::-
    mac_rename_free_predicate(F, P, pn, F_p, P_p),
    mac_get_arity(P, F, A),
    mac_transfer_clauses([P/A-n], p, [P_p], T1),
    mac_transfer_clauses([P/A-n], n, [P_p], T2).
```

The Prolog body is introduced with the `::-` operator, which is defined with a precedence between `::` and the operators used to represent logical formulas. The unary operator `~` represents negation in formulas.[4] The suffix `_p` used for some variable names is translated to the prime superscript in the LaTeX, rendering. We only indicate here the effects of the auxiliary predicates in the Prolog body with an example: The formula $circ(\mathsf{p}, \mathsf{p}(\mathsf{a}))$ expands into:

$$\mathsf{p}(\mathsf{a}) \hspace{6cm} \wedge$$
$$\neg \exists q\,(q(\mathsf{a}) \wedge \forall x\,(q(x) \to \mathsf{p}(x)) \wedge \neg \forall x\,(\mathsf{p}(x) \to q(x))).$$

Second-order quantifier elimination can be applied to compute the circumscription for the example:

Input: $circ(\mathsf{p}, \mathsf{p}(\mathsf{a}))$.
Result of elimination:

$$\mathsf{p}(\mathsf{a}) \wedge \forall x\,(\mathsf{p}(x) \to x = \mathsf{a}).$$

As a more complex example, we consider circumscribing wet in kb_1:

Input: $circ(\mathsf{wet}, kb_1)$.
Result of elimination:

$$(\mathsf{rained\_last\_night} \to \mathsf{wet}(\mathsf{grass})) \hspace{3cm} \wedge$$
$$(\mathsf{sprinkler\_was\_on} \to \mathsf{wet}(\mathsf{grass})) \hspace{3cm} \wedge$$
$$(\mathsf{wet}(\mathsf{grass}) \to \mathsf{wet}(\mathsf{shoes})) \hspace{3cm} \wedge$$
$$\forall x\,(\mathsf{wet}(x) \to \mathsf{rained\_last\_night} \vee \mathsf{sprinkler\_was\_on}) \hspace{0.5cm} \wedge$$
$$\forall x\,(\mathsf{wet}(x) \wedge \mathsf{wet}(\mathsf{grass}) \to x = \mathsf{grass} \vee x = \mathsf{shoes}).$$

The first three implications of this output form the expansion of kb_1. The last two implications are added by the circumscription. This particular form was actually obtained by applying a certain simplification to the formula returned directly by the elimination method:

```
:- ppl_printtime(ppl_elim(circ(wet,kb1), [simp_result=[c6]])).
```

---

[4] The standard Prolog negation operator \+ is not suited to represent classical negation as it symbolizes $\not\vdash$, non-provability.

The option [simp_result=[c6]] supplied to ppl_elim effects that the elimination result is postprocessed by equivalence preserving conversions with the aim to make it more readable. The conversion named c6 chosen for this example converts to conjunctive normal form, applies various clausal simplifications and then converts back to a quantified first-order formula, involving un-Skolemization if required. That the last conjunct of the result can be replaced by the more succinct $\forall x\,(\mathsf{wet}(x) \rightarrow x = \mathsf{grass} \lor x = \mathsf{shoes})$ is, however, not detected by the current implementation.

Finding good presentations of formulas, in particular in presence of operations that yield formulas with essentially semantic characterizations, is a challenging topic in general.

7   Expressing Graph Colorability by a Second-Order Formula – *PIE* Macros with Parameters in Functor Position

One of the fundamental results of descriptive complexity is the equivalence of NP and expressibility by an existential second-order formula (with respect to finite models), that is, a first order formula prefixed with existential predicate quantifiers. This view allows, for example, to specify 2-colorability[5] with respect to a relation E that specifies a graph as follows:

$col_2(E)$

Defined as

$$\exists r \exists g\,(\forall x\,(r(x) \lor g(x)) \hspace{4cm} \land$$
$$\forall x \forall y\,(E(x,y) \rightarrow \neg(r(x) \land r(y)) \land \neg(g(x) \land g(y)))).$$

The source of this definition is:

```
def(col2(E)) ::
ex2([r,g],
    ( all(x, (r(x) ; g(x))),
      all([x,y], (E(x,y) -> (~((r(x), r(y))), ~((g(x), g(y)))))))).
```

The macro parameter E appears as a Prolog variable in predicate position.[6] The macro can then be used with instantiating E to a predicate symbol, or to a λ-expression that describes a particular graph (we will see examples in a moment).

Specifying algorithms as (existential) second-order formulas seems very elegant, but so far not established as a *practical* approach to logic programming. *PIE* in its current implementation lets become apparent related desiderata: Instantiation with a predicate symbol should be usable as basis for abstract rea-

---

[5] 3-colorability, which is NP-complete, can be specified analogously. We consider here 2-colorability for brevity of the involved formulas.

[6] *SWI-Prolog* can be configured to permit variable names as functors, which are read in as atoms with capitalized names. The macro processor of *PIE* compares them to actual variable names in the macro definition.

soning. Instantiation with a λ-expression (or conjoining a definition of a graph), should permit successful elimination. If adequate, the problem should then automatically be converted to a form that can be processed by a SAT solver.

So far, in the current implementation of *PIE*, such steps just work in part, e.g., by decomposing the overall task manually into intermediate steps with different manually controlled formula simplifications, as illustrated by the following example. The following macro defines the inner, first-order, component of the above specification of 2-colorability:

$fo\_col_2(E)$

Defined as

$$\forall x \, (r(x) \lor g(x)) \qquad\qquad\qquad \land$$
$$\forall x \forall y \, (E(x, y) \to \neg(r(x) \land r(y)) \land \neg(g(x) \land g(y))).$$

PIE allows to instantiate E in $fo\_col2(E)$ with a predicate constant e and eliminate one of the color predicates:[7]

Input: $\exists g \, fo\_col_2(\text{e})$.
Result of elimination:

$$\forall x \forall y \, (\text{e}(x, y) \to \neg(r(y) \land r(x)) \land (r(y) \lor r(x))).$$

2-colorability for a given graph represented by a λ-expression can be evaluated by *PIE* currently just in two steps with different elimination configurations, as performed by the following Prolog predicate:

```
elim_col2(E) :-
        ppl_elim(ex2([g], fo_col2(E)),
                [elim_options=[pre=[c6]], printing=false, r=F1]),
        ppl_elim(ex2([r], F1),
                [elim_options=[pre=[d6]], printing=false, r=F2]),
        ppl_form(E),
        ppl_form(F2).
```

Options `printing=false` suppress the emission of printed representations of the two invocations of the elimination reasoner. Only the input λ-expression and the final result are pretty-printed with calls to `ppl_form`. Options `pre=[c6]` and `pre=[d6]` effect that preprocessing based on conversion to CNF and DNF, respectively, is applied for elimination. Invoking

```
:- ppl_printtime(elim_col2(lambda([u,v],((u=1,v=2); (u=2,v=3))))).
```

yields the following output:

$$\lambda(u, v).(u = 1 \land v = 2) \lor (u = 2 \land v = 3).$$

$$1 \neq 2 \land 2 \neq 3.$$

---

[7] One color predicate can also be eliminated from an analogous specification of 3-colorability.

It expresses that the graph described by the λ-expression is 2-colorable if and only if node 1 is not the same as node 2 and node 2 is not the same as node 3.

8   Craig Interpolation

By Craig's interpolation theorem [11,12], for given first-order formulas F and G such that F entails G (or, equivalently, $F \to G$ is valid) a first-order formula H can be constructed such that F entails H, H entails G and H contains only symbols (predicates, functions, constants, free variables) that occur in both F and G. *PIE* supports the computation of Craig interpolants H, for given valid implications $F \to G$. Here is a propositional example:

Input: $\mathsf{p} \wedge \mathsf{q} \to \mathsf{p} \vee \mathsf{r}$.
Result of interpolation:

$$\mathsf{p}.$$

The corresponding directive in the source document is:

```
:- ppl_printtime(ppl_ipol((p, q -> (p ; r)))).
```

The predicate `ppl_ipol` invokes the interpolation reasoner. It takes an implication $F \to G$ as argument and, analogously to `ppl_elim` (Sect. 3), prints an interpolant of F and G.[8] Here is another example of Craig interpolation, where universal and existential quantification need to be combined:[9]

Input: $\forall x\, \mathsf{p}(\mathsf{a}, x) \wedge \mathsf{q} \to \exists x\, \mathsf{p}(x, \mathsf{b}) \vee \mathsf{r}$.
Result of interpolation:

$$\exists x\, \forall y\, \mathsf{p}(x, y).$$

Craig interpolation has many applications in logics and philosophy, as already shown in [12]. Main applications in computer science are in verification [39] and query reformulation, based on its relationship to definability and construction of definientia in terms of a given vocabulary [4,5,48]. For these applications, actually interpolants that are further constrained, in dependency of further restrictions on the input formulas, are relevant. We do not consider these here, but show how basic definability via Craig interpolation can be expressed in *PIE*.

A formula G is called *definable* in a formula F *in terms of* a set of predicates S if and only if there exists a formula H whose predicates are all in S such that $F \models G \leftrightarrow H$. The formula H is then called a *definiens* of G. Consider, for example, the following formula:

---

[8] In certain configurations it can also print several different interpolants.

[9] This is an example which involves an inference step with a constant that occurs only on the left side (a) and a constant that occurs only on the right side (b), which can not be handled by certain resolution-based interpolation systems. See [7,30]. In this particular example, the order of the quantifications in the result is not relevant.

---

kb_2

Defined as

$$\forall x\,(\mathsf{p}(x) \rightarrow \mathsf{q}(x) \wedge \mathsf{s}(x)) \qquad \wedge$$
$$\forall x\,(\mathsf{s}(x) \rightarrow \mathsf{r}(x)) \qquad \wedge$$
$$\forall x\,(\mathsf{q}(x) \wedge \mathsf{r}(x) \rightarrow \mathsf{p}(x)).$$

We can invoke a first-order prover from *PIE* to verify that the formula p(a) is definable in kb_2 in terms of $\{\mathsf{q}, \mathsf{r}\}$:

This formula is valid: $kb_2 \rightarrow (\mathsf{p}(\mathsf{a}) \leftrightarrow \mathsf{q}(\mathsf{a}) \wedge \mathsf{r}(\mathsf{a}))$.

Actually, since a does not occur in kb_2, we can equivalently verify the following implication, whose right side is a universally quantified first-order definition:

This formula is valid: $kb_2 \rightarrow \forall a\,(\mathsf{p}(a) \leftrightarrow \mathsf{q}(a) \wedge \mathsf{r}(a))$.

We can now utilize the features of *PIE* to formally characterize definability and synthesize definientia:

$definiens(G, F, P)$

Defined as

$$\exists P\,(F \wedge G) \rightarrow \forall P\,(F \rightarrow G).$$

The interpolants of the left and right side of $definiens(G, F, P)$ are exactly the definientia of G in F in terms of all predicates not in P. The implication is valid if and only if definability holds. The second-order quantifications in the implication are existential on the left and universal on the right side.[10] Considering that an implication can be understood as disjunction of the *negated* left side and the right side, if F and G are first-order, then $definiens(G, F, P)$ is a formula whose second-order quantifiers are all *universal*. Such a second-order formula is valid if and only if the first-order formula obtained by renaming the quantified predicates with fresh symbols and dropping the second-order quantifiers is valid. This translation is handled automatically by *PIE* such that we can now we verify definability of p(a) by invoking a first-order prover from *PIE*:

This formula is valid: $definiens(\mathsf{p}(\mathsf{a}), kb_2, [\mathsf{p}, \mathsf{s}])$.

And, we can apply Craig interpolation to compute a definiens:

Input: $definiens(\mathsf{p}(\mathsf{a}), kb_2, [\mathsf{p}, \mathsf{s}])$.
Result of interpolation:

$$\mathsf{q}(\mathsf{a}) \wedge \mathsf{r}(\mathsf{a}).$$

---

[10] We actually encountered right side of the implication before in Sect. 4 as the weakest sufficient condition in the macro definition of *explanation*.

The implementation of the computation of Craig interpolants in *PIE* operates by a novel adaption of Smullyan's interpolation method [18,45] to clausal tableaux [57]. Suitable clausal tableaux can be constructed by the Prolog-based prover *CM* that is included in *PIE*. The system also supports the conversion of proof terms returned by the hypertableau prover *Hyper* [41] to such tableaux and thus to interpolants, but this is currently at an experimental stage.[11]

The interpolants H constructed by *PIE* strengthen the requirements for Craig interpolants in that they are actually Craig-Lyndon interpolants, that is, predicates occur in H only in polarities in which they occur in both F and G. Symmetric interpolation [38, Sect. 5] is supported in *PIE*, implemented by computing a conventional interpolant for each of the input formulas, corresponding to the induction suggested with [12, Lemma 2].

It seems that most other implementations of Craig interpolation are on the basis of propositional logic with theory extensions and specialized for applications in verification [4]. Craig interpolation for first-order logic is supported by *Princess* [8,9] and by extensions of *Vampire* [24,25]. The incompleteness indicated in footnote 9 applies to these *Vampire* extensions and was observed by their authors. It also appears that the *Vampire* extensions do not preserve the polarity constraints of Craig-Lyndon interpolants [4].

9   Further Features of *PIE*

In this section we briefly describe further features of *PIE* that were not illustrated by the examples in the previous sections. First we consider the formula macro system. It utilizes Prolog variables to mimic further features of the processing of λ-expressions by automatically binding a Prolog variable that is free after computing the user-specified part of the expansion to a freshly generated symbol. With a macro declaration, properties of its lexical environment, in particular configuration settings that affect the expansion, are recorded. Macros with parameters are processed by pattern matching to choose the effective declaration for expansion, allowing structural recursion in macro declarations.

A Craig interpolant for formulas F and G is extracted in *PIE* from a Prolog term that represents a closed clausal tableau, a proof of the validity of $F \rightarrow G$. *PIE* supports the visualization of such tableaux as graph, rendered by the *Graphviz* tool. Here is an example:

Input: $\forall x \, \mathsf{p}(x) \wedge \forall x \, (\mathsf{p}(x) \rightarrow \mathsf{q}(x)) \rightarrow \mathsf{q}(\mathsf{c}).$
Result of interpolation:

$$\forall x \, \mathsf{q}(x).$$

The respective directive for this interpolation task in the source is:

---

[11] Hypertableaux, either obtained from a hypertableau prover or obtained from a clausal tableau prover like *CM* by restructuring the tableau seem interesting as basis for interpolant extraction in query reformulation, as they allow to ensure that the interpolants are range restricted. Some related preliminary results are in [57].

```
:- ppl_printtime(ppl_ipol((all(x, p(x)), all(x, (p(x) -> q(x))) -> q(c)),
                 [ip_dotgraph=printstyle('/tmp/tmp01.png'),
                  ip_simp_sides=false])).
```

The `ip_dotgraph` option effects that an image representing the tableau is generated. The `ip_simp_sides` option suppresses preprocessing of the interpolation input, which, in the example, would in essence be already sufficient to compute the interpolant, yielding a trivial tableau. The generated image can then be included into the *PIE* document with standard LATEX means, here, for example as Fig. 1. Siblings in the tableau represent a ground clause used in the proof. As the tableau is used for interpolant extraction, decoration indicates whether the clause stems from the left or the right side of the input formula. The decoration of the closing marks indicate the side of the connection partner. The Skolem constant `sk1` is converted to a quantified variable in a postprocessing operation. For a description of the interpolant extraction procedure, see [57].

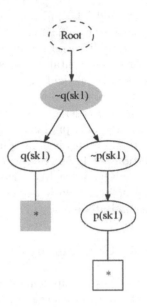

Fig. 1. A clausal tableau.

Aside of the shown representation of quantified first-order formulas by Prolog ground terms, the system also supports a representation of clausal formulas as list of lists of terms (logic literals), with variables represented by Prolog variables. The system functionality can be accessed by Prolog predicates, also without using the document processing facilities.

Practically successful reasoners usually apply in some way conversions of low complexity as far as possible: as preprocessing on inputs, potentially during reasoning, which has been termed *inprocessing*, and to improve the syntactic shape of output formulas as discussed in Sect. 6. Abstracting from these situations, we subsume these conversions under *preprocessing operations*. Also the low complexity might be taken more or less literally and, for example, be achieved simply by trying an operation within a threshold limit of resources. *PIE* includes a number of preprocessing operations including normal form conversions, also in variants that produce structure preserving normalizations, various simplifications of clausal formulas, and an implementation of McCune's un-Skolemization algorithm [37]. While some of these preserve equivalence, others preserve equivalence just with respect to a set of predicates, for example, purity simplification with respect to predicates that are not deleted or structure preserving classification with respect to predicates that are not added. This can be understood as preserving the second-order equivalence

$$\exists q_1 \ldots \exists q_n \, F \;\equiv\; \exists q_1 \ldots \exists q_n \, G,$$

where F and G are inputs and outputs of the conversion and $q_1, \ldots, q_n$ are those predicates that are permitted to occur in F or G whose semantics needs *not* to be preserved. If $q_1, \ldots, q_n$ includes all permitted predicates, the above equivalence expresses equi-satisfiability. Some of the simplifications implemented in *PIE* allow to specify explicitly a set of predicates whose semantics is to be preserved, which makes them applicable for Craig interpolation and second-order quantifier elimination.

In addition to the implementation of the *DLS* algorithm, *PIE* includes further experimental implementations of variants of second-order quantifier elimination. In particular, a variant of the method shown in [33] for elimination with respect to ground atoms, which always succeeds on the basis of first-order logic. A second-order quantifier is there, so-to-speak, just upon a particular ground instance of a predicate. The *Boolean solution problem* or *Boolean unification with predicates* is a computational task related to second-order quantifier elimination [42,44,56]. So far, *PIE* includes experimental implementations for special cases: Quantifier-free formulas with a technique from [16] and a version for finding solutions with respect to ground atoms, in analogy to the elimination of ground atoms.

10   Conclusion

PIE tries to supplement what is needed to use automated first-order proving techniques for developing and analyzing formalizations. Its main focus is not on proofs but on *formulas*, as constituents of complex formalizations that are composed and structured through macros, and as computed outputs of second-order quantifier elimination, Craig interpolation and formula conversions that preserve semantics with respect to given predicates. All of these operations utilize some natural relationships between first- and second-order logic.

The system mediates between high-level logical presentation and detailed configuration of reasoning systems: Working practically with first-order provers typically involves experimenting with a large and developing set of related proving problems, for example with alternate axiomatizations or different candidate theorems, and is thus often accompanied with some meta-level technique to compose and relate the actual proof tasks submitted to first-order reasoners. With the macro system, the supported document-oriented workflow, LATEX pretty-printing, and integration into the Prolog environment, *PIE* offers to organize this in a systematic way through mechanisms that remain in the spirit of first-order logic, which in mathematics is actually often used with schemas.

Aside of the current suitability for non-trivial applications, *PIE* shows up a number of challenging and interesting open issues for research, for example improving practical realizations of second-order quantifier elimination, strengthenings of Craig interpolation that ensure application-relevant properties such as range restriction, and conversion of computed formulas that are basically just semantically characterized to comprehensible presentations. Progress in these issues can be directly experienced and verified with the system.

References

1. Ackermann, W.: Untersuchungen über das Eliminationsproblem der mathematischen Logik. Math. Ann. **110**, 390–413 (1935)
2. Alassaf, R., Schmidt, R.: DLS-Forgetter: an implementation of the DLS forgetting calculus for first-order logic. In: GCAI 2019. EPiC, vol. 65, pp. 127–138 (2019)
3. Behmann, H.: Beiträge zur Algebra der Logik, insbesondere zum Entscheidungsproblem. Math. Ann. **86**(3–4), 163–229 (1922)
4. Benedikt, M., Kostylev, E.V., Mogavero, F., Tsamoura, E.: Reformulating queries: theory and practice. In: IJCAI 2017, pp. 837–843. ijcai.org (2017)
5. Benedikt, M., Leblay, J., ten Cate, B., Tsamoura, E.: Generating Plans from Proofs: The Interpolation-Based Approach to Query Reformulation. Morgan & Claypool, San Rafael (2016)
6. Bibel, W.: Matings in matrices. Commun. ACM **26**(11), 844–852 (1983)
7. Bonacina, M.P., Johansson, M.: On interpolation in automated theorem proving. J. Autom. Reason. **54**(1), 69–97 (2015)
8. Brillout, A., Kroening, D., Rümmer, P., Wahl, T.: Beyond quantifier-free interpolation in extensions of Presburger arithmetic. In: Jhala, R., Schmidt, D. (eds.) VMCAI 2011. LNCS, vol. 6538, pp. 88–102. Springer, Heidelberg (2011). https://doi.org/10.1007/978-3-642-18275-4_8
9. Brillout, A., Kroening, D., Rümmer, P., Wahl, T.: An interpolating sequent calculus for quantifier-free Presburger arithmetic. J. Autom. Reason. **47**(4), 341–367 (2011)
10. Conradie, W.: On the strength and scope of DLS. J. Appl. Non-Classsical Logics **16**(3–4), 279–296 (2006)
11. Craig, W.: Linear reasoning. A new form of the Herbrand-Gentzen theorem. J. Symbolic Logic **22**(3), 250–268 (1957)
12. Craig, W.: Three uses of the Herbrand-Gentzen theorem in relating model theory and proof theory. J. Symbolic Logic **22**(3), 269–285 (1957)
13. Delgrande, J.P.: A knowledge level account of forgetting. J. Artif. Intell. Res. **60**, 1165–1213 (2017)
14. Doherty, P., Łukaszewicz, W., Szałas, A.: Computing circumscription revisited: a reduction algorithm. J. Autom. Reason. **18**(3), 297–338 (1997)
15. Doherty, P., Łukaszewicz, W., Szałas, A.: Computing strongest necessary and weakest sufficient conditions of first-order formulas. In: IJCAI-01, pp. 145–151. Morgan Kaufmann (2001)
16. Eberhard, S., Hetzl, S., Weller, D.: Boolean unification with predicates. J. Logic Comput. **27**(1), 109–128 (2017)
17. Engel, T.: Quantifier elimination in second-order predicate logic. Master's thesis, Max-Planck-Institut für Informatik, Saarbrücken (1996)
18. Fitting, M.: First-Order Logic and Automated Theorem Proving, 2nd edn. Springer, Heidelberg (1995). https://doi.org/10.1007/978-1-4612-2360-3
19. Gabbay, D., Ohlbach, H.J.: Quantifier elimination in second-order predicate logic. In: KR 1992, pp. 425–435. Morgan Kaufmann (1992)
20. Gabbay, D.M., Schmidt, R.A., Szałas, A.: Second-Order Quantifier Elimination: Foundations, Computational Aspects and Applications. College Publications (2008)
21. Ghilardi, S., Lutz, C., Wolter, F.: Did I damage my ontology? A case for conservative extensions in description logics. In: KR 2006, pp. 187–197. AAAI Press (2006)

22. Grau, B.C., Horrocks, I., Kazakov, Y., Sattler, U.: Modular reuse of ontologies: theory and practice. J. Artif. Intell. Res. **31**(1), 273–318 (2008)
23. Gustafsson, J.: An implementation and optimization of an algorithm for reducing formulae in second-order logic. Technical report LiTH-MAT-R-96-04, Univ. Linköping (1996)
24. Hoder, K., Holzer, A., Kovács, L., Voronkov, A.: Vinter: a Vampire-based tool for interpolation. In: Jhala, R., Igarashi, A. (eds.) APLAS 2012. LNCS, vol. 7705, pp. 148–156. Springer, Heidelberg (2012). https://doi.org/10.1007/978-3-642-35182-2_11
25. Hoder, K., Kovács, L., Voronkov, A.: Interpolation and symbol elimination in Vampire. In: Giesl, J., Hähnle, R. (eds.) IJCAR 2010. LNCS (LNAI), vol. 6173, pp. 188–195. Springer, Heidelberg (2010). https://doi.org/10.1007/978-3-642-14203-1_16
26. Kaliszyk, C.: Efficient low-level connection tableaux. In: De Nivelle, H. (ed.) TABLEAUX 2015. LNCS (LNAI), vol. 9323, pp. 102–111. Springer, Cham (2015). https://doi.org/10.1007/978-3-319-24312-2_8
27. Kaliszyk, C., Urban, J.: FEMaLeCoP: fairly efficient machine learning connection prover. In: Davis, M., Fehnker, A., McIver, A., Voronkov, A. (eds.) LPAR 2015. LNCS, vol. 9450, pp. 88–96. Springer, Heidelberg (2015). https://doi.org/10.1007/978-3-662-48899-7_7
28. Knuth, D.E.: Literate programming. Comput. J. **27**(2), 97–111 (1984)
29. Koopmann, P., Schmidt, R.A.: Uniform interpolation of $\mathcal{ALC}$-ontologies using fixpoints. In: Fontaine, P., Ringeissen, C., Schmidt, R.A. (eds.) FroCoS 2013. LNCS (LNAI), vol. 8152, pp. 87–102. Springer, Heidelberg (2013). https://doi.org/10.1007/978-3-642-40885-4_7
30. Kovács, L., Voronkov, A.: First-order interpolation and interpolating proof systems. In: LPAR-21, pp. 49–64. EasyChair (2017)
31. Letz, R.: First-order tableau methods. In: D'Agostino, M., Gabbay, D.M., Hähnle, R., Posegga, J. (eds.) Handbook of Tableau Methods, pp. 125–196. Kluwer Academic Publishers (1999)
32. Lin, F.: On strongest necessary and weakest sufficient conditions. Artif. Intell. **128**, 143–159 (2001)
33. Lin, F., Reiter, R.: Forget It! In: Working Notes, AAAI Fall Symposium on Relevance, pp. 154–159 (1994)
34. Ludwig, M., Konev, B.: Practical uniform interpolation and forgetting for $\mathcal{ALC}$ TBoxes with applications to logical difference. In: KR 2014. AAAI Press (2014)
35. Lutz, C., Wolter, F.: Foundations for uniform interpolation and forgetting in expressive description logics. In: IJCAI 2011, pp. 989–995. AAAI Press (2011)
36. Löwenheim, L.: Über Möglichkeiten im Relativkalkül. Math. Ann. **76**, 447–470 (1915)
37. McCune, W.: Un-Skolemizing clause sets. Inf. Process. Lett. **29**(5), 257–263 (1988)
38. McMillan, K.L.: Applications of Craig interpolants in model checking. In: Halbwachs, N., Zuck, L.D. (eds.) TACAS 2005, pp. 1–12. Springer, Heidelberg (2005). https://doi.org/10.1007/978-3-540-31980-1_1
39. McMillan, K.L.: Interpolation and model checking. In: Clarke, E.M., Henzinger, T.A., Veith, H., Bloem, R. (eds.) Handbook of Model Checking, pp. 421–446. Springer, Heidelberg (2018). https://doi.org/10.1007/978-3-319-10575-8_14
40. Otten, J.: Restricting backtracking in connection calculi. AI Commun. **23**(2–3), 159–182 (2010)

41. Pelzer, B., Wernhard, C.: System description: E-KRHyper. In: Pfenning, F. (ed.) CADE 2007. LNCS (LNAI), vol. 4603, pp. 508–513. Springer, Heidelberg (2007). https://doi.org/10.1007/978-3-540-73595-3_37
42. Rudeanu, S.: Boolean Functions and Equations. Elsevier (1974)
43. Schmidt, R.A.: The Ackermann approach for modal logic, correspondence theory and second-order reduction. J. Appl. Logic 10(1), 52–74 (2012)
44. Schröder, E.: Vorlesungen über die Algebra der Logik. Teubner (1890–1905)
45. Smullyan, R.M.: First-Order Logic. Dover Publications, New York (1995). Corrected republication of the original edition by Springer-Verlag, New York (1968)
46. Stickel, M.E.: A Prolog technology theorem prover: implementation by an extended Prolog compiler. J. Autom. Reason. 4(4), 353–380 (1988)
47. Sutcliffe, G.: The TPTP problem library and associated infrastructure. From CNF to TH0, TPTP v6.4.0. J. Autom. Reason. 59(4), 483–502 (2017)
48. Toman, D., Weddell, G.: Fundamentals of Physical Design and Query Compilation. Morgan and Claypool, San Rafael (2011)
49. Wernhard, C.: Semantic knowledge partitioning. In: Alferes, J.J., Leite, J. (eds.) JELIA 2004. LNCS (LNAI), vol. 3229, pp. 552–564. Springer, Heidelberg (2004). https://doi.org/10.1007/978-3-540-30227-8_46
50. Wernhard, C.: Circumscription and projection as primitives of logic programming. In: Technical Communications ICLP 2010. LIPIcs, vol. 7, pp. 202–211. Schloss Dagstuhl-Leibniz-Zentrum für Informatik (2010)
51. Wernhard, C.: Projection and scope-determined circumscription. J. Symbolic Comput. 47, 1089–1108 (2012)
52. Wernhard, C.: Abduction in logic programming as second-order quantifier elimination. In: Fontaine, P., Ringeissen, C., Schmidt, R.A. (eds.) FroCoS 2013. LNCS (LNAI), vol. 8152, pp. 103–119. Springer, Heidelberg (2013). https://doi.org/10.1007/978-3-642-40885-4_8
53. Wernhard, C.: Computing with logic as operator elimination: the ToyElim system. In: Tompits, H., et al. (eds.) INAP/WLP -2011. LNCS (LNAI), vol. 7773, pp. 289–296. Springer, Heidelberg (2013). https://doi.org/10.1007/978-3-642-41524-1_17
54. Wernhard, C.: Second-order quantifier elimination on relational monadic formulas – a basic method and some less expected applications. In: De Nivelle, H. (ed.) TABLEAUX 2015. LNCS (LNAI), vol. 9323, pp. 253–269. Springer, Cham (2015). https://doi.org/10.1007/978-3-319-24312-2_18
55. Wernhard, C.: The PIE system for proving, interpolating and eliminating. In: PAAR 2016, pp. 125–138. CEUR-WS.org (2016)
56. Wernhard, C.: The Boolean solution problem from the perspective of predicate logic. In: Dixon, C., Finger, M. (eds.) FroCoS 2017. LNCS (LNAI), vol. 10483, pp. 333–350. Springer, Cham (2017). https://doi.org/10.1007/978-3-319-66167-4_19
57. Wernhard, C.: Craig interpolation and access interpolation with clausal first-order tableaux. ArXiv e-prints (2018). https://arxiv.org/abs/1802.04982
58. Wielemaker, J., Schrijvers, T., Triska, M., Lager, T.: SWI-Prolog. Theory Practice Logic Program. 12(1–2), 67–96 (2012)

KBSET – Knowledge-Based Support for Scholarly Editing and Text Processing with Declarative LaTeX Markup and a Core Written in *SWI-Prolog*

Jana Kittelmann[1] and Christoph Wernhard[2(✉)]

[1] Martin-Luther-Universität Halle-Wittenberg, Halle (Saale), Germany
[2] Berlin, Germany

Abstract. *KBSET* is an environment that provides support for scholarly editing in two flavors: First, as a practical tool *KBSET/Letters* that accompanies the development of editions of correspondences (in particular from the 18th and 19th century), completely from source documents to PDF and HTML presentations. Second, as a prototypical tool *KBSET/NER* for experimentally investigating novel forms of working on editions that are centered around automated named entity recognition. *KBSET* can process declarative application-specific markup that is expressed in LaTeX notation and incorporate large external fact bases that are typically provided in RDF. *KBSET* includes specially developed LaTeX styles and a core system that is written in *SWI-Prolog*, which is used there in many roles, utilizing that it realizes the potential of Prolog as a unifying language.

1 Introduction

In the age of Digital Humanities, scholarly editing [11,12] involves the combination of natural language text with machine processable semantic knowledge, typically expressed as markup. The best developed machine support for scholarly editing is the XML-based TEI format [14], a comprehensive markup language for all sorts of text, mainly targeted at rendering for different media and extraction of metadata, which is achieved through semantics-oriented or declarative markup. Recent efforts stretch TEIby aspects that are orthogonal to its original *ordered hierarchy of content objects (OHCO)* text model, through support for entities like *names, dates, people, and places* as well as structuring with *linking, segmentation, and alignment* [14, Chap. 13 and 16]. Also ways to combine TEIwith Semantic Web techniques, data modeling and ontologies are investigated [3]. In accord with these directions we observe a number of apparently open desiderata for the support of scholarly editing in today's practice and in future perspective, which we explicitly address with our environment *KBSET* (**K**nowledge-**B**ased **S**upport for Scholarly **E**diting and **T**ext Processing):

© Springer Nature Switzerland AG 2020
P. Hofstedt et al. (Eds.): DECLARE 2019, LNAI 12057, pp. 178–196, 2020.
https://doi.org/10.1007/978-3-030-46714-2_12

1. It should be possible for users from the application domain to *create, review, validate and maintain source documents* of the edition project. That is, documents with annotated text, with metadata, and with data on relevant entities such as persons and locations. Text markup should be exposed to the users as far as it is relevant and interesting for the application field. Source documents must be stored and versioned. Since source texts with XML markup are hardly readable, in the TEI/XML approach typically an additional user-interface layer is added to the workflow, where apparently only a single – non-free – software system is suitable.[1] On the other hand, outside the Humanities, with LaTeX the direct use of text with markup is widespread, well supported by many free tools and supplemented by numerous free packages of high quality.[2]

2. It should be possible to generate *high-quality* print and hypertext presentations in a *reproducible* way, based on published source documents created in the edition project as well as additional documents and programs that are freely available and can be precisely identified.

3. Not just "final" presentations should be well-supported but also *internal tools* for developing the scholarly edition and *intermediate presentations* used there should be of high quality. This is in particular relevant as many edition projects take several years.

4. It should be possible to couple object text with associated information in ways that are *more flexible than in-place markup*: It may be convenient to maintain text annotations separately from the commented text sources. Markup can be by different authors, automatically generated, or for some specific purpose. Some queries and transformations should remain applicable also after changes of the markup.

5. It should be possible to incorporate advanced semantics related techniques that inherently deliver result that are *fuzzy, imprecise,* or *incomplete.* For example, named entity recognition or tools for statistics-based text analysis.

6. *Linking with external knowledge bases* should be supported. These include results of other edition projects as well as large fact bases such as authority files like *Gemeinsame Normdatei (GND)*,[3] metadata repositories like *Kalliope*,[4] domain specific bases like *GeoNames*, or aggregated bases like *YAGO* [5] and *DBpedia* [9].

---

[1] The *Oxygen XML Editor*. See also https://en.wikipedia.org/wiki/Comparison_of_XML_editors, accessed Nov 19 2019.

[2] In fact, [14, Sect. iv] notes that *"the TEI encoding scheme itself does not depend on this language [XML]; it was originally formulated in terms of SGML (the ISO Standard Generalized Markup Language), a predecessor of XML, and may in future years be re-expressed in other ways as the field of markup develops and matures".*

[3] http://www.dnb.de/gnd. The *GND* is maintained by the German-speaking library community and contains information about various entities, in particular about more than 11 million persons in more that 160 million fact triples. It is in the public domain (CC0) and can be downloaded as an RDF/XML document whose decompressed size is more than 18 GB.

[4] http://kalliope-verbund.info.

7. A digital edition project involves, more or less explicitly, the creation of data, in other words, the assertion of facts about relevant entities like persons, locations, dates, events and units of text such as, for example, letters as components of a correspondence, or distinguished positions in texts. Such data can be project-specific or obtained through combination with external fact bases. As a result of an edition project, such *data should be made explicit and accessible* in a way that facilitates to associate with them *machine processable semantics*, that is, meanings based on some logic that is supported by tools from automated reasoning and knowledge processing. Ontology reasoning in description logics is important here, but, by itself, not sufficient, as classification seems not a main operation of interest in the field. The *GND* fact base on persons, institutions and works, for example, gets by with a quite small ontology of 64 classes.

KBSET approaches these desiderata successfully through the involvement of two technologies: LATEX and Prolog. More specifically, we defined a dedicated small set of descriptive markup elements that is tailored to the application domain, in our case the scholarly edition of correspondences of the 18th and 19th century, in the form of LATEX commands and environments, and use *SWI-Prolog* [17] as a *single environment and language* to implement all tasks that involve parsing and composition of documents and fact bases in various formats, querying with respect to documents and fact bases, and evaluation of complex application constraints.

The current version of *KBSET* supports two flavors of application: The first, *KBSET/Letters*, is a practical environment for scholarly editions of correspondences. Implemented support covers in particular editions of correspondences from the 18th and 19th century in German language. The second, *KBSET/NER*, is a prototype system that allows to experiment with various advanced features centered around named entity recognition. *KBSET/Letters* is currently applied in a large project, the edition of the correspondence of philosopher and polymath Johann Georg Sulzer (1720–1779) with author, critic and poet Johann Jakob Bodmer (1698–1783), which will be published in print as [13, Vol. 10] in summer 2020. Including annotations and indexes, it spans about 2000 printed pages. The online HTML edition, also generated with *KBSET/Letters* from the same sources, will be published in parallel. In addition, *KBSET* is applied in a long-term project, *www.sulzer-digital.de*, a digital representation of Sulzer's complete correspondence, edited successively with *KBSET*. To illustrate the use of *KBSET/Letters*, the distribution of *KBSET* includes the edition of a small correspondence. For *KBSET/NER* it includes as an example a draft edition of a 19th century book. *KBSET* is available as free software from its home page

http://cs.christophwernhard.com/kbset.

The 2016 version of *KBSET/NER* was presented at DHd 2016 [7]. The Sulzer-Bodmer edition project and its use of *KBSET/Letters*, as well as related further interdisciplinary research topics, are described (in German) in [8]. Some components of *KBSET/Letters* were derived from an earlier collaboration of the authors, *www.pueckler-digital.de* [6].

The rest of the paper is structured as follows: In Sect. 2 we describe *KBSET/ Letters*, the environment for preparing scholarly editions of correspondences in practice, and in Sect. 3 the more experimentally oriented *KBSET/NER* flavor of *KBSET* centered around named entity recognition. We conclude the interdisciplinary paper in Sect. 4 with discussions of the *KBSET* environment from three different perspectives: Tools for scholarly editing, the role of *SWI-Prolog* as a unifying practical technology, and some encountered issues that might be of interest for future research on logic-based knowledge processing.

2   *KBSET/Letters*

The *KBSET/Letters* environment is at its current state of development adequate for scholarly editions of correspondences from the 18th and 19th century that are in German language and where the edited texts are represented in a character-preserving (*zeichengetreu*) but not position-preserving (*positionsgetreu*) way.

2.1   Descriptive Application-Specific Markup in LATEX Notation

Figure 1 shows an overview on *KBSET*: Inputs, functionalities of the core system that is implemented in *SWI-Prolog*, and outputs. For creating a scholarly edition of a correspondence, the inputs are documents with domain specific markup expressed as LATEX commands and environments, representing object texts of the edition project, that is, letters, and annotations by the editors that refer to the object texts, respectively (box I1 and I2 in Fig. 1). The parsimonious set of declarative markup elements *KBSET/Letters Markup*[5] is tailored to the requirements of such scholarly editions. Through the specialization, creating the markup is perceived by users as expressing statements of interest rather than a technical burden. Through the LATEX notation, the marked-up text remains fairly readable and can be directly created by users with any text editor that supports LATEX, such as, for example, *GNU Emacs*, which is free software and shown as representative tool in the figure.

Letters and annotations are represented by LATEX environments. Here is an example of a letter environment:

```
\begin{letter}{bs:1745-02-14}{bodmer}{sulzer}{zuerich}{14. Februar 1745}
...
Der Hr.~\xperson{lange}{Pastor Lange von Laublingen}, hat mir, noch
 \xl{brief:lange}{ehe er den Brief von E~Hochedl. empfangen}, berichtet,
...
\end{letter}
```

---

[5] A specification draft is available from the KBSET home page.

Inputs

I1: Object Text Documents
Format: LaTeX with domain-specific descriptive markup

Tool: GNU Emacs

I2: Annotation Documents
Annotations that are maintained externally from object text

Format, Tool: Same as for object text documents

I3: Application Fact Bases
About, e.g., persons, works, locations; bibliography

Formats: Prolog, LaTeX markup, BibLaTeX

Tools: GNU Emacs, JabRef

I4: Assistance Documents
To configure and adjust *KBSET*

Format: *KBSET*-specific, Prolog-readable

Tool: GNU Emacs

I5: Large Imported Fact Bases
E.g., *GND*, *GeoNames*, *Yago*, *DBPedia*

Formats: E.g., RDF/XML, CSV

Core system

C1: Text Combination
- Reordering object text fragments, e.g., letters by different writers in chronological order
- Merging with external annotations
- Merging with automatically generated annotations

C2: Consistency Checking
E.g., for void entity identifiers, insufficient or implausible date specifications, duplicate entries in fact bases

C4: Register Generation
- Indexes for print presentations
- Overview and navigation documents for Web presentation

C3: Named Entity Identification
Persons, locations, dates

Outputs

O1: Display of Identified Entities
Tool: GNU Emacs

O2: Fact Bases
Formats: E.g., RDF/XML, Prolog

O3: Print-Oriented Presentation
Formats: LaTeX, PDF

O4: Web-Oriented Presentation
Format: HTML

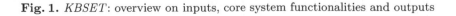

Fig. 1. *KBSET*: overview on inputs, core system functionalities and outputs

Identifier bs:1745-02-14 is declared to denote the represented letter. Arguments of the \begin{letter} statement provide essential meta data: Identifiers of writer, addressee and location, as well as the date in a human readable but parsable form. The tilde for non-breaking space is transferred from LATEX to the *KBSET/Letters* markup. The phrase *Pastor Lange von Laublingen* is marked-up as denoting the person with identifier lange. Identifiers used here can be mnemonic as they are local to the project. The identifier brief:lange is declared to denote the marked-up occurrence of the phrase *ehe er den Brief von E Hochedl. empfangen* in the letter. Its scope is the letter environment. The following example shows an annotation environment:

```
\begin{annotation}{bs:1745-02-14}
  ...
  \ksection{Stellenkommentar}
  \begin{klist}
  \kitem{brief:lange} Der Brief Bodmers an Samuel Gotthold Lange ...
  ...
  \end{klist}
\end{annotation}
```

The annotation block is about the example letter above, associated through the argument bs:1745-02-14 of the \begin{annotation} statement. In the annotation environment the identifiers like brief:lange that were locally declared in the letter environment are re-activated for referencing. This permits a convenient way to express annotations that refer to specific places in the text of letters (*Stellenkommentare*).

Also fact bases can be written with special markup commands in LATEX notation. For example, the referenced person lange can be declared with the following statement:

```
\defperson{lange}{Lange, Samuel Gotthold (1711--1781)}
```

Person names in these declarations must be compatible with the regularities used by the *GND*.[6] They can be directly used in indexes and, with years of birth and death, allow to automatically determine the global *GND* identifiers of persons represented in the *GND*. These global identifiers make metadata maintained, for example, in the *GND* and *Wikipedia* available, relieving the edition project from the need to replicate them explicitly.

So far, the user perceives the project as a collection of documents with letters, annotations and fact bases in the specialized descriptive LATEX markup. Indeed, *KBSET* provides an implementation of the specialized markup in form of a LATEX package that is sufficient to generate a PDF representation of the letters and annotations with fairly high quality just by a pure LATEX workflow. In the result, letters and associated annotations are connected through PDF hyperlinks. References like \xperson{lange}{...} to identifiers declared in a

---

[6] We do not demand in full the principles of the *GND* for choosing *preferred* names, as *"Colombo, Cristoforo"* or *"Homerus"* is unusual in German texts.

fact base are converted to index entries processed by *xindy*. The bibliography is handled by *BibLaTeX*. The involved LaTeX processors already ensure validity and consistency of the documents to some degree.

2.2 From LaTeX to Prolog for Further Consistency Checking and Text Combination

The *KBSET* core system includes a LaTeX parser written in Prolog that yields a list of items, terms whose argument is a sequence of characters represented as atom, and whose functor indicates a type such as *word, punctuation, comment, command,* or *begin* and *end of an environment*. A special type *opaque* is used to represent text fragments that are not further parsed, such as LaTeX preambles. LaTeX commands and environments can be made known to the parser to effect proper handling of their arguments. The parser aims to be practically useful, without claiming completeness for LaTeX in full. It does not permit, for example, a single-letter command argument without enclosing braces. The parser is supplemented by conversions of parsing results to LaTeX and to plain text.

So far, additional syntactic checks at parsing and various semantics-oriented checks that are applied after the parsed documents are converted to Prolog fact bases are implemented (box C2 in Fig. 1). Further ways of consistency checking can be realized with respect to the generated HTML documents discussed below in Sect. 2.3.

Source documents with letters and with annotations are maintained in a large edition project not necessarily in the same ordering and fragmentation in which these should appear in presentations. Based on the parsed LaTeX, the *KBSET* core system can perform such rearrangements (box C1 in Fig. 1) and write out generated LaTeX documents. The conventional LaTeX workflow applied to these generated documents then results in high-quality PDF documents, which, depending on the configuration, are suitable for publication in print or on-screen reading.[7] Figure 2 shows example output pages.

The functionalities for consistency checking and text combination are available as Prolog predicates in a user interface module, and, for users that do not want to interact with Prolog directly, with *Bash* shell scripts that invoke *SWI-Prolog*.[8]

2.3 HTML Presentation

The parsed source documents are converted to representations as Prolog predicates, which form the basis for generating an HTML representation of the scholarly edition. In general, our Web presentation is designed to open-up the edition, to make it easy to get an overview on the material and on the supported navigation possibilities.

---

[7] Before printing in high quality, LaTeX documents in general need manual adjustments in places that can not be handled satisfactorily by the automated layout processor.

[8] In Microsoft Windows, these scripts can be called from the *Cygwin* shell.

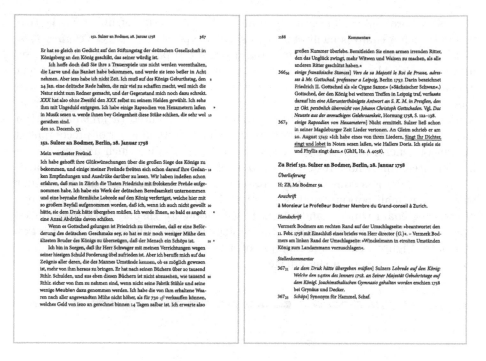

Fig. 2. *KBSET/Letters*: PDF presentation, a letter and an annotation page.

On the basis of the identifiers in the LATEX-syntax source documents, URIs for documents like letters and entities like persons and locations are generated.[9] These can be used as URLs of the respective generated pages, which then can persistently represent the respective document or entity with respect to the edition. An HTML presentation of the project bibliography is generated from the *BibLaTeX* sources via an invocation of the *Biber* processor with options such that it produces an XML representation of the processed bibliography that is then read into *SWI-Prolog*.

The Web presentation just uses static pages, in HTML5, with CSS3 and – very little – JavaScript. This makes the loading of pages fast, requires no maintenance efforts, and facilitates the interaction with search engines, general Web search engines as well as dedicated engines for the online publication.

Some simple but useful means for navigation were realized: Letter pages have links to a chronologically next and previous letter, with respect to the writer and also with respect to the correspondence with the addressee. These four links are always displayed at the same position in the page and thus allow to quickly move within the letters by an author or in a correspondence.

Another realized useful navigation means is what we call *chains* (*Ketten*), or, more explicitly, *result value chains*: The value of a query is often a "chain",

---

[9] This requires a syntactic conversion as "`:`" has a special meaning in URIs.

that is, an ordered set of entities, represented as a series of links. Navigating through such a chain is facilitated by a special type of Web pages, *chain pages*, which just display the chain of links but are invoked parameterized by an index into the chain. They scroll their content automatically such that the indexed link appears at the top. By clicking at some link or a *next* button (for the indexed link) in the chain window the respective linked document is opened in a different window, and the index of the chain window is incremented (a *previous* button has analogous effect). We actually use chains for a finite number of precomputed queries of general interest such as the set of all letters in which a given person is referenced, and whose results are also displayed on the respective entity pages – but are there less convenient to browse through. Chain pages are by default shown in a small pop-up window positioned top left on the screen. If possible, an existing chain window and an existing window for displaying a page linked from a chain window are re-used. Our implementation utilizes the CSS3 `target` attribute. Figure 3 shows an example of a generated Web page representing a letter, accompanied by a chain page.

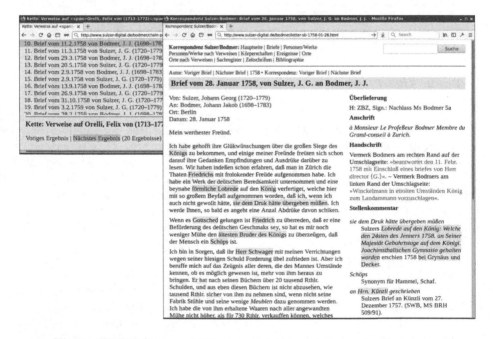

Fig. 3. *KBSET/Letters*: HTML presentation, a letter and a chain page.

2.4   Access from Prolog and Export of Fact Bases

The advanced consistency checking and text combination, as well as the HTML generation can be invoked via *Bash* shell scripts or directly from Prolog. The representation of the parsed source documents as Prolog predicates underlying the HTML conversion can in principle also be applied for other applications, such as conversion to further formats like RDF/XML and TEI/XML, or to export fact bases as indicated with box O2 in Fig. 1. The plan is to specify a suitable set of Prolog predicates such that editions can offer exported data, and also the parsed text, for download. Currently ways to produce RDF and XML on the basis of the internal Prolog predicates are indicated with small examples in the source code.

3   KBSET/NER

While *KBSET/Letters* addresses the practical aspects of comprehensive scholarly correspondence editions, the focus of *KBSET/NER* is to explore experimentally potential future directions of scholarly editing. Specifically the integration of techniques that return non-symbolic, fuzzy or incomplete results, the utilization of large external fact bases from the library community such as the *GND* and from Semantic Web activities such as *YAGO*, *DBPedia* and *GeoNames*, and ways to handle the association of annotations with places in the object text that are not explicitly marked as reference target. The functionality of *KBSET/NER* can be accessed from the Prolog interpreter or with menus and keyboard shortcuts from *GNU Emacs*. A draft edition of *Geschichte der Reaction*, vol. 1, 1852, by philosopher Max Stirner that has been created with these novel techniques is included with the *KBSET* distribution.

3.1   Caching External Knowledge Bases for Access Patterns

The inputs of *KBSET/NER* include, aside of object texts and annotation documents (boxes I1 and I2 in Fig. 1), also large imported fact bases (box I5). Before use, the configured fact bases, which are typically available in Semantic Web formats like RDF/XML or as CSV tables, have to be downloaded, parsed and preprocessed. This can be done with a utility predicate, but, as it may take several hours, for the example application also a TAR archive with the results of the preprocessing can be downloaded from the *KBSET* home page.[10] The preprocessed fact bases are then loaded into the Prolog system. At the first loading they are compiled into *SWI-Prolog's* *quick-load* format. In that format our fact base with 12 million ternary facts on persons born before 1850 extracted from the *GND* takes 7 s to load on a modern notebook computer.

KBSET then accesses these data as Prolog predicates stored in main memory. The indexing mechanisms of *SWI-Prolog* are utilized by maintaining predicates that are adapted to the represented entities, such as persons or locations (in contrast to generic triple predicates as might be suggested by the RDF format), and to access patterns. For example, a predicate for accessing data about a set of

---

[10] Also the original fact bases used for the example application are archived on the *KBSET* home page, as none of them has a persistent URL.

persons via a given last name and another predicate for accessing data about a person via a given *GND* identifier. We call these predicates, which may be in part redundant from a semantic point of view, *caches*. In the current implementation, the caches are in part computed when preprocessing the fact bases and in part when loading them. With this approach, the system can evaluate the several 10.000s of queries against the fact bases required for named entity recognition on the example document in a few seconds. Another useful feature is the semantics-based restriction of the large fact bases at preprocessing them. Since our example edition is a book from 1852, we keep of the *GND* only the facts about persons born before 1850.

3.2   Named Entity Identification

Working with *KBSET/NER* is centered around a subsystem for named entity recognition, which detects dates by parsing as well as persons and locations based on the *GND* and *GeoNames* as gazetteers, using additional knowledge from *YAGO* and *DBpedia*. Persons can be detected in two modes, characterized by names as well as by functional roles like *King of*, *Duke of* and *Bishop of*. Differently from systems like the *Stanford Named Entity Recognizer* [4], *KBSET/NER* does not just associate entity types such as *person* or *location* with phrases but attempts to actually *identify* the entities, hence we also speak of *named entity identification*.

The identification of persons and locations is based on single word occurrences with access to a context representation that includes the text before and after the respective occurrence. Hence an association of *word occurrences* to entities is computed, which is adequate for indexes of printed documents and for hypertext presentations, but not fully compatible with TEI, where the idea is to enclose a *phrase that denotes an entity* in markup.

Figure 4 shows the presentation of named entity identification results in *GNU Emacs*. In the upper buffer, which contains the object text, the system highlights words or phrases about which it assumes that they denote a person, location or date. In the lower buffer additional information on the selected occurrence of *Gleim* is displayed: Links to *Wikipedia* and *GND*, an explanation *why* the system believes the entity to be a plausible candidate for being referenced by the word occurrence, and an ordered listing of lower-ranked alternate candidate entities. Menus and keyboard shortcuts allow to jump quickly between the highlighted text positions with associated entities.

Aside of the presentation in *GNU Emacs*, the results of named entity identification can be output in different formats, in particular merged into a LaTeX source document as annotations. In this merging process also external annotation documents can be considered, where the positions to insert particular annotations are abstractly specified, for example by some form of text pattern. Further supported output formats of the named entity identification results include the presentation as TEI/XML elements merged into a source document, as a Prolog fact base, or, for identified locations, as a CSV table that can be loaded into the *DARIAH-DE* geo browser.

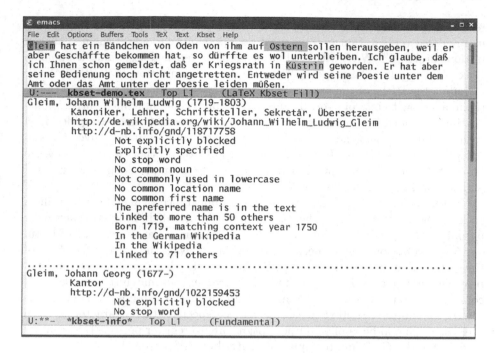

Fig. 4. *KBSET/NER*: named entity identification from *GNU Emacs*.

The named entity identification is controlled by rules which can be specified and configured and determine the evaluation of syntactic features matched against the considered word, for example, *is-no-stopword* or *is-no-common-substantive*, and of semantic features matched against candidate entities, for example, *is-in-wikipedia*, *is-linked-to-others-identified-in-context*, *has-an-occupation-mentioned-in-context*, or *date-of-birth-matches-context*. Evaluation of these features is done with respect to the mentioned context representation, which includes general information like the date of text creation and inferred information such as a set of entities already identified near the evaluated text position. Features that are cheap to compute and have great effect on restricting the set of candidate entities are evaluated first. This allows, for example, to apply named entity identification of persons on the 300-pages example book provided with the system in about 7s on a modern notebook computer. Feature evaluation results are then mapped to Prolog terms whose standard order represent their plausibility ranking. Information about the features that contributed to selection of a candidate entity is preserved and used to generate the displayed explanations shown in Fig. 4.

3.3   Assistance Documents

The automated named entity identification produces incomplete, partially incorrect and, by presenting a ranked list of plausible entities, fuzzy results. Such results may be helpful for developing a scholarly edition but should not remain in a released version. Hence, there must be a possibility to adapt them. This can be done in *KBSET/NER* with configuration files, so-called *assistance documents* (box I4 in Fig. 1). These specify the complete configuration of *KBSET/NER*, including the URLs of the external fact bases, the preprocessing required to use them, and how to bias or override automated inferencing in named entity identification. The idea for the latter is that the user, instead of annotating identified entities manually, lets the system do it automatically and mainly gives hints in *exceptional* cases, where the automatic method would otherwise not recognize an entity correctly. That method was used in the example document supplied with *KBSET*.

In the assistance document the explicit appearance of technical identifiers such as the identifiers from the *GND* should be avoided. This is achieved by permitting to specify a person just by some attributes like name, year of birth, and/or a profession. These specifiers are evaluated with the current fact base of the system, that is, essentially the *GND*. In contexts where a unique person must be designated an error is signaled if no or several persons match the specifier. (Of course, this method is not stable against importing an extended version of the *GND*.) In addition, context properties can be specified that characterize when the biasing should be applied. Other options are to register persons that can not be found in the *GND* and to supplement attributes of persons in the *GND*. Also simple syntactic exclusions, for example that a certain word should not denote a person or location can be specified. Here is an excerpt from the assistance document for the included example. It "assists" the automated named entity identifier in distinguishing two persons named *Tacitus*, classifying *Starcke* (the printer of the book) as a person and identifying him, as well as in identifying the person referenced in the text as *Herzog von Luxemburg*:

```
entity(person,
       [name='Tacitus',
        professionOrOccupation='Historiker'],
       [near_word_in=['Rmern']]),
entity(person,
       [name='Tacitus',
        variantNameForThePerson='Tacitus, Rmisches Reich, Kaiser'],
       [near_word_in=['Adel']]),
entity(person,
       [name='Starcke, Johann Friedrich',
        professionOrOccupation='Drucker'],
       [near_word_in=['Druck']]),
supplement(person,
           [name='Joseph II., Heiliges Rmisches Reich, Kaiser'],
           [biographicalOrHistoricalInformation
            =lang(de,'Herzog von Luxemburg (1765-1790)')]),
```

Like Prolog program files, assistance documents can be re-loaded, which effects updating of the specified settings. Thus, the named entity identification of

KBSET/Letters can be improved in an iteration of adjustments of the assistance documents and reviewing the effects in the *GNU Emacs* presentation.

This mode of interaction has, however, in the Sulzer-Bodmer edition project only been used in occasional cases. Each letter has there been transcribed and extensively commented by scientists, where the manual entity tagging emerged as a by-product. The automated named entity identification has been applied in special situations such as initializing the tagging of locations, examining and completing the manual tagging of persons, and generating auxiliary fact bases that map the project-local entity identifiers to global ones from the *GND* and *GeoNames*.

4 Discussion

We conclude this inter-disciplinary paper with discussions of the *KBSET* environment from three different perspectives.

4.1 *KBSET* in the World of Tools for Digital Scholarly Editing

KBSET has been designed and written within the paradigm of programming and creating mechanizable formalizations in Artificial Intelligence,[11] which is considered there as an integral component of the research activity. The creation of text with markup (LaTeX) is daily routine for researchers in computer science in general, as well as in numerous further fields.

In contrast, in the Humanities the use of formally defined languages entered in the last decade largely from the outside, with the requirement to make publicly funded results openly available in the HTML-based Web. Customizations of TEI/XML seemed the format of choice.[12] Hence the creation of TEI/XML documents became a component of the scholarly editing workflow.[13] However, this should not be misunderstood as equating the creation of digital editions to working with TEI/XML. The text represented in TEI/XML documents is hardly readable and the computational treatment of TEI/XML usually requires familiarity with several dedicated transformation and query languages, such that edition projects are typically large undertakings that are accompanied by support

---

[11] In the sense of the discipline *Artificial Intelligence*, not as synecdoche for its subfield *Machine Learning*.

[12] See for example the DFG (German Research Foundation) document *Förderkriterien für wissenschaftliche Editionen in der Literaturwissenschaft, Ausgabe 11/2015*, https://www.dfg.de/download/pdf/foerderung/grundlagen_dfg_foerderung/informationen_fachwissenschaften/geisteswissenschaften/foerderkriterien_editionen_literaturwissenschaft.pdf.

[13] Scholarly editions of correspondences that offer an openly available TEI/XML presentation include *Alfred-Escher Briefedition* (https://www.briefedition.alfred-escher.ch), *Briefe und Texte aus dem intellektuellen Berlin um 1800* (https://www.berliner-intellektuelle.eu), *Digitale Edition der Korrespondenz August Wilhelm Schlegels* (https://august-wilhelm-schlegel.de), *hallerNet* (http://hallernet.org), and *edition humboldt digital* (https://edition-humboldt.de).

from a specialized IT department, which mediates between the formal languages and the researcher. Observe that this is quite different from research in Artificial Intelligence, where the researcher herself creates mechanizable formalizations and programs. Where should the Digital Humanities go?

As TEI/XML is a general scheme for encoding all sorts of text, *"it is almost impossible to use the TEI schema without customizing it in some way"* [14, Sect. 23.3]. Applications such as scholarly editions of letters typically use project- or organization-specific customizations. Such customizations should be formalized in a schema language and explained in an informal document, both of which should be made accessible with the digital edition ([14, Sect. 23.4] gives very specific notions of this, even claimed to be presuppositions for calling a document *TEI-conformant*). Unfortunately, in current practice such schema specifications and documentations for digital editions are only rarely made easily accessible.[14] The suggested way to associate a TEI/XML document instance with a schema by the `xml-model` processing instruction [14, Sect. v.7.2] seems not used at all.[15]

Writing a conversion from *KBSET/Letters* source documents to some customization of TEI/XML is an easy task based on the extraction process implemented for the HTML transformation. The markup in LaTeX-syntax is there available in parsed form, metadata appear as Prolog predicates, and routines for converting identifiers are already implemented. A module in *KBSET* illustrates the concrete proceeding for XML and RDF conversions of metadata. In fact, a conversion to a TEI/XML customization is much simpler than the HTML translation included in *KBSET*. It is not yet implemented for the reason that, so far, it seems difficult to identify a particular formally defined TEI/XML customization for correspondences for which interesting tools or services are openly available, for example, to generate further presentations or for integration with other editions.

In the light of the standardization efforts via TEI/XML, *KBSET* can be taken as a user-friendly and economic environment for developing scholarly editions that approaches compliance with the desiderata described in the introduction. The generation of a representation in some customized TEI/XML format for interchange and archival is a marginal feature that is easy to add. In the long run, variations of the *KBSET* markup language should perhaps be adapted to reflect some suitable TEI/XML customizations more explicitly, or even be considered as realizations of TEI customizations in LaTeX-syntax.

Vice versa, *KBSET/Letters* can also be taken as a tool for generating presentations. It is not difficult to translate a representation of a correspondence in

---

[14] Actually, the authors were (in November 2019) not able to find any correspondence edition where a formal specification of the used customized schema is referenced from the TEI/XML documents or specified on the Web site. Informal edition guidelines can be found, for example, on the Web sites of *Alfred-Escher Briefedition, Briefe und Texte aus dem intellektuellen Berlin um 1800* and *hallerNet*.

[15] The well-intentioned postulation *"Um die Austauschbarkeit und Nachnutzung zu ermöglichen, werden die projektspezifisch verwendeten XML-Elemente und Attribut-Wert-Paare im TEI-Header dokumentiert"* in the DFG document mentioned in footnote 12 can technically not refer to the `teiHeader` element.

a TEI/XML customization to the *KBSET/Letters* markup (this can be implemented on the basis of the term representations of documents obtained from the XML parser of *SWI-Prolog*) such that the PDF and HTML presentations offered by *KBSET/Letters* become available. Since, as already mentioned, projects use different and hardly documented TEI/XML customizations it is expected that the translations need to be project-specific and some trial-and-error is involved in the development.

KBSET is free software. It depends only on a TEX distribution (it has been tested with *TeX Live*) and on *SWI-Prolog*, both of which are also free software, platform independent, and, moreover, mature, stable and widely used such that the current implementation of *KBSET* can be expected to operate also with future releases of these environments.[16]

The sources of an edition project like the Sulzer-Bodmer correspondence can be published and archived together with the used version of *KBSET/Letters*. The following functionalities are then freely available, through the stability and platform independence of LATEX and *SWI-Prolog* also in the foreseeable future: Generation of various high-quality PDF and HTML representations, generation of fact bases in Prolog representation,[17] and the representation in some TEI/XML customization (which still needs to be implemented). Moreover, if users want to improve or extend these functionalities, *KBSET/Letters* is available as a concrete and working free software environment to begin with.

The use of *KBSET* with other languages than German is supported to some degree: All input documents created for *KBSET* are encoded in UTF-8. The *GNU Emacs* user interface of *KBSET/NER* can be configured to English or German. Some of the word lists included in the implementation are, however, so far provided only for German. Also the presentation templates of *KBSET/Letters* are currently only in German. The *BibLaTeX* configuration included currently with *KBSET/Letters* is based on practices of the Humanities in Germany, but it is no problem to replace it with a different configuration.

4.2 *SWI-Prolog* as a Unifying Practical Technology

The core system of *KBSET/Letters* is written in *SWI-Prolog*, which realizes the potential of Prolog as a unifying language. As noted on the *SWI-Prolog* home page,[18] it considers Prolog *"primarily as glue between various components. The main reason for this is that data is at the core of many modern applications while there is a large variety in which data is structured and stored. Classical query languages such as SQL, SPARQL, XPATH, etc. can each deal with one*

---

[16] Some of the functions of *KBSET* can be invoked in addition from *Bash* shell scripts. A *Bash* shell can be presupposed on Unix-like platforms and can be added, for example with *Cygwin*, to Microsoft Windows platforms.

[17] Considering that there is an ISO standard for Prolog, such fact bases are actually in a *standardized* format. However, the ISO standard for Prolog is only with respect to ASCII encoding. Modern implementations like *SWI-Prolog* support UTF-8.

[18] https://www.swi-prolog.org/features.html, accessed Nov 21 2019.

such format only, while Prolog can provide a concise and natural query language for each of these formats that can either be executed directly or be compiled into dedicated query language expressions. Prolog's relational paradigm fits well with tabular data (RDBMS), while optimized support for recursive code fits well with tree and graph shaped data (RDF)." The particular roles of Prolog, and in particular *SWI-Prolog*, for *KBSET* can be compiled as follows:

1. *Declarative representation mechanism for relational fact bases.* As outlined in Sect. 2.4, we convert the document sources created in scholarly edition projects and large external fact bases to an intermediate representation as Prolog predicates, which are then used, for example, to generate HTML pages, but are also available for other purposes, including export as fact bases or interactive querying on the Prolog shell. The declarative view brings *semantics* into the focus and offers a bridge to the wealth of semantics-based techniques for knowledge representation and knowledge-based reasoning, in particular deductive databases, model- and answer-set computation, first-order theorem proving, and ontology reasoning.

2. *Efficient representation mechanism for relational fact bases.* We utilize the predicate indexing facilities of *SWI-Prolog's* with predicate caches that are specialized to access patterns as outlined in Sect. 3.1.

3. *Query language.* The standard predicates *findall* and *setof* provide expressive means to specify queries in a declarative manner. Complex tests and constructions can be smoothly incorporated, as query and programming language are identical, without much impedance mismatch. Of course, queries written in Prolog can not rely on an optimizer, and have to be designed "manually" such that their evaluation is done efficiently. A further important feature of Prolog is fast sorting based on a standard order of terms, which we quite often use to canonicalize representations of sets and is also the basis of our implementation of ranked answers in named entity identification.

4. *Representation mechanism for structured documents.* As in Lisp, data structures are in Prolog by default terms that are print- and readable, a feature which is supplemented to "non-AI" languages often by XML serialization. In our application context this is particularly useful as it allows to represent XML and HTML documents directly as Prolog data structures, that is, terms.

5. *Parser for XML and Semantic Web formats.* SWI-Prolog comes with powerful interfaces to Semantic Web formats, of which we use in particular the XML parser and the RDF parser, which provides a call-back interface that allows to process in succession the triples represented in a large RDF document such as the *GND* (see footnote 3 in Sect. 1).

6. *Parser for natural language text fragments and for formal languages.* Prolog has been developed originally in the context of applications in linguistics and traditionally supports syntax for grammar rules that are translated into an advanced parsing system. In *KBSET* this feature is used to parse date specifications in various contexts, to parse person specifications by functional roles in named entity identification, and to implement the LaTeX parser.

7. *Practical workflow model.* Workflow aspects of experimental AI programming seem also useful in the Digital Humanities: loading and re-loading documents

with formal specifications as well as invocation of functionality and running of experiments through an interpreter. All of this manageable by the researcher herself instead of further parties.

8. *Programming language.* Not to forget: Prolog is a programming language that is "different, but not *that* different" [10, Introduction].

4.3 Some Issues for Logic-Based Knowledge Processing

KBSET is an implemented system that has been proved workable in an application project and allows to experimentally study further possibilities. Some of the issues encountered in the course of implementing that were solved in specific ways seem to deserve further investigation. One of these issues is the interplay of knowledge that is inferred by automated and statistic-based techniques such as named entity recognition with manually supplied knowledge, which is addressed in *KBSET* so far with the *assistance documents*. Non-monotonic reasoning should in principle be a logic-based technique that is applicable here. Related to this issue is the handling of *ranked* query results used in *KBSET* for named entity identification. This is known in the field of databases as *top-k querying*. Is it possible to add some systematic and logic-based support for this to Prolog and perhaps also bottom-up reasoners like deductive database systems and model generators?

The approach to access fact bases with several millions of facts via preprocessed caches as realized by *KBSET* might be of general interest and could be investigated and implemented more systematically. If queries are written in a suitable fragment of Prolog, they can be automatically optimized, abstracting from caring about indexes (i.e., which cache is used), the order of subgoals, and the ways in which answer components are combined. Recent approaches to interpolation-based query reformulation [1,15] investigate a declarative approach for this. The optimized version of a query is there extracted as a Craig interpolant [2,16] from a proof obtained from a first-order prover. It seems also possible to apply this approach to determine from a given set of queries the caches that need to be constructed for efficient evaluation of the queries.

Digital Scholarly editing involves the interplay of natural language text with formal code and with formalized knowledge bases. From a general point of view, the contribution of the computer in digital scholarly editing may be viewed as a variant of the classical Artificial Intelligence scenario, where an agent in an environment makes decisions on actions to perform: General background knowledge in the AI scenario corresponds to knowledge bases like *GND* and *GeoNames*; the position of the agent in the environment may correspond to a position in the text; temporal order of events to the order of word occurrences; the environment which is only incompletely sensed or understood by the agent corresponds to incompletely understood natural language text; coming to decisions about actions to take corresponds to decisions about denotations of text phrases and about annotations to associate with text components. This suggests that digital scholarly editing is an interesting field for applying, improving and inventing AI techniques.

References

1. Benedikt, M., Leblay, J., ten Cate, B., Tsamoura, E.: Generating Plans from Proofs: The Interpolation-based Approach to Query Reformulation. Morgan & Claypool, San Rafael (2016)
2. Craig, W.: Three uses of the Herbrand-Gentzen theorem in relating model theory and proof theory. J. Symbolic Logic **22**(3), 269–285 (1957)
3. Eide, O.: Ontologies, data modeling, and TEI. J. Text Encoding Initiative **8** (2015)
4. Finkel, J.R., Grenager, T., Manning, C.: Incorporating non-local information into information extraction systems by Gibbs sampling. In: ACL 2005, pp. 363–370. ACL (2005)
5. Hoffart, J., Suchanek, F.M., Berberich, K., Weikum, G.: YAGO2: a spatially and temporally enhanced knowledge base from Wikipedia. Artif. Intell. **194**, 28–61 (2013)
6. Kittelmann, J., Wernhard, C.: Semantik, Web, Metadaten und digitale Edition: Grundlagen und Ziele der Erschließung neuer Quellen des Branitzer Pückler-Archivs. In: Krebs, I., et al. (eds.) Resonanzen. Pücklerforschung im Spannungsfeld zwischen Wissenschaft und Kunst, pp. 179–202. trafo Verlag (2013)
7. Kittelmann, J., Wernhard, C.: Knowledge-based support for scholarly editing and text processing. In: DHd 2016, pp. 178–181. Nisaba verlag (2016)
8. Kittelmann, J., Wernhard, C.: Von der Transkription zur Wissensbasis. Zum Zusammenspiel von digitalen Editionstechniken und Formen der Wissensrepräsentation am Beispiel von Korrespondenzen Johann Georg Sulzers. In: Kittelmann, J., Purschwitz, A. (eds.) Aufklärungsforschung digital. Konzepte, Methoden, Perspektiven, IZEA - Kleine Schriften, vol. 10/2019, pp. 84–114. Mitteldeutscher Verlag (2019)
9. Lehmann, J., et al.: DBpedia - a large-scale, multilingual knowledge base extracted from Wikipedia. Semant. Web **6**(2), 167–195 (2015)
10. O'Keefe, R.A.: The Craft of Prolog. The MIT Press, Cambridge (1990)
11. Plachta, B.: Editionswissenschaft: Eine Einführung in Methode und Praxis der Edition neuerer Texte. Reclam (1997)
12. Sahle, P.: Digitale Editionsformen, Zum Umgang mit der Überlieferung unter den Bedingungen des Medienwandels, 3 volumes, Schriften des Instituts für Dokumentologie und Editorik, vol. 7–9. Books on Demand (2013)
13. Sulzer, J.G.: Gesammelte Schriften. Kommentierte Ausgabe. In: Adler, H., Décultot, E. (eds.) Schwabe (2014–2021)
14. The TEI Consortium: TEI P5: Guidelines for Electronic Text Encoding and Interchange, Version 3.6.0. Text Encoding Initiative Consortium (2019). http://www.tei-c.org/Guidelines/P5/
15. Toman, D., Weddell, G.: Fundamentals of Physical Design and Query Compilation. Morgan and Claypool, San Rafael (2011)
16. Wernhard, C.: Facets of the PIE environment for proving, interpolating and eliminating on the basis of first-order logic. In: Hofstedt, P., et al. (eds.) DECLARE 2019. LNCS(LNAI), vol. 12057, pp. 160–177. Springer, Heidelberg (2020)
17. Wielemaker, J., Schrijvers, T., Triska, M., Lager, T.: SWI-prolog. Theory Practice Logic Program. **12**(1–2), 67–96 (2012)

27th International Workshop on Functional and Logic Programming - WFLP 2019

Structured Traversal of Search Trees in Constraint-Logic Object-Oriented Programming

Jan C. Dageförde[1]([⊠])(ID) and Finn Teegen[2](ID)

[1] ERCIS, Leonardo-Campus 3, 48149 Münster, Germany
dagefoerde@uni-muenster.de
[2] Institut für Informatik, CAU Kiel, 24098 Kiel, Germany
fte@informatik.uni-kiel.de

Abstract. In this paper, we propose an explicit, non-strict representation of search trees in constraint-logic object-oriented programming. Our search tree representation includes both the non-deterministic and deterministic behaviours of executing an application. Introducing such a representation facilitates the use of various search strategies. In order to demonstrate the applicability of our approach, we incorporate explicit search trees into the virtual machine of the constraint-logic object-oriented programming language Muli. We then exemplarily implement three search algorithms that traverse the search tree on-demand: depth-first search, breadth-first search, and iterative deepening depth-first search. In particular, the last two strategies allow for a complete search, which is novel in constraint-logic object-oriented programming and highlights our main contribution. Finally, we compare the implemented strategies using several benchmarks.

Keywords: Constraint-logic object-oriented programming · Explicit search tree · Complete search strategy · Virtual machine implementation

1 Motivation

In constraint-logic object-oriented programming, combining imperative code with features from logic programming causes the runtime to execute parts of the imperative code non-deterministically ("don't know" non-determinism). To give an example, the program (or search region) depicted in Listing 1 has two solutions. The example is written using the Münster Logic-Imperative Language (Muli), which we explain in Sect. 2. The search region declares a boolean logic variable `coin`. Subsequently, evaluating the **if** statement causes the runtime environment to take and implement a decision regarding the potential value of `coin`, thus introducing non-determinism. Consequently, implementing the decision selects a single branch of execution, eventually resulting in one of the two outcomes.

© Springer Nature Switzerland AG 2020
P. Hofstedt et al. (Eds.): DECLARE 2019, LNAI 12057, pp. 199–214, 2020.
https://doi.org/10.1007/978-3-030-46714-2_13

```
boolean flipCoin() {
    int coin free;
    if (coin == 0)
        return false;
    else
        return true; }
```

```
boolean flipTwoCoins() {
    int coin1 free, coin2 free;
    if (coin1 == 0)
        return false;
    else if (coin2 == 0)
        throw Muli.fail();
    else
        return true; }
```

Listing 1. A simple non-deterministic search region in Muli for the demonstration of constraint-logic object-oriented programming concepts.

Listing 2. Muli search region example that comprises two solutions and a failure.

Non-deterministic execution is useful for applications involving search, i. e., an application would usually cause the runtime environment to evaluate more than one branch. To that end, the runtime environment systematically evaluates multiple alternative branches in sequence. Non-deterministic branching dynamically creates an implicit search tree that represents the various execution paths that lead to alternative outcomes of a program. The goal of the present work is to make this search tree explicit at runtime. It encodes the various execution paths of a program, the choices encountered along every path, and every path's outcome (i. e., solution or failure). As there can be paths of infinite length, our search tree representation is non-strict. Our search tree then serves as a basis for structured traversal by arbitrary search algorithms, including iterative deepening depth-first search. Furthermore, by making the search tree explicit, it is possible to inspect the search tree at any given point in time, e. g., after search or even at an intermediate stage. This way, the search tree aids in effective debugging.

This paper provides the following contributions:

- A general *search tree structure* for constraint-logic object-oriented programming that encapsulates execution state (Sect. 4).
- *Search algorithm implementations* that traverse the search tree structure for finding solutions to constraint-logic object-oriented programs (Sect. 5).
- A discussion of the implications of our work for executing object-oriented (imperative) programs non-deterministically (Sect. 6).

First of all, Sect. 2 introduces concepts of constraint-logic object-oriented programming, followed by an outline of the Muli virtual machine in Sect. 3.

2   Constraint-Logic Object-Oriented Programming

Constraint-logic object-oriented programming combines the flexibility of imperative and object-oriented programming with features from constraint-logic programming, namely logic variables, constraints, and search. Muli is a constraint-logic object-oriented programming language that is based on Java [4].

In Muli, *logic variables* are declared in a way that is similar to declaring regular variables. As indicated in Listing 1,

```
int coin free;
```

declares a logic variable of a primitive (integer) type. Instead of assigning a constant value, the **free** keyword specifies that coin is a logic variable. A logic integer variable can be used interchangeably with other integer variables, i. e., they can become part of conditions or arithmetic expressions and can be passed to methods as parameters [3]. In contrast to regular variables, logic variables are used symbolically. Recent work is looking into support for reference-type logic variables [2], but here we focus on logic variables of primitive types.

Constraints are defined as relational expressions, (typically) involving logic variables. For simplicity, Muli does not provide a dedicated language feature for imposing constraints. Instead, a constraint is imposed whenever the flow of execution branches, such as when a branching condition is evaluated. Therefore, constraints are derived from boolean expressions. For instance, in Listing 1

```
if (coin == 0) { s₁ } else { s₂ }
```

coin occurs in the condition and is not sufficiently constrained, so that the condition can be evaluated to either true or false. As a result, the evaluation of the condition creates a *choice*, from which alternatives are evaluated non-deterministically. The runtime environment selects an alternative by imposing the corresponding constraint. In our example, by imposing $coin \neq 0$ the runtime environment can proceed with the evaluation of s_2. The runtime environment leverages a constraint solver for finding solutions as well as for cutting execution branches early as soon as their constraint system becomes inconsistent.

Search transparently performs non-deterministic evaluation in combination with backtracking until a solution is found. Implicitly, following a sequence of choices (and taking decisions at each choice) produces a (conceptual) search tree that represents the order of execution. In such a search tree, inner nodes are choices and leaves represent alternative ends of execution paths. In Muli, an execution path ends with a *solution* (specified by either **return** or **throw**) or with a *failure*, e. g., if a path's constraint system is inconsistent. The full listing of our example in Listing 1 demonstrates how solutions are returned. After search completes, solutions of the example are **false** and **true** (in any given order).

Moreover, applications sometimes require an *explicit failure* denoting the end of an execution path without a solution. In Muli, an explicit failure is expressed by **throw** Muli.**fail**(). Nevertheless, executing that statement will not return an exception. Instead, the statement is specifically interpreted by the runtime environment, resulting in backtracking. Listing 2 provides a slightly extended search region with three execution paths, one of which ends in a failure.

The main program is executed deterministically, whereas all non-deterministic search is *encapsulated*. Encapsulation gives application developers control over search. In addition to coarse-grained control (i. e., requesting either a single solution or an array comprising all solutions), Muli offers fine-grained control by returning a Java stream that evaluates solutions non-strictly. Muli.**muli**() accepts a Supplier and returns a stream of Solution objects. In Java (and, therefore, in Muli), a Supplier denotes either a lambda expression or a method reference (both without arguments). We refer to the method that is passed as an argument as a *search region*, as it will be executed non-deterministically and therefore describes the constraint-logic object-oriented problem. Following the principles of the Java Stream API, solutions can be retrieved from the stream individually on demand [5]. For instance, considering Listing 1, a stream is initialised using

```
Stream<Solution<Boolean>> stream = Muli.muli(self::flipCoin),
```

and the actual search starts as soon as the first solution is requested from the stream.

3   Muli Logic Virtual Machine

The Muli Logic Virtual Machine (MLVM) is a runtime environment for Muli. The MLVM is a custom Java Virtual Machine (JVM) that complies with the JVM Specification (see [10]) for deterministic execution. Moreover, it adds modifications that support Muli-specific extensions, particularly symbolic execution and non-deterministic execution [4]. As in a regular JVM, execution state is represented in the MLVM by a combination of *program counter (PC)*, a *heap*, a stack of executed method frames (*frame stack*), and an *operand stack* per frame. Additional state serves the purpose of supporting non-deterministic execution and constraints. In particular, this includes the constraint stack and the trail.

The *constraint stack* maintains the active constraint system, i. e., the conjunction of all constraints on the stack [4]. Representing the constraint system in a stack structure is beneficial as constraints are added dynamically during execution. Consequently, on backtracking, only the most recently added constraints need to be removed from the stack. Moreover, the *trail* records changes that are made to the virtual machine (VM) state during execution. On backtracking, the information on the trail can be used to revert to a previous execution state. More precisely, using the trail, backtracking achieves the specific state of the choice at which the next decision can be made. In fact, the trail is therefore split up into incremental trails, one per choice, each describing how to backtrack towards the next choice. In addition, in order to be able to not only backtrack to a choice (upwards along a search tree) but to achieve an arbitrary previous state (including downward navigation), the MLVM maintains two trails per choice, one being the inverse of the other [5]. In the following, we call the trail for backtracking *backward trail*, as opposed to the *forward trail* that is used to navigate downwards.

Like a regular JVM, the MLVM reads applications from bytecode and executes bytecode instead of the original source. Muli's bytecode format is compatible with that described in [10], merely adding custom attributes in order to represent logic variables [4]. For instance, the example application from Listing 2

```
 0:  iload_1              // coin1
 1:  iconst_0
 2:  if_icmpne (7)        // coin1 != 0
 5:  iconst_0
 6:  ireturn              // return false
 7:  iload_2              // coin2
 8:  iconst_0
 9:  if_icmpne (16)       // coin2 != 0
12:  invokestatic  #91    // fail()
15:  athrow
16:  iconst_1
17:  ireturn              // return true
```

Listing 3. Bytecode generated by the Muli compiler for the program in Listing 2.

Table 1. Bytecode instructions that may cause non-deterministic branching upon execution. <cond> is a placeholder for specific comparisons, e. g., eq for equality.

Triggering bytecode instruction	Type of choice	No. of decisions
If<cond>, If_icmp<cond>	**if** instruction, integer comp	2
FCmpg, FCmpl, DCmpg, DCmpl	floating point comparison	2
LCmp	long comparison	3
Lookupswitch, Tableswitch	**switch** instruction	1 per case + 1

compiles to the bytecode instructions in Listing 3. Some bytecode instructions exhibit non-deterministic behaviour. For instance, if_icmpne in Listing 3 jumps to the specified instruction if the two integer operands on the operand stack are not equal. Otherwise, execution continues linearly with the following instruction. If one or both operands are logic variables, both *jumping* and *not jumping* are feasible alternatives. As logic variables are used in the current example, the execution of if_icmpne instructions creates choice points that offer two decision alternatives. While **if** instructions always provide two alternatives (i. e., jumping to the **else** branch or not), **switch** instructions result in alternatives according to the number of **case**s plus one for the **default** case, each jumping to instructions accordingly. Table 1 provides a reference of instructions that may exhibit non-deterministic behaviour and counts the decision alternatives from which the MLVM chooses.

Executing a bytecode instruction with non-deterministic branching creates a choice point in the MLVM [4]. Prior to this work, the implementation of the choice point itself was responsible for managing the execution of its branches. More specifically, executing a bytecode instruction created a choice point representation in the MLVM. Consequently, the created choice point contained information about applicable branches, but also implemented the behaviour of search.

That is, upon creation, the choice point representation immediately selected the first decision alternative and applied it, thus committing to a specific branch. The created choice point representations are stored in a stack of choice points. The MLVM referred to the choice point stack during backtracking. Starting from the top, it popped choice points until reaching one with an alternative that had not been evaluated yet. It then immediately committed to this alternative by adding its constraint and following its path.[1] As a consequence, the runtime environment never actually stored an explicit representation of the search tree. Instead, the choice point stack merely maintained a single path through the (implicit) search tree. Therefore, diverting from the currently executed path was not possible, effectively restricting the search capabilities of the MLVM to depth-first search. All things considered, the previous MLVM used a complex, tangled mixture of responsibilities in which bytecode-instruction implementations, choice-point implementations, and the VM realise non-deterministic search in combination.

In a cleaner architecture,

- declaratively executing a bytecode instruction creates choice objects and just returns them to the MLVM (instead of performing a decision right away), and
- choice objects only hold information about available decision alternatives (but no implementation for taking decisions).

As a consequence, the MLVM is the only element that is allowed to change execution state by committing to decisions, instead of sharing this permission with choice objects or instruction implementations. The search tree structure that we discuss subsequently facilitates an explicit representation that holds a declarative representation of choices and of the alternatives that each choice provides. Overall, the structure serves as a clean basis for following arbitrary execution paths through the tree.

4   Search Trees

A declarative, explicit search tree representation lays the groundwork for following arbitrary execution paths instead of limiting execution to depth-first search only. We first explain the conceptual representation, outlining the intuition of the elements that constitute the search tree. Afterwards, we describe how a search tree is constructed dynamically during the execution of a Muli application. Last, we abstractly describe navigation through the search tree as the basis for search.

4.1   Representation

Conceptually, our explicit search tree comprises five distinct node types. There are node types for returned values, thrown exceptions, choices between non-deterministic branches, failed computations, and yet unevaluated search trees.

---

[1] Provided that the constraint system was still consistent. Otherwise, backtracking occurred until the next choice point that offered an unevaluated, feasible alternative.

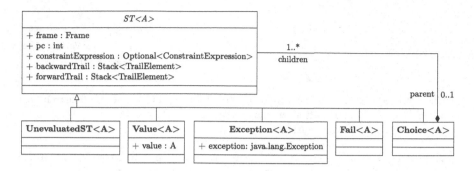

Fig. 1. Class diagram for the representation of search trees.

Figure 1 shows a class diagram for our search tree representation. Basically, this representation corresponds to an algebraic data type and therefore does not implement any decision-taking in contrast to the previously used choice points.

As solutions of a search region, a `Value` node holds the value returned by a computation while an `Exception` node does the same with an exception that has been thrown. A `Fail` node represents either an explicit failure or branches whose constraint system is inconsistent. As a consequence, it does not hold any values. Furthermore, `Choice` nodes store a list of subtrees which, in turn, reference their `parent` choice. Having an explicit reference to each node's parent allows for easy and direct navigation through the search tree. For the root node of a search tree, the `parent` attribute is **null**. Finally, `UnevaluatedST` serves as a proxy for subtrees that have not been evaluated yet, facilitating non-strict usage.

Moreover, each node in the search tree stores fields that prepare for later execution. The `frame` and `pc` fields represent a reference to the (mutable) stack frame and the value of the PC at which the node has been created. Each node holds an optional constraint expression that has to be satisfied in order to reach this node, e. g., as a consequence of non-deterministic branching. Additionally, the backward trail stores the changes to the VM state that were made in order to reach this node (thus preparing for backtracking), whereas the forward trail stores changes that are needed in order to return to this node afterwards. In combination, these fields are used to properly manipulate the state of the MLVM during the traversal of the search tree, which is discussed in detail in Sect. 4.3.

4.2 Construction

The actual search tree is constructed during search. A search strategy is responsible for determining the order in which the search tree is traversed. Regardless of the order, a search strategy evaluates `UnevaluatedST` nodes as long as there are such nodes left and the encapsulating program demands additional solutions. In general, the MLVM evaluates an `UnevaluatedST` node by imposing the node's constraint and executing the bytecode of the search region starting from the PC, which the node points to, until either of the following situations occurs.

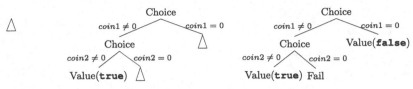

(a) Unevaluated search tree (b) Partially evaluated search tree after encountering the first solution (c) Fully evaluated search tree

Fig. 2. Different evaluation stages of the search tree corresponding to the search region in Listing 2. The constraint of each subtree is noted at the respective edge.

- The computation in the search region returns with a value,
- an uncaught exception occurs during execution,
- the method `Muli.fail()` signals a failed computation, or
- one of the instructions in Table 1 is executed, which results in the creation of a `Choice` object.

In any case, the `UnevaluatedST` node in the search tree is replaced by its evaluated counterpart, i.e., by a `Value`, `Exception`, `Fail`, or `Choice` node. Note that all children of a newly created `Choice` node are unevaluated search trees initially. Furthermore, state changes that were made during this evaluation are received from the MLVM and stored within the new node as its backward trail.

At the beginning of search, the search tree is unknown and therefore initially represented by a single `UnevaluatedST` node. The PC of that node points to the start of the search region, and the optional constraint expression is left empty since no constraints apply to the start of a search region. Similarly, the trails are empty as this node has not yet been evaluated. Figure 2 exemplarily shows three search trees for the program from Listing 2 that all are evaluated to a different degree, and thus illustrate various intermediate evaluation stages that can occur during a search. The illustration assumes a depth-first search strategy; therefore, other search strategies will result in different intermediate stages.

4.3 Traversal

The implementation of any search algorithm requires to be able to navigate through the search tree in any direction, i.e., upwards and downwards. For example, if a branch of a search tree has been fully evaluated, search continues elsewhere. While navigating through the search tree, it is vital to ensure that the MLVM remains in a consistent state. A node's forward and backward trail together with its frame and PC are used for that purpose. In general, navigation takes place from an already evaluated node to another evaluated node, since only evaluated nodes have a trail (see Sect. 4.2). More specifically, a `Choice` node is always the target node or source node when navigating upwards or downwards.

We navigate upwards in a search tree by following references to the parents until we reach the target node (e.g., the root), backtracking the VM state in

```
void navigateUpwards(ST from, Choice to) {
  while (from != to) {
    if (from.constraintExpression.isPresent())
      constraintStack.pop();
    vm.processTrail(from.backwardTrail, from.forwardTrail);
    vm.setFrame(from.frame); vm.setPc(from.pc);
    from = from.parent; } }

void navigateDownwards(Choice from, ST to) {
  Stack<ST> nodes = new Stack<>();
  while (to != from)
    nodes.put(to); to = to.parent;
  while (!nodes.empty()) {
    to = nodes.pop();
    vm.setFrame(to.frame); vm.setPc(to.pc);
    vm.processTrail(to.forwardTrail, to.backwardTrail);
    if (to.constraintExpression.isPresent())
      constraintStack.push(to.constraintExpression.get()); } }
```

Listing 4. Methods for navigating upwards and downwards in a search tree.

the process. In doing so, we remove previously imposed constraints from the constraint stack and undo the changes to VM state by processing the backward trails of nodes along the path. At the same time, the backward trails are converted into forward trails so that a node from which we navigate away can be reached again later when navigating downwards, e.g., for the evaluation of another subtree of that node. Last but not least, the frame and PC of the VM are set accordingly, using the information that was recorded at each node when it was created.

Navigating downwards is slightly more complicated as we first need to determine how to reach a target node from the current (source) node. However, we always have a reference to the target. Therefore, we can use the target's parents in order to find the path to the source. Afterwards, we process the path in reverse order, thus getting from the source node to the target node. We basically do the opposite of what is done in upwards navigation: For each node, we set the frame and PC to what is recorded in the node, apply the forward trail to reapply changes to the execution state, and impose a node's constraint if present. Simultaneously to processing the forward trail, we convert it again into a backward trail to be later able to navigate upwards. For clarity, Listing 4 shows simplified implementations for navigating upwards and downwards, respectively. Subsequently, these general navigation methods serve as primitives for traversal.

```
Choice findCommonAncestor(ST a, ST b) {
  initialise empty set;
  while (b != null) {
    add b to set;
    b = b.parent; }
  while (!set.contains(a))
    a = a.parent;
  return a; }
```

Listing 5. Algorithm for finding the first common ancestor of two nodes.

5   Search Strategies

As a demonstration of how the explicit search tree representation can be employed for the implementation of search strategies, we outline the implementations of three particular ones.

Depth-First Search. The implementation of depth-first search maintains a stack of unevaluated subtrees from the search tree. At the beginning of the search, the initial node (see Sect. 4.2) is pushed to the stack. Then, depth-first search repeatedly pops an unevaluated search tree node from the stack and tries to evaluate it. If its evaluation results in a Choice node, its children are pushed to the stack and search continues by popping the next node from the stack (i. e., a local subtree). Otherwise, if a Value or Exception node is encountered, the search strategy must be able to return the result to the encapsulating program. To that end, it reverts execution state to the state from the beginning of search using navigateUpwards. When search is picked up again, the search strategy uses navigateDownwards in order to evaluate the next node from the stack. Finally, if the node at hand is evaluated to a Fail node, local backtracking is performed, i. e., we navigate upwards to the nearest parent that has at least one unevaluated subtree.

Breadth-First Search. Instead of a stack, a FIFO queue keeps track of unevaluated subtrees. Beginning or resuming search dequeues nodes from the head of the queue. In contrast, when a Choice node is encountered, its children are enqueued at the end. Another difference is the fact that breadth-first search requires navigating between arbitrary nodes within the search tree. While it is, of course, possible to go over the root node, it is more efficient to navigate along a path going over the first common ancestor of the two involved nodes. Listing 5 shows a simple algorithm that determines the first common ancestor of two nodes in the search tree. Once the first common ancestor is found, search combines navigateUpwards (to the found ancestor) and navigateDownwards in order to efficiently navigate between two arbitrary nodes.

Iterative Deepening Depth-First Search. Our search tree can also be used to implement an exciting variant of iterative deepening search. Iterative deepening provides the strength of depth-first search while ensuring that solutions can be found even if there are execution paths of infinite length. In iterative deepening, search is bounded by a constant maximum depth. Search proceeds in a depth-first manner until nodes are reached that are at the maximum depth. In that case, search first evaluates other nodes up to that depth, thus assuming breadth-first search behaviour. Only if additional solutions are required, search increases the bound, again by a constant, and so on. In Muli, aided by the inverse trails, when the bound is increased, the runtime environment does not need to restart computation at the root, which usually leads to a reevaluation of known execution paths (and solutions). Instead, it leverages the (partial) search tree and the recorded inverse trails in order to restart computation from known states that provide further alternatives.

6   Discussion

The implementation of our search tree structure in the MLVM facilitates the non-deterministic execution of imperative (object-oriented) programs in novel ways, using search strategies that could not be implemented without an explicit structure. The existing depth-first search strategy has been reimplemented and is now based on the explicit search tree structure as well. In order to ensure that the required changes do not adversely affect the performance of depth-first search, we first compare the runtime behaviour before discussing novel aspects of search. Note that we measure only performance, not memory consumption. Obviously, maintaining the search tree requires more memory than merely storing the current execution path. However, a possible memory optimisation would be to discard search tree nodes that belong to exhaustively evaluated subtrees—especially in depth-first search strategies.

We are interested in comparing the performance of depth-first search in the new search-tree-based and old choice-point-stack-based implementations. To that end, a set of experiments is conducted in a modified MLVM that contains our search-tree structure as well as in an MLVM without modifications, each executed by OpenJDK 1.8.0_212.[2] Since the MLVM is executed by a JVM, we drop the first 15 executions in order to account for effects caused by just-in-time compilation and take the performance values of subsequent executions. In total, we aggregate performance values of 500 executions per experiment, tackling classic search problems. The first experiment calculates a solution to the 3-partition problem for a fixed set of integer values using a depth-first search strategy. Until the first solution is found, search passes 374 choices. The second finds a solution to the Send More Money puzzle. For reference, we also execute corresponding Curry implementations on PAKCS 2.1.1 using depth-first search. Figure 3 features the average execution times. Our experiment indicates that the

---

[2] Ubuntu 18.04.2 with 4.15.0 x86_64 GNU/Linux kernel; Intel Core i5-5200U CPU.

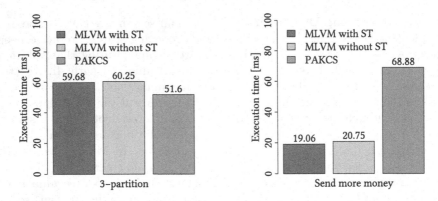

Fig. 3. Comparison of execution times in MLVM with or without explicit search trees, both using depth-first search. Execution times in PAKCS for reference.

```
private static boolean nonTerminatingCoin() {
  int coin free;
  if (coin == 0)
    return true;
  else
    return nonTerminatingCoin(); }
```

Listing 6. Muli search region featuring an infinite amount of execution paths.

implementation and use of an explicit search tree do not negatively affect depth-first search performance. Moreover, the comparison to PAKCS is encouraging, seeing that Muli search regions offer competitive performance while providing support for using side-effects during non-deterministic execution.

Since the use of explicit search trees does not add visible overhead to execution times, we can focus on the benefits of using a search tree representation at runtime. The MLVM now features additional search algorithms beyond depth-first search that all leverage the search tree structure. In particular, using breadth-first search is novel to the non-deterministic execution of imperative programs that have side-effects.

Consider the search region from Listing 6. For lack of a termination condition, there is one infinite execution path. Therefore, it is impossible to evaluate the search tree (or the application) strictly. In our depth-first search implementation, the infinite execution path is the leftmost one. As a result of this structure, depth-first search is unable to compute a single solution. In contrast, several solutions can be returned using a breadth-first or iterative deepening strategy, even though the tree can never be evaluated in full. As a more sophisticated example, we have implemented a search region that finds solutions to the Water jugs problem. Here the MLVM is unable to evaluate a full search tree as there

Table 2. Comparison of search strategies w. r. t. the number of solutions that are returned within ten seconds.

	DFS	BFS	ID-DFS
Simple infinite recursion	0	1469.7	1555.2
Water jug problem	0	29.5	34.4

are cyclic execution paths that result in valid solutions or failures. We have executed these programs using the available strategies 500 times for up to ten seconds each and indicate the average number of solutions in Table 2.

Note that the results do not imply that depth-first search is generally a bad strategy. On the contrary, the combination of increased memory requirements and the time needed for changing VM state using the trail still speaks against using breadth-first search by default. Iterative deepening shares this disadvantage in case that additional levels of the search tree need to be evaluated (but is as efficient as depth-first search if the initial depth is sufficient). Consequently, the results indicate that iterative deepening depth-first search is a good trade-off, if not a better strategy. Further evidence is needed to conclusively argue that iterative deepening is a superior strategy in general. In any case, both are useful strategies in certain situations in which depth-first search falls short.

The search tree structure that is presented in this paper is conceptually similar to the ST structure known from the KiCS2 compiler for Curry [7]. However, Curry search trees only encode evaluation alternatives of an expression. In contrast, search trees for constraint-logic object-oriented programming need to encode the execution behaviour, i. e. VM state changes, that results from different alternatives. Consequently, the state changes are recorded on the corresponding paths that lead to solutions, so that the VM can change state depending on the alternative that is being evaluated. In our current work, we do this by maintaining the forward and backward trails on edges of the search tree.

Prior to our work, the execution state of constraint-logic object-oriented programming in Muli was represented by the PC, frame stack, operand stacks, constraint stack, trail, and choice point stack. Our work results in a slightly altered definition of execution state. What previously was a choice point stack is now replaced by the search tree and a pointer to the current search tree node that is under evaluation. In addition, a search algorithm is responsible for maintaining a suitable data structure that keeps track of the progress of traversing the search tree, e. g., a stack of not-yet-evaluated choices in depth-first search algorithms.

Moreover, the explicit search tree structure is useful for the development of constraint-logic object-oriented programs, as it can be helpful to visualise the structure of search. Specifically, we can visualise at which points different kinds of choices are introduced and which solutions are encountered by the runtime environment. During the development of the MLVM, the search tree structure is useful for ensuring that non-deterministic branching and search algorithms are implemented correctly. In contrast, the structure of the previous approach impeded the diagnosis of problems with non-deterministic execution, as only the current execution path was represented. Consequently, relevant information about previously encountered choices and solutions was lost, whereas this information is adequately represented in the explicit search tree. All in all, the discussed benefits of an explicit search tree structure outweigh the increased memory requirements.

7 Related Work

For software testing, symbolic execution trees describe possible execution paths of an imperative program under test [8,11]. Similar to our search tree, a symbolic execution tree represents choice points where execution branches and collects path constraints. However, a symbolic execution tree usually describes the entire execution of an application. In contrast, our search tree for constraint-logic object-oriented programming describes the execution of specific application parts, namely the non-deterministic execution of a search region. Its leaf node types are tailored to describing the result (i. e., solutions or failures) of execution paths. Moreover, a symbolic execution tree is the result of performing depth-first search, whereas the dual trails of our search tree specifically support arbitrary traversal.

The idea of using an explicit data structure for non-deterministic computations in order to facilitate different search strategies is extensively used in functional logic programming [1,7]. In functional logic programming, search trees cover non-determinism of expressions, i. e., they encode alternatives for the values to which a pure expression can be evaluated. In contrast to that, constraint-logic object-oriented programming is non-deterministic in its execution behaviour, which includes side-effects incurring during execution. Therefore, the present search tree structure has to encode alternative behaviour, including side-effects, in addition to final results. In addition to the representation usually used in functional logic programming, our representation includes node types for exceptions (as a different kind of solution) and unevaluated search trees. The latter types are a prerequisite for the on-demand construction of the search tree during search, which is innately given with the non-strict evaluation in functional logic programming.

An explicit data structure for representing a search tree structure has also been used in a monadic definition of constraint programming [13]. In contrast to our work, it abstracts from side effects and asserts an ordering of subtrees. Another explicit search tree is used for implementing a domain-specific language (DSL) for probabilistic programming in OCaml [9]. As OCaml is strict, the on-demand characteristic of the search tree is modelled explicitly using lambda functions. Although OCaml is not purely functional, the authors disregard backtracking w. r. t. behaviour, modelling only non-deterministic results of pure expressions.

As an alternative to using an explicit search tree, the interface of the probabilistic DSL in OCaml has also been implemented by using continuation passing style and by using delimited continuations, i. e., using shift and reset [6]. Using continuations provides an implementation in a direct style and removes the runtime overhead of the search tree data structure. Therefore, implementing Muli by means of shift and reset is an interesting option for future work. In this case, however, monadic reflection (i. e., inspecting the search tree) is expensive, and its efficient implementation requires additional techniques [12].

The concept of trails has initially been adapted from the trail described for the Warren Abstract Machine (WAM) [14] and has been extended towards dual trails for arbitrary execution state in [5]. Dual trails facilitate their use for backtracking upwards along a search tree as well as for descending towards nodes that have been (partially) evaluated. For their duality, the two trails were originally termed trail and inverse trail. Here we call them backward trail and forward trail, respectively, in order to improve clarity regarding the direction in which they are used. Extending previous work, the present paper leverages dual trails for the implementations of search strategies other than depth-first search.

8   Conclusion and Future Work

Our search tree structure represents the paths of non-deterministic execution of a search region. A runtime environment of a constraint-logic object-oriented language can construct the search tree non-strictly while executing a search region, thus encoding the solutions that are found as well as the execution behaviour of imperative code that leads to solutions or intermediate choices. As a result, the explicit search tree representation can serve several purposes. First, it provides a structure that arbitrary search strategies utilise for traversing the search tree. Furthermore, we found it to make debugging of non-deterministic execution behaviour more productive by allowing developers who use a debugger to introspect intermediate state at breakpoints. More opportunities for utilising the search tree in constraint-logic object-oriented programming will be part of future work.

We also extend Muli's runtime environment, the MLVM, to implement depth-first search, breadth-first search, and iterative deepening depth-first search. Even though they are well-known as search algorithms for tree traversal, they are of particular interest in the context of constraint-logic object-oriented programming where the search tree is not (entirely) known before the program that it represents has been executed in its entirety. The MLVM already supported depth-first search using the previous, unstructured approach, but our evaluation demonstrates that using a structured approach does not add any overhead. On the contrary, the explicit representation provides opportunities for novel search algorithms that could not be used for executing constraint-logic object-oriented programs prior to our work. The modifications have already been integrated into the open source MLVM and are available at https://github.com/wwu-pi/muli.

The current work is the basis for future endeavours. The search tree structure could be used for implementing an interactive search strategy in which a developer could manually decide how to explore the search space when a choice is encountered. This interactivity could be an additional aid for debugging. Moreover, it is interesting to explore alternatives to explicit search trees, such as the use of delimited continuations for the implementation of non-deterministic execution.

Acknowledgements. The initial ideas that led to this work were conceived during the first author's visit to the University of Kiel. The authors appreciate the valuable input of those that participated in the discussions; in particular, Sandra Dylus, Jan Christiansen, Jan Rasmus Tikovsky, and Michael Hanus.

References

1. Braßel, B., Hanus, M., Huch, F.: Encapsulating non-determinism in functional logic computations. J. Funct. Log. Program. **2004**(6) (2004)
2. Dageförde, J.C.: Reference type logic variables in constraint-logic object-oriented programming. In: Silva, J. (ed.) WFLP 2018. LNCS, vol. 11285, pp. 131–144. Springer, Cham (2019). https://doi.org/10.1007/978-3-030-16202-3_8
3. Dageförde, J.C., Kuchen, H.: An operational semantics for constraint-logic imperative programming. In: Seipel, D., Hanus, M., Abreu, S. (eds.) WFLP/WLP/INAP -2017. LNCS (LNAI), vol. 10997, pp. 64–80. Springer, Cham (2018). https://doi.org/10.1007/978-3-030-00801-7_5
4. Dageförde, J.C., Kuchen, H.: A compiler and virtual machine for constraint-logic object-oriented programming with muli. J. Comput. Lang. **53**, 63–78 (2019). https://doi.org/10.1016/j.cola.2019.05.001
5. Dageförde, J.C., Kuchen, H.: Retrieval of individual solutions from encapsulated search with a potentially infinite search space. In: Proceedings of 34th SAC, pp. 1552–1561. Limassol, Cyprus (2019). https://doi.org/10.1145/3297280.3298912
6. Danvy, O., Filinski, A.: Abstracting control. In: Proceedings of the 1990 ACM Conference on LISP and Functional Programming - LFP 1990, pp. 151–160. ACM Press (1990)
7. Hanus, M., Peemöller, B., Reck, F.: Search strategies for functional logic programming. In: Proceedings of ATPS 2012, pp. 61–74, GI LNI 199 (2012)
8. King, J.C.: Symbolic execution and program testing. Commun. ACM **19**(7), 385–394 (1976). https://doi.org/10.1145/360248.360252
9. Kiselyov, O., Shan, C.: Embedded probabilistic programming. In: Taha, W.M. (ed.) DSL 2009. LNCS, vol. 5658, pp. 360–384. Springer, Heidelberg (2009). https://doi.org/10.1007/978-3-642-03034-5_17
10. Lindholm, T., Yellin, F., Bracha, G., Buckley, A.: The Java® Virtual Machine Specification - Java SE 8 Edition (2015). https://docs.oracle.com/javase/specs/jvms/se8/jvms8.pdf
11. Majchrzak, T.A., Kuchen, H.: Automated test case generation based on coverage analysis. In: TASE 2009. IEEE (2009). https://doi.org/10.1109/TASE.2009.33
12. van der Ploeg, A., Kiselyov, O.: Reflection without remorse: revealing a hidden sequence to speed up monadic reflection. In: ACM SIGPLAN Notices, vol. 49, no. 12, pp. 133–144 (2015)
13. Schrijvers, T., Stuckey, P., Wadler, P.: Monadic constraint programming. JFP **19**(6), 663–697 (2009). https://doi.org/10.1017/s0956796809990086
14. Warren, D.H.D.: An abstract prolog instruction set, Technical repot, SRI International, Menlo Park (1983)

Performance Analysis of Zippers

Vít Šefl[✉]

Faculty of Mathematics and Physics, Charles University, Prague, Czech Republic
sefl@ksvi.mff.cuni.cz

Abstract. A zipper is a powerful technique of representing a purely functional data structure in a way that allows fast access to a specific element. It is often used in cases where the imperative data structures would use a mutable pointer. However, the efficiency of zippers as a replacement for mutable pointers is not sufficiently explored. We attempt to address this issue by comparing the performance of zippers and mutable pointers in two common scenarios and three different languages: C++, C♯, and Haskell.

1 Introduction

Some programming techniques make use of the ability to keep a pointer to internal parts of a data structure. Such a pointer is usually called a *finger* [9]. As an example, a finger can be used to track the most recently used node in a tree. Tree operations can then start from the finger instead of starting from the root of the tree, which can lead to a speedup if the program frequently operates on elements that are stored near each other.

However, fingers lose most of their utility when applied to purely functional data structures. Operations that make use of fingers frequently require the structure to contain pointers to parent nodes or require mutability. Pointers to parent nodes create loops which hugely complicate update operations.

A *zipper* [5] is a technique of representing purely functional data structure in a way that allows direct access to an element at a selected position. Different data structures have different zipper representations: we, therefore, distinguish between list zippers, tree zippers, etc. Zippers differ from fingers in a crucial way. Unlike a finger, a zipper contains the data structure. A finger can be removed, and the structure it was pointing to remains intact while removing a zipper removes the structure it contains. As a consequence, while two fingers give direct access to two positions, two zippers do not.

Despite these differences, there is a variety of tasks that can be solved by both approaches. Our goal was to compare the effectiveness of these two techniques. We chose two tasks where the ability to directly access a position inside a data structure and perform local updates is beneficial: traversing a tree in an arbitrary way and building a tree from a sorted sequence. Each task was implemented in Haskell, C++, and C♯, using the programming style common to that language.

This research was supported by SVV project number 260 453.

P. Hofstedt et al. (Eds.): DECLARE 2019, LNAI 12057, pp. 215–229, 2020.
https://doi.org/10.1007/978-3-030-46714-2_14

Note that we compared the performance difference between these techniques, rather than performance across programming languages.

This work is organized as follows. In the next section, we discuss zipper representations. The third section looks at single position zippers in detail. The testing methodology, as well as the programming tasks themselves, are presented in the fourth section. Finally, the fifth section details our findings.

The source code used for performance testing is available online.[1]

2   Related Work

Huet's original zipper technique [5] relies on manually analyzing the data type and then defining the corresponding zipper structure. Listing 1 shows an example of such a zipper.

```
data List a = Nil | Cons a (List a)

data ListZipper a = ListZipper
  { before :: List a
  , focus  :: a
  , after  :: List a
  }
```

Listing 1. List and its zipper

This approach becomes problematic when working with heterogeneous data structures (a structure containing elements of multiple types), or when working with many different zipper representations.

For heterogeneous collections, Huet's zipper can be used to represent only the positions of one type of elements, which is quite limiting. Adams [2] shows how to build a zipper for heterogeneous collections by using generic programming techniques based on the ideas of Lämmel and Peyton Jones [7]. Another benefit of this approach is that new data structures do not need a custom implementation of the zipper structure, which reduces the boilerplate that is usually present when dealing with zippers.

Instead of using an explicit data structure, the zipper can be represented as a suspended traversal of the original structure. Kiselyov [6] uses delimited continuations to implement suspended computation to great effect. Applications include creating a zipper for any type that is a member of Haskell's `Traversable` type class, zipping two data structures for side-by-side comparison and various operations on zippers capable of representing multiple positions.

Another way of dealing with the boilerplate code is to automate the generation of auxiliary data structures. For each regular algebraic data type, the type of one-hole contexts can be obtained by differentiating the original type, not unlike differentiation in calculus [1,8]. A zipper is obtained by combining an element of the original structure and the one-hole context. As a result, the

---

[1] https://github.com/vituscze/performance-zippers

zipper does not need to be defined for each data structure separately [4]. We explore this technique in more detail in the following section.

Ramsey and Dias [11] use zippers to represent control flow graphs in a low-level optimizing compiler. The compiler is written in OCaml, giving the opportunity to use an imperative approach based on mutable pointers as well as a purely functional approach based on zippers. As part of their analysis, the authors also include performance comparison. Zippers are shown to perform slightly better than mutable pointers.

3 Zipper

Huet's zipper is based on the idea of pointer reversal. Reversing all pointers along the path from the root of the structure to a selected position called a *focus* creates a structure that is rooted at the focus. This reversal has multiple advantages. Direct access to the focus allows its modification in constant time. Even in a purely functional setting where in-place modifications are not available, creating a copy of the focused node may be used instead. The rest of the structure stays intact and can be shared.

Similarly, accessing the parent and children of the focus can be done in constant time, which can be used to efficiently move the focus around the structure. Moving the focus is accomplished by reversing the pointers.

Huet shows how to represent this kind of pointer reversal as a purely functional structure. The nodes on the path from the root to the focus are stored in a list. Each element of the list must contain the values and substructures that are not descended into as well as the direction taken when moving towards the focus. The list is reversed, ensuring the parent of the focus is in the head position (instead of the root of the structure).

```
data Tree a = Leaf | Node (Tree a) a (Tree a)

data PathChoice a
  = NodeL a (Tree a) -- Focus is in the left subtree
  | NodeR (Tree a) a -- Focus is in the right subtree

data Context = Context
  (Tree a)        -- Left subtree of the focus
  (Tree a)        -- Right subtree of the focus
  [PathChoice a]  -- Path to the root

data Zipper a = Zipper a (Context a)
```
Listing 2. Binary tree and its zipper

Listing 2 defines a binary tree and its zipper. Listing 3 shows how to move the focus of this zipper to the parent node.

```
up :: Zipper a -> Maybe (Zipper a)
up (Zipper _ (Context _ _ [])) = Nothing
```

```
up (Zipper x (Context l r (NodeL p pr:ps))) = Just $
   Zipper p (Context (Node l x r) pr ps)
up (Zipper x (Context l r (NodeR pl p:ps))) = Just $
   Zipper p (Context pl (Node l x r) ps)
```

Listing 3. Focus movement

However, since the zipper structure depends on the original data structure, these types and operations need to be defined for each structure separately. One way to solve this problem is to automate this process by using data type differentiation [1,8]. We give a brief overview of this technique here.

An *algebraic data type* is a data type defined as a combination of products (tuples) and sums (variants), potentially in a recursive way. Algebraic data types that do not change the parameters in recursive occurrences are known as *regular types*. For these types, the derivative is defined as follows.

$$\partial_x(0) = 0 \qquad \text{(empty type)}$$
$$\partial_x(1) = 0 \qquad \text{(unit type)}$$
$$\partial_x(y) = 0 \qquad \text{(type variable)}$$
$$\partial_x(x) = 1 \qquad \text{(type variable)}$$
$$\partial_x(F + G) = \partial_x(F) + \partial_x(G) \qquad \text{(sum type)}$$
$$\partial_x(F \times G) = \partial_x(F) \times G + F \times \partial_x(G) \qquad \text{(product type)}$$
$$\partial_x(\mu y.F) = [\mu y.F/y]\partial_x(F) \times \text{List}\ ([\mu y.F/y]\partial_y(F)) \qquad \text{(least fixed point)}$$

The expression $[y/x]t$ denotes a capture-avoiding substitution. The variables can be introduced as parameters of the entire type (such as a in List a) or by the least fixed point operation, which is used to define recursive types. The resulting derivative is a type of *one-hole contexts*. A one-hole context is a structure that uniquely describes one position within the original data structure. Zipper then consists of a one-hole context together with an element of the original structure.

For example, a binary tree is a regular algebraic data type, and its zipper can be obtained by computing the derivative.

$$\partial_a(\text{Tree } a) = \partial_a(\mu x.1 + x \times a \times x)$$
$$= [\text{Tree } a/x]\partial_a(1 + x \times a \times x) \times \text{List}\ ([\text{Tree } a/x]\partial_x(1 + x \times a \times x))$$
$$= [\text{Tree } a/x](x \times x) \times \text{List}\ ([\text{Tree } a/x](a \times x + x \times a))$$
$$= \text{Tree } a \times \text{Tree } a \times \text{List}\ (a \times \text{Tree } a + \text{Tree } a \times a)$$

This derivative matches the definition of the tree context given in Listing 2.

The zippers used for performance testing in this work were based on algebraic data type differentiation. The resulting zipper representation was manually adjusted to provide better control over its strictness properties.

4   Performance Testing

To compare the performance of zippers and fingers, we implemented tree traversal and tree insertion in three different programming languages. The approach based on zippers was implemented in Haskell. The approach based on fingers was implemented in C++ and C♯. We included two imperative languages, one with manual memory management and the other with garbage collection, to check how the memory management model affected the relative performance. Unless specified otherwise, when discussing the imperative solutions, we are talking about the C++ solution.

The tasks were chosen to test the performance under two different memory allocation requirements. Tree traversal can avoid memory allocation altogether, while tree insertion cannot. Both tasks were tailored to the finger- and zipper-based approaches, which was done to better represent the common use case of these approaches. In the following, we use the term *cursor* to refer to either a zipper or a finger.

4.1 Tree Traversal

The first task focuses on tree traversal. We are given a binary tree and a vector describing positions within the tree together with replacement values. The goal is to replace the specified elements of the original tree with the given values.

For cursor-based approach, the input vector contains instructions that specify the movement of the cursor relative to its previous position. These movement instructions are interspersed with the replacement instructions. The element under the cursor is replaced with the given value whenever such instruction is encountered. As an example, replacing the left child of the root with 10 and the right child with 20 would be represented as `Vector.fromList [Mov L, Set 10, Mov U, Mov R, Set 20]`.

We compared this approach to a solution where the replacement operation always starts at the root of the tree. The input vector describes the positions relative to the root of the tree. When a replacement value is encountered, the specified element is replaced, and the position is reset back to the root of the tree. The vector corresponding to the previous example would be `Vector.fromList [Mov L, Set 10, Mov R, Set 20]`. We do not allow `Mov U` as it is not necessary to describe a position.

This input format was chosen for better control over the spatial locality of the positions, which allowed us to observe how the cursor-based approach behaves depending on the average distance between positions. This task also allowed us to compare the performance of imperative solutions when memory allocation is not a factor.

Listing 4 specifies the desired behavior of the root- and cursor-based approaches. For simplicity, the specification does not handle incorrect inputs (such as positions outside the tree).

```
data Tree a = Leaf | Node (Tree a) a (Tree a)
data Dir = L | R | U

-- Replace an element at position determined by a list
-- of left/right directions.
replace :: a -> [Dir] -> Tree a -> Tree a
```

```
replace v []        (Node l _ r) = Node l v r
replace v (L:ds) (Node l x r) = Node (replace v ds l) x r
replace v (R:ds) (Node l x r) = Node l x (replace v ds r)
replace _ _        t             = t

data Cmd a = Mov Dir | Set a

-- Specifies the behavior of the cursor-based approach.
cursor :: Tree a -> Vector (Cmd a) -> Tree a
cursor tree = fst . Vector.foldl step (tree, [])
  where
    step (t, ds) (Mov U) = (t, tail ds)
    step (t, ds) (Mov d) = (t, d:ds)
    step (t, ds) (Set v) = (replace v (reverse ds) t, ds)

-- Specifies the behavior of the root-based approach.
root :: Tree a -> Vector (Cmd a) -> Tree a
root tree = fst . Vector.foldl step (tree, [])
  where
    step (t, ds) (Mov d) = (t, d:ds)
    step (t, ds) (Set v) = (replace v (reverse ds) t, [])
```

Listing 4. Tree traversal specification

Imperative Solution. Listing 5 defines the structures used to represent the binary tree. Member functions are omitted for brevity.

```
struct node_t {
  node_t* parent;
  node_t* left;
  node_t* right;
  int64_t value;
};

struct tree_t {
  node_t* root;
  node_t* finger;
};
```

Listing 5. Imperative binary tree (memory layout)

Movement instructions are represented by integer constants to simplify the code. The input vector is processed by iterating over all its elements, applying the corresponding finger operation at each step. We evaluated the imperative solutions on a perfect binary tree of a specified depth.

Functional Solution. The functional solution is more involved. Since the task is meant for a cursor-based approach, the zipper lends itself to this problem naturally. However, the root-based approach presents a few problems that have to be addressed.

The tree and zipper definitions shown in Listing 6 follow the definitions from Listing 2, with the exception that each data type contains strictness annotations. Fields annotated with ! are evaluated whenever the enclosing data constructor is, which ensures that these structures are fully evaluated at all times.

```
data Tree = Node !Tree !Int64 !Tree | Leaf

data Path
  = PathLeft   !Int64 !Tree   !Path
  | PathRight !Tree   !Int64 !Path
  | Nil

data Zipper = Zipper !Tree !Int64 !Tree !Path
```

Listing 6. Binary tree and its zipper (with strictness annotations)

As a consequence, the standard list type is replaced with a custom type. GHC is also instructed to unbox the integer fields, which is done to ensure that the cost of operating on boxed values does not have any impact on the performance. Unboxed vectors from the vector package are used to represent the input vector.

The zipper comes with operations that replace the focused element and move the focus left, right, and up. Processing the input vector is implemented as a strict left fold. The zipper is the accumulator value, and in each step, we apply zipper operation that corresponds to the element of the vector.

When starting from the root, replacing an element of the tree can be done easily with a recursive function that reads the vector in each recursive call and descends into the correct subtree. The problem is propagating the information about how many elements of the input vector were consumed so that the next operation can start from the correct position. To make sure the root-based approach is efficient, we compared a few ways of dealing with this issue.

State Monad Solution. The obvious solution is to use a state monad. Note that laziness in the state is unwanted, and the strict monad version is about twice as fast. Analyzing GHC's core language [10], the monadic code was optimized away, and most values were unboxed. The only value that was not unboxed was the state returned by the replacement operation. Replacing the standard state monad with a handwritten one that uses unboxed integer did not improve the performance in a statistically significant way, however.

ST Monad Solution. Another way of passing the state is to use the imperative ST monad. The standard implementation of STRef is limited to boxed types, which hugely degraded the performance. The standard references had to be replaced with unboxed references from the unboxed-ref package.

findIndices Solution. Instead of propagating the new position via various versions of the state monad, the replacement operation can be given hints on where to start. These hints can be provided by an auxiliary vector containing the positions where each descent starts. We can create this vector by using the findIndices function from the vector package. This solution has a few issues. The input vector has to be traversed twice, and the auxiliary vector has to be stored in the memory.

findIndex Solution. We can avoid the memory allocation by computing the hints as needed, instead of all at once, by using the `findIndex` function.

Precomputed Vector Solution. To measure the impact of the double traversal, we also implemented a function where the vector of hints is a part of its input. The vector is precomputed, and its time requirements were not included in the comparison.

Much like the imperative solution, all functional solutions were evaluated on a perfect binary tree of a specified depth.

4.2   Tree Insertion

The second task focuses on tree building. Building a search tree can be done much more efficiently when the input sequence is sorted. The search for a new insertion point can be skipped since it will always be the leftmost or the rightmost node (depending on the order of the input sequence). This node can be tracked with a finger that is updated each time a new element is inserted. The same can be done with a zipper, although the standard tree insert operation cannot be reused.

To test a zipper for a different structure, we chose 2-3 trees [3] for this task. The structure is redundant: all data is kept in the leaf nodes, and internal nodes contain the minimum of their right subtree (and of the middle subtree, whenever applicable). The task is then to build a redundant 2-3 tree from a descending sequence of a given length. The standard approach starts from the root of the tree when looking for the insertion point. The cursor-based approach starts in the leftmost node and perform no additional search.

Imperative Solution. Listing 7 defines the structures used to represent the 2-3 tree. Member functions are omitted for brevity.

```
struct node_t {
  std::array<int64_t, 2> values;
  std::array<node_t*, 3> children;
  node_t* parent;
  bool is_two_node;
};

struct tree_t {
  node_t* root;
  node_t* last_inserted;
};
```

Listing 7. Imperative 2-3 tree (memory layout)

Tree insertion follows the standard algorithm. We obtain the insertion point and attempt to insert the element into the corresponding leaf node. When the leaf node is full, we allocate a new node and redistribute all the elements from the original node. After this split, we are left with a two-node and a three-node. We take the middle element and the right node and attempt to insert them into the parent node. We repeat this process until no split occurs or the root is reached. Note that splitting an inner node results in two-nodes because the middle element does not need to be duplicated.

The split operation puts the inserted element into a two-node when inserting elements in descending order. As a result, leaf nodes are only split every second insertion. The implementation could be improved to also provide similar benefit for insertion in ascending order.

We also tried the following variations of the tree operations: non-recursive destructor, split operation that allocates the left node, and recursive root-based insertion. The impact on the performance was either detrimental or statistically insignificant.

We repeatedly inserted elements into the tree in descending order and measured the time taken. In the case of C++ solution, this measurement also included the time spent on deallocation, giving a fairer comparison to the languages with garbage collection.

Functional Solution. Listing 8 shows a definition of 2-3 trees with strictness annotations.

```
data Tree
  = Leaf
  | Node2 !Tree !Int64 !Tree
  | Node3 !Tree !Int64 !Tree !Int64 !Tree
```

Listing 8. Functional 2-3 tree

To insert an element into the tree, we recursively insert it into the correct subtree. The result of this insertion is either one subtree or two subtrees and an element. The first case is handled by replacing the corresponding subtree; the second case indicates that a split occurred and is handled similarly to the imperative solution.

To obtain a zipper, we compute the derivative of a parametrized version of the 2-3 tree type.

$$F = 1 + ax^2 + a^2 x^3$$
$$\partial_a(F) = x^2 + 2ax^3$$
$$\partial_x(F) = 2ax + 3a^2 x^2$$
$$\partial_a(\text{Tree } a) = \partial_a(\mu x.F)$$
$$= [\text{Tree } a/x]\partial_a(F) \times \text{List } ([\text{Tree } a/x]\partial_x(F))$$
$$= ((\text{Tree } a)^2 + 2a(\text{Tree } a)^3) \times \text{List } (2a(\text{Tree } a) + 3a^2(\text{Tree } a)^2)$$

If the focus is in a two-node, then there is only one choice for the position, and the context is given by the two subtrees. This case is represented by $(\text{Tree } a)^2$. If the focus is in a three-node, there are two choices for the position (left or right). The context is given by the three subtrees and the element that is not focused, or $2a(\text{Tree } a)^3$.

The path also distinguishes between two-nodes and three-nodes. In the case of a two-node, there are two choices for the focus position (left or right subtree). The context is given by the element and the other subtree. This case is represented by $2a(\text{Tree } a)$. In the case of a three-node, there are three choices for the focus position (left, middle, or right subtree) and the context is given by the two elements and the other two subtrees, resulting in the final term $3a^2(\text{Tree } a)^2$.

Since the insertion algorithm only needs to know the leftmost node and not the particular element, we simplify the zipper by removing this choice point. The type variable is replaced with `Int64` and the list type is replaced with a custom strict list. Listing 9 shows the resulting type.

```
data Nonempty
  = Nonempty2 !Tree !Int64 !Tree
  | Nonempty3 !Tree !Int64 !Tree !Int64 !Tree

data PathChoice
  = Path2L !Int64 !Tree
  | Path2R !Tree !Int64
  | Path3L !Int64 !Tree !Int64 !Tree
  | Path3M !Tree !Int64 !Int64 !Tree
  | Path3R !Tree !Int64 !Tree !Int64

data Path = Nil | Cons !PathChoice !Path
data Zipper = Zipper !Nonempty !Path
```

Listing 9. 2-3 tree zipper

Inserting an element by using a zipper more closely resembles the imperative solution. The key difference is that instead of pointers to parent nodes, the zipper contains a list of choices along the path from the root to the focus. Instead of descending into the tree, the zipper-based insertion needs to descend into this list.

When a node splits and we attempt to add the element and one of the freshly split nodes to the parent node, we also need to include information about the position of the split node in relation to the element. This position is necessary to reconstruct the extra information contained in the zipper. The imperative solution assumes the split node is always to the right.

Much like the imperative solution, we repeatedly inserted elements into the tree in descending order and measured time taken.

5   Results

All experiments were performed on Intel Core i7-4750HQ processor with 24 GB of main memory under Windows 10 operating system. Each program was compiled with the highest available level of compiler optimizations, and in the case of GHC, LLVM backend was used for code generation. Garbage collectors were allowed to only run in a single thread. Each solution was executed with an increasing number of iterations until a time limit of three minutes was reached. The measured times were normalized to one iteration. Mean execution time, as well as standard deviation, were computed. Error bars represent one standard deviation. The raw measurements are available online. [2]

5.1 Tree Traversal

The input files were generated by randomly picking 1,000,000 elements out of a perfect binary tree with 20 levels and outputting the path between them. We evaluated the tree traversal in four scenarios which were obtained by biasing the random generator towards particular areas of the tree: no bias, bottom bias, right bias, and bottom-right bias. One input file was generated for each scenario to ensure any performance differences were not due to different input data.

The results of the functional root-based approach are based on the `findIndex` solution. Its precomputed version is only marginally faster, showing that the double traversal has a low impact on the performance. The state and ST solutions are much slower. Interestingly, the ST solution is slightly slower than the purely functional state solution. Full comparison of these variants can be found in Fig. 1.

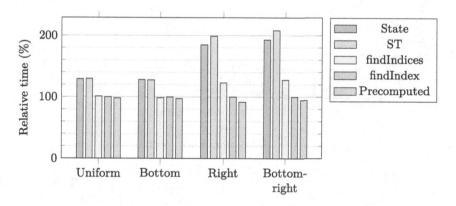

Fig. 1. Tree traversal performance (Haskell)

When the spatial locality is low (Fig. 2 and Fig. 3), the root-based approach shows a clear advantage over the cursor-based approach. The relative gains of the root-based approach are in the range of 50% to 60% for the imperative solutions and around 20% for the functional solution.

---

[2] https://github.com/vituscze/performance-zippers/blob/master/data.csv.

When the spatial locality is high (Fig. 4 and Fig. 5), the cursor-based approach takes over. In the case of the right bias, C++ reaches 150% speedup, C♯ 135% and Haskell 220%. Bottom-right bias increases this gap even more. C++ reaches 205% speedup, C♯ 175% and Haskell 280%.

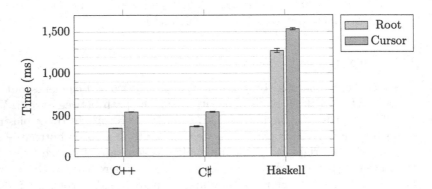

Fig. 2. Tree traversal performance (no bias)

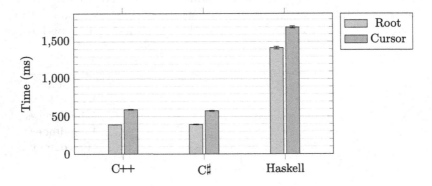

Fig. 3. Tree traversal performance (bottom bias)

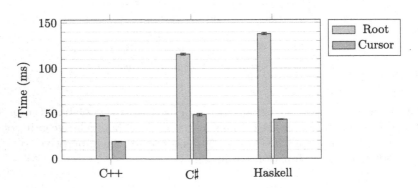

Fig. 4. Tree traversal performance (right bias)

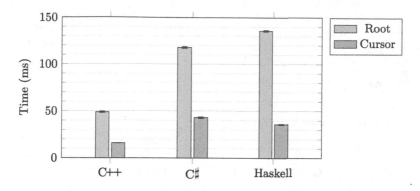

Fig. 5. Tree traversal performance (bottom-right bias)

Notice that the root-based approach also shows a considerable performance boost when the input data has high spatial locality. This boost is a consequence of cache-friendly memory access pattern. In all scenarios, the zipper-based approach exhibits smaller performance losses (low spatial locality) and higher performance gains (high spatial locality) when compared to the finger-based approach.

5.2 Tree Insertion

Evaluating insertion into a 2-3 tree was done by repeatedly constructing a tree containing 10,000,000 elements. The ordered sequence was not part of the input. Instead, the elements of this sequence were generated on the fly and inserted into the tree directly, without any auxiliary structure. As mentioned earlier, this task compared fingers and zippers in an environment where memory allocation is necessary. For this reason, the C++ solution also evaluated the time it took to deallocate the structure, giving a better comparison with C♯ and Haskell.

The results are shown in Fig. 6. All three solutions show a preference for the cursor-based approach. In C++ and C♯, the finger-based insertion is roughly 20% faster than the root-based insertion. In Haskell, the zipper-based insertion is 210% faster.

Note that both the root-based and finger-based insertion allocate $\mathcal{O}(1)$ nodes (amortized) per insertion in imperative languages. The root-based functional solution needs to copy the path from the root to the insertion point, leading to $\mathcal{O}(\log n)$ new nodes per insertion. The zipper-based insertion, therefore, not only avoids the cost of finding the insertion point but also leads to significantly reduced allocation count.

Comparing the C++ and C♯ results did not point to memory management as a major factor. Reducing the size of the tree (by performing fewer insertions) showed that the gap between C++ and C♯ decreased slightly, which hints to a minor performance benefit from using garbage collection.

The C++ solution could be further optimized by using a memory pool instead of the standard **new** and **delete** operators. However, we did not want to deviate

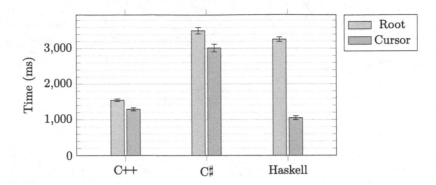

Fig. 6. 2-3 Tree insertion performance

from the standard memory management models. In a similar vein, we decided against fine-tuning the garbage collector parameters for the Haskell and C♯ solutions.

6   Conclusion

While zippers lack the flexibility and ease of use of mutable pointers, they are nevertheless a powerful tool when working with purely functional data structures. However, it was unclear whether zippers offer the same performance benefit as the imperative approach.

We compared fingers and zippers in two scenarios: arbitrary tree traversal and tree insertion. The first test measured the effectiveness of zippers when its imperative counterpart does not have to allocate memory. This test focused on fast access to a selected element as well as the ability to move the focus. The second test considered the case where both the imperative and functional solutions need to allocate memory. This test focused on the pointer reversal aspect of zippers.

We provided evidence that when zippers are used in a functional setting, they offer higher performance gains compared to mutable pointers used in an imperative setting. More importantly, zippers provide this gain without undermining the benefits of purely functional data structures. We hope that this work encourages functional programmers to use zippers before reaching for imperative techniques when optimizing their code.

References

1. Abbott, M., Altenkirch, T., McBride, C., Ghani, N.: ∂ for data: differentiating data structures. Fundam. Inf. **65**(1–2), 1–28 (2004)
2. Adams, M.D.: Scrap your zippers: a generic zipper for heterogeneous types. In: Proceedings of the 6th ACM SIGPLAN Workshop on Generic Programming, WGP 2010, pp. 13–24. ACM, New York (2010). https://doi.org/10.1145/1863495. 1863499

3. Cormen, T.H., Leiserson, C.E., Rivest, R.L., Stein, C.: Introduction to Algorithms, 3rd edn. The MIT Press, Cambridge (2009)
4. Hinze, R., Jeuring, J., Löh, A.: Type-indexed data types. Sci. Comput. Program. **51**(1–2), 117–151 (2004). https://doi.org/10.1016/j.scico.2003.07.001
5. Huet, G.: The zipper. J. Funct. Program. **7**(5), 549–554 (1997). https://doi.org/10.1017/S0956796897002864
6. Kiselyov, O.: Generic zipper: the context of a traversal. http://okmij.org/ftp/continuations/zipper.html (2015)
7. Lämmel, R., Peyton Jones, S.: Scrap your boilerplate: a practical design pattern for generic programming. In: Proceedings of the 2003 ACM SIGPLAN International Workshop on Types in Languages Design and Implementation, TLDI 2003, pp. 26–37. ACM, New York (2003). https://doi.org/10.1145/604174.604179
8. McBride, C.: The derivative of a regular type is its type of one-hole contexts (extended abstract) (2001). http://strictlypositive.org/diff.pdf
9. Brodal, G.S.: Finger Search Trees. In: Mehta, D., Sahni, S. (eds.) Handbook of Data Structures and Applications. Chapman & Hall/CRC, Boca Raton (2004)
10. Peyton Jones, S., Santos, A.: A transformation-based optimiser for Haskell. Sci. Comput. Program. **32**(1–3), 3–47 (1998). https://doi.org/10.1016/S0167-6423(97)00029-4
11. Ramsey, N., Dias, J.: An applicative control-flow graph based on Huet's zipper. Electron. Notes Theor. Comput. Sci. **148**(2), 105–126 (2006). https://doi.org/10.1016/j.entcs.2005.11.042

Adding Data to Curry

Michael Hanus$^{(\boxtimes)}$ (iD) and Finn Teegen (iD)

Institut für Informatik, CAU Kiel, 24098 Kiel, Germany
{mh,fte}@informatik.uni-kiel.de

Abstract. Functional logic languages can solve equations over user-defined data and functions. Thus, the definition of an appropriate meaning of equality has a long history in these languages, ranging from reflexive equality in early equational logic languages to strict equality in contemporary functional logic languages like Curry. With the introduction of type classes, where the equality operation "==" is overloaded and user-defined, the meaning became more complex. Moreover, logic variables appearing in equations require a different typing than pattern variables, since the latter might be instantiated with functional values or non-terminating operations. In this paper, we present a solution to these problems by introducing a new type class **Data** which is associated with specific algebraic data types, logic variables, and strict equality. We discuss the ideas of this class and its implications on various concepts of Curry, like unification, functional patterns, and program optimization.

1 Introduction

The amalgamation of the main declarative programming paradigms, namely functional and logic programming, has a long history. The advantages of such integrated functional logic languages are manifold. One can use the features of functional programming (e.g., powerful type systems, higher-order functions, lazy evaluation) and logic programming (e.g., non-deterministic search, computing with partial information) in a single language which also leads to new design patterns [3,8]. Compared to logic programming, computations can be more efficient due to the use of optimal evaluation strategies [2].

Early approaches to integrating functional and logic programming (see [15] for a good collection of these proposals) used equational logic programming [19,37] as a unifying framework. From a logic programming point of view, equational logic programming extends the meaning of the standard equality predicate "=" by taking user-defined functions into account before checking the equality of both sides of an equation. Hence, both sides are evaluated before they are unified. If the definition of evaluable functions are considered as axioms for an equational theory, this process is also known as *E-unification* [17]. In order to use logic programming techniques (computing with partial information) also for the evaluation of user-defined functions, one can use narrowing instead of reduction [40], i.e., replace pattern matching by unification when a function call should be reduced. In this way, functional logic languages based on narrowing can be used to *solve equations*.

© Springer Nature Switzerland AG 2020
P. Hofstedt et al. (Eds.): DECLARE 2019, LNAI 12057, pp. 230–246, 2020.
https://doi.org/10.1007/978-3-030-46714-2_15

Example 1. Consider the following definition of Peano numbers and their addition (in Haskell [39] syntax):

```
data Nat = Z | S Nat
add :: Nat  →  Nat  →  Nat
add Z     n = n
add (S m) n = S (add m n)
```

In the functional language Haskell, we can only compute the value of expressions, e.g.,

```
> add (S Z) (S Z)
S (S Z)
```

However, if we interpret these definitions as a program written in the (narrowing-based) functional logic language Curry [22,27], we can also solve the equation

```
> add x (S Z) =:= S (S Z)    where x free
{x = S Z} True
```

Here, "=:=" denotes equality w.r.t. user-defined operations (see below for more details) and x is declared as a free (logic) variable which is bound to S Z in order to evaluate the equation to True.

For the practical applicability of functional logic languages, it is important to reduce the computation space by using specific evaluation strategies. Thus, much work in this area has been devoted to develop appropriate narrowing strategies (see [21] for an early account of this research). In order to provide the advantages of lazy evaluation used in Haskell, e.g., optimal evaluation [29] and modularity [30], later research concentrated on demand-driven strategies. Needed narrowing [2] is an optimal strategy [1] and, thus, the basis of the language Curry.

Demand-driven evaluation strategies, like Haskell's lazy evaluation or Curry's needed narrowing, can deal with non-terminating operations that compute infinite data structures [30]. However, this could be in conflict with the equation solving capabilities of functional logic languages discussed above. Standard equality in the mathematical sense is required to be reflexive, i.e., $x = x$ should always hold [37]. Now consider two operations to compute infinite lists of Peano numbers:

```
f1 :: Nat  →  [Nat]
f1 n = n : f1 (S n)
f2 :: Nat  →  [Nat]
f2 n = n : S n : f2 (S (S n))
```

By reflexivity, f1 Z = f1 Z should hold. This means that the infinite lists of all Peano numbers are equal. As a consequence, f1 Z = f2 Z should also hold, but it is unclear to verify it during run time. In early equational logic programming, equations are solved by narrowing both sides to normal forms and unifying these normal forms. However, this does not work here since f1 Z and f1 Z have no normal form. Thus, reflexivity is not a feasible property of equations to be evaluated (more details including issues about semantics are discussed in [18, 36]).

Therefore, contemporary languages interpret equations to be evaluated as *strict equality*, denoted by "=:=" in Curry: e_1 =:= e_2 is satisfied iff e_1 and e_2 are reducible to a same ground constructor term, i.e., an expression without variables and defined functions. In particular, soundness, completeness, and optimality results are stated w.r.t. strict equality [2]. As a consequence, `f1 Z =:= f1 Z` does not hold so that it is not a defect that this equation cannot be solved.

Note that Haskell also offers the operation "==" intended to compare expressions. Although standard textbooks on Haskell define this operation as "equality" [11,31,41], its actual implementation can be different since, as a member of the type class `Eq`, it can be defined with a behavior different than equality on concrete type instances. Actually, the documentation of the type class `Eq`[1] denotes "==" as "equality" but also contains the remark: "== is customarily expected to implement an equivalence relationship where two values comparing equal are indistinguishable by "public" functions." Thus, it is intended that e_1 == e_2 evaluates to `True` even if e_1 and e_2 have not the same but only equivalent values. On the other hand, the documentation requires that the reflexivity property

```
x == x = True
```

holds for any implementation, but this is not true even for the standard integer equality (choose "`last [1..] :: Int`" for x).

This discussion shows that the precise treatment of equality, which is essential for functional logic languages, might have some pitfalls when type classes are used. As long as "==" is defined in the standard way (by the use of "`deriving Eq`"), "==" conforms with strict equality. With the introduction of type classes to Curry, one has to be more careful. For instance, consider the "classical" functional logic definition of the operation `last` to compute the last element of a list by exploiting list concatenation ("++") and equation solving [21,24]:

```
last xs | _ ++ [e] == xs = e
    where e free
```

If "==" denotes equivalence rather than strict equality, `last` might not return the last element of a list but one (or more than one) value which is equivalent to the last element.

In this paper, we propose a solution to these problems by distinguishing between strict equality and equivalence. For this purpose, we propose a new type class `Data` which is associated with specific algebraic data types. We will see that this type class can also be used for a better characterization of the meaning of logic variables and the Curry's unification operator "=:=".

This paper is structured as follows. In the next section, we review some aspects of functional logic programming and Curry. After motivating the problem this paper tackles in Sect. 3, we propose in Sect. 4 a new standard type class for Curry, namely `Data`, as a solution to the problem. In Sects. 5, 6, and Sect. 7,

---

[1] http://hackage.haskell.org/package/base-4.12.0.0/docs/Data-Eq.html.

we discuss how the proposed Data type class affects logic variables, optimization of equality constraints, and non-left-linear rules and functional patterns, respectively. Finally, Sect. 8 discusses related work before we conclude in Sect. 9.

2   Functional Logic Programming and Curry

We briefly review some aspects of functional logic programming and Curry that are necessary to understand the contents of this paper. More details can be found in surveys on functional logic programming [7,24] and in the language report [27].

Curry is a declarative multi-paradigm language intended to combine the most important features from functional and logic programming. The syntax of Curry is close to Haskell [39] but also allows *free (logic) variables* in conditions and right-hand sides of rules. Thus, *expressions* in Curry programs contain *operations* (defined functions), *constructors* (introduced in data type declarations), and *variables* (arguments of operations or free variables). Function calls with free variables are evaluated by a possibly non-deterministic instantiation of demanded arguments [2]. This corresponds to narrowing [40], but Curry narrows with possibly non-most-general unifiers to ensure the optimality of computations [2]. In contrast to Haskell, rules with overlapping left-hand sides are non-deterministically (rather than sequentially) applied.

Example 2. The following simple program shows the functional and logic features of Curry. It defines the well-known list concatenation and an operation that returns some element of a list having at least two occurrences:

```
(++) :: [a]  →  [a]  →  [a]
[]       ++ ys = ys
(x:xs) ++ ys = x : (xs ++ ys)
someDup :: [a]  →  a
someDup xs | xs =:= _ ++ [x] ++ _ ++ [x] ++ _ = x
   where x free
```

Since "++" can be called with free variables in arguments, the condition in the rule of someDup is solved by instantiating x and the anonymous free variables "_" to appropriate values before reducing the function calls. As already mentioned in the introduction, "=:=" denotes strict equality, i.e., the condition of someDup is satisfied if both sides are reduced to a same ground constructor term. In order to avoid the enumeration of useless values, "=:=" is implemented as unification: if y and z are free (unbound) variables, y=:=z is evaluated (to True) by binding y and z (or vice versa) instead of non-deterministically binding y and z to identical ground constructor terms. This can be interpreted as an optimized implementation by delaying the bindings to ground constructor terms [10]. Due to this implementation, "=:=" is also called an *equational constraint* (rather than Boolean equality).

We already used the logic programming features of Curry in the definition of last shown in Sect. 1. In contrast to last, someDup is a *non-deterministic operation* since it could yield more than one result for a given argument, e.g., the evaluation of `someDup [1,2,2,1]` yields the values 1 and 2. Non-deterministic operations, which can formally be interpreted as mappings from values into sets of values [20], are an important feature of contemporary functional logic languages. Hence, Curry has also a predefined *choice* operation:

```
x ? _ = x
_ ? y = y
```

Thus, the expression "0 ? 1" evaluates to 0 and 1 with the value non-deterministically chosen.

3   Equality vs. Equivalence

Type classes are an important feature to express ad-hoc polymorphism in a structured manner [42]. In the context of Curry, it is also useful to restrict the application of some operations to unintended expressions. For instance, in the definition of Curry without type classes [27], the type of the unification operator is defined as

```
(=:=) :: a → a → Bool
```

This implies that we could unify values of any type, including defined functions. However, the meaning of equality on functions is not well defined. The Curry implementation PAKCS [26], which compiles Curry programs into Prolog programs, uses an intensional meaning, i.e., functions are equal if they have the same name. This means that PAKCS evaluates

```
not =:= not
```

to `True` but it fails on

```
not =:= (\x → not x)
```

(since the lambda abstraction will be lifted into a new top-level function). Moreover, the Curry implementation KiCS2 [12], which compiles Curry programs into Haskell programs, produces an internal error for these expressions.

It would be preferable to forbid the application of "=:=" to functional values at compile time. This is similar to the requirement on Haskell's operator "==". Haskell uses the type class `Eq` in order to express that "==" is not parametric polymorphic but overloaded for some (but not all) types. The type class `Eq` contains two operations (we omit the default implementations):

```
class Eq a where
    (==) :: a → a → Bool
    (/=) :: a → a → Bool
```

Hence, the operator "==" cannot be applied to any type but only to types defining instances of this class. We can use this operator to check whether an element occurs in a list:

```
elem :: Eq a => a → [a] → Bool
```

```
elem _ []      = False
elem x (y:ys) = x==y || elem x ys
```

Although type classes express type restrictions in an elegant manner, they might also cause unexpected behaviors if they are not carefully used. For instance, we can define a data type for values indexed by a unique number:

```
data IVal a = IVal Int a
```

Since the index is assumed to be unique, we define the comparison of index values by just comparing the indices:

```
instance Eq a => Eq (IVal a) where
   IVal i1 _ == IVal i2 _ =  i1 == i2
```

With this definition, the operation `elem` defined above could yield surprising results:

```
> elem (IVal 1 'b') [IVal 1 'a']
True
```

This is not intended since the element (first argument) does not occur in the list. Actually, the Haskell documentation[2] about `elem` contains the explanation "Does the element occur in the structure?" which ignores the fact that some instances of `Eq` are only equivalences rather than identities.

This unusual behavior could also influence logic-oriented computations in a surprising manner. If the operation `last` is defined as shown in Sect. 1, we obtain the following answer when computing the last element of a given `IVal` list (here, "_" denotes a logical variable of type `Char`):

```
> last [IVal 1 'a']
IVal 1 _
```

Hence, instead of the last element, we get a rather general representation of it.

The next section presents our proposal to solve these problems.

4   Data

As discussed above, type classes are an elegant way to express type restrictions. On the other hand, it is not a good idea to allow user-defined instance definitions of important operations like strict equality. Therefore, we propose the introduction of a specific type class where only standard instances can be derived so that all instances satisfy the intended meaning. This type class is called `Data` and has the following definition:

```
class Data a where
   aValue :: a
   (===)  :: a → a → Bool
```

Thus, any instance of this class provides two operations:

– The non-deterministic operation `aValue` returns some value, i.e., the complete evaluation of `aValue` yields all values of type `a`.

---

[2] http://hackage.haskell.org/package/base-4.12.0.0/docs/Prelude.html.

- The operation "`===`" implements the standard equality on values, i.e., it returns `True` or `False` depending on whether the argument values are identical or not.

The following definition specifies how to automatically derive a `Data` instance for any algebraic datatype.

Definition 1. *If T is an algebraic datatype declared by*

$$data\ T\ a_1\ ...\ a_k\ =\ C_1\ b_{11}\ ...\ b_{1k_1}\ |\ ...\ |\ C_n\ b_{n1}\ ...\ b_{nk_n}$$

the standard derived `Data` instance has the following form:

```
instance cx => Data (T a₁ ... aₖ) where
  aValue = C₁ aValue ... aValue ? ... ? Cₙ aValue ... aValue
```
$$C_1\ x_1\ ...\ x_{k_1}\ ===\ C_1\ y_1\ ...\ y_{k_1}\ =\ x_1\ ===\ y_1\ \&\&\ ...\ \&\&\ x_{k_1}\ ===\ y_{k_1}$$
$$\vdots$$
$$C_n\ x_1\ ...\ x_{k_n}\ ===\ C_n\ y_1\ ...\ y_{k_n}\ =\ x_1\ ===\ y_1\ \&\&\ ...\ \&\&\ x_{k_n}\ ===\ y_{k_n}$$
$$C_i\ \_\ ...\ \_\ ===\ C_j\ \_\ ...\ \_\ =\ False\ \forall i,j \in \{1,...,n\}\ with\ i \neq j$$

In the instance declaration above, the context cx consists of `Data` constraints ensuring that `Data` b_{ij} holds for each type b_{ij} with $i \in \{1,...,n\}$ and $j \in \{1,...,k_i\}$.

Example 3. For the type of Peano numbers (see Example 1), the `Data` instance can be defined as follows:

```
instance Data Nat where
  aValue = Z  ?  S aValue

  Z    === Z   = True
  S m  === S n = m === n
  Z    === S _ = False
  S _  === Z   = False
```

A `Data` instance for lists requires a `Data` instance for its elements:

```
instance Data a => Data [a] where
  aValue = []  ?  aValue : aValue

  []      === []      = True
  (x:xs)  === (y:ys)  = x === y && xs === ys
  []      === (_:_)   = False
  (_:_)   === []      = False
```

The operation `aValue` is useful when a value of some data type should be guessed, e.g., for testing [25]. The obvious relation to logic variables will be discussed later.

The definition of "`===`" is identical to "`==`" if the definition of the latter is automatically derived (by a "`deriving Eq`" clause). As discussed above, it is also possible to define other instances of `Eq` that leads to unintended results. To ensure that "`===`" always denotes equality on values, *it is not allowed to define explicit*

Data instances as shown above. Such instances can only be generated by adding a "`deriving Data`" clause to a data definition. Note that an instance derivation requires that all arguments of all data constructors have `Data` instances. In particular, if some argument has a functional type, e.g.,

```
data IntRel = IntRel (Int  →  Bool)
```

then a `Data` instance can not be derived.

For ease of use, one could always derive `Data` instances for data declarations whenever it is possible (i.e., functional values do not occur in arguments), or provide a language option to turn this behavior on or off.

With the introduction of the class `Data`, we can specify a more precise type to Curry's strict equality operation "`=:=`". As discussed in [10], the meaning of "`=:=`" is the "positive" part of "`===`", i.e., its semantics can be defined by

$$x \; \texttt{=:=} \; y \quad = \quad \texttt{solve} \, (x \; \texttt{===} \; y) \qquad (1)$$

where `solve` is an operator that enforces positive evaluations for Boolean expressions:

$$\texttt{solve True} \; = \; \texttt{True} \qquad (2)$$

Since expressions of the form $e_1 \texttt{=:=} e_2$ might return `True` but never `False`, "`=:=`" can be implemented by unification, as already discussed in Sect. 2. Such an optimized implementation is justified by the definition (1) above. However, if the semantics of "`=:=`" is defined by

$$x \; \texttt{=:=} \; y \quad = \quad \texttt{solve} \, (x \; \texttt{==} \; y) \qquad (3)$$

as suggested before the introduction of type classes to Curry [9], an implementation of "`=:=`" by unification would not be correct since unification might put stronger requirements on expressions to be compared than actually defined by `Eq` instances.

As a spin-off of definition (1), we obtain a more restricted type of "`=:=`":

$$(\texttt{=:=}) \; :: \; \texttt{Data a => a} \; \rightarrow \texttt{a} \; \rightarrow \texttt{Bool} \qquad (4)$$

This avoids the problems with the application of "`=:=`" to functional values sketched at the beginning of Sect. 3.

5   Logic Variables

When a function call with free variables in arguments is evaluated by narrowing, the free variables are instantiated to values so that the function call becomes reducible. Conceptually, a free variable denotes possible values so that a computation can pick one in order to proceed. With the definition of the type class `Data` and the non-deterministic operation `aValue`, we make the notion of "possible value" explicit. Actually, it has been shown that non-deterministic operations and logic variables have the same expressive power [5,14] since one can replace logic variables occurring in a functional logic program by non-deterministic value generators.

Example 4. Consider the addition on Peano numbers shown in Example 1 which is exploited to define subtraction:

```
sub :: Nat → Nat → Nat
sub x y | add y z === x = z
  where z free
```

We can replace the logic variable z by a value generator:

```
sub x y | add y z === x = z
  where z = aValue
```

The equivalence of logic variables and non-deterministic value generators can be exploited when Curry is implemented by translation into a target language without support for non-determinism and logic variables. For instance, KiCS2 [12] compiles Curry into Haskell by adding only a mechanism to handle non-deterministic computations. Therefore, KiCS2 is able to evaluate a logic variable to all its values. Thus, KiCS2 could exploit this fact by using the following alternative definition for aValue:

$$aValue = \_ \tag{5}$$

This equivalence also sheds some new light on the type of logic variables. Currently, logic variables without any constraints on their types are considered to have a polymorphic type. For instance, the inferred type of aValue as defined in (5) is

```
aValue :: a
```

However, this type does not really describe the intent of this operation, since aValue does not yield functional values. For instance, consider the definition

```
f x = y where y free
```

The type currently inferred is

```
f :: a → b
```

However, it is meaningless to use the result of some application of f in contexts where a function is required. For instance, the evaluation of the expression

$$map (f\,True)\,[0,1] \tag{6}$$

suspends in PAKCS and produces a run-time error in KiCS2 (very similar to the examples described at the beginning of Sect. 3). Furthermore, the inferred type of the definition

```
g x = g x
```

is

```
g :: a → b
```

Thus, it looks very similar to the type of f although g has a quite different meaning: in contrast to f, an application of g never returns a value.

All these problems can be avoided by a simple fix: logic variables are considered as equivalent to the operation aValue of type class Data so that a logic variable without any constraints on its type has type a where a is constrained with the type class context Data a. With this change, the inferred type of f is

```
f :: Data b => a → b
```

As a consequence, expression (6) will be rejected by the type checker since functions have no Data instance.

6   Equality Optimization

Choosing the appropriate kind of equality might not be obvious to the programmer. The difference between identity and equivalence is semantically relevant so that the decision between "===" and "==" is not avoidable. However, "=:=" can be considered as an optimization of "===" so that it is not obvious when it should be applied. In order to simplify this situation, it has been argued in [9,10] that the programmer should always use strict equality (i.e., "===") and the selection of "=:=" should be done by an optimization tool. This tool analyzes the required values of Boolean expressions. If an application of strict equality requires only the result value True, e.g., in guards of conditional rules or in arguments of solve, see (2), then one can safely replace the equality operator by the unification operator "=:=" (see [10] for details). For instance, if last is defined by

```
last xs | _ ++ [e] === xs
        = e  where e free
```

then it can be transformed into

```
last xs | _ ++ [e] =:= xs
        = e  where e free
```

As shown in [10], this transformation can have a big impact on the execution time.

Up to now, this tool (which is part of the compilation chain of Curry systems) considered the optimization of calls to "==". Since this might lead to incompleteness, as discussed above, it has to consider calls to "===" when the type class Data is introduced. However, for backward compatibility and better optimizations, one can extend the optimizer also to calls of the form $e_1 == e_2$: if the types of the arguments e_1, e_2 are monomorphic and the Eq instances of these types are derived with the default scheme (by deriving annotations), the semantics of "==" is identical to the semantics of "===" so that one can replace $e_1 == e_2$ by $e_1 === e_2$ and apply the optimization sketched above.

7   Non-left-Linear Rules and Functional Patterns

The proposed introduction of the type class **Data** together with the adjusted type of the unification operator "=:=" has also some influence on language constructs where unification is implicitly used. We discuss this in more detail in this section.

In contrast to Haskell, Curry allows non-left-linear rules, i.e., defining rules with multiple occurrences of a variable in the patterns of the left-hand side. For instance, this function definition is valid in Curry:

```
f x x = x
```

Multiple occurrences of variables in the left-hand side are considered as an abbreviation for equational constraints between these occurrences [27], i.e., the definition above is expanded to

```
f x y | x =:= y = x
```

This feature of Curry is motivated by logic programming where multiple variable occurrences in rule heads are also solved by unification. However, in Curry the situation is a bit more complex due to the inclusion of functions and infinite data structures. As a matter of fact, our refined type of "=:=" makes the status of non-left-linear rules clearer. According to the type shown in (4), the type inferred for the definition above is

```
f :: Data a => a → a → a
```

Hence, f can not be called with functional values as arguments. This even increases the compatibility with logic programming where unification is applied to Herbrand terms, i.e., algebraic data.

Another feature of Curry, where equational constraints are implicitly used, are functional patterns. *Functional patterns* are proposed in [4] as an elegant way to describe pattern matching with an infinite set of patterns. For instance, consider the definition of last shown above. Since the equational condition requires the complete evaluation of the input list, an expression like last [failed,3] (where failed is an expression that has no value) can not be evaluated to some value. Now, consider that last is defined by the following (infinite) set of rules:

```
last [x] = x
last [x1,x] = x
last [x1,x2,x] = x
  ⋮
```

Then the expression above is reduced to the value 3 by applying the second rule. This set of rules can be abbreviated by a single rule:

$$last\ (\_ \mathbin{++} [x]) = x \tag{7}$$

Since the argument contains the defined operation "++", it is called a *functional pattern*. Conceptually, a functional pattern denotes all constructor terms to which it can be evaluated (by narrowing). In this case, these are the patterns shown above. Operationally, pattern matching with functional patterns can be implemented by a specific unification procedure which evaluates the functional pattern in a demand-driven manner [4]. Functional patterns are useful to express pattern matching at arbitrary depths in a compact manner. For instance, they can be exploited for a compact and declarative approach to process XML documents [23].

A delicate point of functional patterns are non-linear patterns, i.e., if a functional pattern is evaluated to some constructor term containing multiple occurrences of a variable. For instance, consider the function

```
dup :: a → (a,a)
dup x = (x,x)
```

and its use in a functional pattern:

```
whenDup (dup x) = x
```

By the semantics of functional patterns, the latter rule is equivalent to the definition

```
whenDup (x,x) = x
```

Due to the non-linear left-hand side, the type of whenDup is

```
whenDup :: Data a => (a,a) → a
```

Now, consider the operation const defined by

```
const :: a → b → a
const x _ = x
```

and its use in a functional pattern:

$$g\,(\mathtt{const}\,x\,x) = x \tag{8}$$

By the semantics of functional pattern, the definition of g is equivalent to

```
g x = x
```

so that a correct type is

```
g :: a → a
```

Hence, the type context Data a is not required, although the variable x has a multiple occurrence in (8). This example shows that, if functional patterns are used, the requirement for a Data context depends on the linearity of the constructor terms to which the functional patterns evaluate. Since this property is undecidable in general, a safe approximation is to add a Data constraint to the result type of the functional pattern. This has the consequence that the type of last, when defined as in (7), is inferred as

```
last :: Data a => [a] → a
```

Basically, this type is the same as we would obtain when defining last with an equational constraint, but it could be done better: since the functional pattern (_ ++ [x]) always yields a linear term, the type class constraint Data a is not necessary. Hence, one can make the type checking for operations defined with functional patterns more powerful by approximating the linearity property of the functional pattern. Such an approximation has already been used in [4] to improve the efficiency of the unification procedure for functional patterns. However, a significant drawback would be the fact that the inferred type of a function would depend on the quality of the approximation. As a consequence, the principal type of a function [13,28] would become ambiguous under certain circumstances and would depend on a function's implementation.

8   Related Work

We already discussed in the previous sections some work related to the interpretation and use of equality in declarative languages. In the following, we focus on some additional work related to our proposal.

The necessity to distinguish different equalities in the context of functional logic programming and to define their exact semantics has been recognized before. In [16], the authors introduce several equality (and disequality) operations, among others also an operation for strict equality. However, no explicit distinction between equality and equivalence is made as only the former is discussed. Note also that some of these operations became obsolete with [9].

In [33], the author discusses the addition of Haskell-like overloading to Curry. In doing so, a new type class `Equal` that contains the unification operation "`=:=`" is proposed. The intent is to restrict this operation similarly to the equivalence operation "`==`" so that it is only applicable to certain types. In contrast to our proposal, it is not enforced that instances of the `Equal` type class should always have the same form. In the same work, another type class `Narrowable` containing a method called `narrow` is proposed in order to restrict the type of logical variables against the background of higher-rank types. The method `narrow` is very similar to our method `aValue`. But aside from a few downsides of the introduction of such a method, e.g., a possibly fixed order when enumerating solutions, no further consequences for the language itself are discussed in that work.

The idea to use a type relation to restrict the type of logical variables has also been introduced in [35] for a better characterization of free theorems. In [34], a type class `Data` is used for the same reason, but the class is only used as a marker (as in [35]) so that the type class does not contain any methods.

On a side note, there is also a `Data` type class in Haskell. However, this particular type class is used for generic programming in Haskell and shares nothing but the name with our type class [32].

9   Conclusions

In this paper we presented a solution to various problems w.r.t. equality and logic variables in functional logic programs by introducing a new type class `Data`. Instances of this class support a generator operation `aValue` for values and a strict equality operation "`===`" on these values. In contrast to other classes, instances of this class can only be derived in a standard manner and cannot be defined by the programmer. This decision ensures a reasonable semantics: if $e_1 === e_2$ evaluates to `True`, then the expressions e_1 and e_2 have an identical value. Although this is the notion of strict equality proposed for a long time, Haskell-like overloading of the class `Eq` and its operation "`==`" allows to specify that "some expressions are more equal than others" [38].

At a first glance, it might be unnecessary to add a further equality operator and base type class to a declarative language. The advantage is that this supports a clear documentation for all functions depending on equality, as it makes a huge difference in functional logic programming whether one imposes equality or equivalence in a function's implementation. If a programmer is interested in identical values, she or he has to use "`===`".[3] If only equivalence is relevant, "`==`" is the right choice. For instance, consider the operation `elem` to check whether an element occurs in a list. The type

```
elem :: Data a => a  →  [a]  →  Bool
```

indicates that this operation succeeds if the element actually occurs in the list, whereas the type

```
elem :: Eq a => a  →  [a]  →  Bool
```

indicates that it succeeds if some equivalent element is contained in the list.

Unfortunately, these details are often not taken into account. As discussed in this paper, many textbooks and program documentations simply ignore such differences or are not formally precise in their statements.

We showed that our proposal is also useful to type logic variables in a more meaningful way. The type of a logic variable is required to be an instance of `Data` so that one can enumerate the possible values of this variable. Although logic variables are often instantiated by narrowing or unification to appropriate values, there are situations where an explicit enumeration is necessary to ensure completeness. For instance, consider the encapsulation of non-deterministic computations in order to reason about the various outcomes. Set functions [6] are a declarative, i.e., evaluation-independent, encapsulation approach. If f is a (unary) function, its set function f_S returns the set of all results computed by f for a given argument. For instance, `someDup`$_S$ `xs` returns the set of all duplicate elements (see Example 2) occurring in the list `xs`. An important property of a set function is that it encapsulates only the non-determinism caused by the function's definition and not by the arguments. Hence, `someDup`$_S$ `([1,1] ? [2])` yields two different sets: {1} and {}. This property of set functions is important to ensure their declarative semantics. It has the consequence that arguments must be evaluated *outside* the set function. Hence, to evaluate the expression

```
let x free in ...(fS x)...
```

---

[3] As discussed in Sect. 6, the unification operator "`=:=`" does not need to be used by the programmer since it is an optimization of "`===`".

it is not allowed to bind x inside the evaluation of f. As a consequence, x must be instantiated outside in order to proceed a computation where f demands its argument. This can easily be obtained by the use of the operation aValue:

```
let x = aValue in ...(f_S x)...
```

In order to evaluate the practical consequences of our proposal, we implemented it in a prototypical manner in our Curry front end that is used by various Curry implementations. The changes in the type checker were minimal (e.g., adding Data contexts to the inferred types of logic variables). Concerning libraries, only a single type signature had to be adapted in the standard prelude, one of the largest Curry modules: the type of the "arbitrary value" operation gets a Data context:

```
unknown :: Data a => a
unknown = let x free in x
```

In other libraries, only a few types (related to search encapsulation primitives) had to be adapted. With these few changes, even larger Curry applications could be compiled without problems. This demonstrates that our proposal is a viable alternative to the current unsatisfying handling of equality and logic variables in Curry. Usually, no changes are necessary in existing Curry programs. Only in the rare cases of function definitions with polymorphic non-linear left-hand sides or polymorphic logic variables, type signatures have to be adapted.

Acknowledgments. The authors are grateful to Sandra Dylus and Marius Rasch for fruitful discussions during the conception phase of this paper. Furthermore, we thank Kai-Oliver Prott for his efforts in evaluating our proposal by prototypically implementing it.

References

1. Antoy, S.: Optimal non-deterministic functional logic computations. In: Hanus, M., Heering, J., Meinke, K. (eds.) ALP/HOA-1997. LNCS, vol. 1298, pp. 16–30. Springer, Heidelberg (1997). https://doi.org/10.1007/BFb0027000
2. Antoy, S., Echahed, R., Hanus, M.: A needed narrowing strategy. J. ACM **47**(4), 776–822 (2000)
3. Antoy, S., Hanus, M.: Functional logic design patterns. In: Hu, Z., Rodríguez-Artalejo, M. (eds.) FLOPS 2002. LNCS, vol. 2441, pp. 67–87. Springer, Heidelberg (2002). https://doi.org/10.1007/3-540-45788-7_4
4. Antoy, S., Hanus, M.: Declarative programming with function patterns. In: Hill, P.M. (ed.) LOPSTR 2005. LNCS, vol. 3901, pp. 6–22. Springer, Heidelberg (2006). https://doi.org/10.1007/11680093_2
5. Antoy, S., Hanus, M.: Overlapping rules and logic variables in functional logic programs. In: Etalle, S., Truszczyński, M. (eds.) ICLP 2006. LNCS, vol. 4079, pp. 87–101. Springer, Heidelberg (2006). https://doi.org/10.1007/11799573_9
6. Antoy, S., Hanus, M.: Set functions for functional logic programming. In: Proceedings of the 11th ACM SIGPLAN International Conference on Principles and Practice of Declarative Programming (PPDP 2009), pp. 73–82. ACM Press (2009)

7. Antoy, S., Hanus, M.: Functional logic programming. Commun. ACM **53**(4), 74–85 (2010)
8. Antoy, S., Hanus, M.: New functional logic design patterns. In: Kuchen, H. (ed.) WFLP 2011. LNCS, vol. 6816, pp. 19–34. Springer, Heidelberg (2011). https://doi. org/10.1007/978-3-642-22531-4_2
9. Antoy, S., Hanus, M.: Curry without success. In: Proceedings of the 23rd International Workshop on Functional and (Constraint) Logic Programming (WFLP 2014). CEUR Workshop Proceedings, vol. 1335, pp. 140–154. CEUR-WS.org (2014)
10. Antoy, S., Hanus, M.: Transforming Boolean equalities into constraints. Formal Aspects Comput. **29**(3), 475–494 (2017). https://doi.org/10.1007/s00165-016-0399-6
11. Bird, R.: Introduction to Functional Programming using Haskell, 2nd edn. Prentice Hall, Englewood Cliffs (1998)
12. Braßel, B., Hanus, M., Peemöller, B., Reck, F.: KiCS2: a new compiler from Curry to Haskell. In: Kuchen, H. (ed.) WFLP 2011. LNCS, vol. 6816, pp. 1–18. Springer, Heidelberg (2011). https://doi.org/10.1007/978-3-642-22531-4_1
13. Damas, L., Milner, R.: Principal type-schemes for functional programs. In: Proceedings of the 9th ACM SIGPLAN-SIGACT Symposium on Principles of Programming Languages (POPL 1982), pp. 207–212. ACM, New York (1982)
14. de Dios Castro, J., López-Fraguas, F.J.: Extra variables can be eliminated from functional logic programs. Electron. Notes Theor. Comput. Sci. **188**, 3–19 (2007)
15. DeGroot, D., Lindstrom, G. (eds.): Logic Programming, Functions, Relations, and Equations. Prentice Hall, Englewood Cliffs (1986)
16. Gallego Arias, E.J., Mariño Carballo, J., Rey Poza, J.M.: A proposal for disequality constraints in Curry. Electron. Notes Theor. Comput. Sci. **177**, 269–285 (2007). Proceedings of the 15th Workshop on Functional and (Constraint) Logic Programming (WFLP 2006)
17. Gallier, J.H., Snyder, W.: Complete sets of transformations for general E-unification. Theoret. Comput. Sci. **67**, 203–260 (1989)
18. Giovannetti, E., Levi, G., Moiso, C., Palamidessi, C.: Kernel leaf: a logic plus functional language. J. Comput. Syst. Sci. **42**(2), 139–185 (1991)
19. Goguen, J.A., Meseguer, J.: EQLOG: equality, types, and generic modules for logic programming. In: DeGroot, D., Lindstrom, G. (eds.) Logic Programming, Functions, Relations, and Equations, pp. 295–363. Prentice Hall (1986)
20. González-Moreno, J.C., Hortalá-González, M.T., López-Fraguas, F.J., Rodríguez-Artalejo, M.: An approach to declarative programming based on a rewriting logic. J. Log. Program. **40**, 47–87 (1999)
21. Hanus, M.: The integration of functions into logic programming: from theory to practice. J. Log. Program. **19&20**, 583–628 (1994)
22. Hanus, M.: A unified computation model for functional and logic programming. In: Proceedings of the 24th ACM Symposium on Principles of Programming Languages (Paris), pp. 80–93 (1997)
23. Hanus, M.: Declarative processing of semistructured web data. In: Technical Communications of the 27th International Conference on Logic Programming, vol. 11, pp. 198–208. Leibniz International Proceedings in Informatics (LIPIcs) (2011)
24. Hanus, M.: Functional logic programming: from theory to Curry. In: Voronkov, A., Weidenbach, C. (eds.) Programming Logics. LNCS, vol. 7797, pp. 123–168. Springer, Heidelberg (2013). https://doi.org/10.1007/978-3-642-37651-1_6
25. Hanus, M.: CurryCheck: checking properties of Curry programs. In: Hermenegildo, M.V., Lopez-Garcia, P. (eds.) LOPSTR 2016. LNCS, vol. 10184, pp. 222–239. Springer, Cham (2017). https://doi.org/10.1007/978-3-319-63139-4_13

26. Hanus, M., et al.: PAKCS: The Portland Aachen Kiel Curry System (2018). http://www.informatik.uni-kiel.de/~pakcs/
27. Hanus, M. (ed.): Curry: an integrated functional logic language (vers. 0.9.0) (2016). http://www.curry-language.org
28. Hindley, R.: The principal type-scheme of an object in combinatory logic. Trans. Am. Math. Soc. **146**, 29–60 (1969)
29. Huet, G., Lévy, J.-J.: Computations in orthogonal rewriting systems. In: Lassez, J.-L., Plotkin, G. (eds.) Computational Logic: Essays in Honor of Alan Robinson, pp. 395–443. MIT Press (1991)
30. Hughes, J.: Why functional programming matters. In: Turner, D.A. (ed.) Research Topics in Functional Programming, pp. 17–42. Addison Wesley (1990)
31. Hutton, G.: Programming in Haskell, 2nd edn. Cambridge University Press, Cambridge (2016)
32. Lämmel, R., Peyton Jones, S.L.: Scrap your boilerplate: a practical design pattern for generic programming. In: Proceedings of the 2003 ACM SIGPLAN International Workshop on Types in Languages Design and Implementation (TLDI 2003), pp. 26–37. ACM Press (2003)
33. Lux, W.: Adding Haskell-style overloading to Curry. In: 25. Workshop der GI-Fachgruppe Programmiersprachen undRechenkonzepte, Kiel, Germany, pp. 67–76 (2008). Technical report 0811, Institut für Informatik, CAU Kiel
34. Mehner, S.: Tools for reasoning about effectful declarative programs. Ph.D. thesis, Universität Bonn (2015)
35. Mehner, S., Seidel, D., Straßburger, L., Voigtländer, J.: Parametricity and proving free theorems for functional-logic languages. In: Proceedings of the 16th International Symposium on Principle and Practice of Declarative Programming (PPDP 2014), pp. 19–30. ACM Press (2014)
36. Moreno-Navarro, J.J., Rodríguez-Artalejo, M.: Logic programming with functions and predicates: the language babel. J. Log. Program. **12**, 191–223 (1992)
37. O'Donnell, M.J.: Equational logic programming. In: Gabbay, D.M., Hogger, C.J., Robinson, J.A. (eds.) Handbook of Logic in Artificial Intelligence and Logic Programming, pp. 69–161. Oxford University Press (1998)
38. Orwell, G.: Animal Farm: A Fairy Story. Secker and Warburg, London (1945)
39. Peyton Jones, S. (ed.): Haskell 98 Language and Libraries-The Revised Report. Cambridge University Press, Cambridge (2003)
40. Reddy, U.S.: Narrowing as the operational semantics of functional languages. In: Proceedings IEEE International Symposium on Logic Programming, Boston, pp. 138–151 (1985)
41. Thompson, S.: Haskell - The Craft of Functional Programming, 2nd edn. Addison-Wesley, Boston (1999)
42. Wadler, P., Blott, S.: How to make ad-hoc polymorphism less ad hoc. In: Proceedings POPL 1989, pp. 60–76 (1989)

Free Theorems Simply, via Dinaturality

Janis Voigtländer[✉]

University of Duisburg-Essen, Duisburg, Germany
janis.voigtlaender@uni-due.de

Abstract. Free theorems are a popular tool in reasoning about parametrically polymorphic code. They are also of instructive use in teaching. Their derivation, though, can be tedious, as it involves unfolding a lot of definitions, then hoping to be able to simplify the resulting logical formula to something nice and short. Even in a mechanised generator it is not easy to get the right heuristics in place to achieve good outcomes. Dinaturality is a categorical abstraction that captures many instances of free theorems. Arguably, its origins are more conceptually involved to explain, though, and generating useful statements from it also has its pitfalls. We present a simple approach for obtaining dinaturality-related free theorems from the standard formulation of relational parametricity in a rather direct way. It is conceptually appealing and easy to control and implement, as the provided Haskell code shows.

1 Introduction

Free theorems [14] are an attractive means of reasoning about programs in a polymorphically typed language, predominantly used in a pure functional setting, but also available to functional-logic programmers [10]. They have been employed for compiler optimisations [7] and other applications, and can also be used (when generated for deliberately arbitrary polymorphic types) to provide insight into the declarative nature of types and semantics of programs while teaching. Free theorems are derived from relational parametricity [12], and the actual process of deriving them can be tedious. We discuss an approach that side-steps the need to explicitly unfold definitions of relational actions and subsequently manipulate higher-order logic formulae. That there is a relationship between relational parametricity and categorical dinaturality is not news at all [5], and has been used to impressive effect lately [8], but we show that one can do without explicitly involving any category theory concepts, instead discovering all we need along the way. Together with deterministic simplification rules, we obtain a compact and predictable free theorems generator. We provide a neat implementation using the higher-order abstract syntax [11] and normalisation by evaluation [6] principles.

In the remainder of the paper, we are going to explain and discuss the standard approach of deriving free theorems via relational parametricity, first very informally (Sect. 2), then by somewhat superficially invoking its usual formal

© Springer Nature Switzerland AG 2020
P. Hofstedt et al. (Eds.): DECLARE 2019, LNAI 12057, pp. 247–267, 2020.
https://doi.org/10.1007/978-3-030-46714-2_16

presentation (Sect. 3.1), after which we "discover" our bridge to the simpler approach (Sects. 3.2 and 3.3), and conclude with pragmatics and implementation
(rest of Sect. 3 and Sect. 4). As a kind of afterthought, we sketch the precise
connection to dinaturality (Sect. 5).

2   How Free Theorems Are Usually Derived

For the sake of simplicity, we consider only the case of functions polymorphic in
exactly one type variable, i.e., types like $(\alpha \to \mathsf{Bool}) \to [\alpha] \to \mathsf{Maybe}\ \alpha$ but not
like $\alpha \to \beta \to (\alpha, \beta)$. Extension to cases like the latter would be possible.

2.1   Constructing Relations

The key to deriving free theorems is to interpret types as relations [12,14]. For
example, given the type signature $f :: (\alpha \to \mathsf{Bool}) \to [\alpha] \to \mathsf{Maybe}\ \alpha$, we replace
the type variable α by a relation variable $\mathcal{R}$, thus obtaining $(\mathcal{R} \to \mathsf{Bool}) \to$
$([\mathcal{R}] \to \mathsf{Maybe}\ \mathcal{R})$. Eventually, we will allow (nearly) arbitrary relations between
closed types τ_1 and τ_2, denoted $\mathcal{R} \in Rel(\tau_1, \tau_2)$, as interpretations for relation
variables. Also, there is a systematic way of reading expressions over relations
as relations themselves. In particular,

- base types like Bool and Int are read as identity relations,
- for relations $\mathcal{R}_1$ and $\mathcal{R}_2$, we have

$$\mathcal{R}_1 \to \mathcal{R}_2 = \{(f, g) \mid \forall (a, b) \in \mathcal{R}_1. \ (f\ a, g\ b) \in \mathcal{R}_2\}$$

  and
- every type constructor is read as an appropriate construction on relations; for
  example, the list type constructor maps every relation $\mathcal{R} \in Rel(\tau_1, \tau_2)$ to the
  relation $[\mathcal{R}] \in Rel([\tau_1], [\tau_2])$ defined by (the least fixpoint of)

$$[\mathcal{R}] = \{([], [])\} \cup \{(a : as, b : bs) \mid (a, b) \in \mathcal{R}, (as, bs) \in [\mathcal{R}]\}$$

while the Maybe type constructor maps $\mathcal{R} \in Rel(\tau_1, \tau_2)$ to $\mathsf{Maybe}\ \mathcal{R} \in$
$Rel(\mathsf{Maybe}\ \tau_1, \mathsf{Maybe}\ \tau_2)$ defined by

$$\mathsf{Maybe}\ \mathcal{R} = \{(\mathsf{Nothing}, \mathsf{Nothing})\} \cup \{(\mathsf{Just}\ a, \mathsf{Just}\ b) \mid (a, b) \in \mathcal{R}\}$$

and similarly for other datatypes.

The central statement of relational parametricity now is that for every choice
of τ_1, τ_2, and $\mathcal{R}$, the instantiations of the polymorphic f to types τ_1 and τ_2 are
related by the relational interpretation of f's type. For the above example, this
means that $(f_{\tau_1}, f_{\tau_2}) \in (\mathcal{R} \to id_{\mathsf{Bool}}) \to ([\mathcal{R}] \to \mathsf{Maybe}\ \mathcal{R})$. From now on, type
subscripts will often be omitted since they can be easily inferred.

2.2   Unfolding Definitions

To continue with the derivation of a free theorem in the standard way, one has to unfold the definitions of the various actions on relations described above. For the example:

$(f, f) \in (\mathcal{R} \to id) \to ([\mathcal{R}] \to \mathsf{Maybe}\ \mathcal{R})$
$\Leftrightarrow$ ⟦ definition of $\mathcal{R}_1 \to \mathcal{R}_2$ ⟧
   $\forall (a, b) \in \mathcal{R} \to id.\ (f\ a, f\ b) \in [\mathcal{R}] \to \mathsf{Maybe}\ \mathcal{R}$
$\Leftrightarrow$ ⟦ again ⟧
   $\forall (a, b) \in \mathcal{R} \to id, (c, d) \in [\mathcal{R}].\ (f\ a\ c, f\ b\ d) \in \mathsf{Maybe}\ \mathcal{R}$ $(*)$

Now it is useful to specialise the relation $\mathcal{R}$ to the "graph" of a function $g :: \tau_1 \to \tau_2$, i.e., setting $\mathcal{R} = graph(g) := \{(x, y) \mid g\ x = y\} \in Rel(\tau_1, \tau_2)$, and to realise that then $[\mathcal{R}] = graph(map\ g)$ and $\mathsf{Maybe}\ \mathcal{R} = graph(fmap\ g)$, so that we can continue as follows:

   $\forall (a, b) \in graph(g) \to id, (c, d) \in graph(map\ g).\ (f\ a\ c, f\ b\ d) \in graph(fmap\ g)$
$\Leftrightarrow$ ⟦ $(x, y) \in graph(h)$ iff $h\ x = y$ ⟧
   $\forall (a, b) \in graph(g) \to id, c :: [\tau_1].\ fmap\ g\ (f\ a\ c) = f\ b\ (map\ g\ c)$ $(**)$

It remains to find out what $(a, b) \in graph(g) \to id$ means. We can do so as follows:

   $(a, b) \in graph(g) \to id$
$\Leftrightarrow$ ⟦ definition of $\mathcal{R}_1 \to \mathcal{R}_2$ ⟧
   $\forall (x, y) \in graph(g).\ (a\ x, b\ y) \in id$
$\Leftrightarrow$ ⟦ functions as relations ⟧
   $\forall x :: \tau_1.\ a\ x = b\ (g\ x)$
$\Leftrightarrow$ ⟦ make pointfree ⟧
   $a = b \circ g$

Finally, we obtain, for every $f :: (\alpha \to \mathsf{Bool}) \to [\alpha] \to \mathsf{Maybe}\ \alpha$, $g :: \tau_1 \to \tau_2$, $b :: \tau_2 \to \mathsf{Bool}$, and $c :: [\tau_1]$,

$$fmap\ g\ (f\ (b \circ g)\ c) = f\ b\ (map\ g\ c)$$

or, if we prefer this statement pointfree as well, $fmap\ g \circ f\ (b \circ g) = f\ b \circ map\ g$. The power of such statements is that f is only restricted by its type – its behaviour can vary considerably within these confines, and still results obtained as free theorems will be guaranteed to hold.

2.3   Typical Complications

So what is there not to like about the above procedure? First of all, always unfolding the definitions of the relational actions – specifically, the $\mathcal{R}_1 \to \mathcal{R}_2$ definition – is tedious, though mechanical. It typically brings us to something like $(*)$ or $(**)$ above. Then, specifically if our f has a higher-order type, we will have to deal with preconditions like $(a, b) \in \mathcal{R} \to id$ or $(a, b) \in graph(g) \to id$. Here we have seen, again by unfolding definitions, that the latter is equivalent to $a = b \circ g$, which enabled simplification of statement $(**)$ by eliminating the variable a completely. But in general this can become arbitrarily complicated. If, for example, our f of interest had the type $(\alpha \to \alpha \to \mathsf{Bool}) \to [\alpha] \to [\alpha]$, we would have to deal with a precondition $(a, b) \in graph(g) \to graph(g) \to id$ instead. By similar steps as above, one can show that this is equivalent to $\forall x \mathbin{::} \tau_1, y \mathbin{::} \tau_1.\ a\ x\ y = b\ (g\ x)\ (g\ y)$ or $\forall x \mathbin{::} \tau_1.\ a\ x = b\ (g\ x) \circ g$ or something even more cryptic if one insists on complete pointfreeness (to express the condition in the form "$a = \ldots$" in order to eliminate the explicit precondition by inlining). One might prepare and keep in mind the simplifications of some common cases like those above, but in general, since the type of f, and thus of course also the types of higher-order arguments it may have, can be arbitrary and more "exotic" than above (in particular, possibly involving further nesting of function arrows – consider, e.g., we had started with $f \mathbin{::} (([\alpha] \to \mathsf{Int}) \to \alpha) \to \alpha$ as the target type), we are eventually down to unfolding the definitions of relational actions. We can only *hope* then to ultimately be able to also fold back into some compact form of precondition like was the case above.

Moreover, the picture is complicated by the fact that the procedure, exactly as described so far, applies only to the most basic language setting, namely a functional language in which there are no undefined values and all functions are total. As soon as we consider a more realistic or interesting setting, some changes become required. Typically that involves restricting the choice of relations over which one can quantify, but also changes to the relational actions that may or may not have a larger impact on the procedure of deriving free theorems. Specifically, already when taking possible undefinedness and partiality of functions into account, one may only use relations that are strict (i.e., $(\bot, \bot) \in \mathcal{R}$) and additionally has to use versions of datatype liftings that relate partial structures (e.g., $[\mathcal{R}] = \{(\bot, \bot), ([], [])\} \cup \{(a : as, b : bs) \mid \ldots\}$). This is not very severe yet, since strictness of relations simply translates into strictness of functions and connections like $[\mathcal{R}] = graph(map\ g)$ for $\mathcal{R} = graph(g)$ remain intact, so there is no considerable impact on the derivation steps. But if one additionally takes Haskell's *seq*-primitive into account, more changes become required [9]. Now relations must also be total (i.e., $(a, b) \in \mathcal{R}$ implies $a = \bot \Leftrightarrow b = \bot$) and additionally the relational action for function types must be changed to

$$\mathcal{R}_1 \to \mathcal{R}_2 = \{(f, g) \mid f = \bot \Leftrightarrow g = \bot,\ \forall (a, b) \in \mathcal{R}_1.\ (f\ a, g\ b) \in \mathcal{R}_2\}$$

The latter *does* have an impact on the derivation steps, since these typically (like in the examples above) use the definition of $\mathcal{R}_1 \to \mathcal{R}_2$ a lot, and now must manage the extra conditions concerning undefinedness. Also, some simplifications become invalid in this setting. Note that in the first example, in Sect. 2.2, we used that the precondition $\forall x \mathbin{::} \tau_1.\ a\ x = b\ (g\ x)$ is equivalent to $a = b \circ g$. But not in a language including *seq*, since in such a language eta-reduction is not generally valid (e.g., $\forall x.\ \bot\ x = \bot\ (id\ x)$ but not $\bot = \bot \circ id$)! We might still be safe, since the condition $\forall x :: \tau_1.\ a\ x = b\ (g\ x)$ is at least implied by $a = b \circ g$, so depending on where that explicitly quantifying statement appeared in the overall statement we may obtain a weakening or a strengthening of that overall statement by replacing one condition by the other. But such considerations require careful management of the preconditions and their positions in nested implication statements. All this can still be done automatically [1], but it is no pleasure. There is not as much reuse as one might want, different simplification heuristics have to be used for different language settings, there is no really deterministic algorithm but instead some search involved, and sometimes the only "simplification" that seems to work is to unfold all definitions and leave it at that. Moreover, if one were to move on and consider automatic generation of free theorems for further language settings, like imprecise error semantics [13], then the story would repeat itself. There would be yet another set of changes to the basic definitions for relations and relational actions, new things to take care of during simplification of candidate free theorems, etc.

2.4 Some Problematic Examples, and Outlook at a Remedy

Let us substantiate the above observations with some additional examples. First we consider the declaration $f :: (([\alpha] \to \mathsf{Int}) \to \alpha) \to \alpha$. The existing free theorems generator library mentioned above [1], used inside a web UI created by Joachim Breitner [2], produces the statement that for every $g :: \tau_1 \to \tau_2$, $p :: ([\tau_1] \to \mathsf{Int}) \to \tau_1$, and $q :: ([\tau_2] \to \mathsf{Int}) \to \tau_2$, it holds:

$$(\forall r :: [\tau_1] \to \mathsf{Int},\ s :: [\tau_2] \to \mathsf{Int}.$$
$$\quad (\forall x :: [\tau_1].\ r\ x = s\ (map\ g\ x)) \Rightarrow (g\ (p\ r) = q\ s))$$
$$\Rightarrow (g\ (f\ p) = f\ q)$$

Arguably, it would have been more useful to be given the equivalent statement that for every f, g, p with types as above,

$$g\ (f\ p) = f\ (\lambda s \to g\ (p\ (\lambda x \to s\ (map\ g\ x)))) \tag{1}$$

There is another free theorems generator as part of another tool, by Andrew Bromage [3], and it does quite okay here, generating this: $(\forall p.\ g\ (h\ (p \circ map\ g)) = k\ p) \Rightarrow g\ (f\ h) = f\ k$. But if we make the input type a bit more nasty by more nesting of function arrows, $f :: (((([\alpha] \to \mathsf{Int}) \to \mathsf{Int}) \to \mathsf{Int}) \to \alpha) \to \alpha$, then the existing generators differ only slightly from each other, and both yield something like the following:

$$(\forall r, s.\ (\forall t, u.\ (\forall w.\ t\ (w \circ map\ g) = u\ w) \Rightarrow (r\ t = s\ u)) \Rightarrow (g\ (p\ r) = q\ s))$$
$$\Rightarrow (g\ (f\ p) = f\ q)$$

It would have been nicer to be given the following:

$$g\ (f\ p) = f\ (\lambda s \to g\ (p\ (\lambda t \to s\ (\lambda w \to t\ (\lambda x \to w\ (map\ g\ x)))))) \tag{2}$$

which is exactly what the approach to be presented here will yield (modulo variable names). Of course, one could invest into further post-processing steps in the existing generators to get from the scary form of the statement to the more readable, equivalent one. But at some point, this will always be only partially successful. Going from a compact relational expression to a quantifier-rich formula in higher-order logic through unfolding of definitions, and then trying to recover a more readable form via generic HOL formula manipulations, will generally be beaten by an approach better exploiting the structure present in the original type expression – which is what we will do. We will always generate a simple equation between two lambda-expressions, without precondition statements, as in (1) and (2) above.

Moreover, there is still the issue of the variability of free theorems between different language settings. The generator inside Lambdabot [3] does not consider such impact of language features, and thus the theorems it outputs are not safe in the presence of seq. The other previous generator [1,2] does, and thus adds the proper extra conditions concerning undefinedness. For example, for the more complicated of the two types considered above, the output then is (besides a strictness and totality condition imposed on g)[1]:

$$((p \neq \bot \Leftrightarrow q \neq \bot)$$
$$\land (\forall r, s. (\forall t, u. ((t \neq \bot \Leftrightarrow u \neq \bot)$$
$$\land (\forall v, w. (\forall x. v \ x = w \ (map \ g \ x)) \Rightarrow (t \ v = u \ w)))$$
$$\Rightarrow (r \ t = s \ u))$$
$$\Rightarrow (g \ (p \ r) = q \ s)))$$
$$\Rightarrow (g \ (f \ p) = f \ q)$$

In contrast, with the approach to be presented we will get:

$$g \ (f \ (\lambda s \rightarrow p \ (\lambda t \rightarrow s \ (\lambda w \rightarrow t \ (\lambda x \rightarrow w \ x)))))$$
$$=$$
$$f \ (\lambda s \rightarrow g \ (p \ (\lambda t \rightarrow s \ (\lambda w \rightarrow t \ (\lambda x \rightarrow w \ (map \ g \ x))))))$$

which . . .

1. . . . is almost as strong as the more complicated formula above it. The only thing that makes it weaker is that it does not express that the corner cases $g \ (f \ \bot) = f \ \bot$ and $g \ (f \ p') = f \ (g \circ p')$ with p' any of $(\lambda s \rightarrow p \ \bot)$, $(\lambda s \rightarrow p \ (\lambda t \rightarrow \bot))$, $(\lambda s \rightarrow p \ (\lambda t \rightarrow s \ \bot))$, . . ., $(\lambda s \rightarrow p \ (\lambda t \rightarrow s \ (\lambda w \rightarrow t \ (\lambda x \rightarrow w \ \bot))))$ also hold.
2. . . . simply reduces to (2) in any functional language setting in which eta-reduction is valid. So we will not perform different derivations for different language settings. (Rather, eta-reduction, when applicable, can be applied as an afterthought – which is exactly what our implementation will do.)

---

[1] Something we will not mention again and again is that g is also itself non-$\bot$. Disregarding types that contain only $\bot$, this follows from totality of g anyway.

To top the mentioned benefits, the approach to free theorems derivation we will discuss is much simpler than the "relation unfolding" one – simpler both conceptually (and thus also when one wants to obtain free theorems by hand) as well as when implementing it. In fact, the generator code takes up much less than a page in the appendix (without counting the code for implementing the eta-reduction functionality) – a relatively small fraction of the size of the corresponding code in the existing free theorems generators.[2]

There is one gotcha. It is not *always* possible to express a free theorem simply as an equation without preconditions. A typical example is the type $f :: (\alpha \to \alpha) \to \alpha \to \alpha$. Its general free theorem is:

$$(g \circ h = k \circ g) \Rightarrow (g \circ f\ h = f\ k \circ g)$$

Since even for fixed g, neither of h and k uniquely determines the other here, the precondition $g \circ h = k \circ g$ cannot be avoided by some way of inlining or other strategy. The dinaturality-related approach will instead generate the unconditional statement

$$g\ (f\ (\lambda y \to p\ (g\ y))\ x) = f\ (\lambda y \to g\ (p\ y))\ (g\ x)$$

i.e., setting h to $p \circ g$ and k to $g \circ p$ for some p, thus certainly satisfying $g \circ h = k \circ g$, but losing some generality. However, we believe we can say for what sort of types this will happen (see Sect. 3.5).

3   Free Theorems Simply, "via Dinaturality"

So, what is the magic sauce we are going to use? We start from the simple observation that with the standard approach, once one has done the unfolding of definitions and subsequent simplifications/compactifications, one usually ends up with an equation (possibly with preconditions) between two expressions that look somewhat similar to each other. For example, for type $f :: [\alpha] \to [\alpha]$ one gets the equation $map\ g\ (f\ xs) = f\ (map\ g\ xs)$, for type $f :: (\alpha \to \mathsf{Bool}) \to [\alpha] \to [\alpha]$ one gets the equation $map\ g\ (f\ (p \circ g)\ xs) = f\ p\ (map\ g\ xs)$, etc. There is certainly some regularity present: on one side $map\ g$ happens "before f", on the other side it happens "after f"; maybe g needs to be brought in at some other place in one or both of the two sides as well; but the expression structure is essentially the same on both sides. In fact, given some experience with free theorems, one is often able to guess up front what the equation for a given type of f will look like. But to confirm it, one would still be forced to do the chore of unfolding the definitions of the relational actions, then massaging the resulting formulae to hopefully bring them into the form one was expecting. We will change that, by using what we call here the *conjuring lemma of parametricity*.

---

[2] Additional code for parsing input strings into type expressions and pretty-printing generated theorem expressions back into pleasingly looking strings is of comparable complexity between the different generators.

It was previously stated in the setting of deriving free theorems for a functional-logic language [10] (see Theorem 7.8 and Lemma 8.1 there), but will be used for (sublanguages of) Haskell here. To justify it, we need a brief excursion (some readers may want to largely skip) into how relational parametricity is usually formulated abstractly.

3.1   Usual Abstract Formulation of Relational Parametricity

Putting aside notational variations, as well as the fact that the exact form would differ a bit depending on whether one bases one's formalisation on a denotational or on an operational semantics (typically of a polymorphic lambda-calculus with some extensions, not full Haskell), one essentially always has the following theorem (sometimes called just the *fundamental lemma of logical relations*). Some explanations, such as what Δ stands for, are given below it.

Theorem 1 (Relational Parametricity).

1. *If e is a closed term (containing no free term variables, but also no free type variables) of a closed type τ, then $(e, e) \in \Delta_{\emptyset, \tau}$.*
2. *If e is a closed term (in the sense of containing no free term variables) of a type polymorphic in one type variable, say σ containing free type variable α, then for every choice of closed types τ_1, τ_2, and $\mathcal{R} \in Rel(\tau_1, \tau_2)$, we have $(e[\tau_1/\alpha], e[\tau_2/\alpha]) \in \Delta_{[\alpha \mapsto \mathcal{R}], \sigma}$.*
3. *If e is a polymorphic term as above, of type σ containing free type variable α, but now possibly also containing a free term variable x of some type σ' possibly containing the free type variable α as well, then for every choice of closed types τ_1, τ_2, and $\mathcal{R}$ as above, and closed terms $e_1 :: \sigma'[\tau_1/\alpha]$ and $e_2 :: \sigma'[\tau_2/\alpha]$ such that $(e_1, e_2) \in \Delta_{[\alpha \mapsto \mathcal{R}], \sigma'}$, we have $(e[\tau_1/\alpha, e_1/x], e[\tau_2/\alpha, e_2/x]) \in \Delta_{[\alpha \mapsto \mathcal{R}], \sigma}$.*

Now, the promised explanations:

- The notation $\Delta_{\rho, \sigma}$ corresponds to the construction of relations from types (as in Sect. 2.1), where ρ keeps track of the interpretation of any type variables by chosen relations. For example, $\Delta_{\emptyset, \mathsf{Int} \to [\mathsf{Bool}]}$ would be $id_{\mathsf{Int}} \to [id_{\mathsf{Bool}}]$ and $\Delta_{[\alpha \mapsto \mathcal{R}], [\alpha] \to \alpha}$ would be $[\mathcal{R}] \to \mathcal{R}$.
- For any closed type τ, the relation $\Delta_{\emptyset, \tau}$ (in fact, any $\Delta_{\rho, \tau}$) turns out to just be the identity relation at type τ. As such, $(e, e) \in \Delta_{\emptyset, \tau}$ in the first item of the theorem may appear to state a triviality. However, if one explicitly handles abstraction and instantiation of type variables (we have not done so for the exposition in Sect. 2, because we anyway wanted to deal only with types polymorphic over exactly one type variable), then it is less so. One then introduces, alongside $\mathcal{R}_1 \to \mathcal{R}_2$ etc., a new relational action $\forall \mathcal{R}. \mathcal{F} \mathcal{R}$ (for mappings $\mathcal{F}$ on relations), which is defined in exactly such a way that when moreover setting $\Delta_{\rho, \forall \alpha. \sigma} = \forall \mathcal{R}. \Delta_{\rho[\alpha \mapsto \mathcal{R}], \sigma}$, the statement $(e, e) \in \Delta_{\emptyset, \forall \alpha. \sigma}$ reduces exactly to the statement in the second item of the theorem – which then needs not to be explicitly made. The treatment is analogous if one has types polymorphic in more than one type variable, say $\tau = \forall \alpha. \forall \beta. \sigma$, which explains how to deal with that case not considered in Sect. 2.

- The choices of relations $\mathcal{R} \in Rel(\tau_1, \tau_2)$ are not really completely arbitrary, instead depend on the language setting for which the parametricity theorem is stated and proved. As mentioned earlier, $\mathcal{R}$ must be strict to take the presence of partial functions into account, and must be strict and total to take the presence of *seq* into account, and other restrictions may apply in other settings.
- Even the third item of the theorem as stated above, adding the treatment of free term variables, is not yet the most general form. In general, the parametricity theorem is formulated for an arbitrary number of free type and term variables, in straightforward (but notationally tedious) extension of the formulations above. Just for the sake of exposition here, we have chosen the progression between the three items. Of course, usually not all three (or more/further ones) are shown, only one at the level of generality needed for a specific concern. In a short while, we will see that it can even be useful to consider the case where e does involve a type variable, and free term variables of types involving that type variable, but does itself *not* have a polymorphic type.

Also, let us make explicit how Theorem 1 corresponds to the concrete standard derivation approach for free theorems as described in Sect. 2. Given a function f of type scheme σ polymorphic in α, one would use the first or second item of the theorem to conclude $(f_{\tau_1}, f_{\tau_2}) \in \Delta_{[\alpha \mapsto \mathcal{R}], \sigma}$, then unfold the definition of $\Delta_{[\alpha \mapsto \mathcal{R}], \sigma}$, for example $(f_{\tau_1}, f_{\tau_2}) \in (\mathcal{R} \rightarrow id_{\mathsf{Bool}}) \rightarrow ([\mathcal{R}] \rightarrow \mathsf{Maybe}\ \mathcal{R})$ if $\sigma = (\alpha \rightarrow \mathsf{Bool}) \rightarrow [\alpha] \rightarrow \mathsf{Maybe}\ \alpha$, then continue from there, with all the tedious work this entails.

The trick now is to establish a lemma, actually a corollary, that does not even mention the relation construction Δ, and that directly states an equality between expressions rather than something about relatedness.

3.2   The Conjuring Lemma of Parametricity

Before giving the lemma, let us give a brief example of the sort of term e that can appear in it, since without such an example it may be counterintuitive how e could "involve α" but nevertheless have a closed overall type. What this means is that e can be something like $\lambda xs \rightarrow map\ post\ (f\ (map\ pre\ xs))$. In a context in which $f :: \forall \alpha.[\alpha] \rightarrow [\alpha]$ and *pre* and *post* are term variables typed $\tau_1 \rightarrow \alpha$ and $\alpha \rightarrow \tau_2$ respectively, this e has the closed type $[\tau_1] \rightarrow [\tau_2]$, despite the fact that in order to write down e with explicit type annotations everywhere (i.e., on all subexpressions), one would also need to write down the type variable α at some places. Now the lemma, a corollary of the parametricity theorem.

Lemma 1 (Conjuring Lemma).
Let τ, τ_1 and τ_2 be closed types. Let $g :: \tau_1 \rightarrow \tau_2$ be closed and:

- *strict if we want to respect partially defined functions,*
- *strict and total if we want to respect seq.*

Let $e :: \tau$ be a term possibly involving α (but not in its own overall type, which is closed by assumption) and term variables $pre :: \tau_1 \to \alpha$ and $post :: \alpha \to \tau_2$, but no other free variables. Then:

$$e[\tau_1/\alpha, id_{\tau_1}/pre, g/post] = e[\tau_2/\alpha, g/pre, id_{\tau_2}/post]$$

Proof (see also proof of Lemma 8.1 in [10]). The conditions on g (strictness, totality, depending on language setting) guarantee that its graph can be used as an admissible $\mathcal{R}$. To apply the parametricity theorem (in its general form with arbitrarily many free variables), we need to establish $(id_{\tau_1}, g) \in \Delta_{[\alpha \mapsto graph(g)], \tau_1 \to \alpha}$ and $(g, id_{\tau_2}) \in \Delta_{[\alpha \mapsto graph(g)], \alpha \to \tau_2}$. Since τ_1, τ_2 are closed types, these statements reduce to $(id_{\tau_1}, g) \in id_{\tau_1} \to graph(g)$ and $(g, id_{\tau_2}) \in graph(g) \to id_{\tau_2}$, respectively. Both of these hold in all the language settings considered (easy calculations; also note that $g \neq \bot$ if g total), so the parametricity theorem lets us conclude

$$(e[\tau_1/\alpha, id_{\tau_1}/pre, g/post], e[\tau_2/\alpha, g/pre, id_{\tau_2}/post]) \in \Delta_{[\alpha \mapsto \mathcal{R}], \tau}$$

from which the lemma's statement follows by $\Delta_{[\alpha \mapsto \mathcal{R}], \tau} = id_{\tau}$ (recall: τ is closed).

Let us reflect on what we have gained. The conjuring lemma does not mention Δ from the previous subsection. It holds in basically any language setting in which the (or better, a) parametricity theorem holds, no matter what the exact definitions of the relational actions (the unfolding steps employed for a concrete Δ) are. It is enough that a) the *statement* of the parametricity theorem holds in the language setting under consideration, and that b) $(id_{\tau_1}, g) \in id_{\tau_1} \to graph(g)$ and $(g, id_{\tau_2}) \in graph(g) \to id_{\tau_2}$ do hold. Both a) and b) are the case in all polymorphically typed pure functional languages and Δ-definitions we are aware of. This does not just mean partiality and *seq* in Haskell, but also for example the setting with imprecise error semantics as studied in [13]. Even in work on parametricity and free theorems for a functional-logic language [10], where the definition of Δ, including the case $\mathcal{R}_1 \to \mathcal{R}_2$, turns out somewhat differently (since having to deal with nondeterminism and thus with power domain types), the statement of the parametricity theorem and the definition of $\mathcal{R}_1 \to \mathcal{R}_2$ are such that the conjuring lemma holds (for the functional intermediate language used there). Of course, whether the g in the lemma must be strict, or strict and total, or something else, does depend on the language setting, but this is not harmful, since it does not restrict us in our choice of e.

Also, suppose the situation that some new datatype is to be considered. Usually, this requires some new lifting to be defined and used for the relational interpretation of types. Even though there is a standard recipe to follow, at least for run-of-the-mill algebraic datatypes, it is still work, and requires checking and of course building into a free theorems generator, along with appropriate simplification rules. Not so if we use the conjuring lemma, which (while of course requiring an assertion that the parametricity theorem still holds even in the presence of the new datatype – i.e., there must *exist* an appropriate relational lifting) is not itself sensitive at all to how the new datatype is relationally inter-preted. If we can come up with interesting terms e, now possibly involving the new datatype, we are in good condition to prove new free theorems.

Before we consider the question whether we actually can, in general, come up with interesting terms e, let us do so for some specific examples. We have already remarked, just before the conjuring lemma, that given $f :: \forall \alpha.[\alpha] \to [\alpha]$, the term $e = \lambda xs \to map\ post\ (f\ (map\ pre\ xs))$ fits the bill, which means that the conjuring lemma gives us the following statement:

$$(\lambda xs \to map\ g\ (f\ (map\ id\ xs))) = (\lambda xs \to map\ id\ (f\ (map\ g\ xs)))$$

Using the additional knowledge that $map\ id = id$, this is exactly the standard free theorem for said type of f, namely $map\ g \circ f = f \circ map\ g$.

Let us try again, for the type $f :: \forall \alpha.(\alpha \to Bool) \to [\alpha] \to [\alpha]$. We may "know" that we want $map\ g\ (f\ (p \circ g)\ xs) = f\ p\ (map\ g\ xs)$, but do not want to prove that statement via a lengthy derivation. So, imagining where pre and $post$ should be put in order to make both sides of the desired statement an instance of a common term e, we may arrive at $e = \lambda p\ xs \to map\ post\ (f\ (p \circ post)\ (map\ pre\ xs))$, from which the conjuring lemma plus $map\ id = id$ rewriting gives us

$$(\lambda p\ xs \to map\ g\ (f\ (p \circ g)\ xs)) = (\lambda p\ xs \to f\ (p \circ id)\ (map\ g\ xs))$$

Should we also have rewritten $p \circ id$ to p? No, not in general! In fact, $p \circ id = p$ is not valid in the presence of seq, and luckily there is no way to abuse the conjuring lemma for producing the not generally valid statement $map\ g\ (f\ (p \circ g)\ xs) = f\ p\ (map\ g\ xs)$. Only after applying the lemma, when we commit to a specific language setting, we may decide that for us $p \circ id = p$ indeed holds.

To conclude this example exploration, let us consider the nasty type $f ::$ $((((([\alpha] \to Int) \to Int) \to Int) \to \alpha) \to \alpha$ from Sect. 2.4. The choice $e = \lambda p \to post\ (f\ (\lambda s \to pre\ (p\ (\lambda t \to s\ (\lambda w \to t\ (\lambda x \to w\ (map\ pre\ x)))))))$ gives us what we reported there as (2). We also remarked there that the approach presented here does not give us the various positive corner cases relevant in the presence of seq. That is not fully true; actually the conjuring lemma gives us those as well, for example with $e = \lambda p \to post\ (f\ (\lambda s \to pre\ (p\ (\lambda t \to s\ \bot))))$, which is a valid input to Lemma 1, and gives us $g\ (f\ (\lambda s \to p\ (\lambda t \to s\ \bot))) = f\ (\lambda s \to g\ (p\ (\lambda t \to s\ \bot)))$. But in what follows, we want to construct exactly one e for each type of f, and of course we opt for the supposedly most useful one, not for corner cases that "just" happen to also be valid. So for said type of f, we want to, and will, construct the e which gives

$$g\ (f\ (\lambda s \to p\ (\lambda t \to s\ (\lambda w \to t\ (\lambda x \to w\ x)))))$$
$$=$$
$$f\ (\lambda s \to g\ (p\ (\lambda t \to s\ (\lambda w \to t\ (\lambda x \to w\ (map\ g\ x))))))$$

(or with left-hand side $g\ (f\ p)$ in a world in which eta-reduction is valid).

3.3 Constructing e – Discovering Dinaturality

Given some f of polymorphic type, we want to construct an e of closed type. That seems easy, we could simply use $e = 42$. But no, of course we want e to use f in an interesting way. In essence, we want it to "touch" each occurrence of the type variable α in the type of f. For doing so, e can use $pre :: \tau_1 \to \alpha$ and $post :: \alpha \to \tau_2$. Some reflection shows that we should make a difference between positive and negative occurrences of α, in the standard sense of polarity in function types. That is, an occurrence of α that is reached by an odd number of left-branching at function arrows (in the standard right-associative reading of $\to$) is considered a negative occurrence, others are considered positive occurrences. So, for example, in the type $(\alpha \to \mathsf{Bool}) \to [\alpha] \to \mathsf{Maybe}\ \alpha$, the first α is positive, the second one is negative, and the third one is positive. Then, we want to construct e such that negative occurrences of α are replaced by τ_1 and positive ones by τ_2.

This is doable by structural recursion on type expressions. Specifically, the following function $mono_{pre,post}(\sigma)$ builds a term that maps an input of type σ to an output of a type with the same structure as σ, but made monomorphic according to the just described rule about negative and positive occurrences of α. So, for example, $mono_{pre,post}((\alpha \to \mathsf{Bool}) \to [\alpha] \to \mathsf{Maybe}\ \alpha)$ maps an input of type $(\alpha \to \mathsf{Bool}) \to [\alpha] \to \mathsf{Maybe}\ \alpha$ to an output of type $(\tau_2 \to \mathsf{Bool}) \to [\tau_1] \to \mathsf{Maybe}\ \tau_2$. We do not prove the general behaviour, but it should be easy to see that $mono_{pre,post}(\sigma)$ does what we claim. The defining equations we give should also be suggestive of what would have to be done if new datatypes (other than lists and Maybe) are introduced.

$$
\begin{aligned}
mono_{pre,post}(\alpha) &= post \\
mono_{pre,post}(\mathsf{Bool}) &= id \\
mono_{pre,post}(\mathsf{Int}) &= id \\
mono_{pre,post}([\sigma]) &= map\ mono_{pre,post}(\sigma) \\
mono_{pre,post}(\mathsf{Maybe}\ \sigma) &= fmap\ mono_{pre,post}(\sigma) \\
mono_{pre,post}(\sigma_1 \to \sigma_2) &= \lambda h \to mono_{pre,post}(\sigma_2) \circ h \circ mono_{post,pre}(\sigma_1)
\end{aligned}
$$

Note the switching of pre and $post$ in moving from $\sigma_1 \to \sigma_2$ to σ_1. Of course, in that last defining equation, the h must be a sufficiently fresh variable (also relative to pre and $post$).

Given f of polymorphic type $\forall \alpha.\sigma$, we will be able to use the term $e = mono_{pre,post}(\sigma)\ f$ in Lemma 1. It is useful to notice then that (omitting explicit type instantiation and substitution):

- $mono_{pre,post}(\sigma)[id/pre, g/post] = mono_{id,g}(\sigma)$
- $mono_{pre,post}(\sigma)[g/pre, id/post] = mono_{g,id}(\sigma)$

So our overall procedure now is to generate free theorems as follows:

$$
mono_{id,g}(\sigma)\ f = mono_{g,id}(\sigma)\ f
$$

Category theory aficionados will recognise the concept of dinaturality here! For a sketch of the precise connection, see Sect. 5.

Here, let us try out the above for the example $f :: (\alpha \to \mathsf{Bool}) \to [\alpha] \to \mathsf{Maybe}\ \alpha$. We get:

$$
\begin{aligned}
&mono_{pre,post}((\alpha \to \mathsf{Bool}) \to [\alpha] \to \mathsf{Maybe}\ \alpha) \\
&= \lambda h_1 \to mono_{pre,post}([\alpha] \to \mathsf{Maybe}\ \alpha) \circ h_1 \circ mono_{post,pre}(\alpha \to \mathsf{Bool}) \\
&= \lambda h_1 \to (\lambda h_2 \to mono_{pre,post}(\mathsf{Maybe}\ \alpha) \circ h_2 \circ mono_{post,pre}([\alpha])) \\
&\qquad \circ h_1 \circ \\
&\qquad (\lambda h_3 \to mono_{post,pre}(\mathsf{Bool}) \circ h_3 \circ mono_{pre,post}(\alpha)) \\
&= \lambda h_1 \to (\lambda h_2 \to fmap\ post \circ h_2 \circ map\ pre) \circ h_1 \circ (\lambda h_3 \to id \circ h_3 \circ post)
\end{aligned}
$$

So the free theorem we get from this by instantiation is:

$$
\begin{aligned}
&(\lambda h_2 \to fmap\ g \circ h_2 \circ map\ id) \circ f \circ (\lambda h_3 \to id \circ h_3 \circ g) \\
&\quad = \\
&(\lambda h_2 \to fmap\ id \circ h_2 \circ map\ g) \circ f \circ (\lambda h_3 \to id \circ h_3 \circ id)
\end{aligned}
$$

There are ample opportunities for further simplification here, but let us try to be systematic about this.

3.4 Simplifying Obtained Statements

The terms generated by $mono_{pre,post}(\sigma)$ contain a lot of function compositions, both outside and inside of map- and $fmap$-calls. Moreover, many of the partners in those compositions will be id, either up front because of the cases with σ a base type, or later when pre or $post$ is replaced by id (and the other by g). So our primary strategy for simplification is to inline all the compositions, and while doing so eliminate all id-calls. Additionally, all lambda-abstractions introduced by the $mono_{pre,post}(\sigma_1 \to \sigma_2)$ case will be provided with an argument and then beta-reduced. There is no danger of term duplication here since the lambda-bound h is used only linearly in the right-hand side.

These considerations lead to the following syntactic simplification rules, to be applied to terms produced as $mono_{id,g}(\sigma)\ f$ or $mono_{g,id}(\sigma)\ f$. As usual, where lambda-bound variables are introduced, they are assumed to be sufficiently fresh.

$$
\begin{aligned}
\lfloor id\ t \rfloor &= t \\
\lfloor map\ f\ t \rfloor &= map\ (\lambda v \to \lfloor f\ v \rfloor)\ t \\
\lfloor fmap\ f\ t \rfloor &= fmap\ (\lambda v \to \lfloor f\ v \rfloor)\ t \\
\lfloor (\lambda h \to body)\ t \rfloor &= \lambda v \to \lfloor body[t/h]\ v \rfloor \\
\lfloor (f \circ g)\ t \rfloor &= \lfloor f\ \lfloor g\ t \rfloor \rfloor \\
\lfloor f\ t \rfloor &= f\ t
\end{aligned}
$$

The last line is a catch-all case that is only used if none of the others apply. In the case where the simplification function $\lfloor \cdot \rfloor$ is applied to a term of the form $(\lambda h \to body)\ t$, note that we are indeed entitled to eta-expand the beta-reduced version $body[t/h]$ into $\lambda v \to body[t/h]\ v$ (in order to subsequently apply $\lfloor \cdot \rfloor$ recursively). Said eta-expansion is type correct as well as semantically correct, since by analysing the $mono_{pre,post}(\sigma)$ function, which is the producer of the subexpression $(\lambda h \to body)$, we know that $body$, and hence also $body[t/h]$, is a term formed by function composition, and since $f \circ g = \lambda v \to (f \circ g)\ v$ is a valid equivalence even in language settings in which eta-reduction is not valid (and in which thus $f = \lambda v \to f\ v$ would not be in general okay). The eta-expansions on the function arguments of map- and $fmap$-calls (again done to enable further simplification on $f\ v$) are also justified, since map and $fmap$ use their function arguments only in specific, known ways: $map\ f\ t$ is indeed semantically equivalent to $map\ (\lambda v \to f\ v)\ t$, since map does not use seq. These considerations should convince us that $\lfloor \cdot \rfloor$ transforms a term into a semantically equivalent one, hence is correct. But is it also exhaustive, or can we accidentally skip transforming (and thus, simplifying) some part of the term produced by $mono_{pre,post}(\sigma)$? The best argument that we cannot, actually comes from the Haskell implementation given in the appendix, and will be discussed in Sect. 4.

Let us be a bit more concrete again, and consider an example. In the previous subsection, we generated $mono_{pre,post}(\sigma)$ for $\sigma = (\alpha \to \mathsf{Bool}) \to [\alpha] \to \mathsf{Maybe}\ \alpha$. Let us now calculate $\lfloor mono_{id,g}(\sigma)\ f \rfloor$ from this (of course, $\lfloor mono_{g,id}(\sigma)\ f \rfloor$ would be very similar). See Fig. 1. The result is not yet fully satisfactory. For one thing, $\lfloor map\ id\ v_2 \rfloor$ was "simplified" to $map\ (\lambda v_4 \to v_4)\ v_2$. Of course, we would prefer it to be simplified to just v_2. This is easy to achieve by adding simplification rules like $\lfloor map\ id\ t \rfloor = t$. In fact, our implementation does something more general, namely replacing the original first simplification rule $\lfloor id\ t \rfloor = t$ by the following one: $\lfloor f\ t \rfloor = t$ whenever f can be syntactically generated by the grammar $\mathsf{Id} = id \mid map\ \mathsf{Id} \mid fmap\ \mathsf{Id} \mid \mathsf{Id} \circ \mathsf{Id}$.

$$
\begin{aligned}
&\lfloor (\lambda h_1 \to (\lambda h_2 \to fmap\ g \circ h_2 \circ map\ id) \circ h_1 \circ (\lambda h_3 \to id \circ h_3 \circ g))\ f \rfloor \\
&= \lambda v_1 \to \lfloor ((\lambda h_2 \to fmap\ g \circ h_2 \circ map\ id) \circ f \circ (\lambda h_3 \to id \circ h_3 \circ g))\ v_1 \rfloor \\
&= \lambda v_1 \to \lfloor (\lambda h_2 \to fmap\ g \circ h_2 \circ map\ id)\ \lfloor f\ \lfloor (\lambda h_3 \to id \circ h_3 \circ g)\ v_1 \rfloor \rfloor \rfloor \\
&= \lambda v_1\ v_2 \to \lfloor (fmap\ g \circ \lfloor f\ \lfloor (\lambda h_3 \to id \circ h_3 \circ g)\ v_1 \rfloor \rfloor \circ map\ id)\ v_2 \rfloor \\
&= \lambda v_1\ v_2 \to \lfloor fmap\ g\ \lfloor \lfloor f\ \lfloor (\lambda h_3 \to id \circ h_3 \circ g)\ v_1 \rfloor \rfloor\ \lfloor map\ id\ v_2 \rfloor \rfloor \rfloor \\
&= \lambda v_1\ v_2 \to fmap\ (\lambda v_3 \to \lfloor g\ v_3 \rfloor)\ (f\ \lfloor (\lambda h_3 \to id \circ h_3 \circ g)\ v_1 \rfloor\ (map\ (\lambda v_4 \to \lfloor id\ v_4 \rfloor)\ v_2)) \\
&= \lambda v_1\ v_2 \to fmap\ (\lambda v_3 \to g\ v_3)\ (f\ \lfloor (\lambda h_3 \to id \circ h_3 \circ g)\ v_1 \rfloor\ (map\ (\lambda v_4 \to v_4)\ v_2)) \\
&= \lambda v_1\ v_2 \to fmap\ (\lambda v_3 \to g\ v_3)\ (f\ (\lambda v_5 \to \lfloor (id \circ v_1 \circ g)\ v_5 \rfloor)\ (map\ (\lambda v_4 \to v_4)\ v_2)) \\
&= \lambda v_1\ v_2 \to fmap\ (\lambda v_3 \to g\ v_3)\ (f\ (\lambda v_5 \to \lfloor id\ \lfloor v_1\ \lfloor g\ v_5 \rfloor \rfloor \rfloor)\ (map\ (\lambda v_4 \to v_4)\ v_2)) \\
&= \lambda v_1\ v_2 \to fmap\ (\lambda v_3 \to g\ v_3)\ (f\ (\lambda v_5 \to v_1\ (g\ v_5))\ (map\ (\lambda v_4 \to v_4)\ v_2))
\end{aligned}
$$

Fig. 1. An example calculation, for $\lfloor mono_{id,g}((\alpha \to \mathsf{Bool}) \to [\alpha] \to \mathsf{Maybe}\ \alpha)\ f \rfloor$

Another issue is the unsatisfactory "simplification" of *fmap* g to *fmap* ($\lambda v_3 \to$ $g\ v_3$) in Fig. 1. To prevent it, but still keep the general rule $\lfloor map\ f\ t \rfloor =$ *map* ($\lambda v \to \lfloor f\ v \rfloor$) t in which the recursive descent can be important (say, if f is not just a function variable), we add the following simplification rule, which applies right after the one about generalised identities introduced above: $\lfloor f\ t \rfloor = f\ t$ whenever f can be syntactically generated by the grammar Simple = v | *map* Simple | *fmap* Simple (where v means any variable, including the g from $mono_{id,g}(\sigma)$, say). As a result, the calculation in Fig. 1 would now yield the simplified term $\lambda v_1\ v_2 \to fmap\ g\ (f\ (\lambda v_3 \to v_1\ (g\ v_3))\ v_2)$.

In summary, we generate the free theorem for a function f of polymorphic type σ as $\lfloor mono_{id,g}(\sigma)\ f \rfloor = \lfloor mono_{g,id}(\sigma)\ f \rfloor$, additionally using the simplification rules introduced and elaborated above. There might still be eta-reducible expressions left in the produced terms. But those are not necessarily safe to reduce in the presence of *seq*, so are left to a separate post-processing.

3.5 About What Generality Is Lost

There is one issue open from (the end of) Sect. 2.4, where we promised to explain for what types the presented approach will not give an as general result as the existing generators, since it is impossible to express the general free theorem for those types as an equation without preconditions. The criterion again depends on the notion of polarity in function types. We believe it is an exact characterisation, but have no proof to show for it.

Let us annotate all parts of a type expression, not just the type variables, with their polarity. So, for example, the type $(\alpha \to \alpha) \to \alpha \to \alpha$ becomes $(\alpha^+ \to \alpha^-)^- \to (\alpha^- \to \alpha^+)^+$, the type $(\alpha \to$ Bool$) \to [\alpha] \to$ Maybe α becomes $(\alpha^+ \to$ Bool$^-)^- \to ([\alpha^-]^- \to$ (Maybe $\alpha^+)^+)^+$, and the type $(\alpha \to$ Bool$) \to$ (Bool $\to \alpha) \to [\alpha] \to \alpha$ becomes $(\alpha^+ \to$ Bool$^-)^- \to (($Bool$^+ \to \alpha^-)^- \to$ $([\alpha^-]^- \to \alpha^+)^+)^+$. The types for which stating a simple equation is not the most general free theorem are those which contain a negative subexpression in which both a positive and a negative α appear. For example, this is the case for $(\alpha^+ \to \alpha^-)^- \to (\alpha^- \to \alpha^+)^+$, but not for the other two types considered above.

4 Implementation

Figures 2, 3 and 4 in the appendix give the Haskell code for deriving free theorems using the presented approach, minus the code for lexing, parsing, and pretty-printing. The actual generation work happens in Fig. 2: *mono* implements $mono_{pre,post}(\sigma)$, *apply* implements $\lfloor f\ t \rfloor$. An eta-reducer is implemented in Fig. 3. To encode lambda-terms (and substitution), we use higher-order abstract syntax, and normalisation by evaluation principles come into play as well.

The generator code is available online [4], and can be installed using standard Haskell package management tools. To see the generator in action, see Fig. 5 in the appendix.

From Sect. 3.4 we still owe an argument that $\lfloor \cdot \rfloor$ is exhaustive, i.e., that we cannot accidentally skip transforming (and thus, simplifying) some part of the term produced by *mono*. So, consider the following. In the implementation, $\lfloor \cdot \rfloor$ (named *apply* there) does not take one argument term, but instead two, and they are differently typed. Specifically, there is one syntax type for terms generated by *mono* and another syntax type for final output terms. The type of $\lfloor \cdot \rfloor$ is such that it always takes an f in the former syntax and a t in the latter syntax, in the form $\lfloor f\ t \rfloor$. The type of *mono* guarantees that it indeed generates f in the former syntax type (in essence, hence, this syntax type characterises a subclass of lambda-terms in which all terms possibly generated by *mono* live). Since it is easy to see by inspection of the implementation that $\lfloor \cdot \rfloor$ does an exhaustive case distinction on all possible forms of its first argument (it handles all constructor cases of its syntax type), and since $\lfloor \cdot \rfloor$'s output type is the one of final output terms, not of *mono*-generated terms, we know that no parts of the $mono_{pre,post}(\sigma)$-term survive untouched. In particular, the syntax and function types in the implementation also tell us that the catch-all case $\lfloor f\ t \rfloor = f\ t$ will not have to deal with any f that still contains *mono*-material. Instead, we know that if the catch-all case is reached, f is a variable or an already simplified final output term (which could have come into place via the substitution in an earlier recursive call $\lfloor body[t/h]\ v \rfloor$).

5   The Precise Connection to Dinaturality

A dinatural transformation, between two bifunctors $\mathbf{F}$ and $\mathbf{G}$ of the same mixed contravariant/covariant kind over the same source category, is an indexed collection of arrows ϕ_X of types $\mathbf{G}(X, X) \to \mathbf{F}(X, X)$ such that for every $g : B \to A$ the following diagram commutes:

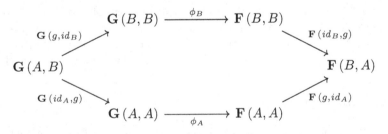

One possible instantiation is to let all categories involved be **Set**, let $\mathbf{G}$ be the constant functor to the final object $\mathbf{1}$, and let each ϕ_X be the lifted constant $f_X : \mathbf{F}(X, X)$, for a given indexed collection f_X. By this, the above diagram specialises to the following one:

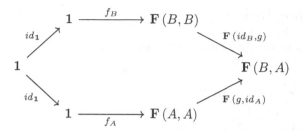

Consequently, we have

$$\mathbf{F}\,(id_B, g)\ f_B = \mathbf{F}\,(g, id_A)\ f_A$$

if f_X is (polymorphically) typed $\mathbf{F}\,(X, X)$ for a bifunctor $\mathbf{F}$ of appropriate kind. Using the *Hom* bifunctor, we can indeed turn type schemes σ into such bifunctors, as follows:

$$
\begin{aligned}
\mathbf{F}_\alpha \quad & (X, Y) = Y \\
\mathbf{F}_{\mathsf{Bool}} \quad & (X, Y) = \mathsf{Bool} \\
\mathbf{F}_{\mathsf{Int}} \quad & (X, Y) = \mathsf{Int} \\
\mathbf{F}_{[\sigma]} \quad & (X, Y) = [\mathbf{F}_\sigma\,(X, Y)] \\
\mathbf{F}_{(\mathsf{Maybe}\ \sigma)} & (X, Y) = \mathsf{Maybe}\ (\mathbf{F}_\sigma\,(X, Y)) \\
\mathbf{F}_{\sigma_1 \to \sigma_2} \quad & (X, Y) = Hom(\mathbf{F}_{\sigma_1}\,(Y, X), \mathbf{F}_{\sigma_2}\,(X, Y))
\end{aligned}
$$

So now we have that if $f :: \forall \alpha.\sigma$, then

$$\mathbf{F}_\sigma\,(id_B, g)\ f_B = \mathbf{F}_\sigma\,(g, id_A)\ f_A$$

for the bifunctor arising from the recursive definition above. Taking into account that the action of *Hom* on arrows is that $Hom(f, g)$ is the function $h \mapsto g \circ h \circ f$, this is exactly the statement

$$mono_{id, g}(\sigma)\ f = mono_{g, id}(\sigma)\ f$$

which was used earlier, since one can then show that the relevant definitions are related by, on the arrow level, $\mathbf{F}_\sigma\,(pre, post) = mono_{pre, post}(\sigma)$.

Acknowledgements. Many of the ideas here, most notably the conjuring lemma (including that name), but also the criterion proposed in Sect. 3.5, originated during past collaboration with Stefan Mehner.

A   Implementation

See Sect. 4 for some explanation of the implementation.

```
module Generate (mono, apply) where
import Syntax (Type (..), Func (..), Term (..))
mono :: Type → Func v → Func v → Func v
mono Alpha      pre post = post
mono Bool       pre post = Id
mono Int        pre post = Id
mono (List t)   pre post = Map "map" (mono t pre post)
mono (Maybe t)  pre post = Map "fmap" (mono t pre post)
mono (s 'To' t) pre post = Lambda (λh → mono t pre post
                                        'Comp'
                                        Embed h
                                        'Comp'
                                        mono s post pre)
apply :: Func (Term v) → Term v → Term v
f              'apply' t | isId f              = t
f              'apply' t | Just f' ← isSimple f = f' 'Apply' t
Map name f 'apply' t = Const name 'Apply' Lambda' (λv → f 'apply' (Var v)) 'Apply' t
Lambda f   'apply' t = Lambda' (λv → f t 'apply' (Var v))
(f 'Comp' g) 'apply' t = f 'apply' (g 'apply' t)
Embed f    'apply' t = f 'Apply' t
isId :: Func v → Bool
isId Id            = True
isId (Map _ f)     = isId f
isId (f 'Comp' g) = isId f && isId g
isId _             = False
isSimple :: Func (Term v) → Maybe (Term v)
isSimple (Embed f@(Var _))                    = Just f
isSimple (Map name f) | Just f' ← isSimple f = Just (Const name 'Apply' f')
isSimple _                                    = Nothing
```

Fig. 2. Module Generate, generation and simplification of free theorems

module Syntax (Type (..), Func (..), Term (..), *etaReduce*) **where**
import Control.Monad.State
data Type = Alpha | Bool | Int | List Type | Maybe Type | Type 'To' Type
data Func v = Id | Map String (Func v) | Lambda ($v \rightarrow$ Func v) | Func v 'Comp' Func v
      | Embed v
data Term v = Const String | Var v | Term v 'Apply' Term v | Lambda' ($v \rightarrow$ Term v)
etaReduce :: Term String $\rightarrow$ Term String
etaReduce $t = evalState$ ($go\ t$) ['*' : $show\ n \mid n \leftarrow [1..]$]
  where $go\ t$@(Const _) = *return t*
        $go\ t$@(Var _)   = *return t*
        go (f 'Apply' t) = *liftM2* Apply ($go\ f$) ($go\ t$)
        go (Lambda' f) = **do** $vars \leftarrow get$
                         let v = *head vars*
                              vs = *tail vars*
                        put vs
                        body $\leftarrow go$ ($f\ v$)
                        case *body* **of**
                          t 'Apply' Var v' | *not* (*freeVar v t*) && $v' == v$
                                    $\rightarrow$ *return t*
                        _ $\rightarrow$ *return* (Lambda' ($\lambda v \rightarrow evalState$ (go ($f\ v$)) vs))
     freeVar _ (Const _)   = False
     freeVar v (Var v')   = $v' == v$
     freeVar v (f 'Apply' t) = *freeVar v f* || *freeVar v t*
     freeVar v (Lambda' f) = *freeVar v* (f "")

Fig. 3. Module Syntax, datatypes for types and different forms of (higher-order abstract syntax) terms, and eta-reduction

module Main $(main)$ **where**

import Syntax (Type $(..)$, Func $(..)$, Term $(..)$, $etaReduce$)
import Parser $(parse)$
import Generate $(mono, apply)$
import Show ()

import System.IO

$sigma$ :: Type
$sigma$ = (Alpha 'To' Bool) 'To' ((Bool 'To' Alpha) 'To' (List Alpha 'To' Alpha))

$main$ :: IO ()
$main$ = **do**
   $hSetBuffering$ $stdout$ NoBuffering
   $putStr$ \$ "function type (or Enter for default): "
   $sigma \leftarrow getLine \ggg \lambda s \rightarrow return$ \$ **if** $s ==$ "" **then** $sigma$ **else** $parse$ s
   $putStrLn$ ""
   $putStrLn$ \$ "f :: " $+\!\!+$ $show$ $sigma$
   $putStrLn$ \$ $replicate$ 66 '-'
   $putStrLn$ \$ "e = " $+\!\!+$ $show$ ($mono$ $sigma$ (Embed "pre") (Embed "post")) $+\!\!+$ " f"
   $putStrLn$ \$ $replicate$ 66 '-'
   let $lhs = mono$ $sigma$ Id (Embed (Var "g")) 'apply' Const "f"
       $rhs = mono$ $sigma$ (Embed (Var "g")) Id 'apply' Const "f"
   $putStrLn$ \$ "free theorem:"
   $putStrLn$ \$ " " $+\!\!+$ $show$ lhs
   ...

Fig. 4. Module Main, putting the generator together with input and output

```
*Main> main
function type (or Enter for default):

f :: (alpha -> Bool) -> (Bool -> alpha) -> [alpha] -> alpha
------------------------------------------------------------------
e = (\h1 -> (\h2 -> (\h3 -> post . h3 . map pre)
                  . h2 . (\h4 -> pre . h4 . id))
          . h1 . (\h5 -> id . h5 . post)) f
------------------------------------------------------------------
free theorem:
  \x1 x2 x3 -> g (f (\x4 -> x1 (g x4)) (\x5 -> x2 x5) x3)
  =
  \x1 x2 x3 -> f (\x4 -> x1 x4) (\x5 -> g (x2 x5)) (map g x3)
------------------------------------------------------------------
free theorem, eta-reduced:
  \x1 x2 x3 -> g (f (\x4 -> x1 (g x4)) x2 x3)
  =
  \x1 x2 x3 -> f x1 (\x4 -> g (x2 x4)) (map g x3)
```

Fig. 5. An example session

References

1. http://hackage.haskell.org/package/free-theorems. Accessed Sept 2019
2. http://free-theorems.nomeata.de. Accessed Sept 2019
3. http://hackage.haskell.org/package/lambdabot-haskell-plugins. Accessed Sept 2019
4. http://hackage.haskell.org/package/ft-generator. Accessed Sept 2019
5. Bainbridge, E., Freyd, P., Scedrov, A., Scott, P.: Functorial polymorphism. Theor. Comput. Sci. **70**(1), 35–64 (1990)
6. Berger, U., Schwichtenberg, H.: An inverse of the evaluation functional for typed lambda-calculus. In: Logic in Computer Science, Proceedings, pp. 203–211. IEEE Press (1991)
7. Gill, A., Launchbury, J., Peyton Jones, S.: A short cut to deforestation. In: Functional Programming Languages and Computer Architecture, Proceedings, pp. 223–232. ACM Press (1993)
8. Hackett, J., Hutton, G.: Programs for cheap! In: Logic in Computer Science, Proceedings, pp. 115–126. IEEE Press (2015)
9. Johann, P., Voigtländer, J.: Free theorems in the presence of seq. In: Principles of Programming Languages, Proceedings, pp. 99–110. ACM Press (2004)
10. Mehner, S., Seidel, D., Straßburger, L., Voigtländer, J.: Parametricity and proving free theorems for functional-logic languages. In: Principles and Practice of Declarative Programming, Proceedings, pp. 19–30. ACM Press (2014)
11. Pfenning, F., Elliott, C.: Higher-order abstract syntax. In: Programming Language Design and Implementation, Proceedings, pp. 199–208. ACM Press (1988)
12. Reynolds, J.: Types, abstraction and parametric polymorphism. In: Information Processing, Proceedings, pp. 513–523. Elsevier (1983)
13. Stenger, F., Voigtländer, J.: Parametricity for Haskell with imprecise error semantics. In: Curien, P.-L. (ed.) TLCA 2009. LNCS, vol. 5608, pp. 294–308. Springer, Heidelberg (2009). https://doi.org/10.1007/978-3-642-02273-9_22
14. Wadler, P.: Theorems for free! In: Functional Programming Languages and Computer Architecture, Proceedings, pp. 347–359. ACM Press (1989)

Improving the Performance of the Paisley Pattern-Matching EDSL by Staged Combinatorial Compilation

Baltasar Trancón y Widemann[✉] and Markus Lepper

semantics GmbH, Berlin, Germany
baltasar@trancon.de
https://bandm.eu/

Abstract. Paisley is a declarative lightweight embedded domain-specific language for expressive, non-deterministic, non-invasive pattern matching on arbitrary data structures in Java applications. As such, it comes as a pure Java library of pattern-matching combinators and corresponding programming idioms. While the combinators support a basic form of self-optimization based on heuristic metadata, overall performance is limited by the distributed and compositional implementation that impedes non-local code optimization. In this paper, we describe a technique for improving the performance of Paisley transparently, without compromising the flexible and extensible combinatorial design. By means of distributed bytecode generation, dynamic class loading and just-in-time compilation of patterns, the run-time overhead of the combinatorial approach can be reduced significantly, without requiring any technology other than a standard Java virtual machine and our LLJava bytecode framework. We evaluate the impact by comparison to earlier benchmarking results on interpreted Paisley. The key ideas of our compilation technique are fairly general, and apply in principle to any kind of combinator language running on any jit-compiling host.

Keywords: Pattern matching · Embedded domain-specific language · Staged compilation

1 Introduction

In declarative programming languages with algebraic datatypes, *constructing* and *querying* structured data are symmetric tasks, handled by languages features of equal expressiveness, the latter namely by *pattern matching*. Semantics are given by a clean, reversible *algebraic* interpretation.

In object-oriented languages, by contrast, the query side is markedly deficient in expressiveness [4,12]. This is due partly to shortcomings in language design, partly to the doctrine of *data abstraction* which is generally incompatible with algebraic semantics.

© Springer Nature Switzerland AG 2020
P. Hofstedt et al. (Eds.): DECLARE 2019, LNAI 12057, pp. 268–285, 2020.
https://doi.org/10.1007/978-3-030-46714-2_17

Paisley [11] is a solution for this dialectic problem. It is a lightweight embedded domain-specific language (EDSL) that raises the pattern-matching expressiveness of the host language Java considerably, without breaking either the imperative control flow or the abstraction of object-oriented data models.

The present paper summarizes the design of Paisley in Sect. 1. Its main contribution is the description and evaluation of a novel compilation technique, presented in Sects. 2 and 3, respectively.

1.1   Basic Design and Usage of Paisley

The lightweight implementation of the Paisley EDSL is a pure Java library that runs on a vanilla Java platform requiring neither compiler nor runtime extensions, and that *reifies* pattern matching primitives by a collection of Java classes. Constructor terms for objects of these classes form a declarative language, but since they denote plain Java objects and thus first-class citizens, patterns may also be configured algorithmically by meta-programming in the host system.

In the following presentation, all code samples are in Java 8, which we assume the reader is basically familiar with. We shall take the liberty to add a keyword **partial** for partial type definition fragments that add up throughout a collection of sources, borrowed from C#, in order to focus on distinct aspects of the APIs according to the flow of discussion.

The Paisley design aims at representing the imperative object-oriented view on Java data objects faithfully. Thus it is concerned with the full spectrum of *operational* semantics of data query operations, of which the implementation of algebraic semantics is merely a particularly well-behaved special case. The basic API is deceptively simple:

```
partial abstract class Pattern⟨A⟩ {
  public boolean match(A target);
  public boolean matchAgain();
}
```

A pattern is an object that can be attempted to match against some value target of the parameter type A, and will indicate success by its **boolean** return value. All additional information, such as extracted pieces of data, needs to be communicated via side effects.

Patterns are potentially non-deterministic; additional matches beyond the successful first, each with their own observable side effects, can be obtained by iterating matchAgain until it fails. Note that patterns are required to store the information needed for backtracking as private mutable state, thus they are reusable sequentially but not concurrently.

The event of a successful match, together with the collection of all observable side effects, is called a *solution*. The sequence of all solutions is the primary behavioral semantics of a pattern.

```
Variable⟨V1⟩ v1 = new Variable⟨⟩();              // (1)
// ...
Variable⟨Vn⟩ vn = new Variable⟨⟩();              // (1)
Pattern⟨A⟩ p = createPattern(v1, ..., vn);       // (2)
if (p.match(target)) do                          // (3a)
    doSomething(v1.value, ..., vn.value);        // (4)
    while (wantingMore() && p.matchAgain());     // (3b)
```

Fig. 1. Basic usage template for Paisley patterns

The single most important pattern class is the Variable, which can be bound to data obtained from the target. A variable pattern simply matches any target deterministically, and records it as a side effect:[1]

```
partial class Variable⟨A⟩ extends Pattern⟨A⟩ {
    A value;
    public boolean match(A target) { value = target; return true; }
    public boolean matchAgain()    {                  return false; }
}
```

The power of these variables comes from the ability to be nested inside complex patterns, and hence record selected parts of the overall target data, under controlled conditions. Note that variable binding is by ordinary imperative assignment; there are no declarative concepts such as *single assignment* (which would prevent transparent sequential reuse) or *unification* (which is ill-defined for arbitrary non-algebraic data APIs).

The basic usage template consists of four steps: (1) allocate pattern variables to hold results; (2) construct a complex pattern over the variables; (3) attempt one or more matches; (4) on success, proceed using the result values; see Fig. 1.

Here createPattern is problem-specific producer code that may build on operations from the Paisley library, doSomething is arbitrary consumer code that does not need to know about patterns, and the greyed-out part is optional for the case of exhaustive search of matches for non-deterministic patterns. Note that the API is statically type-safe for both targets and results, and backtracking is subject to explicit imperative control flow, including the user-defined condition wantingMore.

1.2   Summary of Features

This section gives a brief overview of the features of the Paisley core library. It is not intended as a detailed or complete introduction, but rather to convey an intuition about the operational principles and recurring idioms, as well as the scope of the task of developing a compiler for the Paisley language.

---

[1] This is the only solution-relevant side effect discussed in this paper, but others could be implemented by user-defined combinators.

Paisley is a *combinatorial language* in the sense of Schönfinkel and Curry. Each primitive is either a full-fledged pattern that can be used on its own, or an operator that builds new patterns from one or more existing ones. The core library can be extended as needed by giving new implementations (subclasses) of the existing APIs.

Logic. The most basic Paisley combinators are both and either, which implement the logical conjunction and disjunction of patterns, respectively.

The pattern both(p, q) produces all solutions of q for each successive solution of p in order, both applied to the same target. Since q may observe the variable bindings established by the successful match for p, the solution semantics of the combinator is a *dependent sum* rather than just a Cartesian product of the individual semantics.

The pattern either(p, q) produces all solutions of p followed by all solutions of q, both applied to the same target. This is the most straightforward way to introduce non-determinism. Since q is only invoked after solutions for p are exhausted, the latter can not observe the former, and the solutions semantics of the combinator is just the concatenation of the individual semantics. Note that a variable can only be considered bound in each solution of —either(p, q)— if it is bound by *both* p and q.

Projections. Any data access operation that can be reified as an instance f of the Java standard interface Function⟨A, B⟩, such as a getter for a field of type B from objects of class A, contravariantly induces a transform from Pattern⟨B⟩ p to Pattern⟨A⟩ transform(f, p) — namely, transform(f, p).match(a) should behave equivalently to p.match(f.apply(a)). This allows patterns operating on parts of a data structure to be lifted to patterns operating on the whole, by transforming them with the appropriate access operation.

Tests. Any data access operation that can be reified as an instance t of the Java standard interface Predicate⟨A⟩, such as a **boolean**-valued getter or an **instanceof** test, induces Pattern⟨A⟩ guard(t) — namely, guard(t).match(a) should behave equivalently to t.test(a). Thus, the pattern matches a target deterministically and without extra side effects, if and only if the underlying predicate is satisfied.

Encapsulated Search. An important usage of non-deterministic computations embedded in a conventional deterministic program is *encapsulated search*: locally enumerating all solutions of a non-deterministic subproblem, without leaking backtracking control flow to the consumer. Paisley provides convenience operations for encapsulating the ubiquitous special case of patterns with a single variable. An expression of the form v.bindings(p, a) enumerates the values of variable v for all solutions of p.match(a). Both eager and lazy evaluation are supported:

```
partial class Variable⟨A⟩ {
    public ⟨B⟩ List⟨A⟩      eagerBindings(Pattern⟨B⟩ pattern, B target);
    public ⟨B⟩ Iterable⟨A⟩  lazyBindings (Pattern⟨B⟩ pattern, B target);
}
```

```
Motif⟨Integer, Integer⟩ pos       = Motif.guard(n → n > 0),
                        pred      = Motif.transform(n → n − 1),
                        countdown = Motif.star(pos.andThen(pred));
System.out.println(countdown.eagerBindings(10));
```

⤳ [10, 9, 8, 7, 6, 5, 4, 3, 2, 1, 0]

Fig. 2. Relational programming on numbers

Pattern Algebra. For meta-programming with patterns, it would be desirable to be able to substitute a Variable⟨B⟩ v occurring in a Pattern⟨A⟩ p with another Pattern⟨B⟩ q. Since patterns are specified by an abstract API and in general have no discernible term structure, this is not straightforward. If v is definitely bound in p however, we can have the next best thing: an external data-flow composition v.bind(p, q) — namely v.bind(p, q).match(a) should behave equivalently to b → q.match(b) iterated disjunctively over the elements of v.lazyBindings(p, a). Note that lazy evaluation ensures that computations from p and q are interleaved in the expected order [6].

Substitution in turn is good enough to define a lambda operator for pattern function abstraction. Considering functions on patterns (*motifs*) as first-class citizens raises the level of abstraction considerably:

partial interface Motif⟨A, B⟩ **extends** Function⟨Pattern⟨A⟩, Pattern⟨B⟩⟩ { }
partial class Variable⟨A⟩ {
  public ⟨B⟩ Motif⟨A, B⟩ lambda(Pattern⟨B⟩ body);
}

Besides the basic composition operations for point-free construction, such as point-wise lifted transform() and guard()), motifs also provide Kleene star() and plus() operators for full-fledged relational programming [14]. These operations implement unbounded iteration of a pattern transparently by lazy cloning, and thus increase the expressive power of Paisley considerably. See Fig. 2 for a concise example. [2]

Standard Data Bindings. The API design of Paisley is modular and open, such that pattern primitives that bind to actual data APIs can be added as needed. For convenience, the core library comes with predefined bindings for some of the most common Java datatypes: objects (equality, type checks); numbers (comparison, arithmetic); strings (substrings, regular expressions); collections and arrays (shape checks, element iteration); XML (DOM trees, XPath relations).

1.3 Bottom-Up Optimization

A major downside of highly generic and reusable combinators is that, without a specialization framework, their implementation is quite hard to optimize. By

---

[2] The `javap` disassembly of the compiled bytecode is given in Sect. 5.

the very compositional nature of the combinators, the code that implements the operational semantics of each is a small fragment, and has hardly any metadata about its context that could be exploited for optimization.

We shall take a short detour to demonstrate the optimization potential given by even the most rudimentary bottom-up context information. The remainder of this paper is then the description of a complementary, technologically more sophisticated solution that also takes the more powerful top-down metadata flow into account.

The Paisley API specifies a single item of heuristic metadata, namely a flag that indicates whether a pattern is statically guaranteed to be deterministic, i.e., not to match any single target more than once:

```
partial class Pattern⟨A⟩ {
  public boolean isDeterministic();
}
```

This information is exploited by the pattern combinator both(p, q) that implements the conjunctive sequential combination of patterns p and q (analogous to the Prolog comma operator (p, q)). If p is *not* certainly deterministic, then storage for backtracking (analogous to a frame of the Prolog choice stack) must be allocated, for restarting q for each solution of p. Otherwise, both the choice-point storage and the corresponding fragment of a global backtracking algorithm can be elided. Note that possible non-determinism of q is irrelevant, as it must be realized further down.

The choice between the generic, backtracking implementation and the optimized, semi-deterministic one is made at pattern construction time, depending on the value returned by p.isDeterministic(). Figure 3 depicts both implementations in horizontal synopsis. The subpatterns p/q are stored as left/right, respectively. It is easy to see that the optimized version is significantly superior in terms of space and time efficiency, and that this optimization is crucially necessary for ensuring that Paisley non-determinism does not impose prohibitive costs where it is not needed.

2   Compiling Paisley

The basic mode of Paisley pattern execution is by a modular interpreter; each object in the graph making up a complex pattern encapsulates the code and the state variables required for a particular step of the overall pattern-matching algorithm. While elegant and lightweight, this technique has evident limitations regarding performance.

Fortunately however, combinators have the ideal structure for a well-known compilation technique, namely *partial evaluation*. The inputs to each fragment of implementation are clearly distinguished into two categories of binding time: Combinator arguments make up the pattern structure, and are bound at pattern *construction* time; targets are bound at pattern *application* time. Thus a pattern may be specialized after construction, exploiting the information of the former,

```
private A target_save;                      // no mutable fields, but
private boolean left_matched;               // assert left.isDeterministic();

public boolean match(A target) {            public boolean match(A target) {
  return (left_matched = left.match(target))  return left.match(target)
    && matchNext(target_save = target, false);  && right.match(target);
}                                           }
public boolean matchAgain() {               public boolean matchAgain() {
  return left_matched                         return
    && matchNext(target_save, true);             right.matchAgain();
}                                           }
private boolean matchNext(A target,
                         boolean again) {
  if (again ? right.matchAgain()
            : right.match(target))
    return true;
  else
    while (left_matched = left.matchAgain())
      if (right.match(target))
        return true;
    return false;
}
```

Fig. 3. Pattern conjunction, non-deterministic (*left*) and semi-deterministic (*right*)

to obtain the code of a residual program that just inputs the latter — that is, an equivalent monolithic pattern.

Compiling an interpreted language by explicitly controlled partial evaluation of the interpreter is a ubiquitous and well-proven technique, ultimately haling back to Futamura's first projection [5], but more recently known as *staging* [10].

2.1   Design of the Paisley Compiler

The user perspective on Paisley pattern compilation is an extremely simple API that subsumes interpreted and compiled patterns transparently, and requires no configuration or global context:

```
partial class Pattern⟨A⟩ {
  public Pattern⟨A⟩ compile();
}
```

Here p.compile().match(a) should behave equivalently to p.match(a), although hopefully with less computational overhead, as returns on the resources invested in compilation. Semantic equivalence implies that p.compile() shares pattern variables with p, but higher-level combinators may have been fused to a single object, whose code can be executed without internal dynamic function calls and field indirections, and thus optimized far more aggressively by the jit compiler.

2.2   Implementation of the Paisley Compiler

The Java language and virtual machine (JVM) have no native support for partial evaluation, and are in general not a suitable candidate either, due to their complex imperative semantics. Thus *homoiconic* staged meta-programming, where object and meta code share the same syntax, is not an option. The JVM does, however, support dynamic extensions of the code base through class loaders. Given an expressive JVM bytecode synthesis tool, partial evaluation can be implemented for well-behaved reified languages, in particular declarative lightweight EDSLs such as Paisley, with reasonable effort.

We have implemented such a tool based on our LLJava [15] framework. LLJava defines both a low-level JVM programming language and an abstract bytecode model, and translation tools that can be used as compiler, disassembler and bytecode manipulation library. Our experimental new tool, LLJava-live provides a convenient front-end to the LLJava bytecode model, particularly tailored to the purpose of modular synthesis of code for immediate use. Paisley is its first completed application.

Generator modules interact with LLJava-live through a CompilationContext API that serves both as a source of context (such as variable bindings) and as a sink for code (such as instructions and scoping blocks). Generated code fragments are organized at the intra-method level by default, and connected in a data-flow network: The enclosing scope of each fragment denotes m input and n output variables, which are statically typed and can be realized in bytecode transparently as fields, parameters, temporary local variables, or arbitrary access code. For fragments corresponding to methods, m equals the number of parameters and n equals 1 or 0 for a return value or **void**, respectively.

For local data flow, the fragment may read the inputs and must write the outputs and terminate. In the process, local variables may be allocated, and nested fragments inserted and connected. For non-local data flow, fragments may allocate and share state variables which are realized as **private** fields of the enclosing class.

The virtual instruction set understood by the context comprises both the operand-stack style (*load/store*) and the register style (*move*). Basic block generators are passed as Runnable callbacks, such that the context can rearrange them as needed. The code base of the host program can be referred directly via the standard reification as Class and Method objects. See Fig. 4 for an example where a (highly contrived) code fragment foo is compiled, including a subfragment bar.

The overall organization of generated code into methods and the API of the generated class is handled by an application-specific compiler entry point. LLJava-live provides a generic service for generating the actual bytecode, loading the class and instantiating it via reflection.

Compilation API. In order to preserve the modularity of Paisley, the compiler is distributed over the classes that implement pattern combinators, completely analogous to the interpreter. Thus, for every method related to interpretation, we have added a companion method that generates the equivalent code:

boolean foo(**int** n) {
  bar(n + 1);
  return true;
}
 	
void bar(**int** m);
	void compileFoo(CompilationContext context) {
	  Variable n = context.getInput(0),
	           tmp = context.createLocalVariable(**int**.**class**);
	  context.store(tmp, () → {
	    context.load(n); context.load(1); context.add();
	  });
	  context.block(asList(tmp), asList(), // *I/O variables*
	           () → compileBar(context));
	  context.move(**true**, context.getOutput(0));
	}

Fig. 4. Code fragments (*left*) and LLJava-live generator (*right*).

```
partial class Pattern⟨A⟩ {
    protected void compileMatch      (CompilationContext context);
    protected void compileMatchAgain(CompilationContext context);
}
```

Calling the entry point Pattern.compile() generates a new subclass of Pattern and populates its API methods by invoking each of the companion methods of the pattern to be compiled with a corresponding context. In the following, we discuss a few selected issues to be addressed for the effective compilation of EDSLs in general, and of Paisley in particular.

Variable Capture. As usual in partial evaluation, the program fragments produced by the construction stage may capture host-language variables of their context. For primitive types, a constant corresponding to the environment value can simply be injected into the target class. But capturing references to live Java objects is another matter. We use a staged version of the same technique also employed by the Java compiler for variable captures in local classes: The target class is *closure*-converted, that is, captured variables are represented as **private final** fields, and properly initialized with the environment values when the class is instantiated for proceeding to the application stage.

Fallback Strategy: Staged Eta Expansion. For incremental upgrading of the Paisley core library to compilation, but also for users who wish to extend the language but not be bothered with LLJava-live code generation, there is a fallback mechanism that allows any combinator without a specific code generator, and its arguments, to be embedded in a tree that is compiled as a whole. This fallback is defined as the default implementation of code generation methods, which can either be overridden specifically or simply inherited.

The technique is essentially a staged variant of eta expansion, or *reverse stubs* in virtual machine terminology: by default, any API method of a pattern compiles into a call of itself, thus reverting from compiled to interpreted mode. This entails the capture of a reference to the original pattern. As a special case, pattern variables are always compiled in this way, since their identity is crucial to the external work flow (see Fig. 1), and must not be "optimized" away such that remote interactions via observable side effects are severed.

Avoiding Code Explosion. Partial evaluation frameworks typically draw their power from two related top-down heuristics: The first is *inlining*, where a function call is replaced by the function body, specialized by substituting the actual parameter values for the formal ones. The second is "the Trick" [2], where a fragment of code depending on an unbound variable with few distinct possible values, is replaced by a case distinction over the variable, with the original fragment specialized repeatedly by substituting one possible value per branch.

Both involve the duplication of code in environments with more bound variables than the original place of definition, trading the potential for subsequent simplification for the danger of combinatorial code explosion. For example in Fig. 3 (*left*), consider the double occurrence of the inlinable call to method right.match(target), and the parameter variable **boolean** again that is subject both to inlining globally and to the Trick locally.

Because of the highly self-similar nature of combinator trees, any local duplication of code can easily lead to exponential growth. In the context of the JVM, where the bytecode size of a method is tightly limited to 64 kiB, and the resource-constrained verifier and jit compiler are liable to choke on far less, this becomes a problem very quickly. Thus duplication of bytecode must be strictly controlled for the compilation of nestable combinators.

The Paisley compiler has an all-or-nothing policy regarding code duplication: when the compilation step for any combinator finds that it would call the same substep more than once, a **private** auxiliary method is created instead, populated once and called from every occurrence. The decision whether to inline such methods (where cheap enough) is left to the jit compiler, which has sophisticated code-size budgeting heuristics anyway.

2.3 Motif Compilation

Surprisingly, lifting compilation to the function level, that is from patterns to motifs, requires hardly any effort. An obvious naïve solution would be to compile any motif point-wise:

```
partial interface Motif⟨A, B⟩ {
  public default Motif⟨A, B⟩ compile() {
    return p → this.apply(p).compile();
  }
}
```

But this would redundantly create a *new* class for every application of a motif. Fortunately, we can do much better by reducing the general task to a clever treatment of lambda abstractions, v.lambda(p), that escapes the modular code generation scheme in a substantial but transparent way.

Assuming that v actually occurs in p, the compilation of p will include the staged eta expansion of v. Hence v will occur in the environment of the compiled closure. All we need to do is to defer the actual constructor call for the closure, and return a motif that calls the constructor when applied, substituting its argument for p in the environment. In short, v.lambda(p).compile().apply(q) should behave equivalently to p.compile(), except that the latter's environment reference to v is rerouted to q.

No other motif combinator needs to be implemented manually. Any complex motif m can be compiled monolithically by instead compiling its eta expansion, m.etaExpand().compile(), where the above procedure can be applied to the body.

```
partial interface Motif⟨A, B⟩ {
  public default Motif⟨A, B⟩ etaExpand() {
    Variable⟨A⟩ x = new Variable⟨⟩();
    return x.lambda(this.apply(x));
  }
}
```

The only catch is that the variable x is naturally considered deterministic in the construction-time analysis of p, as discussed above. Thus for non-deterministic patterns q backtracking glue code needs to be inserted. The implementation of compile() for eta-expanded motifs deals with this transparently.

3   Evaluation

We evaluate the performance of the Paisley compiler and its results by reiterating previously published benchmarks of (interpreted) Paisley applications.[3]

3.1   Cryptarithmetic Puzzles

In [13] we demonstrated the use of Paisley for embedded logic programming by considering *cryptarithmetic puzzles*. Given a natural number b, an injective mapping of letters to values in $\{0, \ldots, b-1\}$ induces a b-adic notation of natural numbers disguised as words. A puzzle is a sum equation of n words, and the solutions are the mappings that satisfy the equation. The classic example is $SEND + MORE = MONEY$, with $b = 10$ and $n = 2$, which has the unique solution $O = 0$, $M = 1$, $Y = 2$, $E = 5$, $N = 6$, $D = 7$, $R = 8$, and $S = 9$ [3].

Our approach to solving cryptarithmetic puzzles with Paisley is based on one pattern variable for each letter, and the set of possible digits as the target object. Various generic non-deterministic combinators from the Paisley library span the search tree, and a few problem-specific *constraint* patterns prune it. (Constraint patterns do not examine the target object, but the bindings of variables, exploiting the dependent nature of the both combinator.)

In [13] we considered three increasingly sophisticated search-plan construction algorithms for arbitrary cryptarithmetic puzzles:

---

[3] All results reported here have been obtained on the same test equipment, namely a Core i7-5600U @ 2.60 GHz CPU with 16 GiB of RAM, running CentOS Linux 7 and OpenJDK 8u202.

Table 1. Solving the SEND+MORE=MONEY puzzle with Paisley patterns.

Strategy	Run Time		Speedup	Compilation			
	interp.	compiled		time	bytes	flds	mths
naïve	4 029 ms	3 530 ms	1.14	17.8 ms	8 339	35	29
injective	636 ms	279 ms	2.28	23.4 ms	21 932	91	85
modular	1 719 µs	813 µs	2.11	23.5 ms	23 892	99	93

1. A *naïve* generate-and-test strategy that exhausts the Cartesian space of variable bindings by brute force, and checks the injectivity and arithmetic constraints for each at the very end.
2. A strategy that exploits *injectivity* by inserting pair-wise inequality constraints for bound variables as early as possible.
3. A strategy that additionally exploits *modular arithmetic* by binding variables in right-to-left order of occurrence, inserting approximative checks for the sum modulo b^k, for increasing k, as early as possible.

We have re-run the cryptarithmetic puzzle solver application, using out-of-the-box compilation support for all generic combinators of the Paisley core library, but strictly no additional problem-specific generator code. Table 1 summarizes our benchmarking results. For each strategy the following data are given:

- run times of the original pattern and its compiled variant, and their ratio;
- times for compilation, including bytecode generation, class loading and verification and object initialization;
- size of generated class, measured in overall bytes, number of state fields and matching-related methods (match, matchAgain and their auxiliaries).

All reported times are wall-clock times, each obtained with the precision of System.nanoTime(), as the median of a specific, suitably large number of iterations to allow for jit-compiler warm-up. See Sect. 4 for further discussion.

3.2 Document Object Model Navigation with XPath

XPath [1] is a declarative non-deterministic domain-specific language for navigation in XML document trees, suitable for embedding in various more high-level XML technologies such as XQuery and XSLT. In [14], we demonstrated how a straightforward translation of XPath 1.0 abstract syntax to Paisley motifs yields a lightweight lazy XPath execution engine, which is not only highly educational, but even in interpreted form competes well against the heavyweight XML tools shipped with the Java platform. As benchmarks, we used a selection of test cases from the XMark [9] suite, see Table 2.

We have re-run the tests, using compilation support for all generic combinators of the Paisley core library, as well as for bindings to the standard Java XML DOM. Table 2 summarizes our benchmarking results. For each test the following data are given:

Table 2. Executing XPath queries from the XMark suite with Paisley patterns.

Test	XPath Expression
Q00	`//node()`
Q01	`/site/open_auctions/open_auction/bidder[1]/increase/text()`
Q06	`//site/regions//item`
Q15	`/site/closed_auctions/closed_auction/annotation/description/` `parlist/listitem/parlist/listitem/text/emph/keyword/text()`
Q16	`/site/closed_auctions/closed_auction[annotation/description/` `parlist/listitem/parlist/listitem/text/emph/keyword/text()]`

Test	Run Time			Overhead			Solutions
	interp.	comp.	baseline	interp.	comp.	speedup	
Q00	99.56 ms	64.05 ms	13.71 ms	6.26	3.67	1.71	1 877 979
Q01	11.16 ms	6.78 ms	5.44 ms	1.05	0.25	4.27	4 310
Q06	162.85 ms	84.52 ms	62.11 ms	1.62	0.36	4.50	8 700
Q15	7.13 ms	4.07 ms	3.62 ms	0.97	0.12	7.80	68
Q16	9.43 ms	4.55 ms	3.92 ms	1.41	0.16	8.75	59

- run times of the original motif and its compiled variant;
- the baseline run time of a hand-coded eager traversal algorithm that efficiently implements that particular XPath expression;
- the relative overhead of the interpreted and compiled Paisley variants over the baseline, and their ratio;
- the number of solutions

... in a fixed pseudo-random input document, generated by a tool supplied by the authors of XMark.[4]

All reported times are obtained as above. The results show that the generic Paisley implementation of XPath expressions approximates the performance of specific one-off Java implementations gracefully.

The overhead is noticeable in case Q00, where a trivial query literally matches all nodes, and thus yields a huge number of solutions. Here the cost of lazy backtracking, as opposed to eager traversal, has an impact that can not be compensated fully by our compilation technique. On the upside, the lazy search can be suspended arbitrarily after each solution, at no additional cost. For the other cases, where significant amounts of traversal take place between solutions, the Paisley overhead is moderate. Furthermore it can be improved to near insignificance by compilation, such that the costs of actually calling into the target data API completely dominate.

---

[4] The official XMark home page is no longer online, but can be retrieved from https://web.archive.org/web/20070810005114/http://www.xml-benchmark.org/.

4   Conclusion

We have demonstrated how staged compilation can improve the performance of Paisley, a modularly interpreted combinator EDSL par excellence. The compiler mirrors the structure of the interpreter and generates bytecode that can be immediately loaded and eventually jit-compiled by the JVM. Compiled and interpreted Paisley interface transparently in both directions, and dealing with compilation is completely optional for user extensions. The approach is generally suitable also for accelerating any other declarative EDSL.

Benchmarks indicate that the speedup by compilation is significant, even for legacy applications, and can approximate hand-written data query code. We foresee that long-running applications with complex internal data models, such as information systems and document servers, could benefit the most from this technology. This is because their usage mode fits the assumptions of staged compilation perfectly: *construct early, reuse often.*

In a multi-stage pipeline such as the jit-compiled JVM, there is more to consider than just the run time of the compilation step. For pattern compilation to pay off in the end, the compiled patterns must be (re-)used often enough for the jit compiler to consider them worthwhile for machine code generation. Otherwise they are executed compiled at the level of the embedded language Paisley, but interpreted at the level of the host, in contrast to the original patterns for which the situation is the converse. Thus one-off applications such as the cryptarithmetic puzzles are purely academic, and for more heterogeneous realistic applications empirical validation is required.

4.1   Related Work

Many different approaches to pattern matching in Java exist. We have already compared our approach to the most significant ones, in particular the historically relevant JMatch [8] in previous papers [12,16]. More modern, quasi-algebraic solutions, such as adt4j[5] or derive4j[6], do not properly address object-oriented data abstraction and non-determinism, the focus of Paisley in general, or compilation, the focus of the present paper in particular.

On the JVM, the Scala language supports non-algebraic pattern matching via dedicated syntax and the magic method unapply. As a core part of the language and its compiler, this mechanism is much more tightly integrated than Paisley can ever hope to be, and naturally compiles both predefined and custom pattern code. But the comparison is not exactly fair, as Scala patterns are neither non-deterministic, nor point-free, nor dynamically meta-programmable.

A very recent work [7] on parser generation has inspired us to complete the work presented here. They also improve the performance of a combinator language, often drastically, by intermediate compilation of a construction stage.

---

[5] https://github.com/sviperll/adt4j.
[6] https://github.com/derive4j/derive4j.

Their approach, like ours, combines the benefits of bottom-up heuristic meta-data (a variant of LL(1) analysis) with those of top-down code specialization. However, the MetaOCaml host language framework they use is markedly different in nature: On the one hand, it natively supports staged meta-programming, for which we have had to build a custom tool onto Java's dynamic bytecode loading. On the other hand, OCaml does not have the benefit of a jit compiler that could optimize both combinators and generated code heuristically, which makes their compilation stage proportionally even more effective.

5   Bytecode Disassembly of Countdown Example

```
public class Pattern$compiled$1cll1f extends eu.bandm.tools.paisley.Pattern {

    private final  eu.bandm.tools.paisley.Pattern env$0;      // Motif.eagerBindings()
    private final  java.util.function.Predicate    env$1;     // lambda (n → n > 0)
    private final  java.util.function.Function      env$2;    // lambda (n → n − 1)


    private        java.lang.Object                 state$0;  // choice stack for Pattern.either()
    private        boolean                          state$1;  // choice stack for Pattern.either()
    private        eu.bandm.tools.paisley.Pattern   state$2;  // lazy clone for Motif.star()

    public Pattern$compiled$1cll1f(eu.bandm.tools.paisley.Pattern,
                                   java.util.function.Predicate,
                                   java.util.function.Function);
        Code:
           0: aload_0
           1: invokespecial  #20        // Method eu/bandm/tools/paisley/Pattern."⟨init⟩":()V
           4: aload_0
           5: aload_1
           6: putfield       #22        // Field   env$0:Leu/bandm/tools/paisley/Pattern;
           9: aload_0
          10: aload_2
          11: putfield       #24        // Field   env$1:Ljava/util/function/Predicate;
          14: aload_0
          15: aload_3
          16: putfield       #26        // Field   env$2:Ljava/util/function/Function;
          19: return

    public boolean match(java.lang.Object);
        Code:
           0: aload_0
           1: aload_1
           2: putfield       #30        // Field   state$0:Ljava/lang/Object;
           5: aload_0
           6: aload_1
           7: iconst_0
           8: invokespecial  #34        // Method aux$0:(Ljava/lang/Object;Z)Z
          11: ireturn
```

public boolean matchAgain();
    Code:
      0: aload_0
      1: getfield   #38   *// Field   state$1:Z*
      4: ifeq   25
      7: aload_0
      8: getfield   #30   *// Field   state$0:Ljava/lang/Object;*
     11: astore_2
     12: aload_0
     13: aload_0
     14: getfield   #30   *// Field   state$0:Ljava/lang/Object;*
     17: iconst_1
     18: invokespecial #34   *// Method aux$0:(Ljava/lang/Object;Z)Z*
     21: istore_1
     22: goto   33
     25: aload_0
     26: getfield   #53   *// Field   state$2:Leu/bandm/tools/paisley/Pattern;*
     29: invokevirtual #62   *// Method eu/bandm/tools/paisley/Pattern.matchAgain*
                                         //   :()Z
     32: istore_1
     33: iload_1
     34: ireturn

private boolean aux$0(java.lang.Object, **boolean**);
    Code:
      0: iload_2
      1: ifeq   16
      4: aload_0
      5: iconst_0
      6: putfield   #38   *// Field   state$1:Z*
      9: aload_0
     10: getfield   #38   *// Field   state$1:Z*
     13: goto   32
     16: aload_0
     17: aload_0
     18: getfield   #22   *// Field   env$0:Leu/bandm/tools/paisley/Pattern;*
     21: aload_1
     22: invokevirtual #40   *// Method eu/bandm/tools/paisley/Pattern.match*
                                         //   :(Ljava/lang/Object;)Z
     25: putfield   #38   *// Field   state$1:Z*
     28: aload_0
     29: getfield   #38   *// Field   state$1:Z*
     32: ifeq   40
     35: iconst_1
     36: istore_3
     37: goto   99
     40: aload_0
     41: aconst_null
     42: putfield   #30   *// Field   state$0:Ljava/lang/Object;*
     45: aload_0

```
 46: getfield       #24          // Field   env$1:Ljava/util/function/Predicate;
 49: aload_1
 50: invokeinterface #45, 2      // InterfaceMethod   java/util/function/Predicate.test
                                 //            :(Ljava/lang/Object;)Z
 55: ifeq            97
 58: aload_0
 59: getfield        #26         // Field   env$2:Ljava/util/function/Function;
 62: aload_1
 63: invokeinterface #51, 2      // InterfaceMethod   java/util/function/Function.apply
                                 //            :(Ljava/lang/Object;)Ljava/lang/Object;
 68: astore         4
 70: aload_0
 71: getfield       #53          // Field   state$2:Leu/bandm/tools/paisley/Pattern;
 74: ifnonnull      85
 77: aload_0
 78: aload_0
 79: invokevirtual  #57          // Method eu/bandm/tools/paisley/Pattern.clone
                                 //            :()Leu/bandm/tools/paisley/Pattern;
 82: putfield       #53          // Field   state$2:Leu/bandm/tools/paisley/Pattern;
 85: aload_0
 86: getfield       #53          // Field   state$2:Leu/bandm/tools/paisley/Pattern;
 89: aload          4
 91: invokevirtual  #40          // Method eu/bandm/tools/paisley/Pattern.match
                                 //            :(Ljava/lang/Object;)Z
 94: goto           98
 97: iconst_0
 98: istore_3
 99: iload_3
100: ireturn
```

public boolean isDeterministic();
    Code:
```
      0: iconst_0
      1: ireturn
```

public eu.bandm.tools.paisley.Pattern compile();
    Code:
```
      0: aload_0
      1: areturn
```
}

References

1. Clark, J., DeRose, S.: XML Path Language (XPath) Version 1.0. W3C. http://www.w3.org/TR/1999/REC-xpath-19991116/ (1999)
2. Danvy, O., Malmkjær, K., Palsberg, J.: Eta-expansion does the trick. ACM Trans. Program. Lang. Syst. 18(6), 730–751 (1996). https://doi.org/10.1145/236114.236119
3. Dudeney, H.E.: Strand Magazine 68, 97–214 (1924)

4. Emir, B., Odersky, M., Williams, J.: Matching objects with patterns. In: Ernst, E. (ed.) ECOOP 2007. LNCS, vol. 4609, pp. 273–298. Springer, Heidelberg (2007). https://doi.org/10.1007/978-3-540-73589-2_14

5. Futamura, Y.: Partial evaluation of computation process– an approach to a compiler-compiler. High. Order Symb. Comput. **12**, 381–391 (1999). https://doi.org/10.1023/A:1010095604496

6. Hughes, J.: Why functional programming matters. Comput. J. **32**(2), 98–107 (1989). https://doi.org/10.1093/comjnl/32.2.98

7. Krishnaswami, N., Yallop, J.: A typed, algebraic approach to parsing. In: Proceedings 40th PLDI, pp. 379–393. ACM (2019). https://doi.org/10.1145/3314221.3314625

8. Liu, J., Myers, A.C.: JMatch: iterable abstract pattern matching for Java. In: Dahl, V., Wadler, P. (eds.) PADL 2003. LNCS, vol. 2562, pp. 110–127. Springer, Heidelberg (2003). https://doi.org/10.1007/3-540-36388-2_9

9. Schmidt, A., Waas, F., Kersten, M.L., Carey, M.J., Manolescu, I., Busse, R.: XMark: a benchmark for XML data management. In: Proceedings 28th VLDB. pp. 974–985. Morgan Kaufmann (2002). http://www.vldb.org/conf/2002/S30P01.pdf

10. Taha, W., Sheard, T.: Metaml and multi-stage programming with explicit annotations. Theor. Comput. Sci. **248**(1), 211–242 (2000). https://doi.org/10.1016/S0304-3975(00)00053-0

11. Trancón y Widemann, B., Lepper, M.: Paisley: pattern matching à la carte. In: Hu, Z., de Lara, J. (eds.) ICMT 2012. LNCS, vol. 7307, pp. 240–247. Springer, Heidelberg (2012). https://doi.org/10.1007/978-3-642-30476-7_16

12. Trancón y Widemann, B., Lepper, M.: Paisley: a pattern matching library for arbitrary object models. In: Software Engineering 2013, Workshopband. LNI, vol. 215, pp. 171–186. Gesellschaft für Informatik (2013). http://www.se2013.rwth-aachen.de/downloads/proceedings/SE2013WS.pdf

13. Trancón y Widemann, B., Lepper, M.: Some experiments on light-weight object-functional-logic programming in Java with paisley. In: Hanus, M., Rocha, R. (eds.) WLP 2013. LNCS (LNAI), vol. 8439, pp. 218–233. Springer, Cham (2014). https://doi.org/10.1007/978-3-319-08909-6_14

14. Trancón y Widemann, B., Lepper, M.: Interpreting xpath by iterative pattern matching with paisley. In: Proceedings 23rd WFLP. vol. 1335, pp. 108–124. CEUR-WS.org (2015). http://ceur-ws.org/Vol-1335/wflp2014_paper1.pdf

15. Trancón y Widemann, B., Lepper, M.: Lljava: minimalist structured programming on the Java virtual machine. In: Proceedings 13th PPPJ. ACM (2016). https://doi.org/10.1145/2972206.2972218

16. Trancón y Widemann, B., Lepper, M.: A practical study of control in objected-oriented-functional-logic programming with paisley. In: Proceedings 24th WFLP. EPTCS, vol. 234, pp. 150–164 (2016). https://doi.org/10.4204/EPTCS.234.11

ICurry

Sergio Antoy[1] ⓘ, Michael Hanus[2](✉) ⓘ, Andy Jost[1], and Steven Libby[1]

[1] Computer Science Department, Portland State University, Portland, OR, USA
[2] Institut für Informatik, Kiel University, 24098 Kiel, Germany
mh@informatik.uni-kiel.de

Abstract. FlatCurry is a well-established intermediate representation of Curry programs used in compilers that translate Curry code into Prolog or Haskell code. Some FlatCurry constructs have no direct translation into imperative code. These constructs must be each handled differently when translating Curry code into, e.g., C, C++ or Python code. We introduce a new representation of Curry programs, called ICurry, and derive a translation from all FlatCurry constructs into ICurry. We present the syntax and semantics of ICurry and the translation from FlatCurry to ICurry. We present a model of functional logic computations as graph rewriting and show how this model can be implemented with ICurry in a low-level imperative language.

1 Introduction

Functional logic languages [8] provide fast software prototyping and development, simple elegant solutions to otherwise complicated problems, a tight integration between specifications and code [9], and an ease of provability [10,20] unmatched by other programming paradigms. Not surprisingly, these advantages place heavy demands on their implementation. Theoretical results must be proven and efficient models of execution must be developed. For these reasons, the efficient implementation of functional logic languages is an active area of research with contributions from many sources. This paper is one such contribution.

Compilers of high-level languages transform a *source* program into a *target* program which is in a lower-level language. This transformation maps constructs available in the source program language into simpler, more primitive, constructs available in the target program language. For example, pattern matching can be translated into a sequence of *switch* and assignment statements available in C, C++ and Python. We use this idea to map Curry into a C-like language. Our target language is not standard C, but a more abstract language that we call *ICurry*. The "I" in ICurry stands for "imperative", since a design goal of the language is to be easily mappable into an imperative language.

There are advantages in choosing ICurry over C. ICurry is simpler than C. It has no arrays, *typedef* declarations, types, explicit pointers, or dereferencing operations. ICurry is more abstract than concrete low level languages. Because of

© Springer Nature Switzerland AG 2020
P. Hofstedt et al. (Eds.): DECLARE 2019, LNAI 12057, pp. 286–307, 2020.
https://doi.org/10.1007/978-3-030-46714-2_18

its simplicity and abstraction, it has been mapped with a modest effort to C, C++, and Python.

Section 2 is a brief overview of Curry, with focus on the features relevant to ICurry or to the examples. Section 3 discusses an operational model of execution for functional logic computations. This model can be implemented relatively easily in Curry or in common imperative languages. Section 4 presents *FlatCurry*, a format of Curry programs similar to ICurry. FlatCurry has been used in the translation of Curry into other, non-imperative, languages, but it is not suitable for the translation of Curry into an imperative language. Section 5 defines ICurry and its semantics, and discusses its generation and use. Section 6 addresses related work and offers our conclusion.

2 Curry

Curry is a declarative language that joins the most appealing features of functional and logic programming. A *Curry program* declares *data types*, which describe how information is structured, and defines *functions* or *operations*, which describe how information is manipulated. For example:

```
data List a = Nil | Cons a (List a)
```

declares a polymorphic type List in which a is a type parameter standing for the type of the list elements. The symbols Nil and Cons are the *constructors* of List. The values of a list are either Nil, the empty list, or Cons $e\,l$, a pair in which e is an element and l is a list.

Since lists are ubiquitous, a special notation eases writing and understanding them. Curry uses [] to denote the empty list and $e : l$ to denote the pair, where the infix constructor ":" associates to the right. A finite list is written $[e_1,\ldots,e_n]$, where e_i is a list element. For example, $[1,2,3] = 1:2:3:[]$.

Functions are defined by rewrite rules of the form:

$$f\,\bar{p} \mid c_1 = e_1$$
$$\cdots \qquad\qquad (1)$$
$$\mid c_n = e_n$$

where f is a function symbol, $\bar{p}$ stands for a sequence of zero or more expressions made up only of constructor symbols and variables, "$\mid c_i$" is a condition, and e_i is an expression. Conditions in rules are optional. The expressions in $\bar{p}$ are called *patterns*. For example, consider:

$$
\begin{aligned}
&\texttt{abs x | x < 0 = -x}\\
&\texttt{| x >= 0 = x}\\
&\texttt{length []   = 0}\\
&\texttt{length (\_:xs) = 1 + length xs}
\end{aligned}
\qquad (2)
$$

where abs computes the absolute value of its argument and shows some conditions, and length computes the length of its argument and shows some patterns.

In contrast to most other languages, the textual order of the rewrite rules in a program is irrelevant—all the rules that can be applied to an expression are applied. An emblematic example is a function, called *choice*, and denoted by the infix operator "?", which chooses between two *alternatives*:

```
x ? y = x
x ? y = y
```

Therefore, 0 ? 1 is an expression that produces 0 and 1 non-deterministically. In Curry, there are many other useful syntactic and semantic features, for example, rewrite rules can have nested scopes with local definitions. We omit their description here, since they are largely irrelevant to our discussion, with the exception of *let blocks* and *free variables*.

Let blocks support the definition of circular expressions which allows the construction of cyclic graphs. Figure 1 shows an example of a let block and the corresponding graph. Expression oneTwo evaluates to the infinite list 1:2:1:2:...

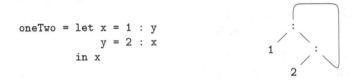

```
oneTwo = let x = 1 : y
             y = 2 : x
         in x
```

Fig. 1. Example of a let block with mutually recursive variables and the graph it defines.

Free variables abstract unknown information and are "computationally inert" until the information they stand for is required during a computation. When this happens, plausible values for a variable are non-deterministically produced by narrowing [6,29]. Free variables might occur in initial expressions, conditions, and the right-hand side of rules, and need to be declared by the keyword **free**, unless they are anonymous (denoted by "_"). For instance, the following program defines list concatenation which is exploited to define an operation that returns some element of a list having at least two occurrences:

```
(++) :: [a]  →  [a]  →  [a]
[]       ++ ys = ys
(x:xs) ++ ys = x : (xs ++ ys)

someDup :: [a]  →  a
someDup xs | xs == _ ++ [x] ++ _ ++ [x] ++ _
           = x      where x free
```

3   The Execution Model

A *program* is a graph rewriting system [16,28] over a *signature*, partitioned into *constructor* and *operation* symbols. We briefly and informally review the underlying theory. A *graph* is a set of *nodes*, where a node is an object with some attributes, and an identity by virtue of being an element in a set. Key attributes of a node are a *label* and a sequence of *successors*. A label is either a symbol of the signature or a variable. A successor is another node, and the sequence of successors may be empty. Exactly one node of a graph is designated as the graph's *root*. Each node of a graph corresponds to an expression in the Curry program.

A *graph rewriting system* is a set of rewrite rules following the *constructor discipline* [27]. A *rule* is a pair of graphs, $l \rightarrow r$, called the left- and right-hand sides, respectively. Rules are unconditional without loss of generality [3]. A *rewrite step* of a graph e first identifies both a subgraph t of e, and a rule $l \rightarrow r$ in which t is an instance of l, then replaces t with the corresponding instance of r. The identification of the subgraph t and the rule $l \rightarrow r$ is accomplished by a *strategy* [4]. For example, given the rules (2), a step of `length [3,4]` produces `1+length[4]` where the subgraph reduced in the step is the whole graph, and the rule applied in the step is the second one.

A *computation* of an expression e is a sequence of rewrite steps starting with e, $e = e_0 \rightarrow e_1 \rightarrow \dots$ Expression e is referred to as *top-level*, and each e_i as a *state* of the computation of e. A *value* of a computation is a state in which every node is labeled by a constructor symbol. Such expression is also called a *constructor normal form*. Not every computation has values.

We have modeled a functional logic program as a graph rewriting system [16,28]. Functional logic computations are executed in this model by rewriting which consists of two relatively simple operations: the construction of graphs and the replacement of subgraphs with other graphs. The most challenging part is selecting the subgraph to be replaced in a way that does not consume computational resources unnecessarily. This is a well-understood problem [4] which is largely separated from the model.

In an implementation of the model, the expressions are objects of a computation and are represented by dynamically linked structures. These structures are similar to those used for computing with lists and trees. The nodes of such a structure are in a bijection with the nodes of the graph they represent. Unless a distinction is relevant, we do not distinguish between a graph and its representation.

The occurrence of a symbol, or variable, in the textual representation of an expression stands for the node labeled by the occurrence. Distinct occurrences may stand for the same node, in which case we say that the occurrences are *shared*. The textual representation accommodates this distinction, therefore it is a convenient, linear notation for a graph. Figure 2 shows two graphs and their corresponding textual expressions.

4   FlatCurry

FlatCurry [17] is an intermediate language used in a variety of applications. These applications include implementing Curry by compiling into other languages, like Prolog [21] or Haskell [12]. FlatCurry is also the basis for specifying

Fig. 2. Graphical and textual representation of expressions. In Curry, all the occurrences of the same variable are shared. Hence, the two occurrences of x stand for the same node. The expression coin is conventionally an integer constant with two values, 0 and 1, non-deterministically chosen. The sets of values produced by the two expressions differ.

the operational semantics of Curry programs [1], building generic analysis tools [22], or verifying properties of Curry programs [19, 20]. The FlatCurry format of a Curry program removes some syntactic constructs, such as nested scopes and infix notation, that make source programs more human readable. This removal still preserves the program's meaning. We ignore some elements of FlatCurry, such as imported modules or exported symbols, which are not directly related to the execution model presented in Sect. 3. Instead, we focus on the declaration of data constructors, the definition of functions, and the construction of expressions. These are the elements that play a central role in our execution model.

FlatCurry is a machine representation of Curry programs. As such, it is not intended to be read by human. For example, each variable is identified by an integer, function application is only prefix, and pattern matching is broken down into a cascade of case distinctions. In the examples that follow, we present a sugared version of FlatCurry in which variables have symbolic names, typically the same as in Curry; the application of familiar infix operators is infix; and indentation, rather than parentheses and commas, show structure and grouping. The intent is to make the examples easier to read without altering the essence of FlatCurry.

In FlatCurry, data constructors are introduced by a type declaration. A type t has attributes such as a name and a visibility, and chief among these attributes is a set of constructors $c_1, c_2, \ldots c_n$. Each constructor c_i has similar attributes, along with an arity and type of each argument, which are not explicitly used in our discussion. The same information is available for operation symbols. Additionally, any operation f has an attribute that abstracts the set of the rules defining f.

The abstract syntax of FlatCurry operations is summarized in Fig. 3.[1] Each operation is defined by a single rule with a linear left-hand side, i.e., the argument variables $x_1, \ldots, x_n$ are pairwise different. The right-hand side of the definition consists of (1) variables introduced by the left-hand side or by a *let block* or by a *case* pattern, (2) constructor or function calls, (3) *case* expressions, (4)

---

[1] In contrast to some other presentations of FlatCurry (e.g., [1,18]), we omit the difference between rigid and flexible case expressions.

disjunctions, (5) *let* bindings, or (6) introduction of free variables. The patterns p_i in a *case* expression must be pairwise different constructors applied to variables. Therefore, deep patterns in source programs are represented by nested *case* expressions.

$$
\begin{aligned}
D ::=\ & f(x_1,\ldots,x_n) = e && \text{(function definition)}\\
e ::=\ & x && \text{(variable)}\\
|\ & c(e_1,\ldots,e_n) && \text{(constructor call)}\\
|\ & f(e_1,\ldots,e_n) && \text{(function call)}\\
|\ & case\ e\ of\ \{p_1 \to e_1;\ldots;p_n \to e_n\} && \text{(case expression)}\\
|\ & e_1\ or\ e_2 && \text{(disjunction)}\\
|\ & let\ \{x_1 = e_1;\ldots;x_n = e_n\}\ in\ e && \text{(let binding)}\\
|\ & let\ x_1,\ldots,x_n\ free\ in\ e && \text{(free variables)}\\
p ::=\ & c(x_1,\ldots,x_n) && \text{(pattern)}
\end{aligned}
$$

Fig. 3. Abstract syntax of function definitions in FlatCurry

Case expressions closely resemble definitional trees [2]. We recall that a *definitional tree* of some operation f, of arity n, is a hierarchical structure of expressions of the form $f\ p_1\ \ldots\ p_n$, where each p_i is a pattern. Since f is constant and provides no information, except to ease readability, we also call these expressions patterns. The pattern at the root of the tree is $f\ x_1\ \ldots\ x_n$, where the x_i's are distinct variables. The patterns at the leaves are the left-hand sides of the rules of f, except from the names of the variables. For ease of understanding, in pictorial representations of definitional trees we add the right-hand side of the rules too. If $f\ p_1\ \ldots\ p_n$ is a branch node, β, of the tree, a variable x in some p_j is singled out. We call the variable x *inductive*. The pattern in a child of β is $f\ p_1\ \ldots\ q_j\ \ldots\ p_n$ where q_j is obtained from p_j by replacing x with $c\ y_1\ \ldots\ y_k$, where c is a constructor of the type of x and each y_i is a fresh variable. For example, consider the usual operation `zip` for zipping two lists:

$$
\begin{aligned}
&\texttt{zip []}\quad\ \ \ \texttt{y}\qquad\ \ = \texttt{[]}\\
&\texttt{zip (x1:x2) []}\qquad = \texttt{[]}\\
&\texttt{zip (x1:x2) (y1:y2) = (x1,y1) : zip x2 y2}
\end{aligned}
\qquad(3)
$$

The corresponding definitional tree is shown below where the inductive variable is boxed.

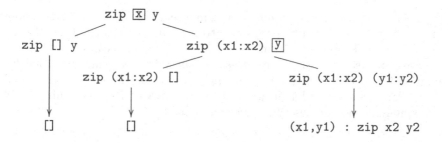

The FlatCurry code of the rules of operation `zip`, closely corresponds to the code in (4). This would be harder for the programmer to write than (3) and less readable, but is semantically equivalent. Every program can be transformed into an equivalent program in which every operation has a definitional tree [3]. There is a relatively simple algorithm [4] to construct a definitional tree from the operation's rules.

$$
\begin{array}{ll}
\texttt{zip x y = case x of} & \\
\quad \{ \texttt{[]} \quad\quad \rightarrow \texttt{[]} \; ; & \\
\quad\; \texttt{(x1:x2)} \; \rightarrow \texttt{case y of} & \qquad\qquad (4)\\
\quad\quad\quad\quad \{ \texttt{[]} \quad\quad \rightarrow \texttt{[]} \; ; & \\
\quad\quad\quad\quad\; \texttt{(y1:y2)} \; \rightarrow \texttt{(x1,y1) : zip x2 y2 }\} &
\end{array}
$$

Expressions are the final relevant element of FlatCurry. As the code of `zip` shows, an expression can be a literal, like `[]`; an application of constructors and operations to expressions possibly containing variables, like `(x1,y1) : zip x2 y2`; or a case expression, like `case y of` ... FlatCurry also has *let blocks* to support the construction of cyclic graphs, as shown in Fig. 1.

FlatCurry programs cannot be directly mapped to code in a C-like target language. There are two problems: case expressions as arguments of a symbol application, and let blocks with shared or mutually recursive variables. A contrived example of the first is:

```
3 + case x of { [] → 0; (y:ys) → y }
```

Since the evaluation of the scrutinee of a case expression might yield a non-deterministic result, it cannot be directly mapped into imperative language constructs. An example of the second is shown in Fig. 1. ICurry proposes a solution to these problems in a language-independent form which is suitable for the imperative paradigm.

5 ICurry

In this section we define ICurry, discuss how to map it to imperative code that implements our earlier model of computation, and show how to obtain it from FlatCurry.

5.1 ICurry Definition

ICurry is a format of Curry programs similar in intent to FlatCurry. The purpose of both is to represent a Curry program into a format with a small number of simple constructs. Properties and manipulations of programs can be more easily investigated and executed in these formats. ICurry is specifically intended for compilation into a low-level language. Each ICurry construct can be translated into a similar construct of languages such as C, Java or Python. This should become apparent once we describe the constructs.

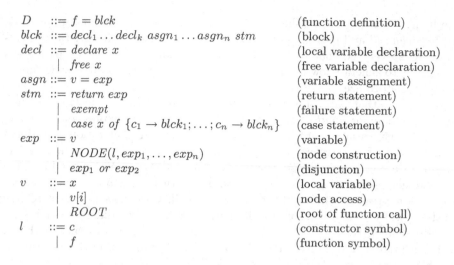

$$
\begin{array}{lll}
D & ::= f = blck & \text{(function definition)} \\
blck & ::= decl_1 \dots decl_k \ asgn_1 \dots asgn_n \ stm & \text{(block)} \\
decl & ::= declare \ x & \text{(local variable declaration)} \\
& \mid \ free \ x & \text{(free variable declaration)} \\
asgn & ::= v = exp & \text{(variable assignment)} \\
stm & ::= return \ exp & \text{(return statement)} \\
& \mid \ exempt & \text{(failure statement)} \\
& \mid \ case \ x \ of \ \{c_1 \to blck_1; \dots; c_n \to blck_n\} & \text{(case statement)} \\
exp & ::= v & \text{(variable)} \\
& \mid \ NODE(l, exp_1, \dots, exp_n) & \text{(node construction)} \\
& \mid \ exp_1 \ or \ exp_2 & \text{(disjunction)} \\
v & ::= x & \text{(local variable)} \\
& \mid \ v[i] & \text{(node access)} \\
& \mid \ ROOT & \text{(root of function call)} \\
l & ::= c & \text{(constructor symbol)} \\
& \mid \ f & \text{(function symbol)}
\end{array}
$$

Fig. 4. Abstract syntax of function definitions in ICurry

ICurry's data consists of nested applications of symbols represented as graphs. ICurry's key constructs provide the declaration or definition of symbols and variables, construction of graph nodes, assignment, and conditional executions of these constructs. Rewriting steps are implemented in two phases, once the redex and rule are determined. First, the replacement of the redex is constructed. This is defined by the right-hand side of the rule. Then, the successors pointing to the root of the redex are redirected [16, Def. 8], through assignments, to point to the root of the replacement.

The declaration of data constructors in ICurry is identical to that in FlatCurry as described earlier. However, the constructors of a type are in an arbitrary, but fixed, order. Therefore, we can talk of the first, second, etc., constructor of a type. This index is an attribute of constructor symbols which we call the *tag*. The tag is used to provide efficient pattern matching. We will return to this topic in Sect. 5.4.

The abstract syntax of operations in ICurry is summarized in Fig. 4. In FlatCurry, the body of a function is an expression. In ICurry, it is a block consisting of optional declarations and/or assignments and a final statement returning an expression. We describe expressions first.

Expressions are nested symbol applications represented as graphs. Therefore, an expression is either a *variable* or a *symbol application*. ICurry makes an application explicit with a *directive*, NODE, that constructs a graph node from its label (1st argument) and its successors (remaining arguments), and returns a reference to the node. Accordingly, there is a directive to access node components: assuming x is a variable referring to a node, $x[k]$ retrieves the k-th successor of the node. An ICurry variable v is a reference to a node n in a graph. When n is a Curry free variable, v is called *free* as well. Otherwise, v is called a *local* variable.

The ICurry format distinguishes between constructor and function application, and between full and partial application. We do not discuss these details in this paper. It is expected that by providing this additional information, processors will be able to generate low-level code more easily, and the generated code should be easier to optimize.

In ICurry, there are only a handful of statement kinds: *declaration* of a variable, and *assignment* to a variable, *return*, and *case* expressions. Following FlatCurry, variables are represented by integers. A declaration introduces a variable which is a reference to a graph node. Successors of a node referenced by x are accessed through the $x[\ldots]$ construct. Arguments passed to functions are accessed through local variables. The return statement is intended to return an expression, the result of a function call. Case expressions in ICurry are structurally similar to those in FlatCurry, but with two differences for algebraically defined types, which have a finite number of data constructors. First, the branches of a case expression are in tag order. We will justify this decision in Sect. 5.4. Second, the set of branches of a case expression is complete, i.e., there is a branch for each constructor of the type.

ICurry code begins with a declaration, and possible assignment, of some variables. It is then followed by either a case statement, or a return statement. Each branch of the case expression may declare and assign variables, and may lead to either another case statement, or a return statement.

Below, we present two examples. The first example is the code of function oneTwo, a constant, of Fig. 1:

```
function oneTwo
  declare x
  declare y
  x = NODE(:, NODE(1), y)
  y = NODE(:, NODE(2), x)
  x[2] = y
  return x
```

Symbol application is explicit through NODE. In the above example, the definitions of the nodes referenced by x and y are mutually recursive, thus either node cannot be completely constructed before constructing the other. We resolve the impasse by partially constructing the node referenced by x (starting with y would be symmetric), constructing the node referenced by y, and finally coming back to x and finish the job. The missing information when the node referenced by x is constructed is the value of the node's second successor, which is addressed by x[2]. This value becomes known when the node referenced by y is constructed. At that point, the missing information is filled in with the assignment to x[2].

The second example is the code of head, the usual function returning the head of a non-empty list:

$$head \ (x : \_) = x \tag{5}$$

The rule of head for the argument [] is missing in the Curry source code. Consequently, the case branch for the argument [] is missing in FlatCurry, too. ICurry has a distinguished statement, exempt, to capture the absence of a rule:

```
function head
   declare arg
   arg = ROOT[1]
   case arg of
      []  →  exempt
      :   →  return arg[1]
```

where ROOT is a reference to the root of the expression being evaluated. This expression is rooted by head, which is the reason why it is passed to function head.

5.2   Operational Semantics of ICurry

In this section, we define a small-step semantics for ICurry programs. We are motivated by the fact that ICurry is very similar to a simple imperative language, but has primitives to support non-deterministic computations. These primitives are the or expression, used to introduce non-determinism, and the exempt statement, used to express a failing branch of a computation.

Non-deterministic choices in a program execution require copying a computation into two branches. In order to reduce the effort for copying, pull-tabbing [5] can be used. Fundamentally, a *pull-tab step* moves a choice occurring in a demanded argument of an operation outside this operation. For instance, if f demands the value of its single argument, then the following is a pull-tab step.

$$f\ (e_1\ ?\ e_2)\ \ \rightarrow\ \ (f\ e_1)\ ?\ (f\ e_2)$$

Although ICurry's non-determinism can also be implemented with other strategies such as stack copying, we use pull-tabbing here due to its limited demand to copy structures. For this purpose, we make the following assumptions:

1. Each ICurry function contains at most one case statement. This can be obtained by replacing nested case statements by auxiliary operations.[2] Therefore, we denote by f^i an ICurry function which demands its i-th argument in a case statement, otherwise the superscript is omitted.
2. A graph might also contain *choice nodes* of the form $?^c(n_1, n_2)$. The expressions n_1, n_2 are the alternatives, and c is a choice identifier which is an integer uniquely determined when the choice node is created. Choice identifiers are necessary to distinguish choices in different computation branches [5,12].

As discussed in Sect. 3, the execution model of Curry is based on graph rewriting. Therefore, the main component of ICurry's run-time system is a graph G. In the subsequent description, we use the following notation. We write $G[n] = s(n_1, \ldots, n_k)$ if n is a node of G with label s and successor nodes $n_1, \ldots, n_k$. The update of a node n of G is denoted by $G[n \leftarrow s(n_1, \ldots, n_k)]$. The label of n is replaced by s and the successors of n are set to $n_1, \ldots, n_k$. In order to implement sharing, it is sometimes necessary to redirect a graph node n to a

---

[2] Some implementations of Curry, e.g., [21] perform this transformation.

node n' of a graph G. We denote this by $G[n \leftarrow n']$. This can be implemented either by a specific "redirection node" or by redirecting all edges pointing to n so that they point to n'. Finally, we denote the extension of a graph G with a new node n by $G \uplus \{n : s(n_1, \ldots, n_k)\}$. The node n does not exist in G and has label s and successors $n_1, \ldots, n_k$.

In order to deal with non-deterministic computations, the run-time system manages a queue of computation tasks, where each task consists of a control block, a stack of pending computations, and a fingerprint [11] managing the consistency of non-deterministic choices for the task. To be more precise, the state of an ICurry computation is a triple (G, Q, R) where the components have the following structure:

- G is graph where each node is labeled with a function, constructor, or the choice symbol, "?". As discussed above, a choice node n has the form $G[n] = ?^c(n_1, n_2)$.
- Q is a queue (list) of tasks where each task is a triple (C, S, F) with:
  - C is the *control* which is either a graph node n to be evaluated or a pair (b, E) consisting of a block of ICurry (see Fig. 4) and an *environment* E (a mapping from local variables to graph nodes).
  - S is a stack where each stack element is a node n labeled by a function symbol. The stack contains the functions to be evaluated by a task.
  - F is a *fingerprint*, which is a (partial) mapping from choice identifiers to indexes of alternatives.
- R is the set of computed results, which are graph nodes. Note that ICurry evaluates expressions to head normal forms, that is graphs with a constructor at the root. This is sufficient since the evaluation to normal form can be implemented by auxiliary operations.

In the following, we use $\phi[x \mapsto v]$ to denote an update of a mapping ϕ for some argument v. If $\phi' = \phi[x \mapsto v]$, then $\phi'(x) = v$ and $\phi'(y) = \phi(y)$ for all $y \neq x$. Furthermore, we use Curry's list notation for states. Thus, an initial state of an ICurry computation has the form

$$(G, [(n, [], \{\})], \{\})$$

where the graph G contains the initial expression with root node n. Thus, there is only one task with an empty stack and fingerprint and an empty set of results. A final computation state has the form:

$$(G, [], R)$$

There are no tasks left and the set R contains the root nodes of all computed results.

We specify the small-step semantics of ICurry by a set of transformation rules on states. Some of the rules use an auxiliary operation *extend* to extend a graph by adding the graph representation of an expression occurring in an ICurry program. Informally, *extend*(G, E, e) extends a graph G with an ICurry expression e w.r.t. an environment E and returns the pair (G', n) consisting of the extended graph and the root node n of the added expression. To define *extend*, we use an auxiliary function *lookup* to retrieve a graph node w.r.t. an environment:

$$lookup(G, E, v) = \begin{cases} E(v) & \text{if } v = x \text{ or } v = ROOT \\ n_i & \begin{array}{l} \text{if } v = v'[i], \ lookup(G, E, v') = n \\ \text{and } G[n] = l(n_1, \ldots, n_k) \end{array} \end{cases}$$

If e is a variable, its binding is looked up in the environment E and returned as n without extending the graph:

$$extend(G, E, v) = (G, lookup(G, E, v))$$

A disjunction e_1 *or* e_2 creates new subgraphs for the arguments e_1 and e_2 and connects them by a new choice node:

$$extend(G, E, e_1 \text{ or } e_2) = G'' \uplus \{n : ?^c(n_1, n_2)\}$$
$$\text{if } extend(G, E, e_1) = (G', n_1) \text{ and } extend(G', E, e_2) = (G'', n_2)$$

Here, c is a new choice identifier. We assume the existence of a global set of choice identifiers so that new unique identifiers can be obtained during the computation. Similarly, a node constructor creates new subgraphs for the argument expressions and a new node connecting these subgraphs. We assume that n_i is the root node for the subgraph created for e_i and G' is the graph containing G and the new subgraphs:

$$extend(G, E, NODE(l, e_1, \ldots, e_k)) = G' \uplus \{n : l(n_1, \ldots, n_k)\}$$

Now we can specify a small-step semantics of ICurry by the following transformation rules:

Function Node: If the control contains a graph node labeled with a defined function whose i-th argument is demanded, the function node is put onto the stack and the control is replaced by the i-th argument:

$$(G, (n, S, F) : Q, R) \ \rightarrow \ (G, (n_i, n : S, F) : Q, R)$$
$$\text{if } G[n] = f^i(n_1, \ldots, n_k)$$

If the control contains a graph node labeled with a defined function which does not demand an argument, the function's body is put into the control together with an environment initialized with the graph node:

$$(G, (n, S, F) : Q, R) \ \rightarrow \ (G, ((b, \{ROOT \mapsto n\}), S, F) : Q, R)$$
$$\text{if } G[n] = f(\ldots) \text{ and } f = b \text{ is a declaration of the ICurry program}$$

Variable Declaration: If the control starts with a declaration of a local variable, it is initialized as a *null* pointer in the environment:

$$(G, ((\mathit{declare}\ x; b, E), S, F) : Q, R) \;\rightarrow\; (G, ((b, E[x \mapsto \mathit{null}]), S, F) : Q, R)$$

Free variables can be handled in various ways. For the sake of simplicity, we implement free variables as non-deterministic generator operations. This technique is also used in KiCS2 [12] and stems from the equivalence of logic variables and non-determinism [7]. For instance, a generator for a Boolean free variable can be defined as:

```
gen_Bool = False ? True
```

Since free variables of different types will have a different generator operation, we denote by gen_x the generator operation of the free variable x.[3] Then a free variable is introduced by initializing it with a node representing the generator operation:

$$(G, ((\mathit{free}\ x; b, E), S, F) : Q, R) \;\rightarrow$$
$$(G \uplus \{n : \mathit{gen}_x()\}, ((b, E[x \mapsto n]), S, F) : Q, R)$$

Assignment: If the control starts with an assignment to a local variable, the graph is extended with the expression and the environment is updated:

$$(G, ((x = e; b, E), S, F) : Q, R) \;\rightarrow\; (G', ((b, E[x \mapsto n]), S, F) : Q, R)$$
$$\text{if } \mathit{extend}(G, E, e) = (G', n)$$

If the control starts with an assignment to successor of a node, the graph is extended with the expression and the successor is set to the created subgraph:

$$(G, ((v[i] = e; b, E), S, F) : Q, R) \;\rightarrow$$
$$(G'[n \leftarrow l(n_1, \ldots, n_{i-1}, n', n_{i+1}, \ldots, n_k)], ((b, E), S, F) : Q, R)$$
$$\text{if } \mathit{lookup}(G, E, v) = n,\ G[n] = l(n_1, \ldots, n_k),\ \mathit{extend}(G, E, e) = (G', n')$$

Return Statement: If the control contains a return statement, the graph is extended with the returned graph and the root of the current function is updated with the returned node:

$$(G, ((\mathit{return}\ e, E), S, F) : Q, R) \;\rightarrow\; (G'[E(\mathit{ROOT}) \leftarrow n], (n, S, F) : Q, R)$$
$$\text{if } \mathit{extend}(G, E, e) = (G', n)$$

Exempt Statement: If the control contains an exempt statement, the current computation is removed from the list of tasks:

$$(G, ((\mathit{exempt}, E), S, F) : Q, R) \;\rightarrow\; (G, Q, R)$$

---

[3] Type-based generators can be implemented with type classes, as described in [23]. Thus, a compiler can easily attach appropriate generators to free variables in ICurry.

Case Statement: If the control contains a case statement, the corresponding branch is selected (this is always possible since the case argument is demanded and was evaluated before invoking the function):

$$(G, ((case \; x \; of \; \{c_1 \rightarrow b_1; \ldots; c_n \rightarrow b_n\}, E), S, F) : Q, R) \rightarrow$$
$$(G, ((b_i, E) : S, F) : Q, R)$$

if $E(x) = n$ and $G[n] = c_i(\ldots)$

Constructor Node: If the control contains a graph node labeled with a constructor symbol, we distinguish two cases. If the stack is empty, a result has been computed:

$$(G, (n, [], F) : Q, R) \rightarrow (G, Q, R \cup \{n\})$$

if $G[n] = c(\ldots)$ for some constructor c

If the stack is not empty, then it contains a function where an argument is demanded. Since this argument, which is the node in control, is evaluated, we invoke this function by putting its body into the control:

$$(G, (n, (n' : S, F) : Q, R) \rightarrow (G, ((b, \{ROOT \mapsto n'\}), S, F) : Q, R)$$

if $G[n] = c(\ldots)$ for some constructor c, $G[n'] = f^i(\ldots)$,
and $f^i = b$ is a declaration in the ICurry program

Choice Node: If the control contains a choice node, we distinguish three cases. If the stack is empty, i.e., the choice is at the top, and the fingerprint already selects a branch for this choice, the choice node is replaced by the corresponding branch:

$$(G, (n, [], F) : Q, R) \rightarrow (G, (n_i, [], F) : Q, R)$$

if $G[n] = ?^c(n_1, n_2)$ and $F(c) = i$

If the stack is empty and the fingerprint does not contain a selection for this choice, we split the current task into two new tasks where the fingerprint is extended in each task:

$$(G, (n, [], F) : Q, R) \rightarrow (G, Q \; ++ \; [(n_1, [], F[c \mapsto 1]), (n_2, [], F[c \mapsto 2])], R)$$

if $G[n] = ?^c(n_1, n_2)$ and $F(c)$ is undefined

Note that we can use any strategy to add the new tasks to the existing ones. Here we put them at the end which corresponds to a breadth-first strategy in the search tree. Putting them at the front of Q corresponds to a depth-first search strategy. Some Curry implementations, like KiCS2 [12], allow the user to select different search strategies.

The final case is a pull-tab step. If the choice is at a demanded argument position, then the stack is not empty, and the graph node identified by the top of the stack is replaced by a choice:

$$(G, (n_0, n : S, F) : Q, R) \rightarrow (G'[n \leftarrow ?^c(n'_1, n'_2)], (n, S, F) : Q, R)$$

if $G[n_0] = ?^c(n_1, n_2)$, $G[n] = f^i(n_1, \dots, n_k)$,
and $G' = G \uplus \{n'_1 : f^i(n_1, \dots, n_{i-1}, n_1, n_{i+1}, \dots, n_k),$
$\qquad\qquad n'_2 : f^i(n_1, \dots, n_{i-1}, n_2, n_{i+1}, \dots, n_k)\}$

Since each transformation step performs only local changes, the implementation effort for these steps is limited when mapping ICurry into an imperative language. This will be shown in Sect. 5.4 where implementations of ICurry in various imperative languages are summarized.

5.3   ICurry Generation

Current Curry distributions such as PAKCS [21] or KiCS2 [12] provide a package with the definition of FlatCurry and a rich API for its construction and manipulation. Therefore, the ICurry format of a Curry program is conveniently obtained from the FlatCurry format of that program.

A fundamental difference between the two formats concerns expressions. Expressions in FlatCurry may contain *cases* and *lets* as the arguments of a function application. These are banned in ICurry which allows only nested functional application. The reason is that the latter can be directly translated into various imperative languages, where the former cannot. Therefore, any *case* and *let* constructs that are the arguments of a function application are replaced by calls to newly created functions. Thus, in ICurry, the replaced constructs are executed at the top level. We replace these constructs during the transformation from FlatCurry into ICurry. However, the same transformation could be performed from FlatCurry into itself, or even from source Curry into itself. Our contrived example below shows the latter for ease of understanding. The code of function g is irrelevant, therefore, it is not shown:

```
f x = g x (case x of ...)
```

is transformed into:

```
f x = g x (h x)
h x = case x of ...
```

The offending *case*, as an argument of the application of g, has been replaced by a call to a newly created function, h. In function h, the *case* is no longer an argument of a function application.

The second major difference between FlatCurry and ICurry concerns case expressions. FlatCurry matches a selector against shallow constructor expressions, where ICurry matches against constructor symbols. Furthermore, the set of these symbols is complete and ordered in ICurry. The transformation is relatively simple, except it may require non-local information. A function in a module M may pattern match on some instance of a type t that is not declared in M. Therefore, the constructors of t must be accessed in some module different from that being compiled.

A third significant difference between FlatCurry and ICurry concerns *let blocks*. They are banned in ICurry, and replaced by the explicit construction of nodes, and by the assignment of these nodes' references to local variables.

In the following, we show an algorithm to translate FlatCurry into ICurry. For this purpose, we define a *pure expression* as an expression that only contains literals, variables, constructor applications, and function applications. Any *or* expression and function application may only contain pure expressions. The scrutinee of a case expression must be a variable, literal, or constructor application. An assignment in a *let* expression must be a pure expression or an *or* expression. The branches of a case expression must match all constructors of a data type in an order fixed by the definition of that data type. Branches missing in the original Curry program contain $\bot$ in their right-hand side.

The algorithm is divided into five functions which are described in Fig. 5. $\mathcal{F}$ translates a FlatCurry function into an ICurry function. $\mathcal{B}$ translates a FlatCurry expression into an ICurry block. $\mathcal{D}$ extracts all of the variables declared in a FlatCurry expression. $\mathcal{A}$ generates necessary assignments for ICurry variables. $\mathcal{E}$ translates a FlatCurry expression into an ICurry expression.

The functions $\mathcal{F}$ and $\mathcal{E}$ are straightforward translations. $\mathcal{F}$ simply makes a block, with the root of the block being set to the root of the function. $\mathcal{E}$ is almost entirely a straight translation, but there is one technical point. In a case expression, each branch must be translated into its own block. However, each of the variables in the pattern of a branch need to be related to the scrutinee of the case. This is achieved by setting the root of the block to the scrutinee of the case.

The function $\mathcal{B}$ creates an ICurry block. Blocks are more complicated to construct. Each block will have a root and a list of variables. The root is the root of the expression that created the block. For a function, the root is the root of the function expression. For a case branch, the root is the root of the scrutinee of the case. The variables of a block are the parameters of a function, or the pattern variables of a branch. After declaring variables, all variables in any *let* expressions are declared with $\mathcal{D}$. Then each variable is assigned an expression with $\mathcal{A}$. If either $\mathcal{D}$ or $\mathcal{A}$ is undefined for some expression, their application does not generate ICurry code. Finally, we translate the expression into an ICurry statement with $\mathcal{E}$.

The function $\mathcal{D}$ declares variables declared in a *let* or *free* expression. If there is a *case* expression, then a new variable x_e is declared.

The function $\mathcal{A}$ assigns variables in a *let* or *free* expression. The expression for all variables in a *let* is translated with $\mathcal{E}$. Next, if there are any variables declared in the *let* block that are used in one of the expressions, they need to be filled in. Finally, if there is a case expression, we assign x_e to be the root of the scrutinee.

A compiler from FlatCurry to ICurry implementing these translation rules is available as package `icurry`. It can easily be installed with the Curry package manager.[4] The tool provided by this package also contains an interpreter for ICurry, based on the small-step semantics specified in Sect. 5.2, which can visualize the graph and machine state during a computation.

---

[4] http://curry-lang.org/tools/cpm.

$$\mathcal{F}(f(x_1, \ldots, x_n) = e) := f = \mathcal{B}(x_1, \ldots, x_n, e, ROOT)$$

$$\mathcal{B}(x_1, \ldots, x_n, \bot, root) := exempt$$
$$\mathcal{B}(x_1, \ldots, x_n, e, root) :=$$
  declare x_1

  $\ldots$

  declare x_n
  $\mathcal{D}(e)$
  $x_1 = root[1]$

  $\ldots$

  $x_n = root[n]$
  $\mathcal{A}(e)$
  return $\mathcal{E}(e)$ (omit *return* if $\mathcal{E}(e)$ is a *case*)

$$\mathcal{D}(let\ x_1, \ldots, x_n\ free\ in\ e) :=$$
  free x_1

  $\ldots$

  free x_n
$$\mathcal{D}(let\ \{x_1 = e_1; \ldots; x_n = e_n\}\ in\ e) :=$$
  declare x_1

  $\ldots$

  declare x_n
$$\mathcal{D}(case\ e\ of\ \{p_1 \to e_1; \ldots; p_n \to e_n\}) := declare\ x_e$$

$$\mathcal{A}(let\ \{x_1 = e_1; \ldots; x_n = e_n\}\ in\ e) :=$$
  $x_1 = \mathcal{E}(e_1)$

  $\ldots$

  $x_n = \mathcal{E}(e_n)$
  $x_1[p] = x_i$ (for each occurrence of $x_i, i \geq 1$, in e_1 at position p)

  $\ldots$

  $x_n[p] = x_i$ (for each occurrence of $x_i, i \geq n$, in e_n at position p)
$$\mathcal{A}(case\ e\ of\ \{p_1 \to e_1; \ldots; p_n \to e_n\}) := x_e = \mathcal{E}(e)$$

$$
\begin{aligned}
\mathcal{E}(x) &:= x \\
\mathcal{E}(c(e_1, \ldots, e_n)) &:= NODE(c, \mathcal{E}(e_1), \ldots, \mathcal{E}(e_n)) \\
\mathcal{E}(f(e_1, \ldots, e_n)) &:= NODE(f, \mathcal{E}(e_1), \ldots, \mathcal{E}(e_n)) \\
\mathcal{E}(e_1\ or\ e_2) &:= \mathcal{E}(e_1)\ or\ \mathcal{E}(e_2) \\
\mathcal{E}(let\ \{x_1 = e_1; \ldots; x_n = e_n\}\ in\ e) &:= \mathcal{E}(e) \\
\mathcal{E}(let\ \{x_1, \ldots, x_n\}\ free\ in\ e) &:= \mathcal{E}(e)
\end{aligned}
$$
$$\mathcal{E}(case\ e\ of\ \{c(x_{11}, \ldots, x_{1m}) \to e_1; \ldots; c(x_{n1}, \ldots, x_{nk}) \to e_n\}) :=$$
$$\quad case\ \mathcal{E}(e)\ of\ \{\ \mathcal{B}(x_{11}, \ldots, x_{1m}, e_1, x_e);$$
$$\ldots;$$
$$\mathcal{B}(x_{n1}, \ldots, x_{nk}, e_n, x_e);\ \}$$

Fig. 5. Algorithm for translating FlatCurry into ICurry

5.4   ICurry Use

The stated goal of ICurry is to be a format of Curry programs suitable for translation into an imperative language. Below, we briefly report our experience in translating ICurry into various target languages. Table 1 shows the size of a Curry program that translates ICurry into a target language. The numerical values in the table, extracted from Wittorf's thesis [30], count the lines of code of the translator. The table is only indicative since "lines of code" is not an accurate measure, and some earlier compilers use older variants of ICurry that have evolved over time. Each ICurry construct has a direct translation into the target language. The following details refer to the translation into C. Declarations and assignments are the same as in C. The ICurry statements are translated as follows: (1) the ICurry *return* is the same as in C, (2) an ICurry *case statement* is translated into a C *switch statement* where the case selector is the tag of a node, and (3) the ICurry *exempt* statement is translated into code that, when executed, terminates the executing computation without producing any result. This is justified by the facts that the evaluation strategy executes only needed steps, and that failures in non-deterministic programs are natural and expected, therefore they should be silently ignored.

Table 1. Number of Curry source lines of code for various translators from ICurry to a target language.

C	441
Python	342
Java	790
JavaScript	632

The ICurry case expressions of a function's code contain a branch for each constructor in the argument's type and a branch for each of the following: the choice symbol, the failure symbol, any function symbol [11, Fig. 2], and any free variable. A dispatch table, which is addressed by the argument's label's tag, efficiently selects the branch to be executed. The behavior of the additional branches is described below, and is the same across all the functions of a program. A choice symbol in a pattern matched position results in the execution of a pull-tabbing step [5,13]. A failure is propagated to the context. A function symbol triggers the evaluation of the expression rooted by this symbol. Finally, a free variable is instantiated to a choice of *shallow* patterns of the same type as the variable. As an example, the evaluation of:

```
head x where x free
```

instantiates x to [] ? (y:ys) where y and ys are free variables. The alternative [] will result in failure. This can be determined at compile time and removed during optimizations.

Compilers from Curry to Python and other imperative languages can be implemented as described above. As Table 1 indicates, the compilers (written in Curry) are quite compact. We observe that FlatCurry covers the complete language, since it is the basis for robust Curry implementations, like PAKCS and KiCS2, and the natural/operational semantics of Curry is defined in FlatCurry [1]. ICurry contains the same information as FlatCurry except type information, since the type correctness of a program has been verified at the point of the compilation process in which ICurry is used.

We have also implemented a translator from ICurry programs into the JSON format. This translator is simpler and shorter than all the translators into imperative languages of Table 1. The translation into JSON is used by Sprite [11], a Curry system under development, whose target language is C++. The JSON format is more convenient than ICurry when the client of the ICurry format is not coded in Curry, hence it cannot read and parse ICurry program using Curry's library functions.

6   Concluding Remarks

Our work is centered on the compilation of Curry programs. As in many compilers, our approach is transformational. To compile a Curry program P, we translate P into a language, called *target*, for which a compiler already exists. This is the same route followed by other Curry compilers like PAKCS [21] and KiCS2 [12].

PAKCS translates source Curry code into Prolog, leveraging the existence of native free variables and non-determinism in Prolog. KiCS2 translates source Curry code into Haskell, leveraging the existence of first-class functions and their efficient demand-driven execution in Haskell. Both of these compilers use FlatCurry as an intermediate language. They have the same front end which translates Curry into FlatCurry. The use of FlatCurry simplifies the translation process, but is still appropriate to express Curry computations without much effort. FlatCurry has some relatively high-level constructs that can be mapped directly into Prolog and Haskell, because these languages are high-level, too.

In order to provide a better basis to compile Curry into low-level imperative languages, we presented ICurry as an intermediate language for this purpose. Before ICurry, a Curry compiler targeting a C-like language would handle certain high-level constructs of FlatCurry in whichever way each programmer would choose. This led to both duplications of code and unnecessary differences. ICurry originates from these efforts. It abstracts the ideas that, over time, proved to be simple and effective in a language-independent way. With ICurry, the effort to produce a Curry compiler targeting an imperative language is both shortened, because more of the front end can be reused, and simplified, because the starting point of the translation is independent of the target and is well understood.

Our work is complementary to, but independent of, other efforts toward the compilation of Curry programs. These efforts include the development of evaluation strategies [6], or the handling of non-determinism [5,13].

There exist other functional logic languages, e.g., $\mathcal{TOY}$ [15,25] whose operational semantics can be abstracted by needed narrowing steps of a constructor-based graph rewriting system. Some of our ideas seem applicable with little to no changes to the implementation of these languages.

Graph rewriting, often supported by graph machines [14,24,26], has been used for the implementation of functional languages. A comparison with these efforts is problematic at best. Despite the remarkable syntactic similarities—Curry's syntax extends Haskell's with a single construct, a free variable declaration—the semantic differences are profound. In particular, there is no textual order among the rewrite rules of a functional logic program, and the notion of laziness is based on needed steps modulo non-deterministic choices. As a consequence, there are purely functional programs whose execution produces a result as Curry but does not terminate as Haskell [8, Sect. 3]. Furthermore, most steps of a functional logic computation are functional steps, but the computation must be prepared to encounter non-determinism and/or free variables. Hence, situations and goals significantly differ.

Future work should investigate ICurry to ICurry transformations that are likely to optimize the generated code. For example, different orders of the declaration of variables in a let block lead to different numbers of assignments. Also, case expressions as arguments of function call can be moved outside the call in some situations rather than be replaced by a call to a new function.

Acknowledgments. The authors are grateful to the anonymous reviewers for their helpful comments to improve the paper. This material is based in part upon work supported by the National Science Foundation under Grant No. 1317249.

References

1. Albert, E., Hanus, M., Huch, F., Oliver, J., Vidal, G.: Operational semantics for declarative multi-paradigm languages. J. Symb. Comput. **40**(1), 795–829 (2005)
2. Antoy, S.: Definitional trees. In: Kirchner, H., Levi, G. (eds.) ALP 1992. LNCS, vol. 632, pp. 143–157. Springer, Heidelberg (1992). https://doi.org/10.1007/BFb0013825
3. Antoy, S.: Constructor-based conditional narrowing. In: Proceedings of the 3rd International ACM SIGPLAN Conference on Principles and Practice of Declarative Programming, PPDP 2001, pp. 199–206. ACM Press (2001)
4. Antoy, S.: Evaluation strategies for functional logic programming. J. Symb. Comput. **40**(1), 875–903 (2005)
5. Antoy, S.: On the correctness of pull-tabbing. TPLP **11**(4–5), 713–730 (2011)
6. Antoy, S., Echahed, R., Hanus, M.: A needed narrowing strategy. J. ACM **47**(4), 776–822 (2000)
7. Antoy, S., Hanus, M.: Overlapping rules and logic variables in functional logic programs. In: Etalle, S., Truszczyński, M. (eds.) ICLP 2006. LNCS, vol. 4079, pp. 87–101. Springer, Heidelberg (2006). https://doi.org/10.1007/11799573_9
8. Antoy, S., Hanus, M.: Functional logic programming. Commun. ACM **53**(4), 74–85 (2010)

9. Antoy, S., Hanus, M.: Contracts and specifications for functional logic programming. In: Russo, C., Zhou, N.-F. (eds.) PADL 2012. LNCS, vol. 7149, pp. 33–47. Springer, Heidelberg (2012). https://doi.org/10.1007/978-3-642-27694-1_4

10. Antoy, S., Hanus, M., Libby, S.: Proving non-deterministic computations in Agda. In: Proceedings of the 24th International Workshop on Functional and (Constraint) Logic Programming, WFLP 2016. Volume 234 of Electronic Proceedings in Theoretical Computer Science, pp. 180–195. Open Publishing Association (2017)

11. Antoy, S., Jost, A.: A new functional-logic compiler for Curry: SPRITE. In: Hermenegildo, M.V., Lopez-Garcia, P. (eds.) LOPSTR 2016. LNCS, vol. 10184, pp. 97–113. Springer, Cham (2017). https://doi.org/10.1007/978-3-319-63139-4_6

12. Braßel, B., Hanus, M., Peemöller, B., Reck, F.: KiCS2: a new compiler from Curry to Haskell. In: Kuchen, H. (ed.) WFLP 2011. LNCS, vol. 6816, pp. 1–18. Springer, Heidelberg (2011). https://doi.org/10.1007/978-3-642-22531-4_1

13. Braßel, B., Huch, F.: On a tighter integration of functional and logic programming. In: Shao, Z. (ed.) APLAS 2007. LNCS, vol. 4807, pp. 122–138. Springer, Heidelberg (2007). https://doi.org/10.1007/978-3-540-76637-7_9

14. Burn, G.L., Peyton Jones, S.L., Robson, J.D.: The spineless G-machine. In: Proceedings of the 1988 ACM Conference on LISP and Functional Programming, pp. 244–258. ACM (1988)

15. Caballero, R., Sánchez, J. (eds.): TOY: A Multiparadigm Declarative Language (version 2.3.1) (2007). http://toy.sourceforge.net

16. Echahed, R., Janodet, J.-C.: On constructor-based graph rewriting systems. Research report IMAG 985-I, IMAG-LSR, CNRS, Grenoble (1997)

17. Hanus, M.: FlatCurry: an intermediate representation for Curry programs (2008). http://www.informatik.uni-kiel.de/~curry/flat/

18. Hanus, M.: Functional logic programming: from theory to curry. In: Voronkov, A., Weidenbach, C. (eds.) Programming Logics. LNCS, vol. 7797, pp. 123–168. Springer, Heidelberg (2013). https://doi.org/10.1007/978-3-642-37651-1_6

19. Hanus, M.: Combining static and dynamic contract checking for curry. In: Fioravanti, F., Gallagher, J.P. (eds.) LOPSTR 2017. LNCS, vol. 10855, pp. 323–340. Springer, Cham (2018). https://doi.org/10.1007/978-3-319-94460-9_19

20. Hanus, M.: Verifying fail-free declarative programs. In: Proceedings of the 20th International Symposium on Principles and Practice of Declarative Programming, PPDP 2018, pp. 12:1–12:13. ACM Press (2018)

21. Hanus, M., et al.: PAKCS: The Portland Aachen Kiel Curry System (2018). http://www.informatik.uni-kiel.de/~pakcs/

22. Hanus, M., Skrlac, F.: A modular and generic analysis server system for functional logic programs. In: Proceedings of the ACM SIGPLAN 2014 Workshop on Partial Evaluation and Program Manipulation, PEPM 2014, pp. 181–188. ACM Press (2014)

23. Hanus, M., Teegen, F.: Adding Data to Curry. In: Proceedings of the Conference on Declarative Programming (Declare 2019). LNCS. Springer (2019)

24. Kieburtz, R.B.: The G-machine: a fast, graph-reduction evaluator. In: Jouannaud, J.-P. (ed.) FPCA 1985. LNCS, vol. 201, pp. 400–413. Springer, Heidelberg (1985). https://doi.org/10.1007/3-540-15975-4_50

25. López Fraguas, F.J., Sánchez Hernández, J.: TOY: a multiparadigm declarative system. In: Narendran, P., Rusinowitch, M. (eds.) RTA 1999. LNCS, vol. 1631, pp. 244–247. Springer, Heidelberg (1999). https://doi.org/10.1007/3-540-48685-2_19

26. José Moreno-Navarro, J., Kuchen, H., Loogen, R.: Lazy narrowing in a graph machine. In: Kirchner, H., Wechler, W. (eds.) ALP 1990. LNCS, vol. 463, pp. 298–317. Springer, Heidelberg (1990). https://doi.org/10.1007/3-540-53162-9_47

27. O'Donnell, M.J.: Equational Logic as a Programming Language. MIT Press, Cambridge (1985)
28. Plump, D.: Term graph rewriting. In: Ehrig, H., Engels, G., Kreowski, H.-J., Rozenberg, G. (eds.) Handbook of Graph Grammars and Computing by Graph Transformation, Volume 2: Applications, Languages and Tools, pp. 3–61. World Scientific, Singapore (1999)
29. Reddy, U.S.: Narrowing as the operational semantics of functional languages. In: Proceedings of the IEEE International Symposium on Logic Programming, Boston, pp. 138–151 (1985)
30. Wittorf, M.A.: Generic translation of Curry programs into imperative programs. Master's thesis, Kiel University (2018). (in German)

Author Index

Printed in the United States
By Bookmasters